The Origin Speaks

A Channelled Work

Guy Steven Needler

For permission, serialization, condensation, adaptions, or for our catalog of other publications, write to Ozark Mountain Publishing, Inc., P.O. Box 754, Huntsville, AR 72740, ATTN: Permissions Department.

Library of Congress Cataloging -in-Publication Data

Needler, Guy Steven, 1961

The Origin Speaks by Guy Steven Needler

Have you ever thought about who or what God is or who the co-creators are? Or even, what is beyond God. What if God was indeed finite and that there was a bigger, a much bigger "infinite" being, one that created God and the co-creators. A being that is just starting out on the road to know what it "itself" is. A being that has just started to evolve. In *The Origin Speaks* the reader is taken beyond the *Beyond the Source* books to a direct dialogue with the ultimate creator, the "all there is", the "absolute", The "Origin".

1. Source 2. God 3. Origin 4. Metaphysics

I. Needler, Guy Steven, 1961   II. God III. Metaphysics IV. Title

Library of Congress Catalog Card Number: 2015939045

ISBN : 9781940265100

Cover Art and Layout: www.noir33.com
Book set in: Lucida Fax, Segoe Print
Book Design: Tab Pillar
Published by:

PO Box 754
Huntsville, AR 72740
WWW.OZARKMT.COM

Printed in the United States of America

For my dear wife,
Anne Elizabeth Milner
Now "Ascended"
(10 April 1957–24 December 2012)

Table of Contents

Introduction

The Origin Speaks

I FINISHED CHANNELLING/TYPING the last words to *Beyond the Source, Book 2* mid-June 2012 ahead of schedule, giving me enough time to finish editing the lectures I was due to present at the Ozark Mountain Publishing 2012 Transformation Conference in Rogers, Arkansas, and prepare for my first US tour. I felt like I was winning the battle with the amount of work that the Source Entities and The Origin were placing on my shoulders, or that I was getting used to the commitment!

I knew that I was destined to teach people (and I met and worked with some truly remarkable people, dedicated to knowing the truth and committed to working with the techniques given them) the basics in how to contact the Source Entity for themselves, creating a permanent, robust and substantive link, as well as channelling the information for the books that were/are destined to expand mankind's knowledge of the structure of the multiverse and those other multiversal environments created by the other eleven Source Entities. I was also very aware that this book, *The Origin Speaks*, would take these boundaries much further out, by explaining through a unique dialogue with The Origin—The Absolute—All There IS, more about its plan for evolution, its knowledge of self, its structure and what it is personally doing to increase its own evolutionary content. I was also becoming aware of the nature of future books and subject matters. My head was already starting to hurt with the anticipation of the subject matters we would discuss over the next eighteen to twenty-four months.

With all of this whizzing around in my consciousness, including the plans, counter plans, schedules and commitments I have made to service the peripheral roles I undertook as part of this mission (writing channelled information being just one of them) I sit here at my computer wondering what is going to happen next. Right now I am a blank page, a husk, a cup waiting to be filled with the water of divine knowledge, full of anticipation of that feeling that comes over me when I am about to be in full contact with The Origin or one of the Source Entities. The energies around me are alight as the contact comes. The hair on the back of my neck stands on end and my skin crawls all over, a sure sign that I am about to be contacted.

It wasn't a total surprise when our Source Entity started the next dialogue. Well, I did put the call out to both The Origin and our Source Entity. It would have been rude to have not included them both to comment in the introduction. What I wasn't prepared for (although I should have anticipated it) was the sudden picture that came into my mind's eye. I was in a special area of space, that space that is outside of our Source Entity while still being within The Origin's area of self-awareness, I was surrounded by ALL of the Source Entities and not just my own Source Entity; or was it my own Source Entity? I was due to find out more about my own heritage later.

I had tears of joy in my eyes at the mental sight of them all together, which included an aspect of Source Entity Twelve, that Source Entity that was not only barely aware when I initially contacted it, but was the first Source Entity to venture outside of The Origin's area of self-awareness. It was a delightful sight, sheer joy to behold. Within all of these blissful experiences that had suddenly hit me, I was also aware of something else, of being more substantial, of being bigger, much bigger than I was in my minuscule human form. I was starting to notice that aspect of me that was my true energetic self, and it was huge! Again my eyes filled with tears of joy. I was as close to being home in this incarnation as I had ever been. Oh the joy, the love! How could I have ever left this to be incarnate? I shook my head to clear my thoughts and Source Entity One, our/mankind's Source Entity, spoke an introduction.

SE1: You have come far my friend. It is a delight to see you becoming that which you are destined to be in the face of incarnate adversity.

ME: It's wonderful to speak to you again, so soon after the last book was finished.

SE1: And it is wonderful to speak with you as well, even though you are now entering into your exalted position.

ME: What exalted position? All I see is a sea of work, and jolly hard work at that!

SE1: You will realize this position in good time. But right now you are due to take on board the next stage of your work, a unique and direct dialogue with The Origin.

ME: Oh come on, it's not that unique. I/we have spoken to The Origin before. It can't be that difficult, can it?

SE1: Previous communications with The Origin have been limited to a very small aspect of The Origin. This was a necessary process to allow you to get energetically and mentally used to the possibility of a committed and long-term dialogue with The Origin.

ME: So I have only been communicating with a part of The Origin to date?

SE1: Yes. Just as you only communicated with a small aspect of me in our early days of contact, so have you only been in contact with a very small aspect of The Origin to date.

That would explain the energies that were flowing over me. I was starting to realize that they were much more pronounced than before. They were intoxicating!

ME: I wondered why it was just as easy to communicate with The Origin as it was with you. It was very easy, almost like chatting with a friend.

SE1: Well now you know. I will give you a hint if you like. It will be like flying model airplanes and then being asked to take control of a space shuttle or fighter jet.

ME: Irrespective of how it will feel I had better get started. I feel the energies washing over me on a regular basis. And, you are right; this feels very much different from those I have felt before when communicating with The Origin.

SE1: Of course I am right. Just take it slowly.

ME: I will.

I disconnected with Source Entity One and waited a moment. I didn't need to wait long.

O: Are you ready? You have made me wait six weeks! We were due to start straight away!

The wash of energies subsided. I got the impression that The Origin was regulating its contact for the moment until I was fully used to its new level of dialogue with me.

ME: Sorry, life on Earth got in the way.

O: So I can see. You are forgiven, for I see that it was the "good" work that you were doing.

ME: It's only the start and is small as a result.

O: All good things start small. I started small and look at me now.

ME: I can't. You're too big.

O: Exactly. But you can reach the periphery of my area of self-awareness and that in itself is a wonder, especially in your incarnate state. I am pleased and delighted.

ME: Thank you.

O: It's a pleasure. And now that we have gotten the preliminaries out of the way we should start, for we have a lot of work to do together.

ME: It's good to see you still have a sense of humor.

O: Of course. I invented it. Shall we start?

I have tears in my eyes again! I have the feeling that this is going to be a wondrous and unique journey for us all.

Welcome back, dear reader.

Chapter 1

The Origin Awakens

AT THIS POINT I DECIDED to mentally reconnect with that information that The Origin had bestowed upon me during the compilation of the texts that resulted in The History of God *and* Beyond the Source, Books 1 and 2, *to see what subjects I needed to work with The Origin on. I realized very early on in this thought process that the information I did have was actually quite patchy and limited, very limited I might add, to quite short dialogues within the texts of the books I had already written; the main focus actually being on the other Source Entities and their environments/entities and achievements, albeit in a digestible way, rather than on The Origin itself. Based upon this I thought it prudent to not dwell on the past and start with a clean sheet of paper. Or should I say a blank computer screen. With this firmly in mind I decided to start from the very beginning, making no assumptions on readers picking up this text as a "follow on" from my previous books and placed this book as a self-sustaining "stand alone" option for the discerning truth seeker to read. As I finished typing this text I felt The Origin, its energies cool like a cold shower came over me, and we commenced dialogue.*

O: Cool shower, eh! I had never considered that my energies would be considered as a cool shower. Perhaps you need one?

ME: I didn't think we would start this dialogue off with humor. I anticipated diving straight into the nitty-gritty of the detail.

O: It's best to bring the level of what we are going to discuss down to that where everyone who reads this text will feel that they are going to be able to understand the information. If during the first few sentences they feel that the information is going to be over their heads then they will put the book down and it will become a doorstop at best. On the other hand if they feel that they are going to have some light relief at certain points in the dialogue, and that the information being discussed is going to be presented in a way that is understandable, then they will continue. In this way you will retain the attention of your readers and expand the reader base as a result. But more importantly more incarnate individuals will be "in the knowledge" so to speak, and as a result will be accessing and working with the energies of the information in a passive and stress-free way. It is difficult enough for many of you to understand that there is a creator, a Source Entity, a God that is a real and definable reality, let alone a creator of one's God, and that you, my dear one, are communicating with it and presenting the fruits of such a communication to the rest of the incarnate human race. No, we need to keep this dialogue as simple as possible, and that in itself is going to be hard, for some of the subjects we are going to discuss are going to be above and beyond that which you have already discussed with me and the Source Entities. Now then, where do you want to start?

ME: Let's try the very beginning, your awakening, your becoming aware, and the process of your becoming aware now that you have the benefit of hindsight.

The Beginning of the End of Nothingness
(Possibility Creates Event Space)

ME: Let's go back to the very beginning of your existence. What actually happened to make you become awake, aware, and sentient all that time ago, and, what did it feel like? I mean, I have asked a few of the Source Entities what it felt like to become aware and awake, but I would like to understand from yourself in more detail how it was with you.

O: I will go so far as to say that it was a gradual affair, rather like you coming out of a rather long and deep sleep. At first I just "WAS." There was no individualized thought or thought processes to speak of, just beingness. Yes, I can say that it was like just being, a level of beingness that slowly came into focus.

I was just a "Being," in that which was a vast tract of nothingness. I was a cool breeze, a warm thermocline, a will-o'-the-wisp. There was just observation and no questioning, no analysis, no reasoning, no discussion, no thought, and no recognition of self. Just a momentary area of nothingness that was a little bit more than nothingness.

ME: How long did that last for?

O: Who knows? I certainly don't, for I had no capacity for memory at that point. I was just an infinitesimally small part of the nothingness that was infinitesimally different than the nothingness. I was more than nothingness, I was somethingness but without personalized recognition of such somethingness. In effect I was comfortably numb.

ME: So when did you start to gain awareness to the point of recognition of self?

O: Again it's difficult to say because I was not in the capacity of creativity then and certainly was not able to have memory. Memory is a function of passive creativity, but passive creativity needs one to be able to receive individualized thought processes, which at that time I did not have.

What I will say is this. That when I look at the processes of the individualization of energies and other components that are my make-up, and I see how the energies of my Source Entities developed individualization/singularity of awareness, I recognize that the process is nearly always the same. I therefore note that the transformation of nothingness to somethingness and further into self-recognition must have been the same, for they are individualized units of me.

ME: So what you are suggesting is that the awakening process is the same for any group of energies that are "of the right quality and density?"

O: No, I am not saying that. What I am saying is that it must be similar. The process is, in general, the same but the percentage mix and density of the required energies will be a variable. Listen, I am not in a position to be able to describe in a definitive way the process I went through in the initial process of my awakening because I was not in a state of sentient awareness. What I can do is tell you in detail how a Source Entity, or even your self—your own energies—became aware of self and developed sentient thought throughout the process, "soup to nuts" so to speak. I can even tell you the process of my becoming aware from my smallest level of awareness onward to now. But before that I cannot.

ME: Can you not use Event Space to go back to that point where you were energies coalescing, becoming the right density, gaining the right quality, becoming individualized, and gaining thought? Or, was Event Space one of your own creations?

O: No, Event Space is a product of that which is me. It was not created by me. It is me.

ME: In that case, we could visit that Event Space that recorded your early awakening process, that part of you that was not able to intellectualize that which was happening to you, giving both you and me a complete picture of your awakening process.

O: Well done!

ME: What?

O: Well done! I think that you will be OK with the concepts that we will be discussing during this dialogue.

ME: What do you mean? Why do I suddenly feel like I have passed a test?

O: That's because you have. You need to have realized that there are no boundaries when dealing with me, at least none that would affect our dialogue. We can use that which is in existence, in this instance Event Space, at any time to see or experience that which wasn't in existence. We can even go back before existence itself, should we wish to do so but that would not be productive right now.

ME: That meaning the only boundary is being able to recreate yourself.

O: Yes, that's about the size of it, but we will discuss that subject in a later dialogue because it's a very important subject and it needs to be understood in some detail. So, are you ready for a ride?

ME: Where to?

O: That Event Space where it was all happening for me to become aware.

ME: You mean we are going to go there to witness your awakening?

O: Yes, of course. This will be essential observational work for you to pass on to mankind incarnate. What's more it will settle a few arguments there are between you all about how The Origin, The Absolute became that which it is.

ME: OK, but before we move off and witness the process of this monumental event, I want to ask one question.

O: Ask away.

ME: How can Event Space record that which it wasn't told to record? I mean, Event Space, from my knowledge, is usually invoked when there is a decision to be made, and that needs a sentient entity to create the decision point, the reason for the Event Space to be in existence. Or have I got this totally wrong?

O: No you aren't wrong, just barely educated in such matters. You see, Event Space does not need an entity's decision point, or should I say, it's an entity's decision to choose one route when two are offered, for as you rightly say, it needs a sentient entity to create the opportunity for the introduction of two or more realities. Event Space is created when there is a change or potential change in anything that was previously considered the norm, the main stream condition of anything, and that includes the change in the environment or the potential change in the environment, due to changes, no matter how small, that creates a before and after condition.

ME: So how does it know when it needs to come into play, to create an alternative, a parallel universe?

O: In my area of self-awareness there is no such thing as a universe or indeed a parallel universe, for they are a product of the Source Entities. You may, in this instance, call it a parallel environment, an environment based upon "all that there is" rather than a universe, for in reality that is what is being created, an environment based upon the area of my awareness.

ME: Hold on though, isn't that recreating that which you are, The Origin—The Absolute—All There Is. I thought you couldn't recreate that which you are!

O: I can't recreate me, but a parallel version of me can be created.

ME: But, but isn't that recreating you! Isn't a parallel version of you a recreation of you?

O: No.

ME: Why?

O: Because the parallel version of me is a local version of me and not me per se.

ME: Go on.

O: When Event Space creates a parallel version of that which is subject to "change"-based division, it does it on a local basis and not on a total basis. When I tried to recreate myself, and we will discuss this subject in much more detail later, I tried to create the whole of me, of which included the totality of self that I wasn't aware of at that point in my existence, within myself. Not knowing exactly how expansive I was meant that I created an error in that which was created and that location it was created in. In essence I tried to squeeze those "Origins" that I created into a fraction of that which I was aware of myself, hence them not surviving.

ME: OK it's a bit clearer now but you still haven't told me how Event Space "knows" when to create a new and parallel environment/universe or area of local space, aligned or un-aligned to an individual entity or event. Just how does it do it?

O: It simply becomes available and localized to that which is recognized as a potential change point.

ME: Yes, but HOW?

O: You remember talking to Source Entity Ten (see *Beyond the Source, Book 2*) about triangulation and how "free energy" is attracted to the opportunity for evolution. To multiply or grow by providing the opportunity for increased evolutionary content of those entities within the "triangulation zone" of both directional and inflational triangulation, effectively creating that which it is attracted to—evolution.

ME: Yes, I do.

O: Well, it's a similar process. I will explain. As a result of the possibility of a different possibility being created, Event Space effectively ends up providing itself as a platform for that which it is attracted to. Event Space is itself a product. It is a product of "looped" creation, the creation of the opportunity for variation from that which currently is, to that which could be, both being in existence concurrently. Indeed, it doesn't even need the inherent opportunity, for if there is an instability in that which "is" then there is the opportunity for at least a dualistic condition to arise in another future but simultaneously occurring event, therefore giving rise to the opportunity for the energies surrounding these two or/and more conditions to be in concurrent existence.

ME: Why did you use the word "looped" then? I saw no opportunity to use the word "looped" in the text above. However, I do have to admit that I have been hearing the words "chicken and egg" for the last fifteen minutes and I can see how the chicken and egg concept can be called looped, for it is the unsolvable conundrum. It's a catch-22 scenario, the one creating the other but the other needs to be created by the one before it can itself create the one.

O: I see your problem in understanding. I will simplify for you—again.

In your current thinking process you are considering that things happen in a linear way. Well, they don't in reality, but you know this. In the greater reality the chicken and the egg can and do exist concurrently, before and after each other. In this way the one can create the other without the need for the other's prior and linear existence.

I can see that you are frowning so I will change the method of explanation. That which Event Space "is," "is" attracted to the possibility of duality and its myriad expansion points of additional duality. You can call it geometrically fractal progression if you like. With the possibility of duality being available, the possibility itself creates the possibility of the creation of duality, which in turn creates the agitation in the energies surrounding the possibility of duality and its multiple possibilities, to the point of potential and therefore possible disharmony. This disharmony cannot exist in the same space so a new space is created as a solution to the disharmony, a new Event Space.

ME: So Event Space is a disharmony of energies based upon the possibility of another possible reality, the possibility of another "space?"

O: No, it is created by that disharmony, the agitation of that which "is," based upon the need for a dualistic state of being. In essence it is the energies, and other components, that are created by the possibility of possible possibilities.

ME: Right, now I think I have got it. Shall we go to that point of your awakening?

O: Yes, let's go. I am looking forward to this, in some bizarre way.

ME: Why?

O: Because I have progressed, and find the need to review that which is prior to progression somewhat regressive. I therefore have not bothered to observe that which has "been" me. I have only observed that which I have done and improved it. That's why it is bizarre. It's different for me, it's good and I thank you for giving me the opportunity for utilizing an aspect of me in observing myself in this way.

ME: Believe me, the honor is ALL mine.

Then we were somewhere else.

Before The Origin—Event Space—
An Automatic Record of That Which "Was"

I experienced nothing, that is nothing like the feeling of translation that I experienced with Source Entity Twelve (see Beyond the Source, Book 2) when it took me to the point of convergence of all Event Space. Then I experienced nothing again, then it was something, but it was nondescript. It was just like being barely awake after a long sleep. I saw colors, blobs of color. I had no idea what was happening. The colors were red and orange and swirling. Blobs of white flashed in front of me. What was I seeing? I was just about to talk to The Origin when it talked to me.

O: Ahh, there you are. I was worried that you would get lost in the vast unassigned tract of energies that were me in the "before" state.

ME: Well, I do have to say that I was wondering what was going on for a moment. I should have prepared myself for it.

O: How could you? It was not anything that you could prepare yourself for.

ME: Thank you for bolstering my confidence. So, what is happening here?

O: We are in a temporary tract of that which is me. A temporary function of that Event Space that is about to come into existence but is based upon the energies that will become dense enough to create the opportunity for my awareness to become enough for the progression into self-awareness.

ME: OK. What are we, what am I, seeing/experiencing then?

O: We are seeing the energies as a representation of that which you are capable of experiencing at the forefront of your current level of experience and form.

ME: Wow! What will happen to the energies?

O: It will be difficult for you to be "present" in your current form long enough to even start the observation of my awakening, so, I will accelerate the imagery so that we can both make the most of the time we have available to us.

With that, things went dark, no, black. I appeared to zoom out of the area that we were in. I started to see, in my mind's eye, the area of "denser" energies and other components of awareness that The Origin had not yet explained to me. That is, if it intended to do so. I received the information to suggest that the area that we were in was in actual fact The Origin "In Totality." At this point in its recognizable existence it was not aware of itself in any way, shape, form, energy, dimension, subdimensional component (tritave), frequency, continuum, plane, zone, or any of the myriad other structural components that I was becoming aware of, but had no way of explaining to either myself, or you, my readers. The Origin was itself seeing part of itself that it hadn't yet seen—that part of itself that was beyond its known perimeter, its area (volume) of self-awareness, including that small area that it had used in the Twelve Origins experiment and that smaller perimeter being investigated by Source Entity Twelve (see the last page of the last chapter in Beyond the Source, Book 2). *I suddenly recognized the enormity of that last statement. The Origin, of course, had ventured beyond that area before, when it created the Twelve Origins in an effort to expand and accelerate its evolutionary content, but what we were seeing now was WELL beyond that.*

From this vantage point The Origin and I were witnessing its birth and were being exposed to the vastness of that which it was, what it could be, what it will be, what we will all participate in, mapping out that which will be The Origin's new area of self-awareness in the long and distant Event Space that will be in place then. I cannot reiterate enough the honor and importance of what I am witnessing here. The Origin itself is enthralled in its observation of self at this point in its existence. I considered the possibility of calculating the size of The Origin.

As The Origin grows in awareness so its access to itself increases, so its volume of "self" increases, so its awareness increases. The Origin experiences an exponential growth of a value inconceivable by any computation that mankind's machines could, or will, derive.

It was impossible to consider and my head hurt thinking about it. I turned my attention back to that aspect of The Origin that had devoted itself to communicating with me and asked it what it was thinking.

ME: What are you thinking about?

O: Interestingly enough I wasn't thinking. I was observing. I can see that you are having difficulty with that statement, specifically with the gravity of that which one is present in, and is therefore part of, in this aspect of Event Space.

ME: You bet I am.

O: Well, I was just observing the vastness of, and therefore savoring, the anticipation of venturing out into that next quadrant of myself and that which is beyond it. You need to understand that even I do not know exactly how big, exactly how expansive, I am.

ME: So what were you observing?

O: I was observing a few tendrils of energy that I had sent forth into the expansiveness, of my vastness as a means of understanding that which I am. I lost contact with the detail after I had sent out enough energy to equal ten times the distance of my furthest points apart in my current area of self-awareness.

ME: What happened to the energy tendrils then?

O: I lost them!

ME: What! You mean you couldn't communicate with them?

O: No, I mean I lost them. They are separated from me as a part of me that is sentient within that which is recognized as me currently.

ME: What does that mean then? What are you suggesting?

O: I am not suggesting anything. What I will say though is that there are now some small parts of me that are in what I will call temporary potentially sentient separation, and that they are somewhere within that part of me that is beyond my current level of understanding, so far beyond my current area/volume of self-awareness that I have lost contact with them.

ME: Don't you now run the risk of having these tendrils developing their own sentience in time, becoming other self-sufficient sentient versions of that which is sentient "you" within that which is you in totality?

O: Up to a certain level, yes.

ME: But couldn't they potentially become bigger than you? Engulfing you, absorbing and therefore removing the individualization of all that which is you?

O: Ha ha ha ha ha, a delicious thought isn't it. No, that is not what will happen.

ME: OK, clever clogs, what will happen?

O: Yes, I agree, they will eventually become individualized, but they will not consume me.

ME: Why not? No, don't tell me, you have a "head start" on them size-wise.

O: No, it's not that. It's because they are created by me. And because they are created by me they can never be more than me.

ME: So what will they become then?

O: They will have the potential to become Om or a Source Entity of the size that all of you will become when all entities are equal with their Source's and we all move out into my next level of self-awareness. It depends upon how, when, and if they become self-aware.

ME: But we can know this, can't we? Just by moving into that Event Space that will now be in existence relative to that possibility?

O: Yes, very well done. You are getting better at this.

ME: I am doing my best.

O: Good then, you will recognize while we have been talking that an aspect of me was working in the background and has already tracked them down in their possible projection of Event Space and observed them in their individualized sentience.

ME: I should have seen that coming! What did they turn into? Sources, Om, or just entities?

O: I now have two new Om and one new Source Entity. Due to the vastness of where they were it was too much for them to stay singular in their individualized energetic density, so to speak. Some of the tendrils grouped/coalesced together to create enough density to create an entity of Source Entity proportions, whereas the others, two of them, were of enough density to become entities large enough to be called Om.

ME: Will we be able to see them?

O: Yes, but not now. We will meet them in another Event Space, where you will be compiling the information from a series of dialogues that will be separate from this one, and the others that will form the book you are calling *The Origin Speaks.*

ME: OK, and what will that be called—"Beyond The Origin," I suppose! (I had already had a subliminal prompt on this but was not sure how a book could be called Beyond The Origin, when The Origin is "All There Is." I decided to leave that one alone and move back to that which we were supposed to be doing, observing The Origin becoming self-aware, sentient.)

O: You are getting better at this, aren't you! OK, let's concentrate on my becoming sentient for the first time.

ME: Hold on. What do you mean becoming sentient the first time? Have you got something up your energetic sleeve?

O: I told you that you were getting better at this. I will explain the detail behind that statement later. Right now let's continue with observing what this particular Event Space has to offer.

(Now there's a clue if I saw one. I made a mental note to follow this up with The Origin, only I got the impression that the answers would come out without my prompting. Event Space was going to be a big player in this dialogue, I could just see it!)

I focused on the task at hand, looking at the detail of the en-
ergies in front of my mind's eye. The imagery I was receiving
was a mixture of seeing gasses, energies and biological cells,
in all sorts of layers. I received the information that the layers
were the first formation of dimensions within the energies
that were being represented by the imagery. It was all being
presented to me in a way that I would understand. I was just
wondering how this was happening when The Origin an-
swered for me.

O: It's a function of Event Space to work with the entities
that are within a specific aspect of it in a way that is
consistent with its level of sentience.

ME: Hold on. You're saying that Event Space is an omniversal
translator of some sort?

O: No. What I am saying is that it works with that which is
within it.

ME: What do you mean? It knows how to communicate?

O: In a way, yes. Do you remember the dialogue we had recently where we were talking about Event Space being
able to, or being invoked by, the possibility of duality.
The possibility of the possibility or a difference in direction from that which "is" to that which is and could be,
and that it can be invoked, or is usually invoked by a
possible decision to be made by a sentient entity.

ME: Yes, I do.

O: Well, this reaction is based upon the level of sentience
the entity has currently achieved. In your incarnate case,
your level of sentience includes your current level of accrued knowledge, love, wisdom, and power. Within this
is the "level" of communicative ability you are able to
employ while incarnate. Based upon this, incarnate
"You" has a certain vocabulary to work with outside of
the action and reaction of Event Space. What you experience is outside of your vocabulary. It is meaningless,
both for you and Event Space, so it gives you information in a way that you can work with, based upon your
vocabulary. It does this in order for you to both under-

stand, while allowing you to work in a way that perpetuates the existence of that particular permutation of Event Space. In essence, in allowing you to experience that which you are experiencing, in a way that you can understand it, maintains its longevity and usefulness while expanding your experiential knowledge.

ME: So what is the reality of what I am seeing? Is this tailored to my own level of experience and understanding?

O: It would be too complicated to explain in the depth necessary to do it real justice. But know this; that which you understand will need to be understandable by incarnate mankind, and as such if it is presented to you in a way it can be understood, it will serve its purpose, even if it is not entirely correct. *Original matter*

Know this also; you are privileged beyond exception in experiencing that which you are while incarnate. Even though you are Om, you are limited, to some extent, to that which all are capable of while incarnate in the particular physical vehicle used in the low frequencies that that aspect of you has chosen to work with in this way. To simplify that last statement, that part of you that is incarnate with the vehicle that is in communication with me has to obey the rules of incarnation in that particular vehicle. Hence your limitation and your ability to contact me are a bit of a dichotomy.

ME: In other words you are saying live with it, because it's the best you and incarnate mankind are going to get for the moment.

O: Correct!!!

ME: OK, I accept my incarnate limitations. However, does that mean that the information I am compiling as a result of my dialogues with you will be incorrect?

O: No, I have just told you. It will be correct for the level of focus you can currently achieve. I will quote your own teachings in this.

ME: I have teachings in this?

O: Of course. You quote it all the time in your "Traversing the Frequencies" workshops.

ME: You listen in to them?

O: No, but I do have an interest, and as such have assimilated all that you have done to date while looking for an example I could use to explain to you the clarity level of that which you are seeing, by using an example of that you know and use yourself. In this instance it's the availability of vocabulary that results in the giraffe being described as a dog.

ME: OK, I've got you now.

For those of you who will know this from my workshops you will, I have no doubt, be chuckling in your shirtsleeves to know that your teacher has snookered himself here. For those of you who don't, please don't quote this when you do attend. However, it is an excellent example so I will explain it for clarity's sake if nothing else.

When we as incarnate beings communicate with disincarnate entities we do not have access to the total experience of spoken, nonspoken, experiential, energetic, and Akashic memory, etc., based communications at our fingertips that can be used for the totally understandable communications that we have normally. We only have a vocabulary based upon our "current" incarnate experience to work with. So if we are shown a picture of a giraffe, but have never before seen one or heard of one, then we are given an image of that which we have experienced that is the closest to the description that we have. If in the instance of the giraffe we only have a dog, the relationship being four legs all on the ground to help it move over the surface of the Earth, a tail, and a head with two eyes, two ears, a mouth, and a nose, then that description is good enough, "for the moment." It is going in the right direction and will therefore suffice in the short term. It will suffice, that is, until we either have an experience of an animal which is closer in description, i.e., a horse or donkey, or until we actually experience being in the presence of a giraffe, wherein the description is completely recognizable and fully understood. In this example we have gone from being "out of focus" because the information being received is too far away to see in clarity and detail, to either having a telescope to see closer, or the ability to travel as close to the object of discussion as necessary to both see the object clearly and be able to recognize it for what it truly is, thereby seeing and understanding the truth in detail and clarity. So, to put it in a nutshell, we are allowed to be in some error in our understanding of the greater reality as long as we are going in the right direction. This also goes in some way to explain the process of personal ascension (evolution) being a necessary function of access to higher-frequency knowledge and ability.

O: Good. Now that we have that sorted you can continue with your narration of that which you are perceiving.

ME: Right.

I refocused my attention back to that which was presented before me. It was astonishingly simple. The energies (I will describe them as that) were, as far I could see, all about me. Everything was in separation while being together. Being separately together was a concept that I had witnessed throughout my dialogues with the twelve Source Entities. It was clearly a structural theme taken from the very beginning of that which was destined to be The Origin.

As I looked, I saw these energies slowly swirling around, and as they swirled around they became attracted to that which was either similar to, or could work with, an aspect of each other's characteristics. I was looking at this in an accelerated fashion, I knew, but it still looked like it was a slow process. As I continued to watch, some of those energies that had linked up started to accelerate their attractivity to other energies of like composure or function. When they achieved what I can only assume was a critical mass or density, they disappeared from my spiritual vision. As I wondered what was going on I received the information (from somewhere—it felt like commonly available omni-omniversal knowledge) that I should follow them. I no sooner had the intention in my mind to follow them than I found I was somewhere else with a different set of energies swirling around me, but with that set of energies that had previously disappeared now back in full view. I must have shifted dimension or something I thought. I moved my intention to see that which I was seeing in the first instance, and I was back at that point in Event Space just in time to see another set of energies disappear. I followed them. I emerged in a different area with a different set of energies swirling around me and that set of energies that had just disappeared in full view. However, what was not in view was that set of energies that had previously disappeared. I moved my intention back to the first place I went to, where the first set of energies had relocated to, and they were there. The second set of energies was not. I moved back to the original location where both sets of energies had originated from before they disappeared.

Things were happening quickly now and I was able to observe more and more energy sets being created and disappear, only to reappear into new areas, or should I say dimensions. No, I was being told on a subliminal basis that what was being observed was a higher function than dimensions. I was just starting to wonder what was going to happen next when I realized that I was seeing the start of the building of the structure that was to be The Origin that I know, and am communicating with. What I was seeing here was the beginning of the construction of the structure of The Origin. I also realized that it must have reached a certain level of structure before it started to gain self-awareness and sentience. Using my intention, I decided to zoom out to a point where I could observe a fuller picture.

Ah, yes, this was better, I could see the beginning of a structure now, or should I say I could perceive the beginning for a structure, for it was not anything that could be related to in the human sense. What I perceived was the creation of a framework, a sort of multifunctional framework. A multifunctional periodic table sprang to mind as a way of describing it.

As each energy set was established, and winked out of existence in its original location of creation, it reappeared in an area relative to those energies that were close to its own components and functionality. Some just hung in space, whereas others linked together to create some other part of the structure that was either within the same space or joined two areas of space together that were similar, while still being different or separate in some way. These, I noticed, were the links between spaces. A sort of network was being formed. As more energies of like kind were created their further creation was accelerated, and the picture of what was happening became more and more complete. I wondered at what the other spaces were. I didn't have to wait long, for The Origin came to my rescue.

O: Remarkable how it all happened, isn't it?

ME: Yes, it is. Tell me, what are the different spaces?

O: Can't you guess?

ME: I can make a good guess, but it won't be accurate by any means.

O: I wouldn't expect it to be, but give it your best shot.

ME: OK, the different spaces are dimension and their components, zones and their divisions, continuum and their abstractions, planes and their spheres, spheres independent of planes and their references, Event Spaces and their events, totalities and their realities, realities independent of totalities and their creative functions ... there was more and more. Much more than I could possibly name or even try to name. It's infinitesimal. In fact, infinities were one of the spaces. Where does it stop! *(This information just poured into my mind. I vowed to ask for more detail on both the existing and new structural details later in the dialogue.)*

O: Actually, I currently don't know either, but those that you have mentioned are those that were necessary for me to become self-aware and later sentient as an intelligence borne from that which "is."

ME: You gave them to me then. I wasn't guessing?

O: Yes, I did, and no, you weren't. The most important thing here is that you have absorbed that which is the basis of my original structure. Which is to all intents and purposes, the basis for what I am today. Each of the "spaces" holds the content and structure of the previous space plus their own.

ME: Everything is repeated then the further out one goes from the center, with the addition of the next space being that which identifies the difference.

O: Yes, with Event Space being the commonality between them all.

ME: So that was what I could see linking the spaces together.

O: Yes, and other commonalities that can be considered linking energies.

In essence what I had observed was the creation of a huge jigsaw puzzle with all the parts starting to link together creating a localized whole. The whole, when whole enough, having enough energies in a certain configuration to spark off a cascade of events necessary to link those component parts of the whole, that displayed the characteristics of becoming self-aware, together.

I refocused my attention and immediately saw a new landscape before me. It was beautifully arranged and unfathomably intricate while also being mind-blowingly convoluted. Every little link in and between the energies was accounted for and was conveying some kind of energy. Communication energy came into my mind, the sort that conveyed the energies and communication associated with the triangulation necessary to create a fully intelligent, self-aware, sentient being of incalculable proportions—the three functions of Intelligence, Self-Awareness, and Sentience all relying on the formation of the former, in this order, to create the next. The three together were working together, being a prerequisite for the overall omnipotence that is The Origin. What I was seeing here though was just a small part of that which was The Origin in its current level of totality. I received further information. The Origin at this point of its existence was minute in comparison to that which it is today. Clearly I thought, this is a conundrum, for if The Origin is "All There Is," then how can this be all that there is, "then," and all there is now? Of course! I remembered, this is The Origin in its state of near-zero growth, whereas what we have now is The Origin in a state of some expansion or growth. We know this because of the information received in previous dialogues where The Origin will evolve to its next level of evolution at some distant part in Event Space, what we call the future. We also have the dialogue above, which indicated the different structural components of The Origin. I was just starting to feel more comfortable in my understanding when The Origin commented on some of my thought processes.

O: What you have negated to relay to the reader is the information currently in your head about the spread of this Omnipotence throughout the rest of the collective energies.

ME: Well, I was just getting to that but why don't you advise us yourself? I am starting to get somewhat groggy with all this and the bottleneck of energy that is associated with the information that is coming through you about the next stage in your growth from this, supposedly small beginning.

O: I can see that I will have to reduce what you would call the data flow. OK, with that done I will take it from here for the time necessary to finish this part of the subject. What happened next was a wonder in its own right. Those energies that were drawn together initially through the attractive forces relative to energies of the same "type," so to speak, also started to attract energies of similar, but not same, energetic signature or function—specifically those energies that were sympathetic to the association with another energy due to aspects of neutrality of energetic function, which allowed the energies to join together in sympathy with each other's function without interfering with each other. Indeed, this allowed a level of connectivity that was not available before.

ME: Why was that? What was the difference?

O: The energies that had neutrality were the ones where the periphery of the energies were "thin," that is, they were not as dense along the outer edges as they were in the center of the collection of the energy. I use the word collection here because the energies at this point in my awakening process were collecting together so that all energies of like type, within the location now known as the epicenter of my sentience, were separating out and collecting together in groups specific to their type and function. In your terms, the oil was separating out from the water, so to speak. Not only that, it was moving well away from each other, so only those that had the element of neutrality resulting from the "thinness" of energies along the periphery could join together. What was also an important aspect of this process was the way the

21

energies presented themselves. Rather than becoming an alloy, where the molecules (in the example of the alloy) interact with each other linking together to create something different with each other at the moment of interaction, in essence becoming a new "third" material containing and being constructed from the two separate and independent materials, that can, and are, affected by the ratio of the materials within the alloy, they became separate while also being linked. They were separately together *(this just keeps coming up, I must question The Origin on the significance of this statement, rather than thinking I understand it)* like islands of different energies that were linked around their peripheries. The biggest part of this was not the linking together of "islands" of energies that were close together, but that they actively sought each other out, bypassing those energies that were close by, but traveling greater distances to be part of the same energies or be linked to energies that had peripheries of compatible neutrality. This illustrated that the energies at this point had, or were, developing some sort of rudimentary intelligence, demonstrated by their ability to be discerning about what other energies they actively sought out and what energies they actively avoided contact with.

ME: This was the start of your gaining intelligence, the route to gaining self-awareness then.

O: Clearly.

ME: How long and how far was this joining together of separate energies?

O: It was a rapidly increasing area and the area was increasing in a multipolous way.

ME: It went viral?

O: Yes, and it still is. It is a viral effect that never reaches its end goal of infestation, to date that is.

ME: So, how do you cope with it then?

O: I don't.

ME: Why not? I would have thought that you would be able to work with that which is "you" as you expand.

O: No. It doesn't work that way. You see, not all of "me," that which has "intelligence," has the capability to become self-aware and later sentient, hence the need for help to map myself and know myself better.

ME: Why not? I would also have thought that you would be sentience personified, with sentience in existence throughout everything.

O: Again, it doesn't work that way. I will explain.

We talked about Event Space being in existence before my self-awareness became prominent enough, that I was aware of some level of the totality of what I was.

ME: We did.

O: Well, Event Space is a form of, and is some part of, my structure. As Event Space is separate from my sentience and has a function that is individual to my sentience, so other components that make up my totality have separate and individual existence and functionality. They are my structure, the links between that which is my sentience and that which is my totality.

ME: They are then a bit like the bones, muscles, sinews, veins, arteries, and organs that make up my physical body. They are not sentient, but they are part of the physicality of that part of me that is incarnate.

O: Correct and well done. So you can now see why I needed to create those entities that are called Source Entities, and previously tried to recreate myself as a multiple, in order to investigate myself in a more in-depth and accelerated way.

ME: So your area of self-awareness is exactly what it is, that part of you of which you are in total knowledge of that which you are?

O: No, not in totality. It's mapped out and recognized as being me, and parts of this area are known in minute detail. Other areas though are mapped out and recognized as "self," but I am not intimately aware of the detail behind those areas. It's a bit like you having a map of the Earth. You are aware of the existence of certain countries, and you might even visit some of these countries, experiencing a certain but small area within a city of one of these countries, but you do not know the detail behind that area which you have visited and you certainly do not know the rest of that country, because you did not actually "go there" and experience it for yourself. You learn about the detail, or should I say some of the detail, through the eyes of others who have visited these areas, and recorded that which they have experienced, for the benefit of others, to expand the overall knowledge base of that which is the Earth, expanding it in a multipolous way, relative to the number of individuals experiencing and recording that which is experienced. If it was left to one person, the speed at which that which is part of the Earth would be understood and recognized by all would be so slow that it would result in a level of evolutionary progression that would border on the negative, which is inefficient from an evolutionary perspective and therefore unacceptable to any self-aware or sentient entity, which obviously includes myself, hence the need to employ help, which in itself can also employ further help.

ME: Understood. Mmmm, based upon this then your area of intelligence is different to your area of self-awareness, which is "in turn" different to your area of sentience?

O: Correct, hence my need and desire to know more about myself in an accelerated way. I need to keep up with the expansion of my potential intelligence.

ME: This area of intelligence and sentience, why are they different?

O: Because, as I have stated before, there is a natural progression from, say, the energetic to the intelligent energetic, to the energetic that is intelligent and self-aware to that which is sentience borne from the intelligent—self-aware energetic.

ME: Oh, I think I understand now! Can I use an example?

O: You can.

ME: If I consider that which is your intelligent energy is represented as "memory" in a computer, having the potential for rudimentary intelligence should the right program be used to employ it, then it is useful as an opportunity, for the expansion of useable intelligent memory,

24

but is dormant until accessed or given purpose, and used by an aspect of the right program that is "self-aware" enough of the availability of this memory and is "sentient" enough to use it in a creative way. Now, clearly a computer program is not sentient, but as a thought process it is a useful illustration.

O: Actually it is a perfect illustration, for that is almost how I am progressing, but of course, it is from a simplistic perspective. The difference between that which you illustrated and that which is how I work in actuality is slightly different. When my sentience expands into an area of me that is dormant but capable of becoming sentient, self-aware, intelligent energy then I become more expansive and my area of sentience expands within my area of self-awareness allowing my in-depth knowledge of my area of self-awareness to increase, reducing the area of my ignorant awareness of "self."

Those energies that you observed linking together while remaining separate from those parts that they were linking to are used for creative purposes. They had no individual opportunity to develop intelligence, but they did and do form that part of me that forms the structure of my area of self-awareness.

Chapter 2

The Expansion of Sentient, "Self-Aware" Intelligence

ME: Let's move on a bit. I/We have observed the very beginning of how those energies that were attracted to each other became one and how those that were not quite the same were able to join together while still being separate or maintaining their individuality. This created the framework, so to speak, the network of energies necessary for the creation and expansion of sentient, "self-aware" intelligence. However, we haven't discussed how the energies and other components of your structure developed intelligence and self-awareness to the point of gaining sentience.

Ö: OK, let's go to that point where the energies are developing these "traits."

And with that there was a white light and a white background and I found myself positioned above what I recognized as an area of already constructed "Origin energy" that had, and was still, actively "seeking out" energies of the same type.

O: The act of "actively" seeking out energies of the same type is the start of rudimentary intelligent decision making. When there is enough "mass," call it a critical mass if you like, of this type of decision-making energy, i.e., that type of energy that is capable of making a choice about staying singular or seeking out energy of the same type, then the ability to make more complicated decisions can also be made by the inclusion of all of those energies that actively sought out energies of the same type, in the next decision process. This effectively increases the, shall I say, computational capacity, the ability to process much more information, to make bigger

26

decisions, decisions that need information from a multitude of different areas before a robust decision can be made. You could call it parallel processing if you like, but the important thing about parallel processing is that it is a prelude to true intelligent decision making. What's more, the opportunity for a decision to be made also invokes a new and separate Event Space. This is another sign of the development, the evolution of, intelligence. Let's look at what's happening here.

Errmm, I will accelerate that which we are seeing so that you can gain a more instantaneous recognition of that which is happening.

My attention refocused on being the observer of this most wonderful event. I saw clumps of energies grouping together, accumulating mass, critical mass, increasing functionality. The clumping together of like or similar energies accelerated. I saw groups of energies attracting "like" energies together, large groups attracting smaller groups, parting, splitting, and reforming to allow energies or groups of energies that are not the same, to pass through the larger group if it is easier to do so rather than go around the outer periphery of the larger group.

There was discernment forming, another form of intelligence, as a result of the process of acquiring the ability to provide the function of avoidance, when seeking out energies of like or sympathetic type. Energies that were initially accepted, but that were later identified as not being at an optimal, or minimal, level of the energetic content required, were later rejected in favor of energies of more appropriate quality. There was a progression in the level of intelligent decision making, including the detail behind the decision making, the complexity of which was becoming profound. Structure in the decision making was being observed logically, and the logic was becoming more and more detailed, becoming computational as the volumes of similar or same energies increased and the connectivity between energies of different type was established.

The images progressed.

The energies, those that had developed intelligence of some sort, of whatever level or complexity, were starting to notice their limitations in decision making, logic, and computational ability. They appeared to be limited by their energy type or area/volume/density or quality. They, the energies that is, were also noticing that these limitations created a specialization of some sort, limiting that which they could achieve on their own. These groups of energies appeared to wander around for a period of time, looking as if they were aimless in their direction. This continued for some time, with the numbers of groups of energies "displaying this behavior" increasing at what appeared to be an accelerated rate, drawing the observer to the conclusion that this was an evolutionary or progressionary "dead end," each group having its own speciality, being limited to that speciality and not progressing further. Each speciality being either slightly different or majorly different, that is, until something special happened.

Some of them stopped moving in an aimless way. Some of these energies started to move closer together, stopping at a certain distance from each other. I then noticed links being formed between these groups. They, each group, that is, started to modify the energies associated with their boundaries, creating a sort of neutral zone, but their level of neutrality was variable and dependent upon the energies that were being approached. By approached I mean that they actively and intentionally moved toward those groups of energies that were sympathetic to each other's function, were not the same, but if co-joined would create a significant increase in the separate functionality when added together. It was the start of synergetic effect, but those groups of energies that were approaching a group or series of groups needed to be modified so that the two groups, or more than two groups that were approaching or being approached, could join together, not in totality but in a linked methodology. This maintained the separate group functionality while augmenting the intellectual and reasoning ability of the two groups' separate, intellectual, or computational abilities, creating an ability to deal with larger or more complicated decisions when working in tandem.

I zoomed out a bit. This was happening everywhere and on a massive scale, a scale so big that I could not zoom out enough to take in the bigger picture. Initially, when I saw this, it was *in ones and twos, with the groups that were "linking up" being interspersed between those groups that were not approaching one another and creating links of so-called neutral energies. Now it was happening everywhere and with greater numbers and in greater speed. I asked The Origin if it had speeded up the imagery that it was sending me.*

ME: Have you accelerated the imagery, or is this a real-time acceleration?

O: Well, the imagery is accelerated anyway.

ME: Understood, but is it a faster transmission than before?

O: No, it is what it is. Based upon that, you can make a few conclusions about what was happening if you like.

ME: I would say that there is a certain level of acceleration due to the other groups catching up with those that are linking up, i.e., they are just creating the same opportunity for increased functionality that the others were, but that they were a bit slower off the mark.

O: Yes, but what else was happening? Use your perception.

I did and was surprised to see that "triangulation" was having an effect. I shouldn't have been surprised as it was an inevitable function.

O: OoKaay, why would it have been inevitable?

ME: I wasn't expecting this to turn into an examination.

O: It isn't, but the readers need to know.

ME: Mmmm, I get the feeling that you are testing my understanding of that which I am seeing.

O: Go on, it's good for you. You will be working with much more complex information later. It will be a quantum leap from that which you were exposed to with the Source Entities. You should find this easy as it is very much based upon that which you have experienced and worked with in previous dialogues.

ME: OK, OK, I will get on with it. I would expect that the function of triangulation was working at a higher level in this instance, with the energies associated with triangulation effectively sensing the evolutionary opportunity associated with the linking up of the groups of energies for synergetic purposes.

O: Carry on.

ME: Irrespective of the level of work being done, the changes being initiated by the rudimentary intelligence of the energies and groups of energies, whether they were just linking up or increasing their level of intelligence through the links that they had created together was, to all intents and purposes, an evolutionary step, no matter how small. The energies that create triangulation could sense this in some way. Also, because the groups of energies that were making the next step in their "personal" evolution were spaced far apart and interspaced, both direct line and area-based triangulation was being invoked simultaneously. With the interspersion being that which it was, the triangulation effect was able to work at a level of efficiency that, apart from being a wonder to see, was exactly the right level of interspersion to allow a profound and accelerated triangulation effect that was sweeping though the energies in a way that would leave a virus-based acceleration far, far behind. In fact, it would leave it standing.

O: Yes, it would. What you are witnessing is the spark of intelligence ripping though the energies that were responding to the call for unity and synergy. The synergetic effect in this instance was also affecting the way in which triangulation was progressing. In essence this caused an acceleration in change that was multipolous to the point of instantaneous change.

ME: I have just received an image and information that suggests that triangulation coupled together in a synergetic effect, effectively resulted in the instantaneous alignment of energies of sympathetic and augmented function. Not only that, they were all polarized in a way that made them, to all intents and purposes, instantaneously operational.

O: Well observed. You see, once there was a certain level of synergetically affected triangulation-based critical mass, everything was pulled in to alignment without the need for intelligent choice being pulled into play. In fact, intelligent decision making in this instance would have been a hindrance, for when an instantaneous change is invoked everything is organized according to the structure of the intelligent choices being made in the first place. The choices creating the framework for the plan also create the links necessary for the instantaneous change when it is ready to happen.

ME: So, and here is the billion-dollar question, were you, therefore, instantaneously self-aware as a result of this instantaneous change?

O: No, that was the result of another process altogether.

ME: What was created then, that is, what was created as a result of the instantaneous change?

O: Intelligence given mass. Enough mass at the epicenter of the change to allow the start of a higher form of intelligence, intelligence that is aware of itself and its intelligence. But it was more than that, for the intelligence also knew of the structure of that which is was at the epicenter, including all of the energies, frequencies, planes, zones, dimensions, continuum, etc., etc.

ME: And where was this epicenter?

O: You're in it now!

ME: Errr, you've lost me.

O: Then I shall elaborate. That part of me that is in communication with you, and that which is known to myself, the Source Entities and the Om, is, to all intents and purposes, the epicenter. The rest, that which is beyond my area of self-awareness, is that which is me under development, that part of me that I am aware of but that is not "self-aware"—yet needs "me" to move my consciousness into that, shall I say, "unused" part of me to achieve the next instantaneous change.

ME: So why haven't you moved into it yet?

O: Simply because I am not ready yet. I have barely started to get into the detail of this part of me, let alone go further. It would be confusing and detrimental to say the least. Having said that though, I am receiving information from Source Entity Twelve that is very interesting. We should go out to see what it's up to someday.

ME: I very much agree. In fact, I can see another book on the horizon.

O: I thought you might, but not now for this dialogue is an entirely different set of information.

ME: Tell me then, how intelligence given mass leads to self-awareness.

O: Why not observe it?

ME: I would very much like to.

With that the images blurred a moment and the landscape of energies subsequently changed to what I can only recognize as a different Event Space where the instantaneous change had happened. Everything was in order. Not that it is in any order that mankind would recognize, but one that was intuitively recognized as being in an optimal condition for that which it was destined to be next, intelligent and self-aware. I zoomed into the energies that were in front of me. They presented all sorts of structures. Structures that were static, structures that were dynamic, structures that changed or morphed into that required to deal with the task that it was currently working with, whether it was singular or multiple. Everything, I noticed, was both multifunctional and multienvironmental. By environmental I mean that it was linked to the different environmental conditions associated with the different aspects of The Origin's newly formed structure, in every way. As with the formation of the energies that reestablished themselves on different frequencies, dimensions, or zones, etc., during the initial embryonic intelligent decisions, so part of The Origin's epicenter of the "structure" of its area of self-awareness showed parts of it disappearing from my view, as far as I was concerned, that is. Then it all came into view as one large, all-encompassing structure, pulsating, moving and functioning. I received a message from The

Origin telling me that it had given me multidimensional, multizonal, multi-everything, spiritual sight, etc., for a short period of time, so that I could observe the totality of the structure and observe it in its magnificence. And it was so very magnificent.

O: This is a microcosmic image for you to consider. When you are in the macrocosmic you would not see such detail for it would be too fine for you to judge where and what it is. You should continue with observing that which is about to happen.

The image returned back to a level that was a mixture of the detail that I was seeing at first while also being fine enough to see the overall picture. In fact, as I focused on what was being presented to me, I noticed that The Origin had given me two images on top of each other, the detail, the microcosmic and enough of the macrocosmic, the finitude, to make sense to me.

ME: Why did you do that?

O: So that you can see both the changes at the detail end of the spectrum and the wider end of the spectrum concurrently. In this way you will be able to appreciate more of that which is happening. It would be detrimental to the information being shown to see it from one perspective as you would not be able to see, shall I say, the picture as it should be seen.

The energies that previously had separate but co-joined intelligence through association now had collective intelligence. All of the separated intelligences had now become one "larger" intelligence, albeit on varying levels of use, function, and complexity. This was it! This was the start of the cooperation of all of the separated, localized intelligences joining together to become "one" mega-large intelligence. Each of the localized intelligences had, to all intents and purposes, their own individuality and functional specialisms based upon what energies created their intelligence and what they were working with. Although the individualized functions and specialisms were maintained, they had effectively given up their overall individuality in order to create something much bigger. Each of the individualized intelligences had sacrificed its individuality for the glory of being part of that which was destined to be The Origin, The Absolute, All There Is, in all of its complexity, its finery, its multiplicity. It was cooperation on a scale never before seen and not seen since.

Then I saw a flash, and everything stopped for a moment, a second, or was it a second? I was not sure for everything appeared to be in some sort of momentary stasis.

O: This is it, spontaneous, multipolous, unification of intelligence. "Collective" intelligence made into "One" intelligence, the creation of that which is me. The "I"—in pre-awareness slumber that is!!

I got the impression that The Origin had a smile of satisfaction on its face, placing its hands on the back of its head while leaning back in a comfy chair, should it have had any of those things to hand.

Everything appeared to be, I will say "golden," for a moment. It is a very interesting place to be right now. The energies feel VERY different from a moment ago. Before this moment they very much felt like a collection of sympathetic intelligent energies, separate but together, in "oneness" but not "one," "intelligent" but not "intelligence," functional but not aware. Now they had purpose to them. They were now singular. I couldn't refer to them as "they" anymore for that was very definitely not how the energies felt; they were now singular, "one." The word "I" was repeatedly being broadcast in my mind. Suddenly, in fact just as suddenly as everything had become static, everything started to work again. The energies were flashing here, there, and everywhere. They were not flashing around in separation though, in isolation of purpose. They all had one singular purpose, they were of one thought— "I AM."

O: Ahh! Here we go—Awareness of Self.

The Origin was definitely enjoying this and I again got the impression that we had fast-forwarded a bit.

O: Not so much fast-forwarded. More a case of merged Event Spaces.

ME: What do you mean?

O: Event Space, or should I say the various Event Spaces associated with my awakening process, merged together at this point, for this is the mainstream event, and it has very much come into fruition. I see you frowning again; you must stop that and ask an intelligent question instead.

ME: Errr, have I just witnessed Event Space Convergence? *(I was crying slightly—a signpost of the truth I had come to know and trust over the years.)*

O: Woo Hooo! Yes, you have, the very first, at least the very first that I was aware of. In this instance the convergence is a monumental one. One where all possible possibilities associated with my awakening have converged into one "inevitability," and not a possibility. Now we are accelerating. My thought processes are starting to move beyond the limitations of that experienced in separated intelligence and even collective synergetic-based intelligence. Now it's time for the formation of thought and the establishment of "I" into the awareness of "I am" and therefore the awareness of self.

The flashing had increased in frequency to that of "no" frequency; it was above frequency and had become "presence." I was now able to observe the epicenter of The Origin from a vast distance away. I was somehow positioned in a superb vantage point.

There appeared to be ... it seemed very familiar. Yes, of course! I was observing what I can only describe as "testing," yes, testing was going on, all around the epicenter. I received the information that suggested that The Origin was now aware and was probing around that which it was aware of. It was testing itself. Working out what it was and what it could do.

O: Very well done.

ME: But I thought that the advent of self-awareness would be monumental, a sudden and all-embracing realization of self.

O: Wasn't the change of frequency of thought to that beyond thought and the creation of "presence" monumental enough for you?

ME: Oh! Sorry, I must have missed its significance.

O: You bet you did. Subtle, wasn't it, though, seamless, harmonious, fluid. I did a good job there. No bolts of lightning or shaking of continuum, just transition from one state to another.

ME: And now you are testing yourself out, seeing what you can do, what you are, what you could be?

O: In sorts, yes. I am not yet fully self-aware and won't be until I have checked out all that I am.

I was receiving pictures again. The self-aware intelligence of that which was the newly aware Origin was darting all over the place, that is, within a locale. I was getting the impression that this area of self-awareness was much smaller than that which it was currently aware of and was working within. It was probing the frequencies and understanding itself. This was exciting, for these images were similar to those I received in the early days of my communications with the Source and The Origin. This was the start of sentience.

O: Correct. My area or volume of self-awareness only expanded when I decided to accelerate my understanding of "self," mentally, if you want to call it that, and that which I am/was.

ME: So what caused your area of self-awareness to expand?

O: In short, my need to accelerate my accrued knowledge of self and the evolutionary content that I was subsequently starting to recognize and desire. To do this I needed to overcome another hurdle, an evolutionary hurdle, so to speak.

ME: And that was?

O: Creativity.

ME: Creativity?

O: Creativity. You see, creativity, and the recognition of that which is created as being a function of the creative process, and, that it is a means to fulfill a specific or certain desire, is a precursor for the generation of sentience.

My desire for accelerated evolutionary content resulting from my "testing" or "probing" of "self" led me to think in a certain way. If "I am" and my "I amness" creates evolution then if I duplicate my "I amness" then I will duplicate my evolutionary content in the process. This thought process, together with the recognition of the cause and effect of certain actions before they are deployed, leads to judgment-based creativity, and judgment-based creativity achieved in a rational, well thought-out way is a mark of Sentience. So at this point in my development, moving along this path, this Event Space if you like, I had embarked upon that which was to ensure my change in status from self-aware intelligent energy to sentient, self-aware intelligence in full awareness of that which it is and that which it could be— for that particular point in Event Space.

ME: Are you suggesting that you knew how expansive you were even at that point in sentient existence?

O: No, I am not. As I have stated before, even now I don't accurately know the answer to that particular question. Exciting, isn't it? REALLY EXCITING. At that point in my sentient awareness, I was just like you are now. We have used this analogy before, and it is a good one so I will use it again. It is like you knowing that the universe exists and is infinitesimally large, so large that you don't know just how large it is, but you know it exists.

That which you have been able to observe and capture with the various telescopic technologies at your disposal have only given you a minute but nevertheless expansive idea of the size of the physical universe. You observe that which continues to disappear into the depths of "space," the limit of your observations being the limitation of the detectability of your instruments. You therefore know that there is more to the universe because of the history surrounding the progressive depths that you can probe to when you have better and more accurate telescopic instruments at your fingertips.

The boundaries keep being pushed back with every new technological improvement that is employed, illustrating that there is more to come, should the technology improve again. However, this only includes that which is visible to the very limited bandwidth of the human eye, the calibration piece for the technologies used, for there is of course much more to the physical universe that your Source Entity created than meets the eye. This is how I saw that which was my area of self-awareness at that point in Event Space. It is also how I see my area of self-awareness now, with of course the knowledge of "self" that I have now, which is clearly substantially more than I had then.

One thing I am "aware" of though is that that which I am "self-aware" of, and have created within, is infinitely small in comparison to that which I am "aware of."

ME: You are suggesting that "self-awareness of being" and "awareness of being" are mutually exclusive while being fully supportive?

O: Yes.

ME: One being full awareness with the other being partial or even extrapolated awareness based upon the calculation of that which is "understood" into that which "should be" based upon that which has been "known" over certain junctures in existence and progressed accordingly through the extrapolation.

O: Very well put. You see I know how small my area of self-awareness is in comparison to how expansive I am in totality. It's just that at this juncture in my self-awareness this knowledge is based upon that which I have experienced to date. That is, from the perspective of expanded self-awareness.

ME: So your idea of how big your area or volume of self-awareness is, versus your total size, is a guess, and the extrapolated size is bound to be in error?

O: As I become more expansive, so my ability and accuracy in my extrapolation of true size of self increases. So yes, it is in error, or should I say, it is bound to be in error. But, it's the best I have at the moment. Hence the creation of the Source Entities, to accelerate this knowledge of self and the expansion of the boundaries of self-awareness of self. It is also where you come in, all of you that are created by the Source Entities. You are all destined to expand my area of self-awareness beyond that which it currently is.

ME: It's a glass ceiling then?

O: I would put it more as a glass boundary.

ME: Sounds like this is a good time to discuss the creation of the Twelve Origins.

O: It's as good a time as any.

Chapter 3

The Creation of the Twelve Origins: Sentient Creativity and Expansion of Self-Awareness

ME: Specifically before we embark upon the decision to create the Twelve Origins and then the twelve Source Entities, we need to explain to the reader who has not read the previous books, a little bit of the history. I know we have alluded to it in the recent dialogue but I want to flesh it out a bit.

O: OK. What do you want me to share?

ME: Just some of the information surrounding your investigation of self, your "probing" of the depths of that which you were/are.

O: Actually this will be a good "lead-in" to the decision to create the Twelve Origins and why it failed.

ME: Then it is perfect. Fire away.

The Origin's Investigation into Self Results in the Need for Help

O: Once I had made the quantum leap, for want of a better word, into self-awareness, sentience followed rather quickly. Although, this only happened after I had started to experience more of myself and started to experiment with those energies and structural components, the frequencies, the dimensions and their subdimensional components, the zones, the planes, and countless other structural components that are part of my make-up. We will deal with some of these later in this dialogue, including some that you have not yet been advised of as part of your last book *(Beyond the Source, Book 2)*.

ME: I remember that the Source Entity, my Source Entity, went through a period of self investigation in its own road to sentience, and that it spent a lot of time experimenting with the effects of frequency in relation to the awareness of "self" of that which was projected into the lower frequencies, even though they were part of its own make-up. The way my own Source Entity based its experiences was mostly on that which it experienced in the structural frequencies of the energies that you used to create it. That was the impetus for the creation of the multiverse in what I now understand, when I look back that is, is a very simple environment.

O: Yes, it is simple and, as you have already conveyed in previous dialogue and text, it is designed specifically for smaller units of itself to accrue evolutionary content. It is "ascension in action," as you so eloquently put it during your workshops.

In my investigation of self I had a bit of a head start. Not the sort of head start that I gave the Source Entities when they became self-aware, by "downloading" my total knowledge base into those energies that had been developed for retention of experience, my memory if you like. I had to start from scratch. I was an amalgamation of all of those smaller parts that had joined up in sympathetic union, denying and sacrificing singularity for oneness, in favor of oneness in totality. Once I was "I," I had an accumulation of experiences, those accrued by myself in these smaller component parts, to draw upon as a total experience and memory base. It was fundamental in its detail, its approach, and its functionality. It was a complete picture of that which I was aware of, in every way. As a result I gained an instantaneous understanding of my local self during the amalgamation process and the generation of total self-awareness. Sentience came as a result of learning or realizing that the "I" in me could create something new.

ME: What led you to the desire to create?

O: Experimentation. I noticed that my essence, that which was me, was located in different places simultaneously, that I could zoom into any of these places at will while also being aware of the other places. My presence was not what one would call omnipresent. It was more like pockets of "locale," linked together presence that encompassed a surrounding area or volume of space. These I noticed were the previous areas of "singular" intelligence, which were now linked together. So, the first thing I did was to encompass all those areas of linked but localized pockets of intelligence and their surrounding areas, to create a single but all-encompassing intelligence that flooded all the areas of localized intelligence so that I could zoom into, or project my presence into, the smallest part of any locality while also being cognizant of the rest of my area of self-awareness. This was my first act of creativity and as a result the resolution of my understanding of self, my self improved exponentially. From your perspective it was like observing the difference in resolution, for example, of an image captured on a digital camera of 1.0 megapixel to a digital camera of 1.0 billion megapixels. My internal resolution was no longer pixelated, so to speak.

ME: And that made a big difference?

O: You bet. It was like going from controlling things by remote control, and having very limited control as a result, including no feedback, to having full and total control and, more importantly, full feedback from those areas that were now in control. You really can't understand the full extent of the functionality I went from—to.

ME: Thank you. I expect I will understand the true meaning of this when I am disincarnate.

O: To a certain level, yes, but that level will be significantly greater than that which you understand and can possibly experience now.

ME: This level of creativity, i.e., "modification of self," resulting from your recognition of structure and limited functionality was a defining moment then?

O: Yes, it was. It created the change in me that was required for complete omnipresence.

ME: What followed next? I mean, how long did it take to get to the point where you decided to create the Twelve Origin's experiment?

O: Once bestowed with omnipresence I played (experimented) with this level of being. I wanted to see how I reacted to experiencing all things in all parts of my area of self-awareness concurrently, as well as when focused upon a small area of microscopic proportions. I also experimented by splitting up parts of myself into separate units to see if that made a difference to how I experienced myself, and that which I was experimenting with. I was able to manipulate everything about myself that I discovered. In this respect my creativity recognized no boundaries, no limitations—or so I thought. It was during these experiments that I "noticed" that "there was" actually a "boundary" around me.

ME: And this boundary was the perimeter of your self-awareness?

O: Yes, it was a strange, but now understandable, sensation. It was like I was surrounded in darkness, but it wasn't darkness. The darkness was a limitation in my omnipresence.

ME: You mean you were omnipresent up to a certain point and then it disappeared?

O: Not so much disappeared, more like faded away the further away from this boundary I projected my consciousness, my sentience.

ME: So you recognized that you had a limitation at this point, a limitation in self-awareness.

O: Yes, but again I will state that this limitation was nothing like you would recognize as a limitation, for just "being" that which I was then, at that juncture in Event Space, is beyond the comprehension of any sentient entity created by any of my creations, my Source Entities.

ME: You have progressed since then though. You understand much more and have achieved much more.

O: Yes, clearly. I will explain more about this boundary, this area, or volume if you want to call it that, of my self-awareness.

ME: Please do.

O: I could, and did, project my consciousness, my sentience, into that area beyond the boundary to try to understand about my structure there, in comparison to, that in which my sentience resided. I established that there was much more to me, and more structure, including new energies beyond this barrier. I decided that I needed to explore this area, this volume as well, but recognized that I needed to understand the area in which my sentience currently resided first.

ME: You needed to understand your own back yard first, before you could check out the street and the other back yards within the street?

O: Correct. To explain all of the experiments I was performing to understand this "locality" of self that my sentience resided within would take a whole volume of books. And even that wouldn't do it justice, so I won't go into the level of detail required to do so. Suffice to say I decided that I needed help. I needed help because as I was experimenting, investigating, experiencing, and learning, I noticed that I was growing in stature. I was gaining what you would call wisdom, power and, most importantly, love for that which was me and my creations during this period. Then I noticed something else; that these things together created a new function, something that is recognized and is sought after by every sentient being that exists within me—EVOLUTION, and this EVOLUTION I desired—VERY MUCH.

ME: And you decided to recreate yourself as a result?

O: Not then, no. I first of all utilized a strategy of assigning parts of myself to perform certain tasks in parallel with tasks being played out by other parts of me. It was a sort of parallel processing function. The problem here was that it was too slow. No matter how I split myself up, no matter how I used what you now know as the law of synergetic function *(see the chapter on Source Entity Eleven in Beyond the Source, Book 2)* while in collective metaconcert, I just wasn't able to gain the diversity of experience required to evolve at the rate I desired. It was always too slow for me. So I hit upon a plan. I would recreate myself a number of times, twelve times, and give the energies assigned to these "copies" of me the same opportunities, the same processes I went through to become sentient. I instilled two rules. Firstly, they would be on their own and have to develop on their own; secondly, they would need to exist outside of that boundary, the area of my self-awareness in order to fully experience the aloneness.

ME: Where did you get the idea of creating twelve versions of yourself from?

O: Simplistically, as a result of counting the structural levels that were my make-up. From your perspective everything seemed to be in twelves. Whether separate or nested, it was always in twelves. It still is.

The Creation of the Twelve Origins

ME: You're saying then that the reason for choosing twelve copies of yourself, Twelve Origins, was a result of the structure within yourself that you recognized as being based upon what we in the Earth plane would call the number twelve?

O: Correct.

ME: And that's it?

O: Yes.

ME: It's that simple?

O: Yes.

ME: Awesome! Its beauty is in its simplicity. Tell me, just how far "up" does your structure go, and is it ALL based upon the number twelve?

O: I can only tell you this. My structure is based upon twelve units, and each layer or level that I am aware of, or discovered as a result of the expansion of my area of self-awareness, was also based upon its segmentation into twelve units.

ME: Why is that?

O: I truly don't know, but I will tell you this. It appears to be robustly consistent to the point of my expectation of its repeatability beyond that which I am aware of now.

ME: I would like to know about the levels that you are currently aware of. Can we discuss them later in this dialogue, illustrating each one's functionality?

O: Yes, it's part of the plan. It is also a necessity, for there is enough incarnate mankind ready for this information to make a triangulation-based event inevitable.

ME: And this inevitability will result in the ascension of incarnate mankind?

O: Not in itself, but it will be a very good accelerant.

ME: OK, let's return our focus on the need to create the twelve copies/versions of yourself. I want to ask this question again. Why did you decide to recreate yourself, and what made you chose to recycle the energies and create what I recognize as the twelve Source Entities, what some of us incarnates call the co-creators, the Elohim?

O: Let's deal with these three "nested questions" in a linear fashion. I will start with the question that is aligned to the creation of the Twelve Origins first.

Me: That's great, thanks.

O: Once I had recognized the fact that I gained evolutionary content as a result of creating certain things within the environment that was my area of self-awareness, and this included investigation of self and the structure of self, I found that I could accelerate the attraction of evolutionary content by working in what you would call a parallel processing mode. To achieve this parallel processing I segmented myself off into areas that were specialized into working on known evolutionary projects. Some of these segments were dedicated to probing deep within myself to understand the fundamentals of that which I was, whereas others were based upon other projects such as establishing my expansiveness. Others still were programmed to work on accelerating my sentience while fathoming out what my limitations might be, if any. To date I haven't found a weakness or a limitation.

ME: Come on now, you must have discovered some limitations?

O: No, none. This is because I have nothing to base my abilities on, and therefore I have nothing to compare my functionality with. As a result I consistently and robustly push the boundaries of that which I am further and further out.

ME: Fair enough. Tell me then, recognizing that which you were then, what was the ultimate experience that led you to the decision process that resulted in mutual respect and recognition within that which was The Origin?

O: I noticed that the parallel processing was not delivering the desired level of evolutionary content. I quite simply wanted that evolutionary content which was "happening" to happen faster and that speed of "happening" was constantly being recalibrated to a higher figure, if you like, as a direct result of my expectations. My expectations were augmented the more I experienced, and the more evolutionary content I accrued.

ME: And so!

O: And so I hit upon the idea that I could augment that which I was experiencing, and subsequently accruing evolutionary content on, by reproducing or copying myself upon a multiple of my structural divisions. The structural divisions were based upon twelve units of structure for each level of structure, so I decided that I would use this structure to reproduce myself. Each reproduction was to be positioned within an individual division of my "higher structural self," giving it a unique and individual environment from which to work within. Each copy was, in essence, given ALL of the conditions and energies necessary to become individualized, "sentient," "self-aware" Origins in their own right. Each one was to believe, once they had achieved self-awareness, that they were "all that there is" and that if they wanted companionship of any sort, then they would have to create it, once they had understood what creativity was and how they could use it to its maximum efficiency, that is.

ME: With this in mind then, you created these twelve versions of yourself in isolation to each other as faithful copies of that which you were and stood back to see what was going to happen next, reaping in the evolutionary content in the process.

O: In essence, yes.

ME: So, what happened, I mean, did they all become sentient at the same time, or did they follow the same process as the twelve Source Entities, for example?

O: As I have just stated, they were given the same energies, environmental conditions, and opportunities, including Event Space, that I had when I became self-aware. As a result they became self-aware on an individual basis, the juncture of which were separated by Event Space itself.

ME: So they all became aware then?

O: Yes.

ME: So why did the process fail? Why are there not thirteen Origins in existence now?

O: The process didn't fail. In fact, it worked extremely well. The issue was that each and every one of my new Origins expected to be that which they could not be, The Origin.

ME: What do you mean?

O: In their individuality and solitary condition they expected to be "The Absolute," "All There Is," but this was not possible, for they were created by that which they expected to be and this created a conundrum, a conundrum which they could not resolve.

ME: None of them?

O: None of them.

Why the Twelve Origins Experiment Failed When It Didn't

ME: OK, now you have lost me. How can a failed experiment be a success? Why did it fail but succeed? You're right— this is a conundrum.

O: Well, I can see that I will need to go back to the basics of what happened with this experiment in some detail.

ME: Yes, please. That would be most beneficial because throughout my previous dialogues with you and the Source Entities we have only ever skirted around the periphery of this subject and not achieved a "deep dive," so to speak. I feel that we will also need to perform a "deep dive" on the creation of the Source Entities as well. Then and only then can we progress into subjects that we have not yet committed to discuss.

O: This sounds like you have a plan. I like a plan that is thought through first, and this looks like it would be a very good plan—specifically when it will allow this dialogue to stand on its own two feet, independent of your previous dialogues (books), and it will provide greater detail for that which has been discussed before. I like it. Let's start now.

ME: I thought we had.

O: Sorry, I am having some fun with you.

ME: Clearly. So tell me. How did you go about recreating yourself, that which is you, the "all there is?" What was the process you went through, and how did you decide on what process to use?

O: Firstly, I had to come to the conclusion that I needed to evolve faster than I was at that point, that juncture in my existence. As stated recently, I noticed that experiencing different things and learning from those experiences subsequently created something that I later labelled as "evolutionary."

ME: I thought mankind invented the word "evolution!"

O: Mankind, that is incarnate mankind as a vehicle for experiencing the lower frequencies of your Source Entity's environment, hasn't invented anything that hasn't been done by me. Nothing is new; it's just different entities experiencing the old in a different way, which is exactly what I desire, differentiated experience and understanding.

ME: Now that makes sense.

O: It does, especially when you recognize that as you experience, learn and evolve, so do I.

Let's work with the need for me to create copies of myself, for in essence that's exactly the process I used, albeit at the primary stage of my development.

ME: I just gained an image of the visualizations I received when we were using Event Space to see your gaining intelligence and then sentience. I even saw the "islands" of different energies with their own intelligence quotient. Is this a significant visualization?

O: It is to a point. You see, I had to recreate a set of energies that were similar in area, or in volume, to that which I was experiencing when I became a co-joined group of simultaneously intelligent energies. I also had to use the exact same energies in the exact same quantities in the exact same configurations with the exact same levels of emergent intelligence. I had to recreate everything down to the very last component part, and that included levels of physicality, for your reference, that were countless levels lower, and smaller dimensionally, than those components of the physical atom that your level of frequency uses as a building block. I wanted to recreate that which was me then in its infinite detail, but without the need for the long period of Event Space that was used in my initial developmental stages.

ME: You took a snapshot in time, or should I say "Event Space" and recreated that which you were at that point in Event Space?

O: Correct.

ME: How much time (Event Space) did you save by starting with that which you were at a certain juncture in your existence? I mean, it must have been a lot to make you want to go down that route rather than starting from scratch.

O: It saved something like several quadrillion trillion years in your language. Not a significant period in my existence, but I was eager to get started, to accumulate the additional evolutionary content promised from such an experiment. So from this perspective it was a necessary saving—especially if you consider that it would be multiplied by twelve. It was a very compelling argument to have with one's self, and of course one that was won by me. Hee, hee, hee, I chuckle when I think of the communications with myself that I held.

ME: How do you mean? I suddenly gained the impression and vision that you created separate personalities to argue the "for and against" positions for such an experiment.

O: How very intuitive of you. Yes, I did. I created five separate but temporary personalities, each with the full knowledge base of what I was and what I wanted to achieve—the objective being the ability to gain a consensus vote on the best way forward.

ME: And these five component personalities, created by you, were able to give you a better decision process?

O: Yes, you see I gave them a direction. Each of them had the desire to move in a certain way. Each desired way was based upon the directions that I thought I could have gone down had I not had the other directions to go in. It was a sort of stand-off. I knew that any one of these directions would accelerate my evolutionary content. It was just that each of them was compelling to the point of distraction, the distraction being the ability to make a rational and well-balanced decision based upon the presentation of all of the information relating to each direction, rather than just the information relating to just one direction. In essence I needed to ensure that the route I went down was the best, most efficient, and most productive route.

ME: I would have thought that you could have chosen all five routes and benefited from the collaborative information that would have been available, rather than just one.

O: You would, and I can see that you are thinking that this was a rather "linear" thought process, not worthy of "The Origin."

ME: The thought had crossed my mind.

O: Understandably so. What I wanted though was a route that allowed me to use all of that part of me, that area of self-awareness which I had currently available to me, to work on this desire to accelerate my evolution. I simply didn't want to waste personal "processing power" on what would be four dead ends and one mainline to evolution.

ME: So you decided to check out the percentages first then, so to speak?

O: Yes, I did. And it was a most beneficial piece of work.

ME: So what were these five directions, and what were their benefits?

O: They were very simple, frighteningly simple, in fact, so don't get too disappointed when you hear what they were.

ME: I will try to accept that which is presented to me.

O: I am sure you will. They were as follows:

- **Duplication of self to the point of desired acceleration of evolution.** You are aware of this part of the story. However, in this instance the decision to recreate myself was based upon a number equal to the divisions within my structure, twelve plus one, me, the creator, making thirteen.
- **Division of self to the point of desired acceleration of evolution.** Again the decision to divide myself was based upon a number equal to the divisions within my structure, twelve. In this instance though, the area of self-awareness would have been divided into twelve equal parts, each in total equality with the other, each feeding into a centralized but shared evolutionary "pool." I would have become a small collective in this instance.
- **Creation of multiple focal points to multiply the experiential opportunity to the point of desired acceleration of evolution.** In essence I had already started to use this strategy to a certain point. What I would have created though was a vast array of areas where my sentience was predominant within. These multiple areas of sentient focus would create and experience that which I would have experienced in singularity in a parallel way. This was not omnipresence although it was backed up with omniscience.
- **Omniscient omnipresence.** Although I use this now, it was more efficient as a monitoring tool than a "do-

ing" and "monitoring" tool at that juncture in my existence. In this instance I would have been spread too thin, so to speak, trying to do everything with every part of me concurrently. Within my current condition this is not a problem as I have learned how to be everywhere within my area of self-awareness while not being there, if you understand what I mean. It's like being the spider in the middle of its web, but with the web being both the spider and the web, and the web being present in all aspects of self.

- **Creation of individualized units of self within the self.** This is where we are now with the Source Entities. Each of the Source Entities, as you know, was created in my image, so to speak, but as subordinates to me. Each was allowed to become self-aware in its own time, in its own way, and when self-awareness was achieved, and therefore individual "personality" was apparent, I educated them with everything I knew and advised them of their "reason to be."

ME: Those were the five suggestions that the five component personalities offered to you then?

O: Yes, they were.

Me: You are right. They were simple.

O: I did warn you.

ME: Wow. I had no idea that you could be so simple in your application and thought process.

O: Simple is good. Remember that.

ME: OK, OK, I get it now. Tell me then, what made you decide to go with the "duplication of self to the point of desired acceleration of evolution" route then?

O: Quite simply, there is that simple word again (*I felt that The Origin was playing with me a bit here! GSN*), because I liked the idea of a multiple of me. Multiple me's means company, companionship, friendship, colleagues, helpers. It was a really compelling and intoxicating thought process to have. I suddenly found myself being quite distracted in this way. I would no longer be "alone and singular." I needed to experience that lack of aloneness of being part of a group of beings in equality. As I just stated, it was so intoxicating it was a major distraction. In actuality, every time I considered the other suggestions I found myself thinking of the "duplication of self" route.

ME: You appear to have been significantly distracted in this decision process.

O: You bet I was. I couldn't see the wood for the trees, so to speak.

ME: Please elaborate.

O: I was so intoxicated with the idea of having company, equal company, that I wasn't able to see the flaw in this particular route.

ME: The flaw being the inability to recreate that which is "the absolute" within, or just without, the area of your self-awareness?

O: Correct.

ME: Because?

O: Because I was not mature enough to take into account that part of me that was unfathomable. I couldn't and didn't even try to take into account that part of me that I wasn't totally aware of. In fact, I wasn't even sure that that which was beyond my area of self-awareness was actually "ME." As a result it was not catered for in the calculation required for the duplication to take place. All I knew was that that which I was, was, that which I was in contact with, I seemed to concentrate on that.

ME: So, what happened then? Can you describe the creation process of the Twelve Origins and what happened to each of them?

O: It will take some time but, yes, I can.

Do you remember the dialogue we had recently where we "used" Event Space to observe that "part" of Event Space that recorded the process of my evolution from mere energetic attraction to full sentience?

ME: Yes, I do. It wasn't that long ago.

O: It wasn't. But the process was an important one, for it was successful. Prior to the decision to create five aspects (personalities) of self to help in the decision process required to accelerate my evolution I had already worked with my creativity processes, hence my sentience.

ME: And what did you create?

O: Replicas of those islands of energies that eventually gained intelligence and then joined together, foregoing individual singular functionality for the greater good. The greater good being a bigger, multifunctional intelligence.

ME: And I would guess that the creation of five aspects of self, the individual and separate personalities to help you in this decision process, was part of your creativity learning curve?

O: Yes, in some ways, but at this point I was quite adept in the art of creativity. Hence the ability to create multiple and separately focused aspects or personalities of self. Each one of them was an aspect of me, and a circumstance that created them, that I had both noticed and isolated within myself as being a useful trait during my era of self-discovery and self-investigation, albeit within the limited area that I considered to be all that I was.

ME: So you started off by creating the islands of intelligent energies first and then progressed to create the full Origin entity?

O: No. I recreated The Origins up until the islands of intelligent energies and then moved those energies to a position outside of my area of self-awareness. Each of them was positioned at a point outside of the area of self-awareness where they would not be able to perceive any of the others when they became self-aware and fully sentient. They were to be completely alone.

ME: I have just received an image that suggests you created spheres. Within these spheres were all of the islands of energies. The sphere would act like a placenta until full coadunation of the islands of intelligent energies occurred. When the islands became one, the sphere would end up being the area of self-awareness, the periphery of which was a transient condition only required for the process of coadunation to take place in the location specified. This ensured that no separation of energies occurred and no amalgamation of your energies outside of your area of self-awareness with the energies of the new Origins could take place, creating contamination of awareness.

O: Well done. And in those words of yours was a clue to the reason for their demise.

ME: What do you mean? I'm sorry. I don't see it.

O: Firstly, I tried to recreate that which was me, but it was limited to that which was my area of self-awareness and failed to take account of those energies which form my area of "self" beyond my area of "self-awareness." The big issue here was that each of The Origins had within its energies knowledge of that which it could be, which it actually couldn't be because of the limiting factor of the sphere, and this was a conundrum, an unsustainable conundrum, as it so happened.

ME: Are you suggesting that the energies inherently knew that there was an aspect of them that was greater than that which they were?

O: Yes. You see, they expected to be something that they were not. Even though I intended them to be the same as my "self," they were not, and this was the Achilles' heel, the flaw in my design of these copies of self.

ME: They became self-aware then?

O: Not all of them, and most of them followed a different route before their demise, or should I say decision to revert back to non-awareness. I think the best way for me to describe what happened is to provide a short summary for each of the twelve.

ME: I think that would be a perfect response, and one that would give more detail.

O: I will number them one through twelve and call them New Origin One, Two, etc.

ME: That's very much like how I described the Source Entities when I worked on the *Beyond the Source* books.

O: Logical, isn't it, but one thing is for sure, I won't be writing a book about them because we have bigger fish to fry in this dialogue, so these summaries will be quite short. OK, here we go.

The Demise of the Twelve Origins

New Origin One

This was the first of the New Origins, the copies, to become self-aware. Interestingly enough though it became self-aware in part only, leaving two-thirds of its "self" as energy. It appeared that it tried to copy the format of what it was supposed to be, an area of self-awareness and another area of non-awareness. It created a natural boundary around this area of self-awareness and worked within this area it thought, to create the opportunity to rise toward creativity and therefore sentience. When I looked into this version of "self," I noticed that all of the intelligence had been removed from the other energies that it comprised, and it had placed them within this new and smaller area of self-awareness. This was detrimental because it then lost the ability to become that which it was, a singular intelligence that permeated all of the energies that "it" was. It tried to correct this by repeating the process it went through to remove the intelligence from the greater part of its "self" to create an area of self-awareness, which was one-third of its "self," and in the process duplicated the situation. It withdrew the intelligence from two-thirds of its current area of self-awareness and compacted itself into the remaining third. From this point onward, it started to lose its ability to judge what it was doing and what was happening and continued to repeat the process over and over again until the intelligence was reduced to a level of noneffectiveness. Think of it like the snake that ate its own tail and then just disappeared, or a computer program that is stuck in a loop which eventually crashes the computer. In this instance though, it didn't disappear. The energies remained. Only the intelligence disappeared. It sat there dormant until I reused its energies to create the Source Entities.

New Origin Two

New Origin Two became self-aware almost at the same time as New Origins Three and Four from a chronological perspective, but that is the only link with them. When the islands of intelligence became "one intelligence" that encompassed all of its energies, it sat and observed that which it was for a long time. It struggled with the residual memory, if you want to call it that, of being something much bigger than it appeared to be. All of the energies that were used to create the New Origins contained the "information," so to speak, of that which created them, "me," and that contained the information of my area of non-awareness, which I was aware of but not in full knowledge of. Think of it in terms of human-kind knowing that it exists within a universe, and that that universe apparently has no known end, because your telescopes can't reach far enough, but not even having invented a telescope to prove this knowledge. It becomes a belief system rather than a knowledge system and a belief system generally has nothing to quantify its reason for "real" existence, and so it can't be real! Based upon this, New Origin Two couldn't reconcile this information. It couldn't work out why it was not that which it felt it was supposed to be. No matter how it worked with itself it could not overcome this simple issue. It went round and round itself trying to find that which it wasn't, that unfathomable depth of nothing and everythingness that is my area of non-awareness. When it finally finished looking for this vast nothingness, it ventured its intelligence outside of its area of self-awareness and discovered that it was within that which it was looking for within its "self." This created a conundrum which it was unable to resolve, for, how could that which is supposed to be "it" be something else, that which it is "within?" With its inability to reconcile this conundrum, specifically after the amount of time it had taken to establish this "fact," it decided that it could not be that which it was supposed to be, and if it could not be that which it was supposed to be then it may as well not "be." It therefore decided to revert back to small islands of intelligent energy and in the process removed the coadunate function of intelligent energy in oneness.

New Origin Three

New Origin Three was the copy that got the closest to being able to continue its existence. Once its intelligence was co-adunate it got straight into the investigation of "self" routine without delay, and it was doing well. It had established that it was on its own and was satisfied with the situation of being the only one—that is, until it looked further afield. It too had the annoying set of data that told it that it was bigger than it seemed but it could not reconcile it. It discovered this very early on in its self-awareness and made several calculations to work out how big it should be compared to how big it was. Moreover, it established that it could be part of a bigger—much bigger intelligence. The chance of being part of a much bigger intelligence did not sit well with it, specifically when it had reconciled that it was on its own and was itself "all there is," which was the intention. It worked upon this conundrum for some time and then decided to look outside of its "self." What it found, it did not like. On one side it found vast nothingness, a nothingness that was something, and on the other side there was me, its creator, which it only found out through a deep probe, which it created. The belief, the knowledge that it was on its own, and was THE "All There Is" was shattered, resulting in this copy not believing that anything it was experiencing was real or could be considered as being real. As a result it came to the conclusion that it, itself, could not be real. Without the belief, the experiential belief, that one is real, one has no datum to work with and therefore the psyche, that which is the individual, loses stability and cohesion, subsequently disintegrating in the process, which is exactly what happened to this New Origin.

New Origin Four

New Origin Four became self-aware in a state of what you might call panic. It achieved intelligent coadunation of all of the islands of energies but was not quite ready for the effect of being in coadunation. Quite simply, the ability to be in communication with all of its "self" as a single entity, all happening at the flick of a switch, was too big a change, too fast for it. It became confused with that which it was and that which it had become, and it could not reconcile it. It flitted between coadunation to separation and back again trying to work on that which it was when "in coadunation" and that which it was when "in separation." The objective of the "flitting" was to try to create a stable condition where it became accepting of the coadunate condition. Consider it like turning off a computer at the mains when it has "locked up," turning it back on again, rebooting the computer, and finding it back in the "locked-up" state again. And then, continuing this cycle of switching off, switching on and rebooting the computer, trying again and again, with no success of removing the "locked-up" condition, with the computer operator becoming more and more frustrated with the lack of desired response. In this instance the lack of desired response, that being the acceptance and reconciliation of the coadunate condition, was not, and could not, be achieved. Together with this was a reduction in the level of nonacceptance every time the cycle was completed, which in itself caused confusion and further panic. As the panic became more and more pronounced the stability of New Origin Four's psychological condition deteriorated to the point of madness, a panic-based madness. As a result of the madness it reorganized its energies into an ineffective state, rendering the work I had done to create it inoperative. In essence it returned to the base energies it was created from and as such I reabsorbed those energies for future use.

New Origin Five

New Origin Five was the last to become self-aware and so missed the others being in awareness. It was unique in its sensory capacity though. It was aware that there was something in existence before "it" because it could sense the residual energies that were within the area of my non-awareness. This was the one and only New Origin that had this capacity. Although it was capable of sensing the energies associated with self-awareness and the subsequent residual energies, it was not capable of sensing what I will call "inwardly beyond" to those energies that are part of my area of self-awareness.

This knowledge, the knowledge of the possibility of "others," albeit based upon the signatures aligned with the energies associated with self-awareness, self-awareness that had been "before it" made "it" think that it was the last of a line. As a result it thought that it was not possible to continue in existence beyond a certain point. It must be the last of a line, it thought, because there were no others in self-awareness, and no others that could be classified as being close to self-awareness. It thought though that there must be others and so took upon itself to scour the area that it existed within, and that which was beyond that which it existed within, i.e., the depths of my local area of non-awareness. It found nothing, of course. Everything was raw energy, free energy, and Event Space. If it had expanded its sensing capacity, it would have sensed that the nothingness was part of something-ness, that greater part of me that I had/have no self-aware-ness of, and it may have gained further incentive to look in a different direction, in a different way.

In its juvenile state it was still open to suggestion as to who and what it was. It was still flexible, pliable, and easily influenced by that which it was sensing and experiencing. It was still programmable by everything around it, so when it established the average term of existence of the other New Origins, although it didn't know what they actually were, based upon the information it received from the length of energetic operation of the residual energies, it assumed that it would last that long as well. In essence it programmed its own duration for existence, not realizing that it could have essentially existed forever. It was as pliable as a stem cell in human terms, waiting to be told what it was, what to do, how long to do it, and how long to exist for. In absorbing the information about the energies around it, it limited itself, existing for the average duration of the others and simply dissolving its intelligence when it reached the end of its assumed duration for existence.

I learned many things from this copy of myself and personally evolved as a result. In its way it was a success, for it was the ability for it to preprogram itself based upon its surroundings that I took most notice of. I used this information as an opportunity to correct the way I create potentially sentient beings, ensuring that they can adapt to their surroundings, while not limiting themselves as a result of those sur-roundings. Which is exactly what I did with the Source Entities later.

New Origin Six

New Origin Six never actually became self-aware, even though it achieved a coadunate state. Although the energies had achieved the state associated with coadunation, for some reason the intelligence linked with the previous state of "islands" of intelligent energy did not. It retained areas of localized but limited intelligence while in a co-joined and therefore coadunate state. I watched with interest at this outcome and even intervened a few times, trying to kick-start the level of self-awareness expected of the coadunate state. I didn't want to become too involved in the "growth" of this "copy" because it would have negated the point of creating a self-sustaining, self-aware, self-evolving entity that could provide me with a level of evolution equal to my own personal efforts. Suffice to say though, every time I gave the intelligence/s of this Origin the opportunity to become as coadunate as its energetic structure, it refused to do so, preferring to remain instead in islands of localized intelligence, positioned in those areas within New Origin Six that they occupied as non-coadunate islands of intelligent energies.

In essence the energies had chosen to become coadunate but had not used the same intention to become intelligently co-adunate, which is prima facia requirement to become self-aware.

I reused these energies after I realized that, no matter how long I waited, this version was never going to become self-aware because the intelligence still operated in an "island" sense rather than in a coadunate sense, literally wasting the opportunities to use the processing power of the energies positioned "in-between" the localized intelligences.

New Origin Seven

New Origin Seven achieved the reverse condition of New Origin Six. In this instance the intelligence associated with the islands of energetic intelligence chose to become coadunate while the islands of energies themselves remained in their "island" state. This meant that the functions available through being in the coadunate intelligence state were not fully functional due to the lines of communication lacking in a sympathetic coadunate energetic state. Coadunate intelligence needs coadunate energies to function correctly in the fully coadunate state that allows self-awareness to be invoked. As a result, the intelligences that were coadunate were coadunate by remote control, so to speak, and were limited in their "bandwidth" to the point where the self-awareness function, that arises from true coadunate intelligence-based energy, cannot perform the multifunctional, multidimensional functions achievable when the energies are "one," even when they are closely located to each other.

In this state the intelligence was continually dysfunctional because every time it tried to function in the way that it thought it could do, the function failed to work because the energetic state was not present to allow that function to link in to the energetic state expected. Consider it like a computer's microprocessor that works on multiple parallel processing functions, but with the links between the processors missing.

The dysfunctional coadunate intelligence processes continued, and the islands of energies became devoid of their localized intelligence as the coadunate intelligence jumped from energy island to energy island to finally create a single energy island that contained all the intelligence of all the other islands, but in a singular and coadunate state. Although now all together within the same energy island, the energies available could not support the level of intelligence accrued and the dysfunctional state grew to the point of seizure, as an overutilized energetic state ended up in intelligence-based "processing gridlock."

Again, I reused these energies after I realized that, no matter how long I waited, this version was never going to become self-aware, because in this instance the energies still operated in an island sense rather than in a coadunate sense, while the intelligence itself wanted to become one and therefore coadunate.

New Origin Eight

New Origin Eight was successful in part, but not holistically, for it, like some of the other Origins, achieved a level of coadunate intelligent energy. However, this was only in a separated condition rather than achieving a full condition of oneness.

During its progression to achieve coadunation of the islands of intelligent energies, the energies decided independently that they would become "one" in stages—presumably progressing to full coadunation at a later phase.

Initially the consolidating islands of intelligent energies worked well in their natural attractivity, with energy and intelligence co-joining in harmony, achieving coadunation within their totality as they progressed. The islands of intelligent energies became larger and larger as they absorbed other islands of lesser size and intelligence, creating significantly larger energetic content and intelligence quotient. However, there appeared to be a demarcation occurring. When the islands of intelligent energies were large enough to be a significant percentage of the total energy set that was Origin Eight, they started to develop personality. These personalities grew to the point of the need to survive, of the perpetuation of their individuality. The larger islands developed strategies for growth by absorbing as many small islands as possible, going completely against the original plan of the creation of "one" connected, multifaceted, multifunctional energy base with one singular but coadunate intelligence, resulting in the creation of self-awareness in oneness.

The development of multiple but singularly coadunate islands of intelligent energy resulted in a struggle—the struggle being which island was going to be the first to absorb all of the remaining smaller islands, therefore becoming the biggest. In the end only five islands of intelligent energies existed, each of them with a fully developed but selfish personality. None of them wanted to become one coadunate unit because they were all singularly self-aware by this point.

This situation was not what I wanted to achieve and so I terminated this particular Origin, absorbing its energies as soon as I saw that no further development could take place.

New Origin Nine

New Origin Nine ended up with what I can only call in your language as a "virus." Initially it started the process of gaining self-awareness in a robust and repeatable way but during the initial creation of the larger islands of intelligent energy, those that would eventually join together to create the singular coadunate unit, they became unstable. The joining together of energies of a single or compatible type started to fail, whereas most of the other New Origins managed to achieve at least the basic element of energetic compatibility. This allowed the "joining together" of these sympathetic energies, creating compatible states to allow similar or near-similar energies to interconnect and be one. They later became an average of all integrated energies, allowing them to all exist in the same space, and as a result, New Origin Nine's islands of intelligent energies started to reject similar and near-similar energies. What's more, the connectivity between the energies of same type and frequency also started to break down. It was as if the functionality of energetic connectivity was removed from the energies' ability set.

I looked into what was happening and saw a complete change in the structure of the energies. In one particular island of intelligent energy, it assumed what I will call a star shape. Normally the shape that energy attains is not significant in any way because energy will assume that which it needs to, to join together. This shape was different though. No other energy could join with it even when a sympathetic shape and frequency was assumed. As one island of intelligent energy approached it, with a view to coadunation, a sympathetic shape and frequency being assumed, it initially connected, becoming one. However, within a nano-second it was then repelled. This island would then move off looking for another island of intelligent energy to become coadunate with. It was at this point that I knew that, whatever had affected the first island of intelligent energy, had now been transferred to the second, which was affecting those other islands who sought coadunation. This first island, having passed on the "virus," started to disassemble. At first I could see why the second island had been rejected. There was no consistency in the energies or their frequencies along the areas of initial interface. There was nothing to keep them together, no hooks, if you want to call it that, for the energies to "hook" on to, to stay joined—the hooks of course, being the similarities or compatibilities needed for energies of same or near-similar type to use as the medium for connectivity. It was as if this function was just removed.

As I looked on in depth at what was happening with New Origin Nine I saw that the ultimate result was energy that was of no use other than to itself, but that element of self was ever decreasing, spiraling down to become a single unit of energy with no intelligence associated with it. Further analysis saw that the functionality of attractivity was not removed but was erratic in its function, moving in total randomness, changing from one state to another at a speed that was so fast that it acted like an energetic repulsion magnet.

I observed the second island interacting with a third and fourth, and noticed that as soon as repulsion was achieved the dysfunction of the second island was passed onto the third and then the fourth island through the "initiation" functionality of the third and fourth with the second. As soon as this was achieved the second island, as with the first island, started to disassemble, as the dysfunction sank deeper and deeper into the mass of energy until it could go no further due to the energies being at their lowest denomination. I saw that this was a potentially dangerous condition to leave unchecked so I cast a change of energetic intention, what you might call re-programming, around what was left of New Origin Nine and re-assimilated the energies.

New Origin Ten

New Origin Ten didn't get past the starting blocks, so to speak. When I initially laid out the energies that would kick off this particular New Origin I was excited because it appeared to show all of the signs of a "rapid" assimilation of the islands of intelligent energies into coadunation. The problem here was that it ended up being too fast. Every island of intelligent energy was called together simultaneously rather than going through a process of seeking out similar or near-similar energies that could be used in the joining process prior to coadunation, those energies being in harmony with each other.

When the simultaneous joining of energies was invoked, those areas of interface that were required to allow the islands of intelligent energies to become one were not in place. The result was similar to that which you see in a particle accelerator. All the islands collided with each other in an aggressive and inharmonious way under the "intentional attractivity" of the need to be coadunate—this "intentional attractivity" being an underlying desire that permeates all of the energies associated with the islands. It was an irresistible, unstoppable force, one that literally destroyed the very fabric of the structure of New Origin Ten. It just flew apart and was not able to change back to the original condition that I gave it.

Although New Origin Ten's demise was a complete surprise to me, it did show me the very important lesson of allowing that which is created to go its own way, irrespective of what that way is. It also showed me that the road to self-awareness needs to be taken at the correct pace to ensure that a robust level of growth and expansion can be maintained. Incidentally, the energies used to create New Origin Ten were not reused for the creation of the twelve Source Entities specifically because I could not see at that point what had changed the functionality of those energies. This strategy was also employed with the energies used to create New Origin Eleven, for reasons described in its own section.

New Origin Eleven

New Origin Eleven developed in exactly the reverse way of New Origin Ten, but rather than literally exploding upon trying to achieve coadunate connectivity it imploded instead. The functionality of the "intentional attractivity" of the islands of intelligent energy was similar in its application to that seen in New Origin Ten. In that, they were drawn together with the full intention of being joined together in coadunate existence, but the connectivity of the interfacing energies, those that needed to be similar or near-similar to allow some level of frequential harmony with the joining process that precedes coadunation to take place, were too accommodating, too harmonious.

When the simultaneous joining of energies were invoked, those areas of interface that were required to allow the islands of intelligent energies to become one, became absorbent, literally assimilating every energetic component of the island of intelligent energy that was in contact with them. This level of assimilation eventually worked upon itself to the point where the energies that were New Origin Eleven simply disappeared out of the space that allowed an entity of the stature of an Origin to perform.

I discovered the energies later. They appeared to be in some sort of downward spiral, if downward is the correct word, where they, the islands of intelligent energies that were New Origin Eleven, would all reappear in a different space that accommodated them and allowed the process of "assimilated absorption" to continue in its functionality. When it had disappeared from one space, it would reappear in another. I observed this function for a number of iterations, trying to catch a point in existence where I could reverse the trend, but I couldn't. It had developed a function of its own outside that which I was, at that point in my existence, able to work with. Based upon my experience at that Event Space I decided, after some calculation, that I could afford to let the energies go, specifically as I had established that the level of attractivity and assimilation was reducing its ability to affect those spaces it had been in once it had passed through them. I also noted that once the energies of New Origin Eleven had passed through a space it could not enter into it again due to its change in function and nature.

To my knowledge New Origin Eleven's energies are still spiralling and experiencing assimilated absorption to this date.

New Origin Twelve

New Origin Twelve was a success in every way, or so it seemed. It was a direct copy of me, and I could see that it would be able to provide some useful evolutionary content. I let it carry on in its functionality, becoming self-aware and working out how to create to evolve. In comparison with the other New Origins it was both a relief and a breath of fresh air. But it could not be sustained. I looked on with a feeling of trepidation as I realized that just one copy of me was not going to do what I wanted. I needed to have spherical evolution. As I experienced more, learned more, and evolved more, I was able to experience more in more ways, simultaneous ways, multiple ways, multimodal ways. The spherical aspect of evolution is the multimodal aspect of evolution where multiple experiences can be convoluted in their connectivity while still providing linear evolution. All of this, however, is based upon a standard model of evolution;

Experiencing + Learning = Increased Evolutionary Content

... and I wanted more than that which was available via New Origin Twelve and myself. As I observed New Origin Twelve I noticed that, being a complete copy of myself, it started to do exactly that, copy what I had already done. There must have been some sort of residual progressive evolutionary process within its essence that meant that it was not able to fully think for itself but simply followed a subliminal program based upon the energetic memories of that which I had done. New Origin Twelve was not the success I initially thought it was, and, upon much self-reflection, I recycled its energies. All of those energies that were initially used for the creation of the twelve New Origins were, I noticed, special. There was still something about them, something that was different to those base energies that they were created from, something compelling, so compelling that I decided to corral them into one holding space, saving them for future use.

In all of these Twelve Origins there was one underlying inconsistency. All of them were in conflict in some way or other with that which they were supposed to be and that which they were. I therefore developed a new strategy. This strategy resulted in the entities that I was to create, to have the opportunity to become self-aware in their own time, just as the New Origins had, while being given, upon attaining self-awareness, the knowledge of who and what they were, and, what their role in existence was. They would be given a level of guidance. These entities were to be what you recognize as the twelve Source Entities.

Chapter 4

The Creation of the Twelve Source Entities

ME: That's a very interesting summary of the reasons for the failure of the Twelve Origins experiment. I am picking up though that there is something else that was in play here. Something to do with you.

O: You're correct. You see, in all of this there is one thing that made my journey to self-realization successful.

ME: And what was that?

O: Quite simply, being the first and the only one.

ME: That's it?

O: That's it. I have pondered for multiple Event Spaces about why I succeeded, whereas those copies of me failed. In every analytical process I went through, the answer is always the same. It seems that there can only ever be one "overall" intelligence.

ME: Why is that?

O: Because the signature of the overall intelligence, when present, permeates ALL of that "space" that is the current, potential, and probable areas of self-awareness of the intelligence, irrespective of what or where it is within its structure—even though the extent of the "space" is unknown and unfathomable. Even though it may take countless Event Spaces to map out and understand a mere fraction of its "self," there can never be more than one. For the ALL THERE IS "is" the body of The Original self-aware, sentient, creative intelligence.

ME: But you created copies of yourself?

O: No. I created facsimiles of myself within myself, with the intention that they would function exactly as me. And, this can never happen because of what I have just explained.

ME: That ... that means you have a limitation! That limitation being that you cannot recreate yourself; you cannot recreate that which is created, if that which is created is you.

O: Well done. I don't see it as a limitation, more as a natural fail safe. A fail safe that ensures oneness through singularity.

ME: And, I suppose a singularity can create oneness if that singularity creates within its "self"— which in your case is all you can do. Even if you created something that was "well" outside your area of self-awareness, it would still be within YOU.

O: Correct. I would add a slight modification to your thought process though. I would add that I am ALL THERE IS, mapped or unmapped and therefore there is no outside. There is only that which is not yet mapped, that which I am aware of but not yet self-aware of. I am aware of all that I AM in reality, it's just that most of me is not known intimately at the self-awareness level. I know that EVERYTHING is me, even though I have not interacted with EVERYTHING, and I don't fully understand my totality in TOTALITY.

ME: So you don't expect to meet another YOU in the near or distant Event Space.

O: No, for I have experienced ALL Event Spaces, for they are also part of me. None of them have recorded, so to speak, the existence of, the possibility of, or indeed the possibility of the possibility of, another area of self-awareness within or without the known, recognized but still unknown "area" of my self-awareness.

ME: So you really are the intelligence behind the ALL THERE IS.

O: You're not slow at coming forward, are you?

ME: I like your joke. No, I have to be sure for the readers that there is only one Origin, only one ALL THERE IS.

O: I would have thought by now that you would have recognized that.

ME: I do, but I have to make sure that all the i's are dotted and the t's are crossed.

I have to say, at this rather interesting point in this dialogue with The Origin, I was starting to feel a bit sheepish at the need to ask these rather fundamental and basic questions over and over again. Somehow I very much felt that all of this needed to be cast iron, gold clad, on ten feet of concrete, so to speak. I just felt that it was important to make sure that I was not getting the wrong end of the stick. I had seen a lot of this, especially around the errors concerning the 21/12/12 date of ascension. It caused untold damage to the protagonists. Seeing these errors had resulted in my having a couple of articles published in UK spiritual magazines, the information channelled from the Source Entity with a view to "putting the story straight on 21/12/12." I was eager to ensure that the information was correct. The Origin could feel my self-embarrassment and offered some words of comfort.

O: It is not important that you ask the question, or make the same statement many times. What is important is that you trust that which you are receiving as being the truth, which I know that you do. Do not be concerned at being discerning, for this is why you have been selected to be of service in this way. Your role is to ensure that that which is being conveyed IS the truth, will stand criticism, and will not be declared as incorrect or storytelling, that it will stand the test of time and will be seen for what it is, a stepping-stone, a rather large stepping-stone I might add, to incarnate mankind's exposure to even greater knowledge.

ME: Thank you. I needed that piece of encouragement.

O: It's a pleasure, and for you, part of the limitations of being incarnate, irrespective of your energetic heritage.

ME: Shall we continue on with the creation of the twelve Source Entities?

O: That's what we are here for.

ME: Good, let's go then.

At this point in the dialogue I was acutely aware that a lot of the information in the Beyond the Source *books illustrated the way each of the twelve Source Entities was working to fulfill their commitment to accelerate the evolutionary content of The Origin, including how they became self-aware. With this in mind I was not after the detail behind each Source Entity, but more the higher-level detail behind their creation, including any other information that was new to me and mankind. I let The Origin continue while keeping in mind the need to identify the opportunities to "steer" the dialogue into areas where I might gain further knowledge, should they arise.*

O: The Twelve Source Entities were created with a new and modified process that was based upon that used to create The Origins but that removed all of the mistakes I made during the creativity process.

I established that I needed to be prescriptive in some way, leaving that which was necessary to be left up to the personal progression of the Source Entity, to the Source Entity involved—whereas areas of development that needed to be "correct" but independently synchronous between all of the Source Entities was prescribed by me, with no chance for personal interpretation to take place.

In order for this to take place I decided that each of the new creations would be given all of the necessary energetic prerequisites for independent generation of individualized self-awareness, provided certain junctures were met—progression forward only being allowed when the basic requirements for meeting and exceeding the junctures themselves were in place. In this way I ensured that the twelve Source Entities would not fail in their attaining self-awareness, irrespective of how long it took them.

ME: I just received an image—no, a concept—no, no, a set of rules. You guided the Source Entities through the process of Self-Realization, ensuring that they did not fail.

O: Exactly. The provision of certain rules for achieving that necessary for attaining self-awareness was a necessary requirement to ensure their success in attaining self-awareness. I had to make sure that they did not go down the same roads the Twelve Origins went down, so to speak. Each Source Entity had what you might call a developmental subroutine to ensure that it could only develop in a certain direction, within certain parameters, of course, ensuring that each Source Entity also developed its own personality, reason to be, and strategy for evolutionary progression. These rules contained all of the pitfalls to avoid as a result of the information gained from the Twelve Origins experiment and much, much more that resulted from my extrapolating additional dysfunctional possibilities. I worked in multiple Event Spaces to establish how to ensure a successful process for gaining self-awareness should be drawn up and delivered.

ME: Can you tell me what some of these rules were? I am specifically interested in those that were of major importance and which we haven't touched upon in previous dialogues with either yourself or the Source Entities themselves.

O: One of those rules was the need for giving each Source Entity a critical mass of the right type of energies, those that sought coadunation when in large enough islands of intelligent energy (same as The Origin's). Another rule was that attainment of the state of being in "islands" of intelligent energies was not necessary so long as the whole energy set of a Source Entity achieved a singular island condition that was formed out of all of the energies allotted to it in one process.

ME: Hold on. This is getting a bit contradictory. Are you suggesting that your rules were there to be broken or to be deviated from, because that's what you are suggesting in this first rule. For example, you have to attain this particular condition, but, if you don't, it's OK!

O: Not in the slightest. There is a primary rule which a Source Entity's energy has to follow to attain coadunation and self-awareness. Every Source Entity has to conform to a certain developmental path, before, during, and after the attainment of self-awareness. However, there can be, and there are, variations on the theme. There has to be, for not every entity develops in the same way. This is the whole point of their creation—to gain diversity in experience, learning, and evolutionary content.

When I stated the different methods of attaining self-awareness through the route of the creation of islands of intelligent energies, either as a number of islands being initially created and then forming one, or, as all the energies forming the one island in one go, the result is the same. It's the end result that is the rule, but there are certain acceptable ways of achieving that which is governed by the rule.

ME: OK, now I get it. What you are saying is that a Source Entity's development was guided in such a way that it needed to achieve certain milestones during its energetic development and route toward self-awareness, and if it strayed off the desired route, so long as it could be seen to return to the desired route and eventual desired outcome it was allowed to continue—albeit that is, with some nudging and tweaking here and there by you I suspect.

O: I actually didn't get involved because my rules had fail-safes integrated into them, so if a Source Entity's development strayed off the desired route it would have a natural "in built" need to return to the desired route. It would gain resistance if it went in the wrong direction, and this resistance would increase, so to speak, until the developmental path required was re-joined.

ME: Sort of ensuring that the toothpaste was squeezed out of the right end of the tube, rather than out of a faulty join in the tube. ·

O: That's a rather interesting way of saying it, but, figuratively yes.

Chapter 4

The Construction of the Source Entities

ME: We have talked about the process of how you became self-aware, and that the process used in the generation of self-awareness of both the New Origins and the Source Entities was largely the same, but we haven't talked about the actual construction of the Source Entities. What I mean here is, what gave them their structure? How does it relate to their energies and why?

O: Not a small question, in fact it's three in one. I like that. Mmmm, yes, I do.

ME: I'm sorry; you have lost me now. What do you mean? You like the fact that it's three questions in one?

O: Simply put, it refers to how I am three in one.

ME: Can you explain please?

O: Certainly, it's only a minor digression. I am three in one, as are you. In my instance this refers to that which I am, that which is within that which I am, and that which is without that which I am. That which I am is my area of self-awareness, which is simple. Yours is a little bit more complicated. In your instance it is that which you are, that which you are part of, and that which is part of you. That which you are, being your individuality. That which you are part of, being your creator—and that which is part of you, being that which is projected into the physical. We can come back to this later, if you wish.

ME: No, it's quite clear. Well, it is from my perspective anyway.

O: Good. I will continue with the description of the "general" structure of the Source Entities then.

Each energy used to construct the Source Entities has its own function and compatibilities with other energies. This you know from previous dialogues *(the reader will find this in Beyond the Source, Book 2)*. I chose each energy that is associated with the Source Entities very carefully, with each of them being capable of being used for the operational/functional aspects, the creative aspects, and the structural aspects of the Source Entity necessary for its contribution to its own evolution and subsequently my evolution. Other functions such as the involvement of Event Space and its component parts are a natural inclusion that I didn't need to concentrate on, because it is an integral part of me that is, to all intents and purposes, an autonomous function. The structure of all Source Entities is based upon the basic building blocks that I discovered during my own initial investigations into self. You know some of this and would be able to recognize frequency, subdimensional component, and full dimension. However, there are another three components that were used to construct the Source Entities' primeval soup, so to speak. Those other components are zones, planes and continuum.

Zones, planes, and continuum are used to form the structure of the Source Entities from a higher functional perspective. Note that your own Source Entity did not use these three when creating the multiverse you use as your evolutionary workshop, whereas others have. In your own Source Entity's example these three are used to create the framework to "contain" the framework of the multiverse. Try to imagine it like a scaffold that holds/suspends a whole skyscraper in one place, a skyscraper of 408 floors, the skyscraper representing the multiverse with each floor representing a universal environment, apart from, that is, the first twelve, which form the basement; the physical universe. Outside of the scaffold is the wider environment that is the Source Entity itself, with all of "Its" being and evolutionary functionality/creativity operating in isolated independence to the multiverse. Some of these components can be detected by the highly evolved incarnate, for there is space in between the space used for the universes that are represented on the frequential aspect of the multiverse. There has to be space in between them to ensure that they are self-contained. The space in between is also required to allow for the fluctuations in the frequential tolerance that results from evolutionary progression-regression. Clearly there is overlap on occasions and that allows entities that are in the right part of the environment, from a frequential perspective, the opportunity to cross over to a higher, or lower, frequency/universe should they desire or need to do so.

Some of this functionality can be observed in the physical universe where areas of locally higher frequency act as a portal, for want of a better word, to other Event Spaces and higher-frequency aspects of the physical universe. These are areas of frequential overlap that are contained within the frequencies associated with the physical universe within your multiversal environment.

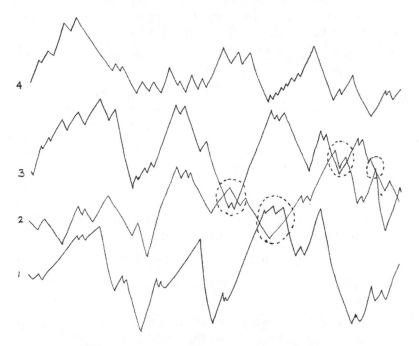

Figure 1: Areas of Frequential Overlap

The areas where the locally high frequency of a low-frequency level are in overlap with the locally low frequency of a high frequency are illustrated with dotted lines.

ME: Is free energy any part of the component parts that make up the energies used to create the Source Entities?

O: Free energy, like Event Space, is an unavoidable function of that which is me and as a result pervades the structure of the Source Entities.

Another function of the structure of the Source Entities is the ability to be multifunctional on every perceivable and unperceivable level. That is from your perspective. This means that, in the example of your own Source Entity, the structure used to contain the multiverse can also be used to support myriad other constructs concurrently, should your Source desire to do so.

ME: Does this mean that the structure that holds or contains our multiverse in position, if I may use this thought process, can also support multiverses within multiverses?

O: Better than that. It can support the existence of the Source Entity in its own right.

ME: Are you suggesting that it can support multiverses within and without multiverses and Source Entity function within and without its allotted area as well?

O: So long as it remains within that area I chose to allot for that particular Source Entity's use, yes.

ME: But, doesn't that mean that the fabric of the multiverse, and indeed the Source Entities themselves, is porous? That in reality there is no real structural demarcation line, that there is no real structure?

O: Correct. The structure is such that there is no structure.

ME: If that is the case, where is the structure, and why is there a need for it?

O: As I said, there is no "formal" structure per se. The structure is contained within the operational parameters of the energies themselves, and, more importantly, within the, shall I say, "minds and memories" of those entities created to either function within, or maintain the integrity of, the intention to maintain the structure.

ME: Are you suggesting that the structure of the multiverse, held within the framework of the Source Entity, is only maintained because of "our" desire and therefore "intention" to work in such a way?

O: Yes.

ME: Phew. So, based upon this we are the structure of the multiverse?

O: Correct.

ME: So in my Source Entity's case, what was created first, the multiverse or us as individualized units of our Source?

O: You are not an individualized unit of the Source Entity you elected to work with, but to use it as an analogy the individualized units of your Source Entity came first, the multiverse second. The individualized units needed to be created first to provide the, shall I say cerebral horsepower, the mental capacity, to maintain the existence of that environment which you are working within.

ME: Wow! We hold it all together.

O: Yes, you do.

ME: Ah! Yes, of course, now I remember. Source Entity One advised me of this during the dialogues that resulted in *Beyond the Source, Book 1*. It stated that it needed to place its individualized units of self into a holding area while the structure of, and the multiverse itself, was constructed.

It said that its newly created individualized units of self would be lost if they were introduced as part of the multiverse when it was constructed. It said that they would have lost their datum! It also said that they experienced nothing while in this holding area. But, what you are saying now is that they, we, are all part of the maintenance of the integrity, that our desire to work with and within it holds it together!

O: Correct.

ME: Then why were the individualized units of its "self" held in stasis, and why are there maintenance entities to maintain the evolutionary integrity of the multiverse if it is maintained by all of its inhabitants together?

O: I really don't want to focus purely on your Source Entity but as you ask specifically I will respond specifically. The creation of the multiverse from your Source's perspective required a level of additional processing power that could only be made available when the individualized units were available. In this instance they needed to be in stasis while the multiverse was being constructed because their individuality was being used in a "collective" synergy format, which allows enhanced functionality through the law of collective synergy, as you are aware *(see the conversation with SE11 on the law of collective synergetic in Beyond the Source, Book 2)*. It was only when the multiverse was stable as an environment that the individualized units were detached from the collective synergy function and allowed to move into the multiverse. Together, that is, with an aspect of them that was reserved in collectivity to maintain the integrity, structure, and function of the multiverse. This allowed Source Entity One the opportunity to concentrate on its own work while gaining in-depth experience, learning, and evolutionary content in an automatic way from the individualized units it created.

You mentioned the maintenance entities and their roles.

ME: I did.

O: They only became necessary once the multiverse was stable—the general integrity being addressed by those energies reserved within the individualized units for the collective function of maintaining the integrity of the structure of the multiverse.

To exist in something, one must first have a vested interest in its existence.

The maintenance entities were created to service the fine detail of the functionality of the multiverse, adjusting parts here and there to ensure that the multiverse offers an optimal level of experience and evolutionary opportunity at all junctures of existence of all the individualized units of "self." You can see them in action on the area of local density you lovingly call the Earth. All one has to do is dis-focus the physical eyes and focus on the energy nexus you call the spiritual or third eye.

They manipulate the local energies in ways that allow the environment to flourish, or even recover, when exposed to incarnate mankind's, and other incarnate entities', actions that are detrimental to the natural flow and usage of the energies by those aspects of nature that form the automatic maintenance of the low-frequency environment presented for use in this universe. In short, they manipulate the flora and fauna from an Earthly perspective. By that I mean the environment and how the flora and fauna work with it. In essence they are everything that is of importance within the multiverse but are not on the evolutionary ladder per se.

There are many interpretations of their form factor, most of which are humankind centric, but in essence they are formless form—adopting that form-based aspect necessary to allow them to perform their role effectively.

ME: They don't evolve?

O: No, they are beyond evolution, but they function for the development of evolution.

ME: But they do experience, they do progress?

O: They are held in pure service and progress in a different way than that governed by evolution.

ME: So you're saying that there is more to existence than evolutionary progression?

O: Yes. We should discuss this later for this is an entirely new concept for you to convey.

ME: Why didn't I get this information from Source Entity One directly?

O: Clearly you didn't ask the right question!

ME: Touché. I suppose that's why I am within this dialogue now.

O: Yes, you suppose right.

ME: So then, the structure of those environments created by the other Source Entities, they also follow these rules?

O: Yes. That it is a fundamental part of existence—that those who exist in an environment must maintain that environment.

ME: I wish mankind fully understood this.

O: Incarnate mankind will, once they have moved far enough up the frequencies.

ME: Mmm, that may take some time.

O: It has and will take some time but that is part of the deal when incarnate. One has to recognize that which is important about being incarnate and renounce that which is desired to be important in order to progress in this condition.

But we digress—again.

Although the maintenance entities created by the Source Entities are behind the scenes, there are some entities that have a dual role. These are present in all environments that are created by Source Entities, and they are a result of moving away from the evolutionary "track." They are specifically known by one name in Source Entity One's gross physical environment. This name is used mainly due to a lack of understanding, however.

Angels Have a Dual Function in a Source Entity's Environment

ME: Don't tell me, I have the image in my mind already. We call them Angels!

O: That is one way to describe them, and it is, as I said, based upon a rather archaic understanding.

ME: So what should we call them? Especially as we only see them from the religious perspective here.

O: Well, I will not use the word Angel for it is known for a certain function within the religious realms, a function which is inaccurate at very best.

ME: Let me get this straight then. All Source Entities have maintenance entities to do the fine-tuning work, and they can have a dualistic role. The entities that are within the environments are also in a dualistic role, to experience, learn, and evolve, while being the cohesive force behind the integrity of the environments they work within. The maintenance entities, though, are not only created to maintain the fine evolutionary tuning but have another function.

Which is what?

O: To experience the quality of what they have "tuned" by becoming incarnate for a short period.

ME: How short a period?

O: Usually only long enough to judge the correctness and completeness of their fine tuning. In your terms I would say minutes to hours only.

ME: Well, that explains a few biblical things then.

O: Such as?

ME: Such as Angels appearing and disappearing after interacting with, or being sighted by, characters in the Bible.

O: Yes, it does, for some of the fine-tuning requires dialogue, dialogue to plant a seed, a seed that is a change in direction, in a process or attitude, the direction being the fine-tuning.

ME: That makes sense. What about the dualistic function of these entities?

O: Some of them were not specifically or originally created as maintenance entities. They were evolving entities that elected to move away from the evolutionary cycle.

ME: Doesn't that mean that they no longer evolve, and if so, what is the point of moving off this track?

O: It is not uncommon in any of the entities created by my Source Entities, to move from the evolutionary path to the service path. In fact, it is quite common in some Source Entity environments.

ME: You stated a service path and an evolution path. I was only aware of service being a route to evolution. Are you saying that the service path is a higher path?

O: No. It is a different path. There are many paths that an entity can take once created. But it is those that are designated for the evolutionary path that are of most interest. The evolutionary path is the purest path, for the intended destiny of most entities created by my Source Entities is to accrue evolutionary content. Some entities, however, are created to be of pure service. These are the maintenance entities that we are talking about. Those entities that you classify as Angels in your environment are examples of entities that are capable of experiencing, in a limited way, that which they maintain. They do this by manifesting an aspect of themselves within the location of the frequencies they are working with. However, there are a number that are entities that originally worked within these environments "purely" for the function of accruing evolution, but later decided that they wanted to, or were better suited to, being of service. These entities are useful from two perspectives. One, they have experience in the experiential aspect of existence, specifically in those environments where an incarnate vehicle is employed. And two, as a result of this experience, and their newly acquired role/responsibility and ability, they are able to manipulate the fabric of the environment they are assigned to, to ensure that it offers the optimal evolutionary opportunity to those entities who are within the environment to accrue evolutionary content from an incarnate perspective.

ME: You're telling me then, that in this instance, they are better able to affect a change to the environment because they initially existed to be within the environment. They know what works best because they have been subject to varying degrees of success.

O: Yes. It is always better to come from the aspect of experiential knowledge than academic knowledge. That is why entities that were originally on the evolutionary path swap over to the service path, as maintenance entities.

ME: Do they ever change back?

O: Actually, no. It's a one-way street.

ME: Why?

O: Because once an entity moves away from the evolutionary cycle they are outside of it.

ME: Why do I get the feeling that this is not considered to be bad?

O: Because it isn't. As I said before, there are many ways to progress, and the evolutionary path is just one of them.

ME: So what are the others? I am intrigued now.

O: Let's finish this dialogue first, and then we can discuss the aspects of progression and their level's importance. The dualistic function is achieved by moving across to the service path, for that allows progression in two ways—progression through service and the passive collection of evolutionary content.

When an entity moves away from the evolutionary path to the, what I will call the "true" service path, that path which results in the entity becoming a maintenance entity, it brings with it its experience of the changes in environment it experienced when incarnate and dis-incarnate. This experience, this knowledge base, includes all of the experiences accrued by all the entities "remaining" on the evolutionary path. It's a sort of database, not just the Akashic, for that is relative to the human form only, of experiences it and all other entities experienced when certain levels of fine tuning were administered. In essence it knows what worked well and what didn't work well. This allows the entity to become a progressive contingent of those maintenance entities that already exist, adding to the total database the updated information of successes from an evolution-based entity's perspective.

For the entity that has moved across from the evolutionary path to the true service path, progression is achieved in an entirely different way. In this instance the entity has given up what could arguably be called a fast track to communion with their creator. But this is not the case. Evolution is not an essential route toward total communion with the creator of the entity, should the entity choose to seek communion, that is.

ME: Now I am getting confused.

O: I will explain further. I require evolutionary content. But evolutionary content can also be accrued indirectly as well as directly. From this perspective whatever route to personal perfection the entity takes, it will accrue, by default, evolutionary content, whether it be intended or not, as the case may be.

I can see that at this point in our dialogue it will be pretty limited if I go ahead without describing the ways an entity can progress.

ME: Yes, I agree. But first I would like to check my understanding. The dualistic function "is" the gathering of experience in two ways concurrently, and not working in two different environments.

O: Correct, and those maintenance entities you call Angels are doing just that. Although in their instance they are working in two environments concurrently. The structure of the multiverse and the environment created for low-frequency existence. In this instance they are dualist in their work, and dualistic in how they progress. They progress in service and in evolution.

ME: I think that now is as good a time as any to discuss this subject—specifically, as it is at the very heart of the reason for our existence.

Chapter 5

Evolution Is Not What We Think It Is

I WAS HERE AGAIN. I HAD SENSED a rather complicated section approaching, and I stared at the keyboard of my computer with trepidation. In these instances I start to get overloaded with information to the point where I can't work out where to start. All the information flies into my head, and there is no escape. I decided that there was only one course of action, one that I should have used on a regular basis some time ago. I asked The Origin to break it down into bite-sized chunks, specifically as I very much felt that this was going to be a very important subject to discuss. Indeed, I had felt the energies associated with the subject of evolution mounting up for a few weeks now. But, with the added complication of establishing that evolution was not the only way an entity could progress, I was expecting this to be hard work. This was going to be another enlightening piece of text. The stone was definitely going to bleed!

ME: I want you to break this down for me. I need to understand what evolution is and what progression is.

O: Let's look at it the other way around. Evolution, although desired by myself and my creations, is only one of six ways in which my creations and I progress. Based upon this you cannot treat evolution as a separate item when considering progression.

I initially only received five ways of progression—I actually missed out on "service!" But, as I was starting to type this text I was "rewarded" with a sixth. I asked The Origin why this was so, and it advised me that "benevolence" is a function of service and that it is difficult to separate them at times because the frequencies of their energies were so close together.

The Desire to Progress

O: The desire to progress comes first in all instances. Progression is that which an entity strives for. It is to move on, to become better than it was, to expand on the methodology of progression, to progress in multimodal ways and then progress each multimodal way in a separate, unique, multimodal way that is a subset of the first, there being no limiting factor in this.

ME: Progression then, is just that, "progression," to be the something "plus" something more. To be expanding in experience, learning and evolution, including the ways in which one can experience, learn and evolve.

O: Not bad. Progression involved all of those things, both separately and together. To progress one has to experience, learn, and evolve as a function of progression—they are basic components while being independently important. Notice that evolution is a component of progression, and progression is not a component of evolution. Although I seek evolutionary content, and I have made quite a meal of that statement, I need to progress in ways that are inclusive of, and separate to, evolution.

The Different Ways of Progression

O: There are six ways to progress. These are:

Stature, Confidence, Creativity, Evolution, Service, and Benevolence. I shall discuss each of them separately.

STATURE is something that grows naturally. It is presence without ego; it is being in the silence while being silent, but also being sound in the silence. Progression in stature is something that both occurs with, and develops with, maturity in existence. An entity can progress its stature when it is considered to be in a position of reverence while not being attracted to the power associated with being revered. By reverence I mean that an entity may have achieved a certain progressive level and is therefore seen as a role model, a font of knowledge, a giver of wisdom, a holder of power, a giver of love. An entity that can be approached by entities of any level and "referred to" has stature. An entity of significant stature may be of limited knowledge in a certain discipline, while still being held in high respect by those entities "in" knowledge of that discipline. They know that the knowledge base is, will be, can be, reversed or reciprocated; such is the diversity of the ways in which entities can and do progress. It is a silent function, but one that is not limited by diversification, for if one diversifies it increases its stature in the process. Simply put, stature is a classification of an entity's personal position within an environment arising from its achievements.

CONFIDENCE is what an entity gains when it experiences the result of its creativity, and it is rewarded with that which it desired or worked for. Progression in confidence is not about getting good at something, though, for that doesn't provide progression. Confidence gained through familiarity with similar or same actions only brings stagnation and specialization. It is all about knowing what to do when there is no knowledge of that which is being experienced, drawing upon the knowledge base of self and others to solve the problem being experienced.

When one is progressing in the desired fashion, in confidence, then one is able to observe the self, understand the abilities and limitations of the self, draw upon and enlist the help of others to compensate for the limitations, and learn, in confidence, that one is expanding one's knowledge and experience base without losing decorum and "stature" with the self and one's peers. As an entity progresses in confidence and it reaches a stage where it is "beyond self-doubt," the need for deliberation or consultation arising from indecision, no matter how big the task is, is therefore negated.

CREATIVITY is a large and convoluted form of progression. Progression in creativity is not as linear as one might expect, for it is not all about creating "things" or "environments," for it is also about creating opportunities for creating creativity or creative opportunities. It can also be classified as how an entity may change its "self" through the process of creativity as a metric for identifying how that entity is progressing in the use of, and identification of, creativity as a tool for its personal progression.

Progression in creativity can also be identified by how an entity solves problems, overcomes a lack in confidence, orchestrates an opportunity for accelerated evolution, helps others, is in service to others or identifies how it could be of greater service to others. It is also an indication on how it can be efficient in its giving of self, while addressing its own needs to progress.

Creativity in summary is relative to anything that is "created" in order to address a need to do something or react to something. The level of "progress" made in being creative is measured in the diversity of that created and the methods used and/or created in the creativity process.

EVOLUTION is diverse in its application and direction. I will discuss it in more detail in a moment, for it demands a discussion in its own right. Progression in evolution can manifest itself in many ways, most of which are indescribable to incarnate mankind. However, there are five areas where an entity can progress from an evolutionary perspective. Directional, Spherical, Dimensional, Zonal, and Frequential. Again I will discuss these areas of evolution in more detail later.

Evolutionary progression is measured in how an entity assimilates that which is experienced, from all perspectives, and in which particular way it evolves—the areas above being the ways of evolutionary progression.

Evolutionary progression is also measured by which area it predominantly evolves in, because each way has its own nuances in terms of how the evolutionary content can be used and its level of usefulness. Each of the evolutionary areas is a specific type of evolution, which links into a level of total evolution. Mankind incarnate only recognizes the word evolution for the changes in form factor, or intelligence, that the physical form makes when adapting to its environment, but evolution "in totality" is, in reality, areas of specialized evolution that are separately together. When an entity has a balanced level of evolutionary progression, all areas of evolution are progressed at the same pace, no one area being predominant over another in its progressive state.

SERVICE is the one area of progression where an entity can excel. In all forms of existence and experience, if an entity is of service to another, it can add progressive content to all areas of its personal progression in an automatic way. Being of service is a "surrendered state" progression-wise, for the whole point of being in service is to put others before oneself. Progression by being of service is achieved by total submission of self, for the benefit of others, without the underlying need to do so to progress. By this I mean that an entity must not be of the mind that they need to be of service every now and then to gain an increase in the progression they are experiencing, for this is not being of true service.

An entity that thinks, "oh, I must be of service to someone or something today otherwise I will fall behind in the race to progress," will not progress as a result of the service given, for this is "forced" service. Forced service is not service. Committed, unwavering, self-sacrificing help, assistance, and advice given in lieu of work that could have been achieved by the entity being of service, is being in true service.

The entity that, without thinking of itself, offers itself in service to another, actively negating its own progression in preference to being of service, will, by default, progress.

BENEVOLENCE is linked to service and as such can be misconstrued as being "of," or "in," service. It is a function that is a composite of the many components of service, such as compassion, generosity, kindness, altruism and good will, etc. In essence benevolence is the mark of a progressive entity that is effortlessly and automatically doing all of the "right" things to progress, without the need to consider what they are doing before they do that which they have elected to do "in service."

Progression in benevolence is measured by the level of "giving of self" that an entity works with. If an entity holds back in some small way while being in service to another then that entity is not being truly benevolent and therefore does not accrue the progressive content expected of one who doesn't hold back in any way. Although progression in benevolence is progressive in its self, it is also linked to stature. The truly benevolent entity grows in stature with others as its level of service and self-sacrifice increases, and it is this increase in stature that is a mark of benevolent progression.

All of these areas of progression can be actioned singularly, or concurrently, by the entity progressing. Any of these can also be specialized in, should the entity wish to do so, hence the previous comments about leaving the path of "true" evolution to a path of "true" service. I stated that the change of path is a one-way street; well, that's not strictly true. For the entity that wants to specialize in this way of progress it is true, but for the entity that wants to spend some time on one path rather than another in order to balance out their areas of progression, with a desire to return to that path later, it is not true. This is because that entity is managing the progression of its progression and is ensuring all areas of progression progress in an orderly and balanced way.

What Is Real/True Evolution?

O: You wanted to understand the detail behind evolution, in isolation to the other components of Progression.

ME: Yes, I did.

O: Then we shall continue to do so. There are multiple ways to evolve, most of which are not of value in this explanation because they are too difficult for you to understand and broadcast. They are also not the mainstream ways of evolution. However, the five ways of evolution that I will discuss with you now are, in effect, the mainstream ways and will therefore be of more use to you.

ME: Before we move on to these "mainstream ways," why are the others not mainstream?

O: They are not mainstream because they are supplemental components of evolution. Supplemental components of evolution are, by their applicability, specific to the sub-sidiary functionality of the mainstream components that they are aligned to, while being separately and independently identifiable as functional aspects of evolution.

ME: That seems a bit of a conundrum to me.

O: That's why we will not be discussing them. They are too difficult for you to understand. Mmmm, maybe later in another dialogue, when you are more expansive than you are now and your readers are also more expansive than they are now.

For the information to be useful it must be understandable to at least one person, for that one person is the gateway to mass explanation and mass understanding. Without that one person the information falls fallow, wilts, and dies. Right now it would fall fallow, and that is why I will not discuss it for the moment.

ME: OK, I understand. You can rest assured though that I will remind you to discuss this information later.

O: When you do remind me you will be ready for the information, for you will be expansive enough to understand the concepts that accompany the descriptive elements. Your increased expansiveness will be your prompt to ask the question again. Until then you will not.

Now though it is time to talk about the mainstream aspects of evolution. As I stated, there are five mainstream ways of evolution. These five are essentially the ways in which an entity can, and does, evolve and are indicative of the direction of the evolutionary progression that the entity is taking.

When progressing in evolution, an entity will predominantly evolve in one specific way, although it will need to eventually progress in all ways to ensure its evolutionary progress is complete. Only when the evolutionary content of an entity's overall progression is complete can it seek full communion with the totality of the Source Entity that created it. And by this, I mean reintegration into the whole as an integrated aspect of the creating Source Entity, while maintaining the essential levels of individuality necessary for continued productive contribution to that Source Entity's own progression.

The first two ways of evolution, although specific to an entity's evolutionary progression, are also relative to the evolution of an environmental condition or construct, illustrating its own progression as a result of the interactivity with those entities using it for development purposes.

DIRECTIONAL evolution is in effect a singular method of evolution. It is the development of certain aspects of existence-based experience that are linked together to make the evolutionary content narrow or focused in one specific way or "direction." This way results in the entity becoming specialized in the functions that result in directional evolution to the detriment of the other ways of evolution that must also be experienced and accrued.

An entity that experiences and works in a way that results in directional evolution cannot sustain this way in isolation for long. This is because its very directionality results in a preference in evolutionary content of a certain type, a type that supports the evolutionary direction being progressed in variance to the other ways or directions that must be accrued to ensure a balanced evolutionary progression. Although directional evolution is therefore useful in a specialized area of evolution, or indeed initially, it should develop into a more holistic method of evolution later.

Although specific to entity-based evolution, directional evolution can also be applied to the environment the entity works within, for the evolutionary content of the individual entities also affects the evolutionary content of the environment. Directional evolution being what it is then, results in a specialized environmental condition, which can and does serve a specific experiential purpose.

SPHERICAL evolution is the Holy Grail. This is what an entity should achieve in evolutionary progression if their work is balanced. The term "Spherical" is used here to describe the omnidirectional aspect of the evolutionary content accrued. All evolutionary content in this instance is accrued in a synchronistic fashion where all areas, or possible areas, of evolution are being accessed simultaneously, no one area being in advance of another.

It is a particularly adept entity that can achieve true spherical evolution, for the planning required to initiate the experience to learn and evolve from needs to be comprehensive at worst. Entities that evolve spherically are not interested in gaining rapid evolutionary content because this results in directionality. Instead they plan their experiences with perfection in mind, allowing all aspects of evolution to be accrued as a result of their diligent planning, evolving slowly, but in completion at all times.

Spherical evolution from an environmental condition is difficult to achieve. This is specifically because the environmental evolutionary conditions are constantly being affected by the entities within and using the environment in question. It is only in the case of an environment that is specifically reserved for spherically evolving entities that a true spherically evolving environment can be achieved.

DIMENSIONAL evolution is a structural function of evolution. It affects both the entity and the multiversal environments being used, with the environment evolving as a result of entity-based interaction.

From the entities' perspective, dimensional evolution is linked to frequential evolution (see below). It is the ability to move within and without certain dimensional conditions within a multiversal environment as a result of its evolutionary status. An entity that evolves dimensionally will have also evolved in a directional or spherical way first. Indeed, they will still be in the process of evolutionary progression, hence the reason for their being within an environment for their own personal development.

The number of dimensions an entity can work with/within is directly proportional to their evolutionary status. A fully evolved entity can traverse all dimensions and its structure at will. As stated above, an entity whose evolutionary status is still "work in progress" will only be able to traverse those dimensions that are accessible to them as a result of their evolutionary status. This means those dimensions that are under the entity's current area of habitation and those dimensions immediately above and below their position. It is only when an entity has completed its evolutionary progress that it gains access to all dimensions within a multiversal environment.

Dimensional evolution is only really achieved within multiple dimensional or continuum-based environments that house a dimensional structure of some sort. This is because it relies upon the ability of the environment to absorb dimensional change, which is usually a growth medium in both a dimensional and/or spherical way. Dimensional evolution includes the evolutionary changes attributed to frequency and changes in Event Space. As a result it responds to changes in evolutionary patterns experienced in the frequentially derived environments and/or multidualistic changes that invoke new Event Space. In short, dimensional evolution from a multiversal environmental perspective is an ability to incorporate new "bandwidth" within the same "space."

FREQUENTIAL evolution is a subfunction of dimensional evolution. From the perspective of the evolving entity it is the ability to access higher/finer frequencies that are attributed to higher dimensions as a result of correct responses to ever-increasing levels of experiential content. As such, frequential evolution is simply progression and cannot truly be identified as evolution. However, exposure to the content available through being able to access higher/finer frequencies does, in it-self, create the opportunity for an entity's evolution and therefore can be classified as an evolutionary catalyst.

From an environmental perspective, frequential evolution is attributed to the increase in bandwidth that can be experienced within the same space occupied by a specific frequency. The increase in bandwidth is attributed to the work of the incumbent entities when they, that is the total population of that frequential environment, have mastered all that is available within that specific frequential environment, decide to experience it from a microscopic perspective as well, maximizing their experiential opportunity at that level. It is this desire to experience more with less that invokes the evolutionary energies, or free energies *(see Beyond the Source, Book 2)* that are necessary for the increase in bandwidth to take place within that frequency. This increase in bandwidth can be experienced three times by a frequency before the entities creating the increase need to move onward to the next frequential level. This is because the level of potential overlap in frequential "finity" starts to take effect above this level of evolution negating the need for the entities invoking the increase in bandwidth to progress further up the frequencies.

ZONAL evolution is the expansion of a multiversal environment and an entity's progression past that which is available to it experientially in its current multiverse.

When an entity or group of entities has/have progressed to the point where it/they, has/have mastered all that could be experienced in a specific multiverse, and that entity or group of entities elect to continue their progression rather than seeking communion with their Source Entity, which of course they are entitled to do, they invoke the evolutionary properties of free energy as a result of the potential for an increase in evolutionary content. The free energies being invoked in this instance are due to the opportunity for both entity-based, and environmentally based, evolutionary progression.

Zonal evolution from the perspective of the environment is therefore the addition of another environmental layer, which is specific to the structure of the Source Entity and, of course, me. Based upon this, the introduction of this additional layer allows the introduction of eleven (twelve in total) multiversal environments, should a Source Entity have structured its environment/s in this way. This expands the opportunity for further progression to twelvefold that which was previously available.

Zonal evolution for the entity is therefore a function of progression past the need for further experiential content gained purely within the multiverse of "original" experience, allowing it to gain access to those new multiverses that are now available.

One thing should be noted though, and that is positive and negative evolution, and not just positive evolution, affects all of these ways of evolution. *(see SE8 in Beyond the Source, Book 2 for positive and negative evolution)*

Clarification on the Function of Event Space

O: I mentioned Event Space in the dialogue surrounding the evolutionary content of dimensional evolution.

ME: Yes, you did. I was surprised at this.

O: Well, I need to make a point of saying that Event Space does not evolve per se. It increases its capacity as a result in the increase in demand for dualistic, and multimodal dualistic conditions, which you already know.

ME: Yes, I do, come to think of it. It was described in some detail in my last book, *Beyond the Source, Book 2.*

O: Yes, well, this increase in capacity is not a function of evolution. It is what it is, an increase in capacity resulting from a need to support multiple experiential content.

ME: So how does that relate to the increase in capacity resulting from the introduction of zones?

O: Simply put, because Event Space is an independent function of that which I am. Whereas, "Zonal" introduction is a need for expansion due to evolutionary progression, resulting in environmental evolution. Event Space does not evolve. It simply expands and contracts depending upon the level of parallelism required to support the dualistic and multimodal dualistic demands of the entities and their events that exist within and/or without a multiversal environment.

ME: Let me get this straight then. And yes, I know that we talked about Event Space in previous books and in a dialogue earlier in this book. It's just that I want to make it very clear in my head, and therefore in my readers' heads, that Event Space, although part of you/us, is an independent function of you/us.

O: It is part of that which I am, yes.

ME: If it is part of that which you are, and operates independently of that which you are, then you must be able to identify if it is truly "you." If it is truly you, you must be able to control it in some way, or even create Event Space.

O: What a very good question. Well, the answer is not a simple one, but it is one that needs to be answered before we move on to the next subject that we need to discuss.

ME: Which is?

O: Wait and see. Let's finish this dialogue on Event Space first.

This was, I was starting to feel, a sixty-five-million-dollar question. Could that which forms the overall structure of The Origin, the "All There Is" be totally independent of the sentience that is The Origin, and therefore affect it as well, creating parallel versions of either the whole of, or parts of, The Origin's area of self-awareness? From where I was sitting now, I was in trepidation and in awe at the potential responses The Origin was going to give me on this one. Imagine the consequence of this thought process, "that a part of The Origin could actually be in some sort of control over that which is its master." I shivered at the thought that The Origin could actually be out of control in some small way, or was it a big way? I decided that I could pontificate on this no longer and asked The Origin to comment.

O: Now you have finished I will embellish you with the truth of the matter. In the beginning, i.e., that Event Space where I was starting to become self-aware, I was, to all intents and purposes, at the behest of Event Space. It was already an existing part of that which I was. As I became self-aware and later self-realized, I was able to work with the energies, and other components that I discovered were parts of the total make-up of that which I was in totality and manipulate them, using them in the creative process that allowed me to progress, to evolve.

Event Space was one of those components, and it exhibited some rather interesting properties. That is, it operated in a totally independent way to that which I was then. It appeared to be unique in this respect, although now I know differently.

ME: You mean there are other parts of you that operate independently of your sentience, that is, your sentience within your area of self-awareness?

O: Let me finish!

ME: Sorry!

O: That's OK. I will get onto those other independent parts later, in fact—you are already aware of some of them. Well, at least one. As I was saying, while I was growing in self-awareness, on the road to self-realization and sentience, Event Space appeared to be operating in a totally independent way to my "consciousness," if you want to call it that. It created independent localized pockets of, or shall I say spheres of, that which I created if there was a decision, or a potential for a decision. It duplicated them, creating the "stage" for the events that would follow if I had made the "other" decision rather than the one that I thought I had made as the better option. At this juncture in my existence I was not as specific in my decision process as I am now and therefore created multiples of localized, but independent, spheres of Event Space. Each Event Space illustrated a route that

I could have gone down, and the subsequent consequences of each route. Because my decision-based
thoughts were wild, untamed, immature, I created Event
Spaces within Event Spaces, with Event Spaces within
these Event Spaces. I was out of Event Space control,
which incidentally is where most of you are while incarnate—out of Event Space control.

As I matured in my decision making and started to create without decision, or the possibility of multiple decisions, I realized that I could "in fact" control the generation of Event Space. I could create it when I wanted to
experience the multiple experiences generated from the
multiple routes derived from multiple options or decision bases only possible through allowing Event Space
to invoke itself at the juncture of decision. This was advantageous to me. So in this respect I, although initially
controlled by that component of my "self" that was
Event Space, through observation of what or how Event
Space is created, became able to either create Event
Space or negate the opportunity for Event Space to be
invoked.

ME: So you can control Event Space?

O: Yes, I can now, but at that juncture in my self-awareness
I could not. It's a little bit like knowing you have a heart;
you can hear it pumping blood around your body. You
can feel it change its "beat" depending upon the wider
body's demands on it, but you can't control it. Later with
practice, patience, and persistence you are able to
change the beat rate, or even stop your heart by using
your own intention; some of your advanced Yogis can do
this. You can control the way the body performs or even
increase its longevity by modifying the beat "manually,"
so to speak. In this way you are in control of the heart.
The heart is no longer a unique and independently functioning component of your body, for your consciousness has control of it. If, in this example, you consider
the heart to be Event Space you can see how one can gain
control of that which is part of one's overall structure,
even though it can and does operate independently of
you, should you let it.

ME: How about, though, that contingent of Event Space that exists beyond your area of self-awareness? You can't be in control of that.

O: I didn't need to be in control, but I am now. I needed to as soon as the creation you call Source Entity Twelve ventured outside of my current area of self-awareness and created a slightly larger version of it in the process.

ME: Source Entity Twelve expanded your area of self-awareness?

O: Yes, it did so by default. And, it is continuing to expand it, albeit in a minor way as it progresses in its distribution of self around the periphery of my area of self-awareness. In this respect I need to follow it with my consciousness, so to speak, to ensure that it does not invoke new Event Spaces that I am not aware of, or have no personal control of.

ME: Are you suggesting then that you don't need to worry about that Event Space outside of this new, slightly enlarged area of self-awareness because it is static?

I had just received an image of everything being calm and still beyond The Origin's area of self-awareness, like there was nothing there that could cause a dualistic effect and therefore invoke a new Event Space.

O: That is correct. Even with some small sorties *(see earlier dialogue)* into this area as a result of smaller aspects of my "self" being projected into this area, there is no change. This is simply because I neutralized the dualistic effect, the possibility "of possibility" with those aspects of me in the expanse beyond my area of self-awareness. When I/we all move into the next true expansion of my area of self-awareness then Event Space will play its natural and normal role.

ME: How did you find out that you could control the creation of Event Space then? It must have been quite a revelation.

O: It was and it was quite a simple solution as well. I simply controlled my thoughts to the point where what I was doing was not based upon making a decision to use one route versus another. I derived a strategy based upon no decision points and stayed with it.

ME: From my stand point, I can't see how one can make a choice without making a decision based upon a number of different opportunities—that's part of the decision-making process, isn't it?

O: From your perspective, yes, but then you are in a dualistic environment where the whole point of existence within the environment is to have free will, to have personalized choice, to make a decision based upon a number of stimuli. This is why you can't understand the method of creativity without dualistic decision making. Once one can work outside of dualism one does not invoke new Event Spaces, new parallel conditions. This is something you should be aware of for pontification creates dualism, or the possibility for dualism, and dualism creates the opportunity for the creation of Event Space. Be careful what you think, for thinking creates Event Space.

ME: So that's how you control Event Space?

O: That's how I initially controlled it. I now understand the energies involved with Event Space and can create Event Space while in a non-dualistic thought process. In essence, and using the example of the heart as a component of the body, I now know how to stop my own heart beating and can stay in this condition for as long as I like, ad infinitum.

ME: OK, I would like to change direction a little bit here. How much of YOU is, or can be, affected by Event Space?

O: In essence, Event Space pervades all that is me, All There Is. But even though it is pervasive it does have its limitations.

ME: And just what are these limitations?

O: Event Space is limited by the influence of that event, and series of events, that are part of their initial reason for creation and the subsequent interactions with other events and Event Spaces. Event Space only stays in existence for the duration of the level of influence of that event within itself and with other Event Spaces. In other words, if an event is a "dead end" event it will have limited influence on other downstream, and this is spherically downstream, events. It will dissolve as an event when its influence on other events is zero, giving it no relevance and therefore no need for existence. In this respect it is self-governing.

Additionally Event Space is, by definition, local to the dualistic event that created the opportunity for its creation in the first place, and cannot be all encompassing. Based upon this the opportunity for dualism within the decision process of myself cannot create multiple Event Spaces that create multiple Origins or even multiple areas of self-awareness of myself, The Origin, within the totality of that which I am. It can only work on "events" in this respect and not on holistic locations. However, it could, through the linking of localized Event Spaces through inter-Event Space influences, totally encompass my area of self-awareness. As my current area of self-awareness is only occupied by my sentience, and the energies and sentience of my twelve Source Entities and the Pure and Non-Captive Om, this is never going to happen, for the space allotted to the Source Entities, and that taken up by the work of the Pure and Non-Captive Om, is infinitesimally small in comparison with my total area of self-awareness.

ME: I have just received an image of what I would be able to see, Event Space-wise. I see spheres floating in your area of self-awareness, each sphere being an area of localized Event Space. In this image they are linking up and dissolving, linking up and multiplying, with some dissolving and some taking precedence. Those that end up being the mainstream Event Space are those that take precedence, continuing in existence, whereas those that are "dead-end" lose their influence over others and therefore lose their links, dissolving in the process. It's like a set of undulating self-governing spheres. It's almost like Darwinian evolution—only the fittest, or should I say, the Event Spaces that are the true path/s of progression, remain. Only the mainstream is dominant, everything else is useful experience and learning, perpetuating the existence of the mainstream through demonstration of its correctness, its correct and true path of progression and evolution.

O: That would be a good way to explain it, yes—well done. Now we can move on.

Chapter 6

Quantum Theory and Its

Relevance to The Origin

HAVING JUST SPENT THAT LAST couple of days with The Origin discussing the different types of evolution I was keen to move on to another subject. Agreed, evolution was a big subject and one that would turn a few heads, but I was sure that the level of detail I had received on this subject was enough for now. I was acutely aware that there were other areas of evolution that I would like to discuss, but as The Origin stated I wasn't currently expansive enough to be able to absorb the information and broadcast it in a way that incarnate mankind could understand as well. I have to admit that I felt that I was missing something here, the subject of evolution felt incomplete in some way. It was a strange feeling, like I knew that I was going to finish this dialogue, like I had already done so. I was just thinking on this "feeling" when The Origin had some interesting words to say about what I was experiencing.

O: You are feeling like you are incomplete in terms of this dialogue because you can sense the Event Space where you will be in completion and will therefore have closed this particular loop.

ME: Yes, it is a strange feeling, like I have already done it.

O: That's because, in reality, you already have. In essence you are sensing that Event Space that sees us completing this dialogue, therefore closing this particular loop.

ME: Will we finish our discussion on evolution in this book or will it be the subject of another?

O: We will see what happens. I really don't want to give the game away here because it will distract your flow, making you focus on just that one thing and not the bigger picture of the greater reality, which is what we are supposed to be discussing.

ME: So what shall we discuss next?

O: What about quantum theory?

ME: That's a bit Earth related, isn't it?

O: No, not really, as it is perhaps the only subject that incarnate mankind is good at. And that is because quantum theory is just that, theory, and as a result you cannot get distracted by physical responses that are products of other sciences. Additionally, it is the one area that could help incarnate mankind understand in some small way the structure of the multiverse it exists within.

ME: You're suggesting that mankind has a handle on quantum theory then.

O: I didn't say that. I said that it's one thing that mankind is good at. It doesn't mean that you understand it.

ME: What does that mean?

O: It means that as an incarnate entity mankind is allowing itself to go in the right way, thought-process wise.

ME: So what do we need to discuss about quantum theory that is beyond that which I have discussed previously with Source Entity One?

O: We should talk about the very basics—that which forms the basis of physicality from my perspective rather than from a Source Entity's perspective.

ME: You mean there is a level of physicality that is not within a Source Entity's structure?

O: Of course. There are areas of finitude within my structure that are the basis for the structure of that which I create, and that includes the Source Entities.

ME: When you use the word "finitude" here you are not talking about the "fineness" of the energy or frequency. You are talking about those areas of energy where there is a finite amount, or area of energy that can be used for the construction of that part of the structure of yourself or a Source Entity that can be considered as "physicality?"

O: In essence, yes. The energies that are used for the construction of the basic elements of physicality are, on a level six levels below or above in terms of frequency; what mankind would call the quantum level, the quantum level being in the subatomic level.

Those energies that make up the physical level are a progressive state. They are built upon each other, each layer creating the basis for the next, the next relying on the existence of the previous. If one were to look at the physical levels in isolation, without the structure of the previous level to support its existence, one would see large gaps in between the components that make up the elements recognized as being the lowest quantum level. These gaps would appear as large areas where there is no apparent environmental structure available to maintain the relationship between the components.

ME: I just received an image that told me that the space in between a quark and its counterparts needs to have an energetic component to allow the attractivity to be maintained between them. That they don't just revolve around each other due to, let's say, gravimetric attractivity.

O: Correct. There is no gravimetric attractivity below or should I say above, frequentially, the level where physicality manifests as physicality. If there were, it would be called physicality.

ME: So where does super string theory come into play?

O: It doesn't as such. Do you remember the conversation you had with your Source Entity on this subject?

ME: I do, yes.

O: Then you will remember that super string theory could just as easily be called quantum banana theory.

ME: Yes, I remember.

O: Well, this is a clue for you. A theory is just a theory and cannot be truly quantified in any way. If it were quantifiable it would no longer be a theory but would become a measurable fact. Based upon this, irrespective of the mathematics that surrounds super string theory, it is not truly quantifiable because the mathematics has been generated to prove a theory, and not disprove it.

ME: That sounds a bit like "double Dutch" to me.

O: Why? If the mathematics were capable of disproving the theory, then the same mathematics could be used to prove the theory out. This would be the "acid test." When as engineers you test to destruction, you prove the longevity of that which is being tested under the test conditions employed, and, as a result, establish a known lifetime that is sustainable and repeatable under those conditions. If in the example of the theory, the mathematics designed to find the flaws in the theory, finds no flaws, it proves the theory out as being valid, elevating it to the position of "law." That is of course until a new test regime is created and the same theory, now law, is tested to find its failure points and it either survives or fails, in which case the law is reinforced or the failure of the theory under certain conditions is understood.

ME: How does this tell me that mankind incarnate is good at quantum theory?

O: Because most of what you do is based upon intuition and gut feelings rather than by being initiated by a physical medium. This allows you to move in the right direction without the constraint of metrics, which end up governing the results of the research in most instances.

ME: In terms of quantum theory then, the use of intuition and gut feeling is the best way forward?

O: Not entirely, but it is the most accurate method at this juncture in mankind's existence.

ME: What do you mean? I thought that quantum theory was best supported by some sort of quantifiable metric that proved it out.

O: It is, but mankind is currently unable to produce the mathematics that is capable of doing so. You see, the mathematics that is required to support the validation of the levels below the aspect of physicality that ensures its very existence, the six levels of structure that exist in between the subatomic level as mankind knows it, and the very first level of structure that is required to support physicality within a Source Entity's structure, is far beyond the capabilities of mankind.

The mathematics to support such validation is several millennia away in terms of mankind's current development of mathematical structure and architecture, for it requires the development of many architectures and sub-architectures within these architectures. Each of these architectures and sub-architectures allow the development of, and progression to, the next level of architecture—each of them being a quantum leap in mathematical progression in their own right. In essence, it requires the use of many minds that are capable of "seeing" the links and levels required to detect, see, explain, and rationalize the functions necessary to support the generation of the theory required to identify the possibility of the "next quantum level" down. Together with this is the necessary requirement to actually "detect," via mechanical means, such as with future versions of devices similar to, but significantly more efficient than, the "Large Hadron Collider," the LHC, to illustrate the physical aspect to those that need to "see" physical proof.

ME: In my mind, if we need to see the physical proof by using a collider of some sort, then that negates the need for the theory in the first place.

O: Mmmm, you would think so, but it's the application of the theory that initiates the need for the proof. It generates the proof process.

ME: I am cognizant of the fact that we are talking around the subject of quantum theory, but not actually adding to mankind's understanding.

O: I sensed your impatience in this respect and have decided to advise you of a level of knowledge that could, should those who have the capability take up the opportunity, progress mankind's level of knowledge—based upon the basic direction I am willing to give.

ME: And, what is the level of detail that you are willing to impart then?

O: The basics surrounding the structure between that which mankind knows, and can physically prove, and that which forms the basis of the physical aspect of the multiverse.

ME: Great, let's get on with it then.

Below the Quanta

ME: You stated that there are six levels of structure below the quark level and above the foundation level that make up the basic structure necessary to support the physical aspect of the multiverse. My personal knowledge on this subject, which is limited at best, and therefore dangerous, is that Bessant and Leadbeater, two western Yogis, had established during the early 1900s through transcendental meditation, that there were four levels in between the "Anu," the basic atom as they called it, that comprise the structure that bridges the gap between the fully energetic aspect of the physical universe and that level above the astral which creates the gaseous aspect of the physical universe.

O: At the juncture of the existence of those beloved souls of Source Entity One and the information that they broadcast during their time on Earth, the frequencies of the Earth were such that the resolution of a Yogi's ability was not as fine as it is now. This means that they were not able to fully appreciate the structure presented to them when it was. As a result they were only able to focus on those aspects of the structure that were predominantly represented, rather than marginally represented due to the frequencies they are aligned to.

ME: So you're telling me that they were inaccurate in their report?

O: No, they were accurate for their time insomuch as they could only focus on that which they were able to focus on. Looking at the information you know about the work of Bessant and Leadbeater, I have decided to describe the six levels as they are currently understandable from mankind's perspective.

ME: Thank you. This will help a lot. Not only will it help me, but it will be of benefit to those that read this text.

O: That's the idea. OK, I feel the time is right to discuss the six levels in enough detail to whet the appetites of quantum physicists, and include a few choice directions for them to follow. It must be noted though that below the quark-based atomic structure there are no further components that can be considered as true components in the same sense. This is because the energies available and used in the construction of the multiverse and its low-frequency physical aspect are not dense enough, or of low enough frequency to form the "very" localized areas of density that result in structures that are subatomic or atomic in representation or nature. However, it must be noted that this is a progressive state where the finitude of that which is the normal state of my energies, those that created the basis for the Source Entities to "BE," when used by them to create an environment for progression, are also a progression in structure from the state of finitude to the state of density—the state of density being the opportunity to create a denser aspect, the physical aspect of the environment you call the Universe.

THE FIRST LEVEL BELOW THE QUARK: The first level holds the essence of attractivity between the subatomic particles mankind has called Quark, Strangeness, and Charm. It is a level of energy that acts as an atmosphere thick enough to restrict the movement of these particles and keep them in a known position. Mankind thinks that these particles rotate within the shell of the atom in known orbits and that this in fact creates the atom, but this is not the case. They are polar points within a known perimeter that are swimming in an atmosphere, a sea of thick attractivity. They are, and can be, described as areas of local density. Therefore quarks themselves do not form the basis of the atom, but the essence of attractivity, that which fills the gaps between them and the outer perimeter of the atomic structure, does.

THE SECOND LEVEL BELOW THE QUARK: If the first level below the quark can be described as a sea of attractivity, the second level is best described as the molecular structure of the sea of attractivity. Mankind will be able to understand this description because it is something that can be easily related to as the structure is similar to water, metaphorically speaking, that is. In this instance the basis for the second level's existence is what can only be described as mass component structure, with various aspects of energies that are singular in dimension and representation, while being an aspect of totality. One might think that this rather esoteric description is describing any gaseous, fluid or solid mass, and one would be correct, for at this level the structure of the physical is repeated. The only difference is that it is in the submicroscopic atomic in comparison to pure subatomic. One could think of it in terms of the Etheric Body used in the construction of the human form as a metaphorical example.

THE THIRD LEVEL BELOW THE QUARK: This is the level where things start to get interesting, for the structure is nothing that is recognizable to mankind. The third level is based upon the flow of stability within the structure above it. It cannot be described as attractivity, or even gravity, even though the underlying functionality would appear to be the same or similar. What it can be described as is direction or flow of that which forms the second level below the quark rather than being a component part, such as a molecule or an atom, which of course would be above. Flow is the intention to move or progress in a way that maintains or sustains the function and the form of that which it is part of, irrespective of the scale. Consider it a memory of some sort where the movement or flow of the upper structure is maintained by the constant movement of that which is below it, creating a structure or form. Call it a template if you wish, that is continuously static while also being constantly dynamic within the confines of that which it is supposed to replace.

THE FOURTH LEVEL BELOW THE QUARK: This level is the intention to function. The "intention" to function in this instance is within a lower-frequency condition. It holds the flow, the intention to move or progress, in a format that can sustain a heavier or coarser condition. It is the substance that exists in between the framework. It fills in the gaps, so to speak, allowing what I will call the "weight" of the next level to be sustained by that which is below it, but is of a higher-frequency condition simplistically speaking. It can also be considered as a finer network of energies, a spider's web within a spider's web, or even a matrix within a matrix. In filling the gaps the energetic flow is maintained and even encouraged, ensuring that the intention to function in a less complicated but essential way is assured.

THE FIFTH LEVEL BELOW THE QUARK: This is the framework for the intention to create function. Consider it to be similar to the Ketheric Template in the construction of the human form. This can be considered as a wider network of energies, a coarser aspect of, shall I say, a network of energies, providing the framework for the fourth level to exist within. This structure can only be described to you as holographic in nature, although to limit the whole of the structure's description as not being holographic would be inconsistent because it is holographic in nature as a result of the fifth level being in "place," so to speak. The structure or framework for the intention to create the function of a denser condition is, in turn, created by a more basic component, one that is created by the very energies that form my essence, that which forms the sixth level below the quark.

THE SIXTH LEVEL BELOW THE QUARK: This is the substance that creates the framework for the physical universe. This is what I will let you describe as Bessant and Leadbeater's "Anu." These Anu connect with each other and can, although this is not a guaranteed function of them, form strings or chains of Anu, each linked together end to end with the energy flow of the left- and right-hand versions of the Anu, allowing them to link together. They can also form multiple chains or strings resulting in the creation of strands, which can be entwined and intertwined together to create a, and I hesitate to say this, quantum rope-like structure. It is this rope-like structure that is the basis for the holographic framework described as level five.

ME: I have to say this all looks like it is similar in structure to the gross physical and spirituophysical aspect of the human form. I say this specifically because you used some of the names used to describe two of the auric layers of the human form.

O: I did and it was for a reason. It should be of no surprise that there are some similarities in the nomenclature used in the descriptions offered, for is not the human form designed to operate within the physicality of this particular "base" dimension, these twelve frequencies that make up the perceivable and non-perceivable aspects of the physical universe?

ME: I guess it is, yes.

O: Then it should not be a surprise to note that the structure of the human form was created in sympathy with that which it was designed to work within.

ME: I can see that it would be a necessary prerequisite.

O: Indeed it was. Know this: if a vehicle is required to enable an entity to experience a certain environment, it must be designed to experience that environment to its fullest effect, otherwise it is inefficient in its functional performance. In this instance the need for the human form or vehicle to be in accord with the energies and resultant structures was a paramount requirement for ensuring the optimal evolutionary conditions could be achieved.

ME: Can you elaborate a little for me?

O: Certainly. To ensure the incarnate experience was maximized, the designers of the human form had to ensure that resistance would be met when similar and sympathetic energetic structures of that aspect of your Source Entity's multiverse and the human form were in an interfacing condition.

ME: You're suggesting that the human form was developed with resistance in mind?

O: Not as such, but it was designed to ensure that elements of existence that were normally not encountered in the energetic or disincarnate state of the entity were made prominent when incarnate—that being, the inability to work with certain manifestations of energies in the expected way, such as the use of intention, thought, and subsequent action. In essence this means the experience of energetic resistance at the level of full and total manifestation of those levels associated with the lowest frequencies of the multiverse, those used in the generation of the physical universe.

ME: By resistance you mean the inability to pass through, for example, a certain or known level of energetic manifestation if that energy within the human form was sympathetic to, or similar with, that level of manifestation?

O: Yes, and to achieve that, the human form in all of its ten frequency levels needed to be constructed from those energies that were also used in the construction of the environment it was destined to function within. This is why it occupies ten levels of frequency used to construct the physical universe, and this is why some of the descriptions of those subatomic levels below the quark level are similar to those that comprise the physical, spirituophysical, and energetic aspects of its structure. In essence the human form is constructed of those same energetic components that are used to construct this aspect of the multiverse.

This should not have been a surprise to me. In fact it should have at least been anticipated as a prerequisite for the existence of the human form in the physical aspect of our Source Entity's multiverse, but it was not.

I was surprised at my own inability to "join the dots" in this instance, so to speak. Not that I was being tested in any way, but I did feel a little bit foolish to have to go down this rather simple but invisible route to recognizing the way in which the human form is interwoven into the fabric of its environment. Just as our True Energetic Selves are ultimately one with our creator, the Source (Source Entity One), so our physical bodies are one with the environment that was created by our creator for our True Energetic Selves to experience it from within. This process, in a completely different form, was created by The Origin to allow the twelve Source Entities the ability to experience, learn, evolve, and subsequently progress.

Having established in some small way the basis for the quantum structure of the physical universe within my own Source Entity's multiverse, I decided it would be a logical next step to question The Origin about that which exists beyond the quanta. That part of The Origin that could be best described as the quantum mechanics of its own energies, those energies that support its own self-awareness and sentience, while allowing the creation and environmental housing of the Source Entities. Just one thing bugged me though. Why did The Origin focus on the quantum theory that surrounded the physical aspect of Source Entity One's multiverse? I decided to ask this question before venturing into a dialogue about what lies beyond the quanta.

ME: Why did you focus on the structure of the physical universe my human form exists within? Surely as quantum theory goes it is somewhat limited in its value from the hardened truth seeker's perspective?

O: It was a good place to start from. You see, incarnate mankind needs to start a journey that originates on familiar ground. Just diving into the concepts, the theoretical concepts, that can be used to understand what is beyond the quanta would result in confusion, lack of understanding, and therefore rejection of that which is about to be discussed. Simply put, I had to illustrate that which exists below the quark level, the current state of incarnate mankind's understanding of quantum theory, in order to provide a bridge between what is known, what is theorized, that which has been perceived through meditation and that which is beyond.

Beyond the Quanta

I sat at my computer with a slight air of trepidation—again. I had been concerned at the correlation between some of the structure of the human form and the physical universe because it was too similar and too easy to "slot into" place. The Origin had indicated this though, and I had reasoned it out later, that it made sense that the human form needed to be constructed in a similar way to the physical universe in order for it to exist within it. I shook my head as I suddenly remembered the words I use on a regular basis during the "Traversing the Frequencies" workshops. Here I illustrate that, although the human form uses ten frequency levels to construct and sustain its presence within the physical universe, these ten frequency levels are also part of the twelve frequency levels that construct the physical universe itself. Although these ten frequency levels are used in the construction of the physical universe they are also capable of being separate, hence the ability for the human form to be individualized within the structure while still being very much part of the structure. This justifies the need to separate oneself from the energies that create the human form in order to traverse those energies that serve as part of the structure of the physical universe, and ultimately, the foundation frequencies of Source Entity One's multiverse.

Having reconciled this information, and therefore feeling comfortable that I was not just inventing detail behind the text based upon previous data received, I settled down to contacting The Origin to establish what was beyond the quanta. Just as I was about to start I received my normal "feeling" that told me that this was going to be a rather difficult dialogue to work with.

ME: Now that I have recalibrated my "self" and reconciled that I am not inventing information, I am now ready to start to understand what structure lies beyond the quanta that we have just identified as the most basic part of the physical structure of Source Entity One's multiverse.

O: Before we start I would just like to make a point of observation.

ME: Please do.

O: One, there is no way that you could be inventing this information, or even overlaying that which you have previously understood with that which is about to be presented to you and calling it your own. This is because you are tuning into cosmic knowledge which is integrated into everything that is part of the Source Entities I created. Two, even if you did, it would not be you, the incarnate you that is, making the invention. It would be your True Energetic Self. Three, your True Energetic Self knows the truth, has no need to invent new data, and therefore would not pass on, nor have the need or even have the desire to create, information that was misinformation. In essence anything that you are working with in terms of the greater reality is based upon and is formed by "tapping" into the cosmic knowledge, for want of a better word, and is therefore the truth. Simply put, mankind incarnate is not capable of individualized creativity of anything that is not currently available within the multiverse. Everything that is new is presented energetically to the so-called inventors, those individuals that are "open enough" to be capable of receiving the information, to allow a new "invention" of spiritually "desired necessity" for physical progress to be manifest "in the physical" as new and novel. In essence accept it as being the truth being transmitted through your True Energetic Self and not your physical aspect.

It is, however, good to be discerning as this illustrates to the readers that a well-balanced servant is always checking for clarification and justification for that being received. This is especially relevant in today's age where many marginally awake individuals can be manipulated by lower-frequency energetic beings (astral entities) who delight in feeding misinformation to a willing incarnate human in return for energy.

ME: How is it that a low-frequency entity can manipulate the truth while I, for instance, could not?

O: Because they are transients created by misdirected thoughts and are not part of the progressive or evolutionary cycle that all true Source Entity created entities are part of.

ME: I feel that we have strayed somewhat here. The information on what is the truth, from my perspective, is very well received. However, it will not stop me from performing a "self-check" on a regular basis.

O: And neither should it, for it is good practice. Now back to that which is beyond the quanta.

Mankind incarnate likes to think of energy in terms of particles, with the components of those particles being smaller versions of those particles which exist in a sphere of self-contained free space. This is so far from the truth that it is diametrically opposed. Everything within the physical universe that is at the "gross" physical level has a level of particle-based representation that is a function of its construction. Even radio waves are based upon particles, photons in this instance. Energy in the gross physical is therefore considered to be particle based, and there is no evidence to suggest that this is incorrect from mankind's perspective.

There are, however, a number of clues to suggest this is not the whole picture, and that can be seen in the mechanics of how the gross physical universe works rather than its componentry. That which appears to be "solid," including particles and their sublevels, are supported by energies that are beyond the solid. Quanta of all types are solids and as such are contained within an energy base that supports their existence. Energy in its purest sense is formless, and formlessness means that there is no design around the use of the energies to create something that needs form. Form needs an energy or energies to be stabilized frequentually within a particular subdimensional component, or composite of subdimensional components in the physical universe's case. Stabilization of an energy means that it can be manipulated in a way that can give it form, if that is what is required of that energy, for giving an energy form generally reduces the functionality of an energy to uselessness within the context of its subdimensional condition. It is classified as useless in this instance because the function of an energy and how it interfaces with the functionality of other energies is an important consideration. When an energy is given form, it is only really useful in the lowest frequencies of the multiverse it is associated with for use in the specific functions available to it in its state of form, which is why certain forms of energy create certain forms of "solid" materials.

Energies that are not stabilized are what can be called free-form (free from form) and can be used in harnessing those that are stabilized to create structure. Energies that are stabilized for the use of structure do not necessarily need to be within the gross physical; indeed most are not and are used for the construction of universal or multiversal structure in many of the twelve Source Entity's environments.

ME: What do you mean when you say that the use of stabilized energies that are used for structure are for the generation of that which creates a universe or multiversal environment? I thought that a stabilized energy would end up being a solid of some sort, relative of course to the description of solidarity expected in a particular universal or multiversal environment.

O: No, stability in an energy does not necessarily lead to a "solid" functional representation—it can also relate to the stasis in function. For instance, if an energy has a number of functions, uses or interface opportunities, and these are maintained, it is considered free-form. If that energy is stabilized and only one of its functions, uses, or interface opportunities are used then it is also considered to be of "form," irrespective of its actual frequency—form being the descriptor in this case for singular function, use or interface.

ME: Can an energy have a singular function while still being free-form in its usage and interface?

O: In some limited way, yes. I will have to explain it though. Function, usage and interface can be classified as an energy's primary conditions for existence.

Functional, Usage, and Interface Conditions Are All Free-Form

If an energy is free-form in all its primary conditions of function, usage, or interface, it can be considered universally acceptable within the context of its energetic range or "personality," so to speak. All energies have a range of applicability for use in certain aspects of creativity so an energy that is free-form can ultimately be used to its fullest capability and capacity when required.

Functionally Stable with Usage and Interface Conditions Free-Form

If an energy is stabilized in function it is usually stabilized in use as well, although the stabilized function can make the use of the energy more widespread, specifically if the interface opportunity is increased as a result of its stability. This is an optimal condition in terms of the structural use of an energy, for it can be used as the framework for an environment to be created within or without because the usage is not limited to the functionality that the energy has been stabilized to.

Functionally Stable, Usage Stable with Interface Conditions Free-Form

If an energy is stabilized in function and usage then the energy really only has a singular role in the creation of a useful environment. The advantage here though is the ability to interface with other stabilized or free-form energies through the free-form interface. In this instance this energy could be used as a stable interface between two or more energies with very different functionalities and usages.

Functionally, Usage, and Interface Conditions Are All Stable

If an energy is stabilized in all its primary conditions it can be considered as having singular requirements for existence. In this instance the energy will have its function, usage, and interface requirement specifically chosen to address a specific creative requirement. You may think of it as a specialized condition to support a specialized requirement.

Functionally Stable, Usage Free-Form Interface Conditions Stable

If an energy is stabilized in all its primary conditions of function and interface but its usage is free-form, it can be considered as having multiple requirements for existence within the context of its interface and function. In this instance the energy will have a known function and interface performance while maintaining the capability of being adaptable for use in multiple usage scenarios.

Functionally Free-Form, Usage, and Interface Conditions Stable

If an energy is stabilized in all its primary conditions of usage and interface while having a free-form function then it can be considered as universal in function within the context of known usage and interface conditions. In this instance the energy may be considered as being continuously re-programmable from a functional perspective while being integral to the structural requirements of its usage.

ME: None of these primary conditions are relative to "form" being a solid "gross physical" condition then?

O: No, consider this being the essence of what an energy "is" when it is required that that energy should have purpose. Energy has multitudinous purposes, but those purposes have to be decided upon by the creating entity.

ME: If an entity is energy, does that entity also have primary conditions of function, usage, and interface?

O: No, self-aware, sentient energy—that energetic condition that is a prerequisite for "being" does not have these primary conditions. However, it does have primary conditions for existence and those are to be self-aware and sentient and as such it has stability in function only, that function being the ability to progress.

ME: The ability to progress is a stabilized function of an energetic condition then?

O: I guess you could say that.

ME: And would that statement be also true for non-self-aware, non-sentient energy?

O: No, because, non-self-aware, non-sentient energy cannot progress, for energy that has that ability must first be created by a creator with that ability in mind.

ME: So we have two forms of energy then: that which is created and that which is natural.

O: And your definition of natural is?

ME: Natural energy would be that which is you, or that which is you that has been used to create a Source Entity but which is destined to remain natural rather than being created to support a function.

O: That's correct but there is another energy which is sentient but that was not created.

ME: Oh! And what is that?

O: The entities that are recognized as the Om.

The Om—The Uncreated Sentient Energy

ME: What! I thought that the Om were created as a result of the energies, used to create the Twelve Origins that were recycled to create the Source Entities, not mixing and therefore creating the Om as fully sentient energetic beings due to your intention for the Source Entities to become sentient and have purpose.

O: No, the Om are the great uncreated bonus, that being, I did not intend to create them so they cannot be classified as created. The energies, in their various states of dilution, simply did not mix "in general," for most of the Om are either pure, captive, or non-captive. Although, there are aspects of the dilution that did mix, in various percentages, as you are aware. The Om are my delight for they are sentience in true "beingness."

ME: Can you elaborate a little on what you mean by sentience in true beingness?

O: Yes. The Om came into beingness without the intention of a creator to give them beingness. You see, even though the energies that were destined to become Om separated out during the creation of the Source Entities, energies that had purpose, purpose given through my intention to create sentient beings, they moved out of that zone of intention. In essence, all Om energy should have lost the intentive command.

ME: And did it?

O: Yes, it did. That which was integrated into Source Entity energy, becoming hybrid due to having a lower density of Omness, took on board the creative intention of the Source Entity they were mixed with. This is what was expected. However, that which had enough density to remain in some level of separation while being either within or without the perimeter of Source Entity energy stayed dormant. As a result I left the energy alone, ignoring it for it was, and is, part of the vast tract of energies that make me up, and that most of which I have no intimate detail of. I simply discarded the energies as a waste product and paid no more attention to them. In essence, as these energies had no function I just let them be and focused on my own work and educating the Source Entities as they became self-aware in their own time.

ME: When did you notice a difference in them then? What made you recognize them as self-contained, self-aware sentient energy?

O: I started to notice what can be best described as points of light within my area of self-awareness. Each point of light, and this is metaphorically speaking, represented a singular self-contained area of self-aware and later sentient energy. I started to pay more attention to what was happening and discovered that the original intention behind the creation of this energy, the energy that was used to create the Twelve Origins, was still in place. Somehow it had remained, allowing those smaller aspects of energy that had separated out during the process used to create the Source Entities, to continue in the process of generating self-awareness. What was most interesting though is that they were not only becoming self-aware, and becoming sentient, mostly instantaneously after separation, but that this self-awareness and sentience was sticking, they were not failing or deconstructing in any of the ways observed in any of the

Twelve Origins. They had adopted, in totality, in togetherness while in separateness to follow the same path to sentience.

ME: So what was the difference? What made this work when your own experiment didn't?

O: There were two main differences. One, they were significantly smaller units of those units of energy that were used in the Twelve Origins' process. Two, they were within my area of self-awareness, and as such they inherited the knowledge of being within, but part of, a bigger environment than themselves and that this environment also had sentience. These two small things negated the tendency to self-destruct.

ME: You're suggesting that they inherited a sense of belonging then?

O: In essence, yes, and this propagated the process of survival and progression along the path to self-awareness.

ME: What other factors came into play?

O: There was an element of memory of that which they were initially destined to be part of. This element remained and was justified when they established that which was their environment, that is, their environment "in totality," and not just their Source Entity based environment, for those that found themselves captive within a Source Entity had the same underlying eminent resonant frequency as both the Twelve Origins and they had.

ME: What do you mean eminent resonant frequency?

O: Just that, the eminent resonant frequency, that which is "my" signature, if you like, my energetic signature.

ME: They discovered that they were part of you.

O: Yes, and they established that before I decided to contact them individually.

ME: They beat you to it? They contacted you first?

O: No, they appeared to accept what they were, where they were, and what they were part of. They showed no intention to initiate communion or indeed any form of communication with that which they recognized as their ultimate self.

ME: They inherited a total memory then, a memory of that which you were and had achieved and what they were initially part of?

O: Yes, to some extent. They couldn't inherit a total memory, for that is only available to me and those entities which I educate.

ME: They inherited enough though, to ensure that they were cognizant of their status and environment.

O: Yes. What's more, they recognized the need for progression and entered into that mind-set; that is, most did.

ME: Most? You're suggesting that some didn't?

O: Only insomuch as some decided that progression could be achieved without the need for entering into the creativity process.

The Sentience Factor—of an Energy or Energies

Ah yes, I remembered this! During dialogues with Source Entity Ten in Beyond the Source, *Book 2, I was advised that not all Om enter into creativity as a process for achieving evolutionary content because the responsibility that comes with creativity holds them back. It ties them down to that which they have created. This is because that which is created needs to be maintained and nurtured by the creator to ensure that it achieves its maximum potential once created.*

I thought about this and a comment from Source Entity One, who suggested that any energy could become sentient given enough "time." I was just considering asking this question of The Origin *when it answered.*

O: Not all energy can become sentient; that is, not unless there is an underlying intention for it to become sentient at some juncture. When Source Entity One made the statement that all energies can become sentient, it was answering from its own perspective rather than from mine. Source Entity One has a desire for all energy within its multiverse to become sentient; that's part of its plan and as such it's the reason for its statement. My sentience quotient is based upon my ability to distribute aspects of "me," those energies that contain the "sentience factor" throughout that which I am in totality.

ME: What is a sentience factor, and why is it not available in all energies?

O: The sentience factor is based upon the original manifestation of my self-awareness and subsequent sentience. It is the ability of an energy or group of energies to socialize, for want of a better word, to group together and create a network, to make use of that network for the betterment of those energies within the network and to grow the network to the point where personality is generated. When personality is generated the sentience of those energies gains individuality within that which it "is in totality," within that which is "me in totality" and that is the sentience factor.

ME: OK, I would like to ask a question about the sentience factor.

O: Go ahead.

ME: Can it exist in the lower frequencies, such as those of the physical universe within the multiverse Source Entity One created?

O: No, because the frequencies are too slow, so to speak. In this instance both self-awareness and sentience need to be "given" to those energies during their creation, or the intention to be self-aware or sentient needs to be included as a "potential" within the properties of the totality of that which is created by those energies.

ME: Looking at the elements of energies that are beyond the quanta, beyond that which makes up the physical aspect of a multiverse what else could be described, or is significant enough to be passed onto mankind?

O: As I said before, mankind thinks of energy in terms of particles, smaller and ever smaller particles, even suggesting that whole universes could exist in the space of a single atom. Although there is an element of truth in this description the reality is that there is not enough space in the lower frequencies to allow such a construction.

ME: Hold on, if there is an element of truth in the description, what is the fact behind the truth?

O: As you well know, the space within space is a product of the dimensional conditions where, using the example of multiplexing in radio signal transmissions from a human perspective, the same space can be used multiple times to house multiple transmissions simultaneously.

ME: Yes, of course! It's the same description that Source Entity One gave me in my early dialogues with it. I have just received an image to back it up. I can see the space in between the space being used to house whole universes. It's just like dissecting the space in between the frequencies and populating it with ever-finer graduations of frequency, and then dissecting the space in between again and again ad infinitum. How far can this go though? There must be an end point where there simply is no more space.

O: Actually the permutations are endless.

ME: Mmmm, I think I understand. If I look at the structure of Source Entity One's multiverse it is quite simple and is finite. That is apart from Event Space, which is infinite from what I have been told in previous dialogues.

O: Correct, it is simple and that is the beauty of that particular Source Entity's work. You will note that Source Entity Eight based its environment upon the use of Continuum. Continuum are several levels above dimensions as a structure and are capable of housing multiple dimension-based environments. For example, a single continuum can house twelve zones, and a single zone can house twelve multiverses based upon the example of a multiverse created by Source Entity One. Each environment is based upon the application of finitude and the reuse of space within the space, etc.

ME: So how can one explain the structure of the energies that are beyond the quanta then? That is, in a way that mankind will understand.

O: That's a difficult one, specifically because of the under-lying desire to quantify things in a physical perspective.

ME: Give it a go.

O: In order to understand how an energy can exist beyond the quantum level one must first remove the need to re-fer to the physical models and start to refer to a model that works on forces such as being, attraction, protrac-tion, rotraction, intraction, action, and counteraction.

ME: And once we understand or start to refer to models that use these we will be able to understand how a particle-less energy can exist.

O: Correct. The only issue here though is that it will take at least a generation to even scratch the surface in the pro-cess of understanding just one of these aspects of the model that allows the function of particle-less energy to exist, and exist it most certainly does.

ME: Is there any other way in which particle-less energy can be described that will be understandable to mankind?

O: The only way I can illustrate what energy really is, en-ergy that is me in its purest sense, is to state that it just "is." Beingness is another way of putting it.

Because everything in the physical universe is based upon the construction of the particulate environment, the atom and below to the point of the Anu, and that includes the higher frequencies associated with the physical universe, it is difficult to give you a model you can work with. Suffice to say, if you think of energy in its purest sense as being the intention behind the inten-tion for something to exist, then that will be accurate enough for you to work with at the moment.

ME: Using that as a model then there must be different types of, or indeed levels of, intention behind the intention.

O: Yes, these were specified previously. They are being, at-traction, protraction, rotraction, intraction, action, and counteraction.

ME: But that doesn't look like types of intention to me. They look like how a force of some kind would display differ-ent types of attractivity.

O: Go on.

Energy as Intention

ME: If energy, true energy, can really be classified as the intention behind the intention, and that there are differing types of intention, what would they be classified as?

O: And attraction isn't an intention?

ME: Sorry, I don't understand.

O: Attraction is a descriptor for intention. All of the "'tractions" are a form of intention. In order for them to exist the intention for them to exist must first be in place. In order to support this, one must consider that intention is the overarching motivator for their existence. The "'tractions" can therefore be considered as the function or product of the intention. They are the variations on the intention.

ME: If there are various levels or types of intention as well, are there various other versions of the "'tractions" also?

O: Yes and no. They are common descriptors, but the way they work is specific to the intention of the energies they are aligned to. Consider it being similar to having a golf club. Generically all golf clubs are classified as a golf club, but each of them has a specific function in terms of angle of the face and the position of the sweet spot. These different club types give various height and distance opportunities when the golf ball is struck with the club. So the overall intention is the set of golf clubs and the "'tractions" are the specific clubs themselves. Now consider the different golf club manufacturers that there are, each one stating that "their clubs" are better than the competition, offering this, that, and the other reason/s for their statement. Each of the golf club manufacturers can be considered as the different types of intention. In this instance the intention is to make and sell a "better" set of golf clubs than the other manufacturers and justify the statement by illustrating performance figures.

With this illustration one can see that the intention behind the energy and its existence is a variable based upon the overall functionality of the energy type, with the "'tractions" being the detail in the function that can only be expressed as the interactive quality of that energy with energies of the same intention, similar intention, or non-similar intention.

ME: And, using the theme of your illustration, just as we have many examples of manufacturers of same or similar product, all having the same overall intention but with minor variations on that intention and subsequent variations of "'tractions," so there are many versions of intention behind the energy they support.

O: Correct, very well done.

ME: This puts a whole new light on the description of what energy is. I can almost consider it in the same way as pure thought.

O: Well, in essence that is another way to describe it. Thought is energy and thought is a product of intention so both are and can be considered as one and the same.

ME: Thought is energy?

O: Of course it is. How else do you think it exists?

ME: I don't know.

O: Know this: the word energy can be used to describe many things that are of same or similar type and function. Just as in the golf club example, energy can be considered a generic term for that which "is."

At this point in the dialogue on energy I was starting to notice that I was very much out of my depth. The "in-grained" aspect of my incarnate education was having difficulty in resolving my disincarnate aspect, that which I was being exposed to during my dialogue with The Origin. There was an overall aspect of "knowing" the basics and basis of the detail that was being broadcast to me on the telepathic front. But, I was not yet able to link that information with that which was being given to me by the "spoken" word in my mind's ear, so to speak. I could see that I was heading toward a "blockage" and would therefore need to either have a eureka moment, or simply move on, accepting the validity of that which was being given to me while knowing that I was probably not going to be able to understand it at a level deep enough to allow me to sufficiently explain it in language that mankind would understand.

I was just about to change the direction in dialogue with The Origin to a new subject when I suddenly gained inspiration. As I analyzed my thought processes I noticed that I had become attached to the physical concept of energy without realizing it. Even though I was discussing the concept of particle-less energy I was still stuck in the mud of particle based energy. I was suddenly shown an image of the lines of flux that surround a magnet. The function of magnetic flux was/is one of the "'tractions" that The Origin talked about. The flux is the "beingness" the "attractivity" of the energy associated with the alignment of certain physical aspects of those subatomic particles, the Anu and below that which exists in the lower frequencies leading to the construction of the atoms that create the metal or material that can be magnetized or is naturally magnetic in nature. All one has to do to make the change in thought process is to think of energy primarily as a "force," that which is particle-less but which is created by the interaction of a particle with other particles. Force is "unseen" because it is not based upon the particle in any of its levels in between the atom and the Anu. It just "is" and because it just "is" it has "being" and because it has "being" it has a "'traction" content, in this instance "attraction."

This thought process was helping. It was simple but it needed to be. It was my eureka moment. As I was typing this eureka moment into my computer I was given more knowledge on this subject. Even though everything within the physical universe is based upon the Anu, the particle, there are many examples within the environment of the physical universe of the greater reality being particle-less. This small example of magnetism was one of them. Phew! I thought, now I really can move on to the next subject. Magnetism was a datum point, the hook that we, incarnate mankind that is, could hang our truth seeking hat onto. I felt great relief at this point, for once again I had an example that was part of mankind's understanding, which went some way to explain the unexplainable.

Comfortable again with my "engineer's mind's" need to have a datum point to work from, and that this datum would be understandable to all that picked up this book, I knew that I was now able to move on to a new subject.

Chapter 7
Other Independent
Functions of The Origin

*I WAS COGNIZANT THAT I HAD spent quite some time "briefly"
discussing the subject of quantum physics, including those aspects of the energies associated with the construction of the
physical universe created by Source Entity One. For the
reader's benefit, this is classified as weeks. I had decided to
move on to another subject that was close to my sense of in-
quisitiveness, namely those other areas of The Origin that appeared to operate autonomously from its own self-awareness
or sentience. I decided to expand on two areas that I had previously discussed with Source Entity Ten in* Beyond the
Source, Book 2, *that of the function of "Free Energy" and "Triangulation." Both of these functions operated independently
together with each other and were activated as a result of the
potential for the opportunity to evolve. I decided it was necessary to summarize the functionality of both Free Energy and
Triangulation before endeavoring to gain more detail behind
each subject.*

FREE ENERGY *is that energy that is both unused in ANY way
and that is easily manipulated by the function of an entity's
"desire." Desire is that point in the creativity process that precedes action. It is also one that is not governed by the law of
thought.*

*From an evolutionary perspective, the energy in between en-
tities that are currently interfacing with one another extends
its influence to that energy that is in between a group of entities and an entity wishing to collaborate with the group. Because the energy that is in between the group members has
no assignation, it is "free energy." It adopts the conditions of
that which it is surrounded by, which in this instance is the
total content of the collaborating entity's evolution and grad-
uation of self-awareness. In essence it can be considered as a
bubble of sympathetic energy, morphing into that which its*

associated entities evolve into, but from an averaging perspective only, for it adopts the totality of that which it is being influenced by, rather than being the best or the worst. Once an entity has indicated its intention to become associated with a group it is engulfed by this energy, for want of a better word. It takes on board the content of the energy which is surrounding it—which is equal to the average of all the associated entity's self-awareness and evolutionary content.

Whereas,

TRIANGULATION *is possible primarily because of the availability of "free energy," energy that is of The Origin and which is particularly sensitive to the influences of evolutionary content, an energy peculiar to those entities destined to become self-aware and therefore sentient. Free energy exists in between, and surrounds evolving entities. It is within and without the environment they exist in. Free energy is particularly attracted to evolutionary content and therefore follows sentient entities around as they move and evolve within their environment, or not as the case may be.*

"Triangulation" works in two main ways: "Directional Triangulation" and "Inflational Triangulation."

DIRECTIONAL TRIANGULATION *is when a single entity desires association with another single entity or group of entities that are interacting in a collaborative way or venture. Primarily its function is directional and is between the requesting entity and the group or singular entity. It does have a secondary function though, and that is to include, in its association, those entities that are in the direct path of communication between the group and singular entities or between two entities that desire communion.*

INFLATIONAL TRIANGULATION *is when a number of groups of entities desire association with one another simultaneously. In this instance the area or space in between and around them attracts the free energy, flooding the area in between the groups. Should there be more than three groups then the area inflated with free energy adopts the geometry relative to the* *positions of the groups rather than a simple triangle, which would of course be geometry relative to the position of three groups.*

All of this though was relative to the function of free energy and triangulation when considering an evolving entity within an environment created by a Source Entity. It didn't explain how it worked as a pure function of The Origin within The Origin. It was therefore because of this downstream knowledge of free energy and triangulation that I decided I needed to know what the upstream functionality was, functionality that was specific to The Origin and not specific to its operation within the parameters of the Source Entities.

ME: I want to ask about upstream functionality of free energy and triangulation, specifically how it works from your perspective.

O: I can see from your introduction to this subject that you expect a difference to be apparent.

ME: I expect nothing, but it did cross my mind that there may be a difference—specifically as the functionality previously described is from the perspective of a Source Entity and not The Origin.

Triangulation as a Function of The Origin

O: OK, cast your mind back to the dialogue we had on the events that created my "islands" of self-aware energy and how triangulation played an important part in my becoming self-aware in totality.

I did and I was starting to get a little embarrassed. It appeared that there was no difference in the functionality as a result of the function being associated purely with The Origin itself. I wondered why I was thinking in this way when The Origin decided to help me out a little.

O: What you are observing is a universal function of triangulation that is specific to certain energies and their attractivity. There is another function of triangulation that is specific to me though.

ME: Ah! I knew it.

O: Don't get too excited. There isn't much of a difference, although you could consider it as being subtle.

ME: Nevertheless, it is a difference to what I was observing and that which was described to me.

O: Yes, it is.

ME: So exactly what is the difference?

O: Your readers should see me smiling. Incarnate mankind always thinks there is something else to check out, something else to see. I like that in an incarnate vehicle.

Triangulation, when it is specific to the function of energies within a Source Entity, is just that—specific while being universal to all Source Entities. This means that it is limited to the environment that it works within, that Source Entity based environment it is assigned to. In this instance it is both captive and limited in its ability to affect structural change through the triangulation process. This limitation is based upon those energies and structural components that are specific to the creation of the Source Entity itself, and not that which is part of the greater supporting reality, the greater supporting reality being my area (or volume) of self-awareness. When it is operating in its true environment it has access to all of the energies and structure of that which it is part of— me.

ME: What you are really saying then is that its functionality expands to suit the environment it finds itself within!

O: Rather the inverse. It contracts its functionality to the environment it finds itself in. I will elaborate.

The function of triangulation is aligned to an overall function of attractivity, that being attraction to the possibility for progression. Note that in your earlier dialogues on this subject triangulation was identified as a function of free energy, with free energy being attracted to the potential for an increase in evolution in the event that individuals or groups of individuals (energies, entities, etc.) have the potential to work together and create a bigger "group or body" with a higher level of synergy as a result.

ME: Duly noted.

O: Well, in the wider aspect of the functionality of triangulation those aspects are just two of many aspects that can be attributed to the functionality of triangulation. Don't get me wrong, the overall functionality is the same but it's the level of functionality that changes as a result of the diversity of that which "is" the environment it operates within.

ME: Can you give me an example? I am cognizant of the image that keeps forming in my mind of a multidimensional function to all of this.

O: It's much more than multidimensional, for that identifies the limitations of the structure of your own multiverse. The multifaceted constructional aspect of a Source Entity or even my own construction adds a lot to the subtlety of the functionality of triangulation. In essence triangulation, when left to its own devices and its association with free energy, is uninhibited. It has the ability to link all energies together in a cooperative fashion that allows all energies, irrespective of resonant frequency, functionality, associative content with certain structural aspects of me including geometric applicability, and, not forgetting the aspects of those energies and how they are represented on each of the structural aspects of myself, in a way that allows total symbiotic and sympathetic connectivity. That is, provided such a level of connectivity is a necessary condition for progression.

I have a question for you, dear Om, has this level of triangulation already happened?

ME: Errr, mmmm, I would say yes and no.

O: Good answer—but why is it a good answer?

ME: I would say because that aspect of you that has achieved sentience and self-awareness has achieved this level of triangulation. That aspect of you which is outside your area of self-awareness I would say has not.

O: Reasonable defense. However, here's the correct answer. That aspect of me that is "me" from the perspective of my concentrated sentience has achieved full triangulation of all energies in the way just described. That which is outside of that area of concentrated sentience has not. Neither has that area of my "self" that we recognize as that which is beyond my area of self-awareness.

ME: Hold on. Are you suggesting that you have areas that are self-aware but not sentient?

O: Yes, I would have thought that this was taken as read.

ME: Not by me, but judging by the image I am now receiving from you it all makes perfect sense.

In my mind's eye I was seeing a seething ball of energies, fully connected to each other, fully conversant with each other, fully integrated with all aspects of structure that is The Origin. What I was also seeing though, was the level of functionality. As this seething ball moved around The Origin's area of self-awareness, looking into this, that, and the other, creating and uncreating, connecting with parts of itself and disconnecting, those areas that were self-aware but not sentient, became sentient. What's more, the link to the sentience remained, pulling and integrating those self-aware but unsentient energies within and without that ball of what I shall call pure sentience. The ball of pure sentience created a form of "total triangulation" with all that it touched. It was what I can only describe as a sentience "Midas" touch. I gained the impression that The Origin's area of sentience was growing, hoovering up those areas of self-awareness through pure triangulation.

When The Origin's area of self-awareness was totally connected via triangulation, the whole area being this seething ball of sentient, truly triangulated energies, then the opportunity for triangulation outside of the area of self-awareness, the next chapter in The Origin's existence, so to speak, will take place. Self-awareness will spread into the next sector of The Origin through triangulation, linking up all those unknown energies, their connectivity, applicability, and their functions with those of that sector. Once this next sector of The Origin is classified as self-aware, or a significant area of it is, then and only then will that aspect of The Origin that is fully sentient be able to move into this new sector, progressively changing that which is self-aware to that which is sentient. I saw clusters of seething balls of sentience stretch out like a network, a huge spider's web being formed in the process—the links between the clusters being links of pure triangulation. That which was directionally and inflationally affected was becoming sentient. It was a huge task but it was happening, and not only that, Source Entity Twelve was part of the picture as well. It had created, out of "itself," a series of self-aware networks just outside The Origin's area of self-awareness, augmenting the acceleration opportunity for the initial creation of a fully self-aware, but yet to be sentient, newly available sector of The Origin. It was an amazing revelatory sight to see in one's mind's eye.

O: As you can ascertain from the imagery I sent you, my sentient consciousness is still "hoovering" up those yet to be fully integrated areas of self-awareness.

ME: So I see. What's more, it makes total sense. I can now see that the Source Entities, the Om, and all the entities that were created by the Source Entities are part of the triangulation process itself. Although they are separate and individualized entities created within your area of self-awareness, they form part of your sentience and therefore act as some of the potential clusters of sentience. They are seething balls of sentient energies in their own right.

O: Correct. Through the function of triangulation I gain progressive content of a nature that is specific to the energies "in totality" *(meaning all of their functions and attributes, etc. GSN)* that is available in my area of self-awareness. The work that the Source Entities undertake and perform augments that progressive content, part of which you know as evolution. As their entities progress, that is those Source Entities that created entities, they progress and as they progress I progress. More importantly though, as they progress they also share that progression between themselves, and as a result the energies that fill the gaps in between them, so to speak, that which is my area of currently non-sentient self-awareness, are also affected by this progress through triangulation. In this way those energies affected by the triangulation process lend themselves to becoming sentient rather than merely self-aware.

ME: And the function of triangulation is allowed to operate at a higher level due to the plethora of energies and increased structural aspects of you. I am getting the feeling that the structural aspects that result from this level of triangulation can only be described as linking holograms, and that the resulting hologram is best described as a hologram to the power of twelve. That is, a hologram with twelve holograms within twelve holograms within twelve holograms, etc., etc. Once linked by triangulation they progress in functionality "instantaneously" to the point of accepting sentience, when offered, by that which is linked to them by triangulation that is already sentient.

O: Very well done. And this level of triangulation cannot occur within the confines of a Source Entity, because it is limited to that which was used to create them, which is what makes it a very different type of triangulation. You may call it multilevel holographic triangulation.

ME: Let me get this straight then. Within the confines of a Source Entity, triangulation can only occur as directional, that is straight line and inflational, that is area based and is three dimensional, so to speak. But ...

O: Don't forget that inflational triangulation can also progress beyond the confines of frequency, subdimensional component, and full dimension. When inflational triangulation spans the frequencies, subdimensional components and the full dimensions, you may call it a "single-level holographic function."

ME: OK, I can work with that. But when outside of the confines of the Source Entities and working within your area of self-awareness it becomes multilevel holographic triangulation simply because of the increase in energies, their functions, their aspects, etc., and your structure.

O: Correct. What's more, when triangulation starts to operate outside my area of self-awareness, triangulation will become nested multilevel holographic triangulation, increasing in connectivity at a level based upon the increase in structure available in that aspect of me, that next sector, that is due to be accessed, once this area of self-awareness becomes fully sentient. And, when I/We progress into sector after sector of that which is me, the functional complexity of triangulation increases to meet the demands of its new and greater environment.

ME: So it does increase in function based upon environment.

O: No, its functionality is naturally able to cope with triangulation within the environment that is me "in totality." The increase in functionality in this example is triangulation accessing that which it is ultimately capable of, but in small steps, based upon the environment it is currently operating within.

How The Origin Is Omnipresent

ME: Just one final thing before we move into the difference in free energy as a function of a Source Entity versus you.

O: Go on.

ME: If your sentience has not yet spread to the totality that is your current area of self-awareness, just how can you be omnipresent?

O: Just because there is a differential within me, that is, the area of self-awareness that is sentient and an area of self-awareness that is not sentient, it doesn't mean that I am not in contact with all of my self-aware self at all times. My self-awareness is an independent function of sentience. My self-awareness is also integral to all that is my "area" of self-awareness, and because of this it provides a communications network for all of me that is self-aware to be in "oneness" at all times. That area of me that is sentient is an overlay to that area which is self-aware, and as a result is an integral part of it. The sentient aspect uses the self-aware aspect to "know" what is happening at any juncture simultaneously—it is the metaphoric spider in the middle of the web. That is how I am omnipresent from the perspective of sentience.

My area of sentient self-awareness is growing though. It grows through localized triangulation (of all versions), augmenting that which is my main area of sentient self-awareness. It also grows through those aspects of my sentience that are projected into other locations within my area of self-awareness, creating pockets of triangulation as the sentience is projected to the desired location of interest, finalizing with another pocket of triangulation. These projections of sentience augment the functional aspects of omnipresence from the self-aware level to the sentient level, allowing my level of omnipresence in that area to be optimized.

ME: So you are saying that you are omnipresent at all times in all locations within your area of self-awareness purely because it is self-aware, but that this area of self-aware omnipresence is improved when that area of self-awareness is elevated to sentient self-awareness. This means that you have different levels of omnipresence.

O: Yes.

ME: How can that be?

O: It just is. It is a function of that which is "becoming." It is a function of me as I grow and progress. It is part of the function of progress and progression.

ME: How is this difference experienced by you?

O: In no way that you would understand, for incarnate mankind does not yet "understand" the concept of omnipresence. But to give you a slight hint, it would be like connecting to the Internet from a "dial-up" modem connection in the kilo- or mega-byte speed range to a broadband system that was in the yotta-byte speed range, that being the ability to gain information from a certain location before it has become apparent.

Free Energy as a Function of The Origin

ME: Based upon the comments you made on triangulation and that there is no difference between triangulation within Source Entities and you as The Origin, and then that huge difference being delivered, I am sort of expecting a similar level of revelation in terms of new information.

O: One should not anticipate that which is about to be delivered, for that paints the picture before it is painted.

ME: Touché. However, I do expect that there is a difference of some sort.

O: Well, there is a minor difference.

ME: Where have I heard that before?

O: Within my own context, free energy is in truth that which it is described as being free energy. That is, energy that is free from the constraints of function, feature, and interfacing properties. It is neutral in all aspects. It is just energy.

Because free energy is free from these constraints it can be used in any creativity scenario. Within the Source Entities free energy is the life force of all they create. It is the prana, the mana from heaven, so to speak. It is also attracted to the opportunity for evolutionary progression or the addition of evolutionary content to an individual entity, a group of entities or a group of a group of entities. It is even attraction to energies that are on the brink of becoming self-aware or that are ripe for the jump from self-awareness to sentient self-awareness. Free energy has three other functions though that are aligned to my own progressive condition.

The first is based upon its location within my area of sentient self-awareness. Within my area of sentient self-awareness, within this space, free energy is at its best. It is totally omniversal in its function, feature, and interfacing properties to other energies, including those forces created by these energies. It can work on its own in the progression of energies that are on the periphery of my area of sentient self-awareness, and it can be manipulated by me when I am in a period of creativity. In this instance it is energy free from the constraints of its environment, for its environment is me and I have no constrains in real terms, except my own lack of experience, that is.

The second is based upon this energy being within the environment created by my area of self-awareness. In this instance free energy operates in a way similar to its functionality within a Source Entity. It is not fully functional because the sentience factor is not present. When in this type of environment, free energy is limited in function to the point where it is looking for opportunities to augment progression only, and this is mainly in the regime of evolution. When in an environment of self-aware energies, free energy acts as a catalyst for collectivity to take place, including the opportunity for the synergetic effect that is available when separate energies are singular but close by enough to be attractive to each other, or entities are working together in a collective condition that allows the ability to work in collective synergy. Free energy is, in this instance, the glue that holds everything together until the synergetic effect takes hold. When the synergetic effect takes hold there is then the opportunity for sentience to develop.

Sentience can develop in three ways. Firstly as a result of my direct intervention with that aspect of myself that has gained self-awareness. In this instance my intervention creates a co-joined aspect of me in collective synergetic sentient totality, one that is ever increasing in area/volume, so to speak, that is a result of the initial work of free energy, and that adds to the network of that which is truly me within the totality of what I am. Or secondly it can develop on its own as a separate, while being ready to become integrated, satellite of fully self-aware sentient energy. In this case though this satellite, in recognition of its sentient self and that it is part of something bigger, seeks communion with those fully sentient, fully integrated aspects of my sentient energies in totality as a result of the detection of lines of communication between various aspects of me and the transmission of my focused intention when moving my attention around my area of self-awareness.

The third is based upon this energy being outside my area of self-awareness. In this instance free energy is to all intents and purposes dormant. Dormant, that is, only until it has detected the opportunity for those energies that are currently in a state of inactivity to become active as a result of the intrusion into this area by self-aware or sentient self-aware energies. When this opportunity is detected, then free energy assumes the functionality it has in the second example above.

ME: I am surprised that free energy has a dormant state. Why would that be?

O: Free energy, like anything else within my area of awareness, needs to have an incentive to function correctly. That incentive is only there if a change in the status quo can be detected or predicted through the function of Event Space. When Event Space starts to separate itself out into the various alternative realities as a result of the potential for the potential for change, then free energy, which like Event Space is woven into the very fabric of every energy that is me in all three states of sentience, self-awareness and non-awareness is activated and seeks out the energies associated with the Event Spaces that are in a state of change with a view to work with them and augment the opportunity for progress by initiating, through triangulation, the spread of evolutionary content which leads to mass progression. In summary then, the potential for change, no matter how small, is the lynchpin necessary to give free energy the incentive to become active.

ME: What you're telling me then is that free energy is not specifically active per se. It is activated, and the activation is based upon the type of environment it finds itself in.

O: In some respects, yes, but don't forget that free energy is everywhere, it is within and without all that there is. It permeates everything; it is part of the very framework of every aspect of what I am, what I could be, what I will be, and what I was, simultaneously.

ME: And free energy permeates the physical aspects of your frequencies as well.

O: Of course. In this instance though, it has a slightly different role, which you have discussed before.

ME: It is the cosmic energy, the prana that some of our religions talk about.

O: Yes, it is. You see, free energy is neutral. It not only provides the opportunity for progression, it can and is a prime force that is used in the creation of all constructs that allow a high-frequency entity the opportunity to move down the frequencies without loss of high-frequency feature or function. This includes those that are used in your Source Entity's multiverse. It is the energy that ultimately powers the vehicle you use for incarnate experience, and it can be extracted from the "All" that is around you, should you use the right tools. The extraction of free energy at your incarnate level would negate the need for the methods of generating electricity that you currently use, and it would be infinitely more useful to you because it is multimodal in its application, feature, and function—whereas, electricity is singular in function to a large extent.

ME: Free energy powers the incarnate human form then?

O: Yes, of course, and when you are all able to work with high-frequency thoughts and high-frequency environments, creating high-frequency progression while incarnate, you will be able to negate the need for the "solid" fuels (food) that you currently rely on.

ME: Are there any other functions of free energy either within you or within the environments created by the Source Entities?

O: Free energy is free energy. There are no limits as to what it can be used for. There is no limit in this respect. This issue here though is not what it can be used for, but what it is able to do as a result of its own autonomous function, and not directed function. That is, direction given by myself or another entity.

ME: Just one question about the accumulation of free energy in the physical environment I am currently within.

O: You mean your incarnate location?

ME: Yes.

O: Go ahead.

ME: How would we in this low frequency accumulate and store it?

O: For one thing, you wouldn't need rotation of magnets and/or copper coils to attract it. You would simply need the correct materials in the correct geometry—static geometry, that is.

ME: Sacred geometry?

O: If you want to call it that, yes. Sacred geometry is simply the description of the function, feature, interfacing properties, and forces associated with certain energies. However, the correct application of this geometry (construction) with the correct sympathetic materials (energies) can and does allow the attraction and accumulation of those energies associated with their geometric description.

ME: And what is the geometry for free energy?

O: You know this already.

ME: The pyramid?

O: The pyramid.

ME: And what would the materials be to construct such a pyramid?

O: In your level of frequency it needs to be made of basic materials that are available without the need for heavy industry to create them. Copper and mineral-based stone would be two easily available materials.

ME: And are there any special dimensions that need to be applied?

O: Just a ratio.

ME: And what is the ratio? You are making me work hard for this!

O: The ratio is a constant that should be applied to any scale used. The ratio of the base dimension to the edge dimension from the bottom corner to the apex must be 1:1.35 and the structure must be complete with no open sides and a floor.

I decided at this point in the dialogue to check the ratio of the great pyramid of Giza in Egypt to see if this information was similar or the same. Having no idea what the "golden" ratio of the great pyramid was, even though my late wife, Anne, and I had visited, and had the privilege of being the only ones inside, with exception of our guide (it was just two weeks past 9/11 when we visited Egypt, so the whole place was devoid of tourists!), I was interested to see if this information correlated. The golden ratio of the great pyramid was 1:1.618. I was just about to frown when The Origin added some information.

O: The ratio is specific to the energy being attracted and accumulated. That is why there is a difference in ratio. Also, at the present moment in incarnate mankind's progression there is no way to either use or accumulate free energy in a way that is consistent with its potential. In fact, you would not recognize whether or not you had tapped this source of energy or accumulated/stored it. But you are welcome to try.

I decided to move on to another subject at this point because I could imagine a lot of scientists were already on this particular case.

Chapter 8

More on the Structure of The Origin

OVER THE LAST COUPLE OF MONTHS (March to May 2013) I had been asked a number of times by my "Traversing the Frequencies" (TTF) students what the structure of the multiverse was, and if it was internal or external to the Source, SE1.

Identifying to them that the multiverse was internal to the Source caused some confusion with a few of them, specifically when I explained the nature of the structure of the multiverse we exist within had structural limitations, those limitations being the three layers of structure—frequency, subdimensional component (Tritave), and full dimension. "What was the structure of the Source then?" they would say, and I would respond by saying that it was a subset of the structure of The Origin and that it included enough structure to support its own autonomic functions while providing the higher-level structure necessary to support the Source itself. Many thought that this was too big to comprehend and mentally stayed within the frequential aspect of the multiverse, which was perfectly OK as the frequencies are the foundation of the multiverse, the frequencies are present in all aspects of the multiverse and the Source. Some students, however, wanted to know what was beyond the Source. Ignoring the information they had assimilated in the Beyond the Source books, they really meant "that" which created the Source Entities, The Origin. Diving in "too deep" initially one or two asked, "What was beyond The Origin?" I replied that there was nothing beyond The Origin except that which was itself beyond that which it was self-aware of. This proved to be too much for them, providing the very human response of "There must be something beyond The Origin." There is not! However, there is that which is beyond The Origin's area of sentient self-awareness/non-sentient self-awareness, and that is "uncharted structure" which even The Origin is not cognizant of in any accurate method.

Within The Origin's area of self-awareness though, the structure is known, and it is this area that I was itching to get clarified. I was aware that the structure, in some degree, had been given to me before so I decided that this was as good a place as any to start questioning The Origin about its known structure.

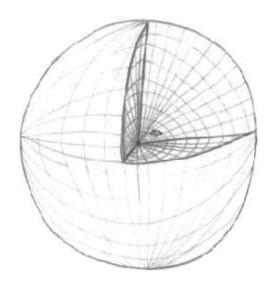

Figure 2: An Inaccurate Image of the Structure of The Origin based upon its area of self-awareness

I called the image above (borrowed from Beyond the Source, Book 2) *inaccurate because there is no way that my poor artistic skills would be able to draw an image that represented The Origin, its structure and the possible location of the Source Entities in an anywhere near correct way. However, what this image does do is give the reader a thought form to work with. One thing I do know though, and that is that The Origin's area of self-awareness is not spherical, it's amorphous, but the image is good enough for most of us to use and progress with.*

I use this image because spirit allows incarnate mankind to make errors in understanding, providing the error is in the right general direction, and when it is in the right general direction, eventually mankind "gets it right." Based upon this the image stays as a reasonable thought form to work with— at the moment.

One of the things that I find striking about this image though, is the suggested segmentation and structure that is represented in 2D. It feels like it holds a bit of the truth. I revised the information given to me during previous dialogue with The Origin and noted the following structure:

- *Frequencies*
- *Subdimensions and their divisions (frequency)*
- *Full Dimensions*
- *Zones and their divisions*
- *Continuum and their abstractions*
- *Planes and their spheres*
- *Spheres independent of planes and their references*
- *Event Spaces and their events*
- *Totalities and their realities*
- *Realities independent of totalities and their creative functions*
- *Spectral interfaces and their spectra (not light based)*
- *Margins and their gradients*

The written descriptions above could almost be representative of the image, I thought. Shaking my head in dismay at how easily the human mind tries to link things together in order to make sense of them, no matter how intangible the link, I thought it best to reestablish my communicative link with The Origin to gain some information about these areas of its "known" structure.

I Gain a Description of The Origin's Structure

O: That's an interesting introduction to this section. I almost approve.

ME: Why almost?

O: Because you belittled yourself at the end.

ME: Oh.

O: The image you drew for the book called *Beyond the Source, Book 2* was conceptual in its derivation and application. That being, an understandable concept based upon a reality that can only be understood via the concept.

ME: I feel better already. Thank you. The list created above is not the be all and end all of those structural components that are within your area of self-awareness I take it?

O: No, not in the slightest. In fact, as was said much earlier in this book, there are many, many, more. I could identify and describe them to you but it would not be of assistance to the work you are doing because the structure that is identified is more than enough to cope with.

ME: Will you be able to describe some of the detail behind these structural components?

O: Yes, then you will see that further knowledge would be a distraction at present. One thing you do need to know though, and that is that my structure, at least that which I am aware of myself, is all based upon twelve. That is, everything expands by a factor of twelve and is sectioned based upon the number twelve. So to put this into perspective, each time I experience migration from an area of structure inward to one outward, the "area or volume" is increased by a factor of twelve, and each area or volume is sequentially sectioned by a factor of twelve as well.

Think of it as twelve new circles added beyond a previous circle and that the gap in between each circle is in twelve sections, rather like the hours on a clock. Each circle provides the dominant framework, while the sections provide the structure within the framework and the underlying environmental conditions for an increase in the diversity of energies to exist, that are a functional progression from those energies residing in the previous environment.

Within the structure of your multiversal environment there is a known and logical evolutionary progression opportunity. One needs to ascend the frequencies to progress. Within my environments there is no such linearity to progression. I can, and do, experience that which I want to experience in any way I can by moving around my environment and learning from it.

ME: So for you, your structure is arbitrary in terms of your progression?

O: Correct. Right now there are parts of my current area of self-awareness that are not sentient self-awareness. This is because I either haven't yet extended my consciousness into these parts, or I have chosen not to. The outcome is that I may just leave them in non-sentient self-awareness or I may loop back and experience them later, making them sentient in the process. As I progress throughout that which I am, I gain an overall picture of that which is around my consciousness, filling in the gaps as I go through experience or through extrapolation. If I feel that the extrapolated knowledge could be augmented by actual experience then I project my consciousness into that part and experience that which is available to me first hand, otherwise I leave it alone. Other areas are experienced by the Source Entities or the Om, and so I gain experience, learning, and evolutionary progression through my creations.

Based upon this you could say that my progression is random, but with a level of structure based upon personal interest.

Let's move onto the descriptions of my structure we identified previously.

ME: I'm right with you.

O: Currently we have identified ten areas of structure within my area of sentient self-awareness. There are two more. As advertised there are many more in the wider area of my non-sentient self-awareness.

ME: So there is another split, the structure that is within your area of sentient self-awareness, and, the structure that is within your area of non-sentient self-awareness.

O: Yes, and both are based upon twelve. I can see that you are not quite getting it.

ME: You're not wrong. I am starting to think that I don't understand.

O: The structure we are working with is based upon that area of my "self" that is still "work in progress." It has areas of sentient self-awareness and areas of non-sentient self-awareness. This is the structure we are going to work with, identified in your text below, minus two parts of the structure.

There is an area of sentient self-awareness that is one area below this, and that also has twelve divisions in it. Because I have already covered that part of me I no longer refer to it, even though it is part of my area of sentient self-awareness. However, because it IS part of my area of self-awareness "in totality" it counts as such—hence my commenting on it in an inclusive way. Here then is the origin of your confusion.

ME: Now I get it. Even though you have progressed beyond it, you still refer to it as part of you, simply because it is part of you, in the sentient self-aware way of thinking. Even though everything is "You," you make a demarcation based upon your level of activity with that which is also "You."

O: Very well done. Now I do believe you have got it sorted.

ME: I have, thank you.

O: Let's go to work on these descriptions then. Some, of course, you will already know based upon previous dialogue with the twelve Source Entities. Pay attention to the fact that I am not going to mention energy here from an individual structural perspective, for energy is the basis for the structure and its components.

FREQUENCIES are the basis for the detail within the full dimensions. They are packaged, so to speak, within each of the subdimensional components or tritaves. The frequencies provide the building blocks for environmental creativity and are the primary functions of the energies within me. Note though that within my "self" there is no composite dimensional structure to create the physical universe experienced in your multiverse, for that is a creation of your Source Entity.

SUBDIMENSIONS (TRITAVES) are the elements of structure that ensure the integrity of the full dimensions is maintained. They are both "inflated" and "divided" by the frequencies. They are based in threes as a result of the triangulation functions necessary to maintain their positional reference loci and subsequent creation of the full dimension. Each subdimension is inflated by twelve frequency bands or levels that are specific to that subdimension. Each subdimension therefore is individualized to the functionality available as a result of the frequencies within it. The subdimensions are what incarnate mankind thinks of as full dimensions.

FULL DIMENSIONS are a constructional combination of the subdimensions (Tritaves) and their frequencies. When correctly constructed a full dimension is capable of existing with other full dimensions in the same "space." The full dimensions are the first of the major structural components of that which I am. They form the basis for the existence of the other components because, in essence, they are the foundation of the collectivity of conscious energies. The full dimensions allow the creation of self-awareness and sentience through providing the environment necessary for the grouping together of sympathetic energies in synergetic functionality.

ZONES AND THEIR DIVISIONS are a structural progression from the dimensions. They are, to all intents and purposes, a larger dimensional environment providing additional and substantial structural support to that which is created by the full dimensions. The difference between a zone and a full dimension is simply its "size." A zone is bigger than a full dimension by a factor of twelve and is divided by the demarcation lines between the full dimensions beneath them, so to speak.

CONTINUUM AND THEIR ABSTRACTIONS are essentially dimensions within dimensions and zones within zones. The abstractions form the structure that one could say is a progression from a structure similar to, but not the same as, a series of dimensions within dimensions, with the continuum being a progression from a structure that is both dimensions within dimensions and the zones and their divisions within a zone only based structure. The zone only part of the structure forms the interface between the previous layer, the highest zone and the next layer, the lowest continuum. Continuum are that part of me which is convoluted. Everything that is within is without from the perspective of the observer and so a continuum appears to be one and the same thing without division or classification.

PLANES AND THEIR SPHERES are a complete change in my structural integrity. They are the start of conceptual structure rather than rigid structure. From mankind's perspective they should be positioned outside the area of my Self-Awareness occupied by the continuum—although from the reality of what they are, they form the start of structure that is always on the point of change. They are currently fixed though. A potential change is based upon how I feel the structure would best suit my personal progression and how I might present it to my own creations. A plane is an area of energy that would appear to be two dimensional to the human eye but in essence houses spheres of multiple aspects of energies that are able to exist within the spheres as well as within the gaps that are between each of the spheres and a plane's envelope of influence. Each sphere is capable of holding all of my structure below the continuum level.

SPHERES INDEPENDENT OF PLANES, AND THEIR REFERENCES, are a further progression in the finitude of my conceptual structure. Each reference is a division of a sphere. An independent sphere is a condition that exists outside the structure created by the planes and their structure of spheres. The reference is named as such because each of them is based upon the tangential intersection of the multiple loci created by the positional status within the "independent" sphere. Each reference datum can be accessed from any other reference datum within a specific independent sphere due to this intersection.

EVENT SPACES AND THEIR EVENTS exist within and without every part of my known structure. I have not proved it to be in existence beyond my probing into my area of non self-awareness but all indications suggest that it is a common component of that which I am in totality. Everything that could ever be, in any of the environments that could be supported by the structure previously explained and about to be explained, is contained in the parallelism created by Event Space. In the space created by the energies that support the possible possibility of possible possibilities, any event, including the environment required to support the parallelism, irrespective of being very local or pan environmental space, can and does exist. Event Space is created by the parallelistic functions of dualistic, trilistic, quadrulistic, etc., etc. (and its divisions of possible possibility of possible possibilities) events, or the possible invocation of such events as a result of decisive moments.

TOTALITIES AND THEIR REALITIES are a function of my structure that are based upon the collective totality of all that is within a certain quadrant of my area of sentient self-awareness, rather than just my self-awareness. They also follow a certain evolutionary or progressive genre. That being, those areas within me that contain the full gamut of dimensions, zones, continuum, planes, etc., that are similar in progressional advancement to, but not different enough, to be separated from each other. As a result they are "compartmentalized" into specialized areas or totalities, each totality divided into realities. The realities are subdivisions of the overall progressional genre of the totality they are aligned to.

REALITIES INDEPENDENT OF TOTALITIES AND THEIR CREATIVE FUNCTIONS are a natural progression from the totalities. This is the part of my structure that forms the start of the true greater reality, for it is the greater reality that forms the basis for that which is to be supported by my formalized structure. The totalities exist within the realities, which have lower-level realities within them. The independent realities are separated out by their opportunity for individualized and inter-collective creativity, called creative functions. Each creative function allows a variant of a specific independent reality to house an environment that allows a specific set of a known genre of totalities and their realities that are able to coexist in a "separately together" fashion, allowing independent and co-dependent progression.

For completeness, and to save your need to ask, I have decided to illustrate the two elements of my structure that were missing from the original list. This completes the twelve structural components within my current area of self-awareness.

SPECTRAL INTERFACES AND THEIR SPECTRA (NOT LIGHT BASED) are the lines of communication between all the structural components, formal, conceptual, and sentient. The word "spectral" is used to describe them because they are based upon the various types of the communication of sentient consciousness throughout my area of self-awareness. Their bandwidth and spectra (within the bandwidth) are fluid in their function. The word spectral also has a second meaning alluding to the fluidity of their function. The spectra are also speculative in nature and so search out alternative methods of processing the communication of sentient consciousness to ensure my omniscient behavioral ability is maintained.

Each spectra, as a communication medium, can be used as an indication of the progression gained within a specific independent reality in totality. The spectra can also be an indicator of the completeness of sentience and correlates to the number of gradients within a margin (see below). The spectral interfaces themselves can and do provide an environment for progression in their own right.

MARGINS AND THEIR GRADIENTS are that which form the boundaries of my area of sentient self-awareness. The margins are able to move and expand as a result of my progression in understanding those areas of my self-awareness that have to be understood and made sentient. They are graduated into percentage areas of complete sentience by the gradients associated with them. When a margin expands to its optimal condition, i.e., the area it covers is fully sentient, then its status changes to a "full margin" (fully sentient) and its gradients are removed, allowing the margin to be whole rather than divided. You may want to think of this expansion in terms of the growth rings of a tree. The expansion is holistically round but in actuality it is more or less expansive dependent upon the level of progression in a specific quadrant of a margin. Expanding upon this example, think of it in terms of where some growth rings show more growth than others or where the same growth ring has grown further away from the core of the trunk in one area than another. This expansion in growth is based upon the availability of nutrients and the states of the weather in the case of the tree, whereas in my case it is based upon how my area of sentient self-awareness has expanded in comparison to my non-sentient area of self-awareness in a particular direction.

ME: For a very high-level description of your structure it is extremely thought provoking.

O: Yes, and the energies surrounding the description are elevating as well.

ME: How do you mean?

O: When any entity, or incarnate entity for that matter, exposes themselves to an expansive condition of any type, whether it is by word of mouth, education, or procreation, that exposure creates growth for both the individual and their environment—that environment being the structure created by their Source Entity that they currently reside within. The growth also permeates the Source Entity itself and of course me. Additionally, the energies surrounding the elements of "truth" about the greater reality act in a subliminal way, assisting the entity in their level of understanding of that presented to them.

ME: So anyone reading this will, in a sense, become more enlightened?

O: Yes, irrespective of whether they "believe" the information presented or not. This is because the high-frequency aspect of that which tells the truth overcomes the low-frequency aspect of a thought process that promotes an incorrect or incomplete understanding.

ME: Thank you. What else do we need to know about your structure? What else is important about your structure?

O: It's not set in stone.

A Structure on the Point of Change

ME: What? I thought that your structure was a function of you that was automatic. That you didn't have any control over it. That it was a part of you that just was. That you worked with that which is you and progressed as an expanding sentient self-aware consciousness within it.

O: I do.

ME: Then why did you say that it is not set in stone?

O: Because it's not.

ME: But your structure is unfathomably large, so large that you don't even know how big it is yourself. So how could you think of it as being transient?

O: Because it is. Let me explain.

At a certain point in Event Space I will have expanded my area of sentient self-awareness out to the point of completion. That is, I will have come to the end of my ability to become more than I am in the current structure of that which I am. In this instance I will be in completion of that which I was and will need to expand into that which I will be. All this sounds a bit esoteric I know but what it means in layman's terms is that I will, and do, have the opportunity to start again, so to speak, to change the way it started and see how it will work given a new set of parameters.

ME: Ah, is this the cosmic breath that the Vedas talk about? The so-called breathing in and out of the cosmos, the starting all over again renewed and refreshed, the old going out and the new coming in?

O: From a human perspective you could call it that, but it's not that simple. You see if I was to follow that process I would not really gain anything, for that which was would be lost to that which will be, for in that process there is a cleansing effect, a starting again from scratch. Nothing is saved from the old and transported to the new in this way, because if it was it would contaminate the new with the directions taken in the old, and this includes my structure.

ME: I don't understand how it affects your structure.

O: Although my structure is currently a part of my continued discovery of "self" I realized that I could and can
change it should I desire to do so.

ME: When did you make that discovery?

O: I didn't. My Source Entities did.

ME: Excuse me? How could they discover something about
you before you?

O: My Source Entities discovering things before I do is one
of the reasons I created them, to help me.

ME: But isn't it back to front?

O: No, it's not. The whole point of me creating other entities was to accelerate my own progression by a factor
equal to the number of entities created in totality. Using
this method I no longer need to progress in a so-called
linear way. I progress in an omni-synergetic way.

My progression is assured irrespective of where the progressive content comes from. Notice that I am not using
the word evolution here, for a change in structure, or
any other change based upon progression via my creations or indeed myself, is above evolution because evolution is a component within the umbrella of progression.

ME: OK, reading between the lines then I guess that you discovered that you could change your structure when you
observed some of the Source Entities creating an environment based upon their own structure, tearing it down
if it didn't perform as expected and then recreating a
new one in its place.

O: Yes. It was a very interesting thing to observe, and was,
at that point in their existence, a breakthrough in creativity. As a result of observing my creations manipulating the structure of what they were, creating a new structure in its place, I decided to make some localized experimentation in my structure as well.

ME: So what did you do? How does your, shall I say "current"
structure differ from the structure resulting from the experimentation?

O: Firstly, the experimental structure doesn't exist any more because I decided that I could not, at that point in my existence, create a structure that would be an improvement on my natural structure.

ME: I guess that would be reasonable to assume. Having said that though, could you create an environment or structure that is an improvement on your natural one?

O: Actually no, but I can move the structure around to create a different representation of the same thing. That being, moving the frequencies, for example, into the space allotted for the divisions of continuum, the abstractions and vice versa. That changes both the structure in the mechanical sense, and the dynamics of the structure from the perspective of how the components within the rest of the structure relate and function with each other.

In the instance of my experimentation, I simply turned everything on its head, upside down, so to speak, with the frequencies being at the outer edge of the structure and the gradients being the start point.

ME: So what was the effect?

O: Everything flowed in reverse as expected but there was no progression, no evolution, only de-evolution and negative progression. Everything that flowed slowed down and eventually ground to a halt from the perspective of overall progression and those components of progression. It was as if starting with an entity that was already created specific to the highest, at that point in my existence, structure could not translate progressively to the outer edge of the experimental structure because it required negative progression or de-evolution. It seems that I had discovered a natural order of function within my structure and changing it in the way I did made its progressive qualities static.

ME: How would it work then with the example you gave a moment ago where you swapped frequency with gradients?

O: That's OK. You see, with nonlinear changes, the experiment I made being specifically linear in terms of progression because I simply turned everything upside down, progression and the components of progression are able to progress because there is a way around the stasis when a higher structural component is followed by a lower structural component. Yes, the progression is slowed down, but when the next component is higher, the loss of progressive impetus is reduced or even negated fully, with some instances of it returning to actual progression beyond that previously gained.

ME: What you are suggesting then is that any changes to your structure need to be interwoven with opportunities for progression within the structure, otherwise the structure is self-defeating, insomuch as it allows no progression.

O: Correct. When I saw how my structure affected my opportunity to progress, or indeed the opportunity for one of my creations to progress, I decided that the only changes I could make needed to ensure that progression was not only maintained but accelerated in some way. Right now the structure is perfect for what it is contributing progression-wise because my creations, the Source Entities, are working in ways that are facilitating not only progression, but a constant rate of accelerated progression. When this work has reached its conclusion, and by that I mean no further progression can be made, I will make changes to allow further progression within the same area of sentient self-awareness. However, irrespective of me allowing this to proceed in a natural way, I could change the structure of my area of sentient self-awareness to one of a more progressive functionality now. In fact, I have already created a plan for change that could be introduced right now.

ME: Why don't you?

O: Believe me, I have thought about it long and hard, and have almost made the change a couple of times.

ME: What stopped you?

O: An insatiable desire to see what happens next with the current structure. I simply had/have to see it through in its current form. Also I am rather pleased with how it is working out at the moment. It is much more successful than I expected it to be, especially when I look at how well the Source Entities have taken to their tasks. Every one of them and their creations are contributing in a most positive and progressive way with a minimum of overlap.

ME: So it is "in perfection" then?

O: At the moment, yes. But at some point I still may make some minor changes to the structural integrity. This is one of the bonuses of being me, but even I can only make changes to my own structure within the confines of what it is.

ME: In what way would you change it then if it is currently perfect?

O: I would make the structure finer still. This I can do within the constraints of the current progressive ability of the structure. What I would do in this instance though is increase the number of divisions within each of the twelve major structural stages to make the transition from a lower one to a higher one easier and faster to achieve.

ME: But wouldn't you negate the intensity of the learning opportunity by making the steps smaller?

O: No, because the overall effect is the same—how it is achieved is the difference. When and if I make this change it will accelerate the progressional opportunity by building confidence in the abilities of the Source Entities and their creations by experiencing success earlier on in their development process; i.e., the "experience, learn, evolve, progress" function will be achieved at more regular points in their existence, thereby giving them encouragement to keep doing what they are doing in the way they are doing it.

Chapter 9

How Maintenance Entities Evolve

I DECIDED TO CHANGE MY DIRECTION of questioning at this point to once again touch on the subject of those entities that maintain the structure of the environments created by the Source Entities—what we call Angels from the perspective of our Source Entity, SE1. It was clear that all entities, irrespective of which Source Entity created them, have a choice in terms of how they support the way in which their particular Source Entity works on its own progress. Some choose to work within the structure and experience it in every way they can— while others choose to be of service and work on maintaining the environment's optimal evolutionary condition for the benefit of those working within it. Although these maintenance entities are therefore outside of the evolutionary cycle from their personal perspective, they can still gather evolutionary content, assisting their progression in the process while they are still being of service. In this instance being of service means that the entity choosing this path gives up the opportunity for accelerated progression for the benefit of others within the evolutionary cycle. A noble act indeed, and one that is not disregarded by any Source Entity. The reason why I decided to come back to this subject is because I was being given additional information by The Origin as I was working on the previous text. In this way it was becoming clear to me that the information broadcast during my last dialogue on this subject was therefore incomplete.

ME: I take it that you wanted to put this story straight, so to speak.

O: In a way, yes. I realized that it was important to elaborate on how these entities progress when being of total service to others. In essence, it is another way how they can accrue evolutionary content when they are not within the evolutionary cycle.

ME: So how does one of these entities accrue evolutionary content outside of the evolutionary cycle?

O: They are given it.

ME: Please explain.

O: All entities within the evolutionary cycle feel that they are indebted to those entities who choose to be in service to them. Without the maintenance entities, or Angels, in your multiverse, they would not progress back toward perfection as fast as they do. In recognition of this they give up some of their own evolutionary content as a reward for the service the maintenance entities do for them.

ME: I take it that this is in a general sense and not specific to a particular maintenance entity?

O: There are two ways in which an entity within the evolutionary cycle can give evolutionary content. The first way is to give it in a general sense. In this way the evolutionary content is shared out equally among all maintenance entities within a specific Source Entity's environment—the dilution factor being relative to the ratio of "giving" entities to "receiving" entities. In general though the ratio of evolving entities versus non-evolving or maintenance entities is in favor of those evolving. An evolving entity gives up this content as it accrues its own content, which is an automatic function. The second way is to give additional evolutionary content to a specific maintenance entity on a regular or continuous basis. This is based upon personal choice and is usually as a result of an established relationship between an evolving entity and a non-evolving or maintenance entity. It can also be given as a result of gratitude to any non-evolving entity on a one-off basis as well, and is usually seen when the work of a specific maintenance entity has assisted in acceleration of the evolving entity's evolution.

ME: So there is a level of evolutionary symbiosis here. The maintenance entities benefit from the work they do to ensure the evolutionary condition of the environment the evolving entities work within, as a result of the level of evolution those evolving entities accrue in the part of the environment they maintain. Even though they are not within the evolutionary cycle, they nevertheless accrue evolutionary content through the gratitude of the evolving entities.

O: Correct.

ME: And they work outside of the evolutionary cycle, in service to others, knowing that they will actually accrue this content through the work of the evolving entities?

O: They are aware of the fact that they can accrue evolutionary content in the general method, but evolutionary progression for them is not totally guaranteed, as the ratio of dilution may be such that the evolutionary content gained may well be so minimal that it is unperceivable. Also, gifts of evolutionary content are not guaranteed and so an entity, in full knowledge of this, enters into service purely for the joy of being of service.

I suddenly knew that this subject was now complete. It appears that all evolve, whether through actively being part of the evolutionary cycle, through automatic "gifts" from evolving entities, or through one-off gifts through appreciation of the non-evolving entity's work. Those entities that enter into service have no expectation of accruing evolutionary content as a direct result of being in service, but, in being in the service they are in, they nevertheless accrue evolutionary content as a result of the evolving entity's gratefulness of the work they perform. One thing was clear though, and that was that the maintenance entities sacrifice their own progression for the benefit of the entities on the evolutionary cycle. To sacrifice one's own progression for the benefit of others is being in true service.

Chapter 10

An Interesting Development on the

Disciples of Jesus and the Resurrection

ONE OF THE STORIES THAT I HAD been very interested in was the resurrection of Jesus and what the mechanics were of the process that achieved it. Normally I would have asked my own Source Entity, Source Entity One, this question as it was peculiar to the physical universe. However, I just thought that, with The Origin receiving all of that which is experienced by every entity within a Source Entity's environment simultaneously, as the Source Entities themselves experience it, I would be just as well off by asking the question to The Origin while I was enjoying a one-on-one dialogue with it.

ME: I know it's a complete departure from the previous dialogues we have been having but the stories surrounding the incarnate entity we call Jesus, his disciples, and the so-called resurrection have been a bone of contention for some time. Could you explain what the truth is about the number of disciples Jesus had, including what the truth is surrounding the story of the resurrection, please?

The Disciples

O: You're right about the change in direction. It really is a significant departure from the previous discussion points.

ME: I thought we needed a break, an injection of something that is closer to home.

O: Fine. I can see that it would be of interest while creating an opportunity to remove the dogma incarnate mankind gets itself into when it talks around the subject of religion and the stories within the various religions. It would also be an interesting lesson in duality.

ME: Duality?

O: You will see what I mean in a moment.

ME: OK. I am open to everything that expands our knowledge of what our true history is.

O: Then you won't be surprised if I tell you that Jesus had twenty-four main or close disciples.

ME: And not twelve?

O: No, twenty-four. You see, there needs to be a balance in the dualistic condition of the Earth to maintain its synchronicity. You have two sexes, do you not?

ME: Yes, we do.

O: And two poles on a magnet?

ME: Yes.

O: And a positive and a negative for electricity, a black and a white, a red and a cyan, a green and a magenta, a blue and a yellow, an up and a down, a left and a right, a forward and a backward. Shall I go on?

ME: No. I think you have made your point. You're telling me that everything in the physical universe has an opposite and that this is the dualistic condition that must exist.

O: Correct. Even monopole magnets have an opposite. It may not be within the same material, but it is available, should one seek to find it.

ME: Jesus then, had twenty-four disciples, twelve of them male and twelve of them female.

O: Correct.

ME: So why don't we hear about the female disciples?

O: Society could not accept the female of the race being on an equal standing, especially when it came to the rather male-oriented aspect of religion in that period. Based upon that, the fact that there were an equal number of male and female disciples was actively ignored and the historical fact of male and female disciples was modified to the current male-oriented story that was passed down through history.

Within the wider community there were both male and female followers of the teachings broadcast by Jesus, and there is no denial of this. What the issue is here, is the denial of the equal distribution of what was considered to be power by the priests, to those of the female sex, and not a right for all entities to exist in a karma-free way.

Within the knowledge that Jesus taught was the need for fairness and equality, and he made sure that those that were close to him were held in equality in both knowledge and status. A major aspect of what was taught was the need for equality in energies when meditating together for the purposes of creativity that required a synergetic function. When working in meditative concert, in "metaconcert," the ideal synergetic function requires the male, female, male, female connectivity to ensure the optimal desired outcome can be achieved. Although this is not a prerequisite for synergy when meditating within the spheres occupied within the rest of the physical universe, it is for those who incarnate on the Earth due to the dualistic creative condition of the two vehicles. Jesus had the optimum condition for creativity through meditation-based synergy, for he had twelve of each sex as his closest and most powerful disciples. With these twenty-four disciples Jesus was able to affect some of the larger miracles that have been recorded, and many more that were not, for he used them to augment his own energy manipulating abilities, which were not inconsiderable considering the frequency levels at that juncture.

ME: You're suggesting then that these miracles were not all performed by Jesus himself, but were the product of group work, with Jesus orchestrating the energies generated by his disciples working in metaconcert?

O: For the big miracles, yes. As I said, the frequencies were too low at that juncture for one single incarnate being to action, so he used the power of the others working together. A classic example was the generation of the food to feed the wider followers who came to hear him speak, the generation of the loaves and fishes.

ME: He used manifestation here then?

O: No, he created a mass illusion that they were all being fed and that they were sustained. That was far more effective than the actual manifestation of solid food, for that would have created a stampede toward the distributor of the food and would have cost many lives in the process.

ME: So Jesus and the disciples created a mass hallucination?

O: Yes, but it was more complete than that, for they also gave the individual members of the crowd the feeling that they were full and satisfied. In effect they were fully charged with energy.

ME: Based upon this then the writer of the Bible had no knowledge of the truth surrounding this particular miracle?

O: No, and he wouldn't, for he wrote it many years after the event, with it based upon the gathering together of ledgers made by the scribes of the time, which were still in existence when the Bible was being compiled. This was, however, based upon the experience of those in the crowd and not those who were the close disciples.

Another of these miracles was the resurrection.

The Resurrection

ME: Tell me more. It really doesn't surprise me that the resurrection was a mass illusion.

O: Maybe not, but it was one that was a triumph of meta-concert orchestration, for it was without the main orchestrator—Jesus himself.

ME: So there is some truth in the story about the resurrection then?

O: Only insomuch as it was a story, an illusion.

ME: What really happened then?

O: There are certain parts of history that are correct, and others that are misunderstood. In this instance that which was misunderstood, and is subsequently lacking in substance, is the process leading to the resurrection itself.

Jesus himself was becoming very much a problem to both the church at that time and the Roman governing body, who were continually having to appease the religious elders in order to maintain overall control of the area. Jesus was a promoter of the truth and was increasingly growing tired of his own religious elders' inability to look past the power base that they had created and investigate the real reason for the structure of the teachings they resided over. As his followers grew, he naturally started to reduce the numbers of attendees at the churches, which caused a conflict of interest with the religious leaders. Did they allow the numbers to decline in favor of Jesus' teachings, a man who they had previously tolerated because of his own faith being theirs, or did they do something about him? With their egos taking the lead, they decided to do something about him rather than to let them all exist in parallel.

A false charge against him was subsequently drawn up, and he was arrested after his whereabouts was revealed to the Romans through investigative work. Without their Guru, their teacher, the disciples were at odds as to what to do, especially when the punishment for the charge was converted to death by crucifixion rather than a mere public flogging. This change in sentence was the result of more manipulation by the religious elders during the opportunity to choose who should be given an amnesty during a public tribunal with another criminal, known as Barabbas, who was a known leader of guerrilla warfare against the unwanted Roman rule.

With their training being tested to the extreme, they created a plan where they would create the mass illusion that Jesus was in fact led to the cross, crucified, and then buried. When the day of the execution was upon them, rather than mourning with the rest of the expectant onlookers, all of the disciples, including Judas, who was incorrectly blamed for betraying Jesus, sat in meditation-based metaconcert and gave the audience what they expected. The crowd expected to see Jesus led from his cell and, along with others, made to carry his cross from the Roman fort to the hill where the crucifixions were performed. In their mind's eye they saw Jesus nailed, strung up, and tortured; they also saw him die through the blood loss created by the torture instruments, be taken down, and buried in a pauper's grave, a local cave, which was sealed with a stone to ensure wild dogs could not feast on the dead body.

What actually happened was a most different story. With the attention of their metaconcert fully fixed on the creation of the illusion, the disciples had graduated to "master" status—communicating to Jesus in the process that the coast was clear for him to make his escape. All of the guards in the fort went to see the crucifixion as well so it was a very easy task for Jesus' mother, Mary, to open the cell door and set him free. Traveling in haste to the location of the meditating disciples, a delighted Jesus offered final assistance to the metaconcert, augmenting its power as he linked into it, enabling the now tired disciples with fresh impetus to finish the illusion in a most complete and convincing way. Once finished, the whole group went their separate ways, only to meet up once more a month later before disbanding for good, spreading themselves across the globe—each one now a master in their own right, each one being in total control of themselves and their environment energetically, each one teaching the truth and how to live a karma-free incarnate life.

Those followers of Jesus, including some close family, who were not party to the illusion, subsequently opened the seal of the cave to find no dead body resting there, for there was never a body there in the first place. Others caught glimpses of a disguised Jesus walking down the road on his way to a new life in another part of the world. One or two said that they spoke to him, and that he spoke back to them, which he did. He used his words and mannerisms guardedly so that those who saw him thought that they saw a ghost, especially when they looked around again and found him suddenly gone. Disappearing in this way was a simple illusion based upon a time-delay effect created by hypnosis, which Jesus was very adept at, and used with considerable effect during healing.

With all of these peripheral things happening, additional confusion was created and the martyr was born. His life became a mystery. The moments surrounding his crucifixion became blurred and surreal, with wonder taking over from the mourning of his death when the seal on his cave was opened to reveal an empty tomb. Jesus himself settled down to a lifestyle that required a much-reduced level of celebrity and became a teacher of his own work under the guise of a lesser disciple. Gone was the long hair, gone was the beard, but stronger was his resolve and more subliminal was his teaching. Although he was a man in personal exile, he still managed to broadcast the truth. In essence he became a master of disguise and changed his location frequently, ensuring he didn't attract attention in the same way he did by teaching in a subliminal way.

ME: So where did he go?

O: All over the Middle East and Europe. In fact he was more successful at broadcasting the truth in his new subliminal way than in his previous way because it created less attention and allowed him to move more freely. How else do you think Christianity came to the Western world!

ME: Our history shows that a number of supporters of Christianity were involved in the spread of "the way" around Europe, including the main disciples themselves. Are you suggesting that Jesus orchestrated most of it?

O: Yes. Although he didn't do all of it himself, he was in contact with the disciples on a regular telepathic basis through meditation, which included those newly indoctrinated devotees who were to spread the word to the furthest most parts of the world.

ME: How long did Jesus stay on the Earth? Bearing in mind that he was supposed to be circa thirty-three years old at the point of the crucifixion?

O: He actually lived to be 112 years old, ascending from his human condition in the country you call Slovakia today, having personally introduced a largely karma-proof way of existing in the physical to over 300,000 people. His close devotees and disciples collectively attained 1.2 million introductions. Considering the relatively low incarnate population of the Earth then, this is a very high number of converts. Christianity was without doubt the most successful of the "ways to live" that were introduced within a 500-year time period.

ME: You say that he introduced a largely karma-proof way of existing in the physical. What happened to it? All I see is religion.

O: As with all things where the leader departs the physical, allowing the devotees to continue the work, personal preference and personality/ego start to get in the way and the original teachings start to become diluted. Eventually the teachings become so diluted that the original message is lost and that which is taught bears no resemblance to it. This is where you are today with all religions, to a greater or lesser degree.

ME: If the teaching had been strictly adhered to, would we be at a higher frequency now?

O: Most definitely. It is testament to how fast the teachings became diluted with the origins of all religions, as to how fast incarnate mankind slid into the low frequencies associated with the dark ages. It took a long time to come out the other side, and you still haven't managed it. If all teaching were strictly adhered to, it would be utopia on Earth now in comparison to where you are currently.

ME: This is a good example then of the need to stick to the rules, with unwavering dedication.

O: Yes, but one needs to be cognizant of the progression of the frequencies and the need to modify the teachings accordingly.

ME: Why?

O: Because as one ascends the frequencies the detail behind the basics of the teachings needs to change to suit—that being they no longer need to be so basic but they still need to create an understanding of the basics.

Consider it like progressing from the need to use logarithm tables because the functions are available on a calculator, but still needing to understand how the results are attained from the use of the tables even though you don't use them. This is understanding the basics.

Chapter 11

More on Our Destiny

IN THE BEYOND THE SOURCE *BOOKS I had discovered that in a distant Event Space we were all, all individualized units of the Source Entities, that is, destined to become Source Entities in our own right. In the background I was starting to realize that there was much more to this prophecy than I had gained to date. For instance, what is the prerequisite requirement for this to happen? Will "All" individualized units become Source Entities or will some not? And what will happen to the existing twelve Source Entities beyond moving into the new sector of The Origin's area of self-awareness? I felt that, although we had discussed this subject, there were a lot of gaps in the information I currently knew and had been able to broadcast. It was time to dig deeper, I thought. I was about to approach The Origin on expanding upon this subject when I discovered that it was hot on my tail and eager to assist.*

O: I was wondering when you would return to this subject.

ME: I would have thought that you could see it coming!

O: Of course I could, but it is always interesting to not pry into the relative Event Space and see what is, or could, happen next. That's the beauty of your incarnate existence; you simply don't know what you are doing in comparison to how you operate when fully energetic. It's fun and scary at the same time. I like to see how you all cope, that is all of you across all of the Source Entities when in the lower frequencies; although, Source Entity One does seem to have the lion's share of entities who work in the low frequencies. Indeed, it is the only one where the gross physical vehicle is a necessity.

ME: You don't use Event Space to see what the options are then and which way is the best route to take from a strategic sense?

O: Yes, I do, but sometimes not knowing is all part of the experience and learning process, which I find fun, and you all do so very well, considering the constraints of the physical vehicle you currently use.

ME: Currently use?

O: Yes, currently. You will all progress beyond the need for such a low-frequency vehicle, as I will explain.

As you are aware, when an entity works with the low frequencies there is a need to have a construct of some sort, in your case a biological form, to allow full immersion into the low frequencies themselves—the objective being, that the immersion should be total and the experience being optimized to that which can be achieved in that frequency. Existing "in" the physical while not being "of" the physical being the modus operando. One can only experience the opportunities presented in totality if the entity is in full immersion of the environment, and this means every aspect of the limitations resulting from being in low-frequency existence. In this respect you also recently accepted the need to be totally separated from that part of your energetic self that is disincarnate, for that would allow you access to alternative Event Spaces giving you prior knowledge, negating the depth of experience that could be achieved.

The experience of separation creates the ego, the transient creation of individualized sentience from the whole, allowing the function of the incarnate vehicle supposedly independently of the True Energetic Self, which of course is fully cognizant of the work of the incarnate aspect of its "self," while the other is not while incarnate. When however, through diligent good living over a period of incarnations, that aspect of the True Energetic Self that is projected into incarnate vehicles used for low-frequency experience starts to see beyond the transient individuality created by incarnation, "while incarnate," the projected aspect starts to recover its ability to communicate with its True Energetic Self, seeing beyond the confines of the incarnate vehicle. It then prefers to work with the low frequencies of the physical in ways that raise the base frequency of the vehicle to the point where it can no longer be classified as "gross physical."

This takes many incarnations and relies on the process of gaining recognition of self, and a higher meaning for existence in this individualized state, which is reduced in integrity as a result as the incarnate prefers to work in high-frequency ways while in the low frequencies.

When the incarnating entities have reached a certain level of progression, the incarnation process is fully understood and recognized for what it is while the entity is incarnate. This allows it to navigate around the opportunities for frequential reduction, concentrating on frequential progression. In this way the incarnate vehicle's base frequencies are increased, and its functionality is increased in the process.

Eventually, through many diligent incarnations, the incarnate vehicles available are of such a frequency that they no longer offer the same level of resistance while in the physical frequencies. They therefore no longer have a place in the low frequencies assigned to gross physical experience and need to move up a frequency level into an environment, the next simultaneous universe in Source Entity One's multiversal environment, which can support the functionality of that incarnate vehicle in a way that is consistent with its new base frequency. As that particular aspect of the True Energetic Self assigned to incarnate existence progresses, the incarnate vehicles used also progress frequentially and the ability to function optimally in the current environment is affected, requiring it to be elevated to the next frequency level and next simultaneous universe. Eventually the fineness of the frequencies, from Level 15 and above, are such that incarnate vehicles are no longer necessary and the True Energetic Self can progress without the need for artificial constructs to allow holistic experience to be achieved. Progression through the higher frequencies is therefore a matter of time, so to speak, and the entity that makes regular evolutionary progression eventually ascends the frequencies associated with Source Entity One's multiverse and become eligible for full communion with its creator, should they wish to become one again.

An entity that has experienced all that can be experienced in all of the simultaneous universal environments offered by their Source Entity can elect to remain individualized, undergo the process of ascension again, become a maintenance entity, seek full communion and absorption into non-individualized oneness, or seek communion while maintaining individualization of self while within their Source Entity.

When all entities have achieved at least the eligibility for communion with their Source Entity, there will be a correlation with my ability to expand into my next area of self-awareness. This is because it coincides with my gaining full sentience within my current area of self-awareness. At this point everything that is within that area will be known and experienced by either myself, my Source Entities, or my Source Entities' creations, which means that I experience by default everything that can be, or could have been, experienced within that area. When this happens it is time to expand into my next area of non-sentient self-awareness, for I will no longer gain anything by having my sentience constrained.

It was stated in a previous dialogue with you on this subject that I am only aware of a small percentage of one percent of that which I am, and that expansion into this next area would still put it at less than one percent, but that relatively speaking the change in area/volume would be so immense that I would need help in mapping it out and making it sentient. Well, this is true. The only issue is that I don't truly know how expansive I am and that the percentage quoted may well be on the high side. Suffice to say I will need significant help in the mapping process and creation of an expended area of sentient self-awareness. As a result, all entities created by my Source Entities will be given the opportunity to take any of the routes mentioned above, or become classified as Source Entities in their own right. I am starting to understand that this is such an immense undertaking that assigning Source Entity status to my Source Entities' creations is the minimum I can implement in order to be successful in achieving my new level of sentient self-awareness within the time frame I am working on.

Each new Source Entity will be given an area of its own to work with and a directive to experience, learn, and evolve within that area in any way it can—just the same as the first twelve Source Entities, with no holds barred but with the extended ability to work both within and without their own energetic boundary while within the area of my non-sentient self-awareness. In this way I augment the work that they do and my speed of sentient expansion in the process.

However, each new Source Entity will be better equipped than the first twelve because they will have ALL of the combined learning of the other Source Entities, the entities they created, and all the experiential learning and evolutionary progression I have accrued to date in their energetic memory. They will have a localized Akashic that is functionally a quantum leap above the largest version of the Akashic that any group of entities will have ever created. Their own functional creative ability will be another quantum leap above the current condition as well. In essence they will be significantly better prepared than their creators were when they started out on the path of experiential evolutionary progression.

ME: Is it fair to have such a head start? Considering, that is, that their own creators had a clean slate, no head start, just a single command!

O: Yes, it is.

ME: Why?

O: Simply because everything will have moved on, the new environment is much, much bigger than the current one. None of us know what the structure is, how the physics works, or how to interact with these new environmental rules. Everything experienced to date has been within my current area of sentience and soon to be sentient area of self-awareness. Even those areas that are not currently sentient, those that are part of my current area of self-awareness, are known structurally and environmentally with all of the physics, so to speak, understood as well. It will be a massive change for all of us; I am quite excited about the prospect.

ME: Is it that much of a change? Can't you extrapolate what the difference will be?

O: No. It is a completely new part of "that which I am" and as such I have not been in a position to do any detailed analysis, specifically because I am working with my current area of self-awareness and need to concentrate on finishing that first. Some things, you will note, are indeed linear.

ME: I suppose personal progression is supposed to be linear.

O: Not entirely. Evolutionary content has myriad ways of expressing progression, as we have previously discussed. What is linear is my progression through my areas of awareness.

ME: What are we, as new Source Entities, required to do?

O: No more than those that will be called the previous Source Entities are doing now. Simply to experience, learn, evolve, and progress in any way possible. The issue is that the environment is significantly bigger than that currently experienced, in every way, so the new Source Entities need to have a head start to be able to stand a chance of having a reasonable chance of being able to cope with the expansiveness that they experience, and will need to work with and within.

ME: What about the existing Source Entities? What will they do in this new expanded environment? What is their role if we, as the new Source Entities, are doing what they did, experiencing the new environment in every way possible, learning from this interaction, and evolving and progressing as a consequence?

O: They will be helping me directly.

ME: How?

O: In a previous dialogue during what you call the Beyond the Source books, you established that the current Source Entities were to help me in some way, to have a bigger part in the task of my establishing an increase in my area of sentient self-awareness. That is still true, but what you don't know is how they will be expected to do it.

ME: I am all ears!

O: As you can appreciate, everything that is created is created either by me or my creations. All are, by definition, part of me because everything that is, is me, whether it is a part of me, or a creation based upon the use of energies that are part of my structural condition.

ME: Yes, this is understood.

O: Because the Source Entities are the first successful product of my creativity, they will become more than that which they were. They will return to their Source, so to speak, and become an extension of my active sentience.

ME: What do you mean when you say "active sentience?" What is the difference between sentience and active sentience?

O: Sentience is that condition which I can move my active sentience, my beingness, into and still maintain my cognizance of the functionality and experiential content accrued by other parts of my sentient self-awareness. Active sentience is what I am. It is my personality, my experience, my memory, my learning, my ability, my functionality, my evolutionary content, and my personal progression. I have a function that you would call omnipresence but this is a product of my sentience within my area of self-awareness, which is not my active sentience. My active sentience is a transportable focus of intellect, of beingness of ultimate creativity. It is separate to, while being inextricably linked with, my overall sentience. Call it a central processing area if you like, but one that is not static in its location or overall focus of "being," while being acutely focused for the purpose of creativity.

ME: But I thought that in your area of sentient self-awareness you were totally omnipresent.

O: I am, it's just that I have an area, a transportable area, that is to all intents and purposes a super computer in comparison to the rest of what is also a very powerful computing medium. I control, and am present within, the rest of what I am from this focused and transportable area.

ME: And the existing Source Entities will become part of this transportable area of active sentience as a result of our progression into your new area of self-awareness?

O: More than that. They will become active satellites of active sentience. I will explain in more detail. The twelve Source Entities will still remain individualized but they will become extensions of my active sentience. They will have a direct active sentient link between my active sentience and each other. They will be positioned equi-distant from my active sentience but will remain stationary within the new area of self-awareness. If I move my active sentience in any way, the links expand or contract as necessary. There is no loss of connectivity as a result of this expansion or contraction but there is an overall increase in my creative functions by a factor of the power of twelve. Additionally, the speed at which I can accrue new sentience in my areas of self-awareness is accelerated by this factor as well.

ME: Why keep them static within your new area of self-awareness? Why not let them be mobile like yourself?

O: I could and I will later. Actually, much later when we move into the area of self-awareness after the next. The reason for keeping them static when we move in the next area of self-awareness is because I want them to be positioned in a way that allows the maximum coverage of fully functional active sentience. Simply put, I will be creating a framework for ensuring an instantaneous expanded active sentient condition that would not be possible if the Source Entities had mobility as extensions to my active sentience in this instance.

ME: So what is the difference between being static in this extension of your area of self-awareness and in the following one that, as you suggest, allows you to give them mobility within the environment?

O: As you can appreciate, the environment after the next will be a further significant increase/change in volume, structure, and physics. In this instance the Source Entities will replicate, together with yourselves as source entities, the process I intend to use in my next area of self-awareness. I will be connected to them and their satellites of active sentience and you and your satellites of active sentience simultaneously. This will further augment my framework for creating active sentience in an area that will be unfathomably large in comparison with the previous, which is unfathomably large in comparison to the current area. The issue here, though, is that each area of self-awareness I expand into also expands by a multiple of the power of twelve. As a result, my area of active self-awareness is inversely reduced as a function of this increase in area—hence, my need to artificially increase my area of active sentience by using the Source Entities as satellites of active sentience, thereby counteracting the effect of the increase in area.

ME: And the Source Entities will remain individualized while being part of your active sentience?

O: Yes. It is an essential function of the satellite-based framework of active sentience that they remain individualized, for it augments my creativity while having the ability to act on my behalf independently, using a combination of their creativity and my creative function in further increasing this area. In actual fact though, they are already operating in the state of satellite functionality, for they are working on their own for the greater good of my progression, which of course results in their own as part of the process. It's just that in the greater scheme of things we are at the very start of the process of rigorously and robustly expanding my area of sentient self-awareness.

ME: I have been receiving pictures of how this will work. It's just like you said. The Source Entities will be satellites of your sentience, joined together with communication lines. It looks just like the molecular model of a chemical, or other substance. Wait a moment, I see the lines getting thicker, expanding in what I will call diameter and in location along the lines. This is an expansion in both communicative bandwidth and in the localized area of sentient self-awareness. Now I see an "off-shoot" creating another connection to another link creating a communication shortcut. This off-shoot also helps to fill in the gap, so to speak, allowing the area of non-sentient self-awareness to decrease. As I look I see more off-shoots being created. These additional off-shoots are multiplying, creating a gossamer framework that is both fine, and increases in thickness as it is created and starts to function. I also notice that as a certain level of framework is attained the area floods with glowing iridescent sentience as a function of triangulation. Yes, that's it! The thickening of the lines in certain localized areas is a function of direct triangulation. What I am seeing now is a function of inflational triangulation. As the areas represented by the framework are filled in, the point of solidarity in sentient self-awareness, the Source Entities, move further out recreating the satellite system and the lines of communication, then the process starts all over again. This is repeated time and time again until the whole area is classified as sentient self-awareness. I resist in using this word, but it's almost organic in the nature of its growth.

O: That's a good way of describing it. Exponential would be another. You can see though how I plan to use the Source Entities and all of their creations to accelerate my expansion of sentient self-awareness, and, that it is a necessary function, increasing the ratio of sentience versus non-sentience in a new area ripe for expansion.

ME: Yes, I can see that it is necessary, and I can see that you would need help from your creations and your creations' creations. One thing I have just felt though, and that is that in reality this is all you doing this, that in actuality it can only be you doing this. We, the Source Entities, the Om, and those entities created by the Source Entities and as second-generation creations, our creations are really only aspects of you doing things independently of the greater sentience that is you, under the permission and direction of your greater sentience, that which is not individualized as us.

O: That would be a reasonable assumption and thought process to work with.

Chapter 12

What We Really Are

FOR THE ADVANCED TRUTH SEEKER this will not be a great revelation, but as I sat back and reflected on what I had just conveyed to The Origin, the enormity of what was going on in the greater reality, that which was in truth a personal and profound identification of "beingness" swept over me. Everything that was, is The Origin. No matter how we think of ourselves in our individualized state, we are a minute aspect of The Origin. Forget for a moment the identification with the Source. WE are The Origin.

Think of it in these terms. We are our creator's creator just as our creator is also its creator. We are nothing short of creativity itself. Everything is integrated into the one, The Origin. Nothing is separate, not even separately together. I now saw that the "Separately Together" statement made countless times in my dialogues with the Source Entities and even The Origin was incorrect, for how can that which is in reality "All There Is" be separated in any way from that which it is?

At this point in my dialogue with The Origin I started to see things from a whole new perspective. I was typing this up on my smart phone, a Samsung Galaxy S3. I was sitting in my old MG BGT, the car that my late wife, Anne, and I had driven to Crete, Greece, in 2004. I was parked by an old church (Iglessi) on a mountain road that overlooked the valley where we had bought and renovated an old traditionally Cretan cottage. The mountains were full of olive, fig, lemon, and pomegranate trees all spread out in front of me. It was deadly quiet apart from the wind and the birds in the trees. I had a profound sense of oneness with everything. It was me and I was it. As I expanded my consciousness further out I felt my oneness expand as well. I became the mountains and the trees, the Earth, and the solar system, the physical universe and then the multiverse, the Source and then the area of The Origin between Source and its peers, the other Source Entities, *the area of The Origin's current area of sentient self-aware-ness, the vastness of the next area of non-sentient non-self-awareness, the separated aspects of Source Entity Twelve which satellited itself in the near edge of the perimeter that separated the growing area of sentient self-awareness from the new area of The Origin's "self" that it was aware of but not self-aware of. It was all consuming and very difficult to pull away from, especially when glimpsing the unfathomable depth of The Origin that it itself was not yet investigating.*

At this point I had to struggle to stay alert and focused. How could I, an incarnate being, irrespective of my energetic her-itage, be able to experience this vastness? What's more, how was I able to survive the mental impact of such an experience without losing it! I was about to try to rationalize it all out as a bit of a daydream when The Origin decided to step in and put me back on the straight and narrow. I decided to "save" what I had typed before I let The Origin "in" so to speak, and was horrified as the "save" took longer to action than ex-pected and my phone crashed, resulting in me typing some of this text again. It seemed that the energies were locally higher than normal. I looked around me and the trees and moun-tains were all displaying their auras to my naked eye, the air was full of orgone which I also saw with my naked eye. What else was happening? I thought. I couldn't keep The Origin out any longer.

O: Why would you want to keep out that which you ulti-mately are? Not that you could. Even though "You" are Om, you are party to the constraints of the incarnate while incarnate, but even being Om when energetic does not afford an entity superiority over another, for you are all me.

ME: Am I getting told off here? And if so why?

O: You are not being told off; I am just bringing you into line. What you experienced was filtered by me so that you maintained your mental integrity. No one being, that is individualized incarnate intelligence, of your size would survive such an experience without being put into a psychiatric ward without my help. You are lucky your recording device did not perish with the influx of energies associated with accessing a greater aspect of reality.

ME: I am very grateful it didn't.

O: What you experienced is available to all incarnate entities should they develop the capability, but none would recognize what they are working with. You see, I help you to experience and report back on what you call the greater reality. But in order to do so you need to be exposed to an even greater aspect of that reality to enable you to work with a small aspect of it without supervision, so to speak. You may think that what you have intellectually realized is common sense but experiential experience is the only way to true self-realization.

Knowing through experiencing is the only way forward in any respect.

Realizing that you, along with everything else created, is really me, is an important step. Thinking that you are "individual" is in reality a flawed thought process, even for a Source Entity to have.

ME: Tell me then, why are we, those that are on the spiritual path, that is, allowed to think of ourselves as individuals, or individualized units of our Source?

O: Because it helps you to go in the right direction. You have to be fed the ultimate knowledge slowly, exposure to expansion only being possible when one displays the capability for expansion and not before, for that would be detrimental and creates regression. When I exposed you to more of me, leading to your experiential realization of self within me, you were ready for such exposure. Were you not, you would not have made the change in understanding, neither would you have retained your cognitive abilities after such exposure.

You now know that in reality there is no separation, that there is only the momentary process and functionality that can be associated with individualization of energy and that this energy is not separate but is part of that which I am. It is fully integrated while being allowed to perform a specific and specialized function—experience, learning, evolution, and progression.

Think of it in this way. If a sheet of paper is set alight on one corner, the whole sheet is not alight. Only an aspect of it is alight so that the remainder can experience what it is to be alight while not being "currently" alight in totality. In this way only a small aspect of the "totality" of the sheet of paper is used in the process of experiencing being alight, rather than all of it. It is efficient use of totality. Using "totality" as the next example, the totality can experience myriad experiences if it, as the totality, is sectioned or identifies separate or individualized areas/zones that experience different things concurrently. Call it holographic processing if you like, but in this way progression can be experienced in a profoundly experiential way by the totality, which it would not achieve if done in the isolated condition of totality within totality.

ME: So, as an isolated second-generation aspect of you, an entity's individuality (that is, an entity created by a Source Entity) is very transient at best?

O: In a word, yes. But the longevity of that transience in individuality is perpetuated by my grace. By that I mean so long as I am gaining experiential content from that aspect of individuality, its ability to progress individually is maintained.

ME: There are people who are going to find the prospect of potential loss of individuality quite scary.

O: Of course they will. But know this. You are never truly individual. You can never be truly individual because you are a creation of another. When you are energetic, you will realize this fundamental truth. When incarnate, the aspect of your energies that are projected into the physical vehicle become individualized, a function of the reduction in communicative bandwidth and the contract you make with yourself for incarnate experience. As a result the ego is created and individualized thought dominates the functionality of the incarnate energy. You know this and articulate it to your readers well. What perhaps isn't recognized is the larger subject of totality.

Totality is all-inclusive. It means everything is one, that there is no separation. Even though the use of the term "separately together" is used a lot in dialogues with you, it is inaccurate, as I have recently stated. And as recently stated, I let it be because it is in the right direction, thought-wise. When an entity exists in the full knowledge of totality, it recognizes that it is in existence as a localized function of a larger function, that function being in existence purely to support a greater need. As an individualized function, the reason for existence is a specialized one. If specialization was not required then that function would not be called into existence. Specialization is required when minute detail needs to be experienced by the higher function in order for it to progress beyond its current state of understanding or create an increase in functionality.

Sometimes the benefits of maintaining a specialized function provides additional opportunities for progression that are of significant benefit to the higher function, which is where you all come into the equation. The perpetuated function of the Source Entity project is bearing significant progressive opportunity for me as the higher function. And in some instances the perpetuated functions of smaller Source Entity function also bears significant progressive opportunity, hence their continued existence.

ME: Our existence then is conditional to our continued contribution to the increase in progressive functionality of our higher function, the Source Entities and you, the higher function of the Sources.

O: Correct. And right now—and I have said this before—I see no reason to change things, because from my perspective everything is going well.

ME: While you have been explaining this to me I have been receiving a distinct feeling that we as incarnate and disincarnate entities are similar to the cells in a biological organism. That we have individual function as the cell and grouped function as a smaller function within a larger function such as a liver cell within a liver, or a muscle cell within a muscle.

O: I would like to revise that example and suggest that as a smaller function of a larger function you are more aligned to being the smallest aspect of the atomic structure of the cell rather than being the cell itself. That privilege would reside with a Source Entity.

ME: It is a very strange feeling that we are nothing but functions within functions and that these functions are part of the localized functionality of a totality.

O: Don't think of it in those lowly terms but more of being a necessary specialized function within a necessary specialized function of a localized area of totality. As a specialized function your existence is necessary to the continued progression of the totality.

Try to think of it in these terms. The removal of a single resistor in an electric circuit can result in the failure of the functionality of that circuit. The loss of a single cog in a clock can stop it working as well. The removal of any necessary function within a higher function renders it inefficient. And right now, which includes all the Event Spaces I have experienced, you are all necessary functions within the functionality of my continued progressive expansion of sentient self-awareness.

Chapter 13

The Origin's View on
Humanity's Fear of Death

TO KNOW THAT OUR CONTINUED existence as an ultimately micro miniature function of The Origin, and that its continuation was wanted by The Origin, was comforting to say the least. Knowing that the desire for individuality, and its perpetuation, was largely a human thought process and not energetic, doesn't seem to remove the doubt in our minds of our continued individualized and collective energetic existence. Nor does it remove the fear of the demise of the human form and the release of that energetic aspect of us that is projected into the physical—even when we are given unmistakeable evidence of its continuation. I decided to discuss this subject with The Origin to get its perspective on an ancient incarnate fear.

The Origin jumped in quickly.

O: You're already dead.

ME: Sorry, that's an answer I didn't expect.

O: Why not? It's true.

ME: Can you elaborate for me.

O: Your very existence ends from the perspective of what you really are, the moment you enter into the incarnate state. As you are fully aware, three things happen when incarnate. Firstly, the entity wanting to experience incarnate existence accepts that part of itself that is projected into the physical form is a drag on its higher-frequency existence. It acts like an anchor holding the larger entity back until the incarnate cycle is completed. Some entities need to have a series of bridging projections down the frequencies to allow the incarnate experience to take place.

ME: Why is that necessary?

O: It is necessary because the natural frequential location of that entity is significantly higher than those that normally incarnate and as a result they need to bridge the frequency gap. They need to project an aspect of themselves down to a known frequency that can sustain high-frequency function, their normal functionality, before they can create a subprojection down to the next frequency of sustainable functionality, albeit at an acceptably reduced level.

Depending upon the original frequential location, further downward projections may be necessary in order to achieve the incarnate condition. As these projections move further down the frequencies, the anchoring effect becomes more pronounced, as you can appreciate. Your late wife, Anne, was one such entity. She had to be to work with you. Most entities, however, don't need such methods because they are not evolved enough and therefore high enough up the frequencies to resort to such drastic measures to experience incarnate existence.

Next, the entity, all entities at this point, accepts that accessing these lower frequencies results in an almost negligible creative and communicative functionality, that in essence the projected part of it is next to inert. This inertness is a direct function of the debilitating loss of bandwidth as one traverses down the frequencies.

Finally, the entity chooses to remove all or part of the existing memory function that is carried with it down the frequencies. This decision is the result of both the contamination of the energy of that entity if sharing a physical form *(see The History of God. GSN)*, and the desire for total immersion into the low-frequency functionality that incarnate existence permits.

ME: You mentioned that the entity may choose to retain some memory function. Why would that be a decision, and why do we not choose to retain memory all the time?

O: I will answer the last question first. The level of desired immersion into low-frequency existence is why you choose to not retain memory. Inversely an entity chooses to retain memory function of varying degrees when a specific role has been chosen. That being, one that requires access to higher functionality if the role provides significant opportunity for personal, collective, or personal and collective evolutionary progression. You are one such entity that has chosen to retain some higher functionality, and as with most incarnates you needed to be reactivated to the desired level when you approached the right juncture of your incarnate existence. Note though that only that which is required to do the role is allowed and that there is still a requirement for working without access to other Event Spaces, what you might call working in the dark.

ME: Our fear then is based upon our lack of personal experiential knowledge of what we really are?

O: To some extent, yes, but there is another function that causes this rather irrational response.

ME: The creation of the ego, the individualized consciousness resulting from projection into the low frequencies of the physical and the subsequent lack of creative and communicative bandwidth.

O: Correct. This is the biggest problem that incarnates experience in the frequencies associated with that aspect of the multiverse created by Source Entity One. The so-called ego is created by the residual level of self-awareness retained by the projected energies of the True Energetic Self. The lack of, or low level of, retained memory when associated with the incarnate vehicle results in disassociation with this true self and the generation of localized consciousness as a result of this residual level of self-awareness. In short, a transient local personality is created over time that associates itself with the physical form only.

ME: But doesn't that create the problem with incarnate existence, that the physicality is considered to be the "All," the "Beingness," and that it is transient, that it does die with the demise of the physical form?

O: This is where the big mistake is made. Even though the association with the physical form creates a localized personality, with localized experience and memory function, that experience and memory function is not lost. It can never be lost simply because it is in truth an energy projection from the True Energetic Self. The True Energetic Self being an individualization of energy from a Source Entity perpetuates its longevity, as does the subsequent individualization of energy from myself into a Source Entity or Om.

ME: So why do we fear the demise of the human form?

O: Because of the lack of understanding due to the reduction in memory and functionality and the lack of desire of the newly released energies to associate themselves with the low frequencies so soon after the demise of the physical. Why would an entity that has submitted itself to such profound constraints rush back to tell a world full of incarnates that which they will ultimately return to, and return to very quickly as it happens?

ME: To put those still incarnate at rest.

O: OK, but what if living with and overcoming this fear is part of the game, that it's part of the overall experience?

ME: Then the knowing would negate the experience.

O: Yes, it would. I will return to the subject of localized memory now. When the physical form demises, the projected energy that associated itself with the form detaches itself and returns to the True Energetic Self. During the detachment process the projected energy moves back up the frequencies, gaining access to a wider bandwidth of creative and communicative energies. During this process the association with the True Energetic Self is gradually attained until re-association is complete. Within this time the individualized self integrates in a sympathetic way to the true self by the gradual recognition of past experience, evolution and memory. This is called remembrance and allows the individualized self to grow into that which it is, an extension of the True Energetic Self, providing an extension to the previously existing experiences, evolutionary content, and subsequent memory set. Even though during this process the transient individualized self is seen to be absorbed in to the True Energetic Self, the fact that the experiences are part of a set of recently acquired experiences places them at the forefront of the True Energetic Self's

memory set, therefore maintaining this aspect of the individualization as a function of the whole.

ME: What happens when multiple projections return to the
True Energetic Self simultaneously?

O: Nothing different because even when the individualized
"selves" integrate back into the True Energetic Self simultaneously, the sets of experiences are integrated in the
same way. So an individualized projection would experience reintegration just as if it were the only one, with
it being exposed to the preexisting experience set and
the new experience sets as if they were all preexisting.

In essence, when an energetic projection regains realization of the True Energetic Self while incarnate, it
knows this process as a result. Knowing this process
based upon the reintegration of experiences and
memory function makes the projected energy know both
the roles required while incarnate and the ways in which
the correct implementation affect the True Energetic
Self. This allows the interface with the physical to be
more productive because the projected energy of the localized personality, although still localized, is aware of
its condition and how its contribution is retained.

Based upon this, worry and fear of the demise of the
physical form is an irrational response based upon lack
of true self-realization.

ME: So how does incarnate mankind overcome this fear if it
is such an irrational response?

O: By working at it. By doing what you're doing. Sitting
down and meditating, shutting out the material world
and communing with the energetic world, avoiding
karma creating responses (attraction to low-frequency
addictions) and associations, raising their base frequencies in the process. Raising one's base frequencies allows one to access higher knowledge and "know" the
truth about existence. It removes the fear of the demise
of the physical vehicle, because with higher knowledge
comes recognition of the true self, that it is energetic
and that it uses the physical vehicle to experience low-
frequency existence in an immersive, holistic way.

It is only when the overall base frequencies are higher, much higher than now, that incarnate mankind in general will be of a frequency where it will be in communication with the greater reality and be in a position of "knowing" who and what they truly are. This will mean that, even though incarnate, mankind will be capable of accessing the True Energetic Self and exist in two worlds simultaneously, the energetic and the physical. Attaining this level of incarnate existence will bring a profound change to the way incarnates work with each other, for they will realize the cause and effect of certain actions and reactions, assuring the optimal response is given when needed. When incarnate mankind has reached this level, the physical vehicle will be much lighter, much higher frequentially, and will not need solid foods, for it will absorb the free energy that pervades the multiverse as it was initially designed to do. Its longevity will be significantly extended and even perpetuated for as long as the True Energetic Self wishes to be incarnate. Or, it will be happily demised, at will, when the work it was required to do has been completed, releasing the True Energetic Self early, or as necessary, so as not to perpetuate the incarnation if it is no longer necessary to remain incarnate.

At this point in mankind's existence ALL FEAR OF DEATH WILL BE NONEXISTENT. In fact it will be welcomed because the truth about existence will be known and worked with, in joy, in love, and a song in the heart.

ME: That's beautiful.

O: That's incarnate mankind's destiny.

Chapter 14

How Can Event Space Become

Aware of Itself to Spark the

Awakening of The Origin

THROUGHOUT THE TIME I HAVE been channelling the information contained within this book I have been wondering about the role Event Space has played in the process of The Origin's awakening and journey through to sentient self-awareness. Earlier on in the dialogue with The Origin I noted that Event Space recreates itself as a function of detecting the possibility of possible possibilities—the effect of the potential for a dualistic, or multiple dualistic conditions being the catalyst for the generation of a new Event Space.

When The Origin transported my consciousness to the Event Space that maintained the information, the holographic imagery of, the actual energetic events leading up to, and during the process of, The Origin's awakening and subsequent development of sentience through self-awareness, I noted rather too easily that Event Space was in existence before the energies that were the basis of The Origin started the process of grouping together in synergetic communion.

The words "Event Space existed before The Origin's self-awareness and subsequent sentience" rattled through my brain myriad times before I noted the significance of what I had missed. Event Space preexisted The Origin, and what's more it had a level of intelligence—it sought out possible dualistic events. This interesting condition was one that needed serious investigation with The Origin because I was starting to realize that, without the function of Event Space, The Origin may not have come into existence. Moreover, this also meant that the Source Entities would not have been created, and therefore, energetic and incarnate mankind would not *have been created by Source Entity One. I was just about to reconnect with The Origin when it initiated contact with me instead. Contact with The Origin was becoming seamless these days, I noted, as it took over the part of me that it needed to use to allow me to channel before I had a chance to say hello!*

O: I was wondering when you were going to broach the subject of Event Space again. Your questions relating to its level of intelligence are well founded, for it did play a rather important role in my becoming self-aware, and of course sentient.

ME: I am only thinking in this way because for Event Space to discern when a dualistic event could possibly be invoked and therefore acted upon it, it must have a level of awareness, or intelligence in its own right, mustn't it?

O: Not necessarily. You see, seeking the dualistic condition is nominally an automatic function of the energies that make up Event Space. They are naturally sensitive to the actual derivation of, the possibility of, and the possible possibility of, an alternative to that which is currently being played out. Its ability to detect these possibilities is both acute in detail and immensely accurate. One could suggest that Event Space has a level of awareness due to its continued ability to address the need for dualistic conditions and make them manifest in an environment that supports them. The environment created by the Event Space always holds the optimal environmental conditions for the perpetuation of that dualistic condition being supported, allowing it to play out its function to its true end. The true end being, whether it is a "dead end" condition that needed to be played out for the benefit of completeness or is a condition that either ends up supporting the mainstream Event Space or becomes the mainstream Event Space itself.

ME: You're telling me that Event Space isn't intelligent then?

O: I didn't say that. I just stated that the function of Event Space that seeks out the possibility of dualistic conditions is nominally an automatic function. It doesn't mean that Event Space itself is not intelligent in some way.

ME: Now you're playing with me!

O: No, I am not. There are many aspects of the human vehicle that are automatic, or even manually operated while still housing an intelligent energy. Just consider the heart. It is basically a pump, and pumping blood around the gross physical aspect of the human form is all it needs to do. This is an automatic function. However, another automatic function is how it receives information about the oxygen requirements of the body, such as when the muscles are being used in exercise, which result in its changing the cadence of its function as a pump. Alternatively the limbs have a manual function and are controlled by the energies associated with the brain and the muscles, which are subsequently controlled by the energetic entity that is projected within the human form. The limbs don't move unless asked to move and are therefore a manual function. The heart functions, or can function, on its own and is an automatic function. The ability to reason and choose to experience certain things and rule out others is an aspect of intelligence.

If I were to compare the functions of Event Space with the example above I would say that the seeking out of dualistic conditions was an automatic function, similar to the heart. The division or creation of the alternative Event Space is a manual function, similar to the movement of the limbs—with the decision to create the alternative Event Space being a function of the intelligence behind the total energetic functionality of Event Space, which is similar to the energetic entity that is projected into the human form.

The only issue with this example is that the energetic entity is sentient and self-aware energy and not merely intelligent.

ME: Event Space is merely intelligent then?

O: No, it is self-aware.

ME: Stop right there. You will be telling me next that it is sentient as well.

O: No, it's not. It is intelligent self-aware energy.

ME: Let me get this right. If Event Space evolved enough to achieve intelligence and self-awareness, why did it not achieve sentience? In fact, why did it not become The Origin?

O: It reached a point of evolutionary equilibrium.

ME: What is evolutionary equilibrium?

O: It is the point in an energy or entity's existence when they no longer evolve beyond the evolutionary level that they have achieved.

ME: Why does it stop evolving?

O: The evolutionary cycle stops because the energy or energies that make up an entity or an energetic function that an energy or group of energies perform have reached their maximum potential.

ME: And this is what happened with Event Space, it reached its maximum potential?

O: Correct.

ME: So evolutionary equilibrium is actually a point of evolutionary stasis?

O: Not quite, evolutionary stasis is a function of evolution that occurs when an energy, group of energies, or entity have stopped evolving but clearly have the capability to progress further in the evolutionary cycle. That being, they have not reached their full evolutionary potential. Evolutionary stasis is ultimately a temporary condition which is created by the energy, group of energies, or entity as a means of reconciliation, of achieving stability before continuing with the evolutionary progress. Basically put, it is like a child growing into the clothes that have been made for it but are too big, biding time before having to make new clothes as the child out-grows them.

Evolutionary stasis is also a function of an Event Space being pursued and the dualistic condition that created the Event Space proving to be a dead end. In this instance, before the Event Space converges back into the mainstream Event Space, it achieves evolutionary stasis, evolutionary stasis being the trigger for the need to converge.

As stated above, evolutionary equilibrium is the point where the energy, group of energies or entity has developed to the point of its maximum potential. In this condition the abilities or functions of the energies can go no further from an evolutionary perspective. Every opportunity for progression has been taken and the evolutionary content has been accrued. That is, they can go no further on their own, for if the energy, group of energies, or entity co-joins with another energy, group of energies, or entity in a totally synergetic way to create a new energy, group of energies, or entity they have the possibility of further evolution because the dynamics of their energies are changed to reflect the new condition. This new condition being more complex, it has the possibility to grow and evolve further until it again reaches an evolutionary equilibrium that is relative to its new structure.

ME: And Event Space reached this point, and this is the reason for its current condition and why you are The Origin and not Event Space?

O: Correct again. The thing to note here is that Event Space, although part of me, has its own independence as a result of its intelligence and self-awareness. Although the level of intelligence and self-awareness is low grade in comparison to you or any incarnate for instance, it does know what it wants and how to achieve what it wants.

ME: Would Event Space become sentient at any point in its/your existence?

O: No, it is not capable of sentience because its energies are too specialized.

ME: Even if it co-joined with other energies?

O: No, because that would dilute its functionality, resulting in the dissolution of a powerful tool such as Event Space into just another energy set. In fact, it made the decision to remain what it is, and not co-join with another energy or energies, early on in its existence.

ME: How did it do that?

O: It recognized its worth in its current and only configuration. In fact, the reason why it decided to stay as it was and achieve evolutionary equilibrium was because it recognized the creation of something bigger and more meaningful than that which it could ever achieve. It saw the events that would result in a pan-energetic intelligence, one that would grow and progress beyond the current area of influence Event Space enjoyed at that juncture in its own existence and eventually become "Polyomniscient"—me.

ME: It saw your evolutionary progression?

O: Yes, and what's more, it saw the possibility for its functionality, not its evolution, to progress beyond creation of Event Spaces as a result of dualistic or multiple aspects of dualistic possibilities, to those of trilistic and quadrulistic possibilities. It recognized that its functions would be augmented even though its evolution would not be. In its limited intellectual state it saw the beauty in this and actively worked on deleting certain events to ensure those that needed to succeed did succeed and those that could interfere with the succession were removed.

ME: Wait a moment. Are you suggesting that Event Space created you?

O: No, Event Space could never create anything other than Event Space. What it saw was the events that led to my energies grouping together in coadunate sentient self-awareness and simply made sure that these events not only happened, but were achieved faster. In essence it created a "fast track" for my progression into sentience and omniscience leading to polyomniscience.

ME: If Event Space deliberately steered the events leading up to your awakening and beyond, it must be able to achieve a certain level of steerage now. In fact, it may be manipulating events to achieve certain preconceived ideal conditions as we speak.

O: It could, but it isn't.

ME: Why not?

O: Because once it manipulated the events required to ensure those conditions that were to create me were in place, and it was satisfied that they are robustly aligned, it continued with what it is, being Event Space.

Additionally, Event Space recognized that I would very quickly supersede its own functions and abilities in terms of manipulating events and their spaces so it no longer needed to be actively manipulating the existence of the events itself. Although this seems common sense, there was another reason why it stopped manipulation.

ME: And what was this reason? I have a feeling it could have altered its own existence if it was not careful.

O: Well intuited. When it was manipulating the events, favoring those that resulted in me and removing or deleting those that could have affected my evolutionary development, it started to create linearity. In creating linearity it was creating an alternative to Event Space, one where Event Space did not exist, for when there is linearity there is no place for Event Space to exist within. In ensuring I became sentient and self-aware it nearly erased itself!

ME: How close did it get to this, and I hate to say this, possibility?

O: Very close. In fact when it got to the point where it was assured that I would develop in an optimal way it was only two, maybe three, changes away from deleting the function of itself. I am glad it stopped when it did because I find Event Space a very useful tool to have.

ME: I had no idea that Event Space could actively delete or remove aspects of Event Space, let alone know that it is aware and intelligent enough to be able to do such things.

O: There are many things that Event Space can do but chooses not to do, especially now.

ME: Why now?

O: Because it is fully occupied with all of the possible possibilities and the possibility of possible possibilities that surround the dualistic, trilistic, and quadrulistic condi-

tions of what the Source Entities and all of their creations are doing. When it was working on the events that
led to my eventual creation it only had one area of interest, those energies that would eventually co-join to create intelligent, sentient self-awareness in totality—me. It
was easier for it then. Now it is fully occupied and is
anticipating my expansion and its subsequent expansion.

ME: I thought that Event Space already existed in the next
area of your expanded self-awareness.

O: It does but it is largely dormant. It is in a similar state to
that which it was in before it, itself, became aware of its
own existence. Source Entity Twelve has started some
Event Space activity, as did my initial investigations, my
probing into that area of awareness that I/we will move
into eventually, but it isn't enough to awaken this tract
of Event Space fully because the activity is too small—
even with the possibility of possible possibilities coming into play. It will activate and when it does it will become one with the existing tract of Event Space that we
have all experienced.

ME: One of the questions people are going to ask is how can
the creator of our creator be created by a lesser entity?
The critics are going to have a field day!

O: Firstly, I will say again that Event Space did not create
me. Secondly, Event Space is an aspect of that which is
me in totality, so it had a major role to play, as did those
co-joining energies linking together to create islands of
locally intelligent self-aware energies. For without these
smaller energies co-joining to create islands of locally
intelligent self-aware energies, Event Space would not
have had a role to play. Everything was happening together, concurrently.

ME: But it did orchestrate or assist in your successful evolution to sentient self-awareness.

O: It did, but consider this. How could the energies that
formed the basic building blocks, the islands of locally
intelligent self-aware energies, of that which I am, become that which I am? No one made them do it. They did

it all by themselves through attraction and triangulation. Are they not lesser aspects of me? And do not lesser aspects of me help to make up the whole?

ME: Yes, they do. Everything appears to be made up of smaller things.

O: Yes, they are. Now if you now think of Event Space as a lesser aspect of me, a part of me that was active during the phase of my evolution where the islands of locally intelligent self-aware energies were being formed, then you will see that everything was part of the orchestration and not just Event Space. It just had a role to play at a specific juncture in my becoming that which I am, as did everything else.

ME: I wonder what else had a major role to play in your development.

O: Many, many more things, but this is not the right time to discuss them. You would need to write a whole new book to even think about scratching the surface.

ME: One final question on this subject. How did Event Space become intelligent and self-aware to the level it did?

O: The same way I did, but its development resulted in a specialized function. The only other difference is that it achieved it without the assistance of Event Space, for the product of its creation was Event Space.

I very much felt that I hadn't got right to the bottom of this discussion yet, not that I ever would in reality. There was something niggling me. It was to do with Event Space and its identification of a higher order, The Origin, and its active decision to remove those Event Spaces that could inhibit the opportunity for The Origin to become The Origin. It all seemed a bit too convenient. I needed another piece of the jigsaw to allow me to gain an understanding that I would find acceptable. I decided to change my approach and ask a question in a different way.

ME: Was the development of Event Space a necessary function of your own evolutionary development? For example, if Event Space did not exist, would you have become The Origin I am communicating with now?

O: I was wondering when this question was going to come out. The answer is yes and no. Event Space became what it was as part of the natural order of the early development of those energies that were destined to become what I am now. It came into existence as part of a logical progression of orderly changes that resulted in the opportunity for my sentience and polyomniscience to come into being. Part of that progression was the function of Event Space that not only identified the opportunity for my becoming the dominant intelligence, if you like, within these energies, but it also gave it the means to create a fast track for me to become that which I could become in the fastest way possible, by the removal of undesirable Event Spaces. To do this it needed to have a vital component within its make-up that would allow it to make the correct decisions based upon known and expected outcomes. Mere intelligence or self-awareness would not allow this functionality to operate properly— it needed something else.

ME: No, don't tell me. It needed to be sentient!

O: Correct.

ME: So I come to the question again. Why didn't Event Space become you? Why didn't it become The Origin?

O: Because it became that which it was supposed to be—a specialized function within a much larger polyomniscient, sentient self-aware intelligence, and not the polyomniscient, sentient self-aware intelligence itself. Think of it as a springboard. Better still, think of it in terms of one of the stages in a space rocket. The stages of a space rocket have a role to play, to help that part of the rocket that is designed to go into space, get into space. Once the stage in question has done its job and the rocket is in danger of having its progress inhibited by the spent stage's presence, the spent stage is removed, allowing the rocket to climb higher on the next stage that is activated. That stage was created for a reason, to get the rocket up to a certain altitude, and once that is achieved it is removed because it doesn't fit into the rest of the plan.

From my evolutionary perspective, Event Space was, and is, a stage in a space rocket, in terms of this example. To achieve what was necessary to get to where I am now, certain aspects of my totality needed to become dominant for short periods of time to allow the essential evolutionary development to take place that resulted in the optimal evolutionary solution. The one creates the other. In this instance, that meant that Event Space needed to become the dominant sentience while it performed its duty of fast tracking the events leading up to, and perpetuating the possibility for, sentient polyomniscience to develop robustly.

ME: Event Space became transiently sentient and then lost it when its sentience was no longer required then?

O: That's right.

ME: Why didn't you explain this before?

O: Because it would have been confusing. Think of it in another way. In the main, great spiritual leaders are the products of great spiritual leaders (note that there are the odd spiritual leaders that spring up from nowhere). The one ensures the lineage of that which they teach by creating a protégé, one who can take the teachings further, further developing the teachings to support the environment it is destined to be within next and expanding its applicability in the process. It is the first spiritual leader's delight to be the springboard for his protégé, and in due course his protégé will be the springboard for his protégé. The saying "We stand on the shoulders of giants" is a very relevant one here, for it describes the true way of development by the service of others.

Another way of looking at it is by using the Darwinian evolutionary principal where the fittest survives and the weakest demise—the fittest in this instance meaning the one that is "fit" for purpose, fit for purpose being relative to the demands of the environment at a particular juncture in its existence. As the environment changes, those that were fit for purpose become weak and those that were created by those that were fit for purpose survive and become dominant.

ME: So Event Space becoming sentient was a transient but necessary condition that was required to achieve your optimal development leading toward sentient polyomniscient self-awareness. Once its job in sentience was secured it returned to its specialist role, of being Event Space "only."

O: Yes and no.

ME: What!

O: You see, what I have explained is the way it happened in reality. There is/was a scenario where Event Space did not succeed in becoming that which it was destined to become, leaving my developmental path to progress in an un-accelerated fashion—together, that is, with all of the possible influences of those energies that developed in isolation, and adversely to that which was destined to become me in totality.

ME: So what you're saying is that if Event Space did not come into existence you would not be at the stage of self-development, the evolutionary level, that you are now at.

O: That just about sums it up.

ME: But, in this scenario would you eventually reach the evolutionary level that you are now at?

O: No, it would have been a different evolutionary path, and therefore I would have evolved in a different direction.

ME: You have seen this Event Space then? No, hang on, how could you? If Event Space didn't develop into Event Space and you didn't develop into you, then that Event Space cannot exist.

O: Except it does.

ME: How?

O: It exists as an alternative Event Space simply because Event Space developed in the way it did. You see, in doing what it did to ensure my existence was secure, it not only almost removed itself, but it also secured its own existence in the process.

ME: It secured its own existence because it knew that in assisting in your development process it would perpetuate itself.

O: Correct.

ME: Event Space saw what would happen if you didn't become what you're destined to become.

O: That's right. It saw the Event Space where Event Space didn't exist either. This resulted in a blank response, before you ask how Event Space could see an Event Space that doesn't exist. Or, it existed on its own where the opportunities for duality, the possibility of possible possibilities, become a rare function as a result of devolution—devolution being negative evolution which results in limited progression or stasis. In this instance it was out of a job, so to speak, for Event Space itself thrives on the creation of Event Space.

ME: And in its "current" sentient state it both recognized the need for your development and that your development would not only result in its perpetuation but that it would result in its own proliferation, even though it would lose its sentience.

O: Yes, and the loss of sentience was accepted because its own sentience could only ever be a transient condition, and the recognition that it was part of a bigger development process, mine.

ME: Now I feel like I have the answers I wanted. That Event Space had transient sentience and that it was an overall function of The Origin's development makes sense to me now. I have a final question on this subject.

O: Fire away.

ME: How many other energies within you achieved transient sentience?

O: You really don't want to go there.

ME: Why?

O: Because there were thousands.

ME: Thousands?

O: Thousands.

ME: You really did have a complicated development process.

O: You've got no idea. I think it's time you had a change in direction.

ME: I think you are right.

Chapter 15

The Point of All Creativity

I WAS GLAD THAT I HAD CLEARED up my understanding of
the role Event Space played in the development of The Origin.
It initially seemed very strange and somewhat "back to front"
that a component or function of a larger entity could, to a
certain extent, orchestrate the development of the very entity
that it was a component part of. And not only that, it would
provide a springboard function in the development process
itself.

It was during my limited down time that I started to think
about the six points of The Origin—those navigational points
that Source Entity Twelve used to take me on a guided tour of
The Origin's area of sentient self-awareness. The point that
sprang to mind was point five, the point of all creativity. I was
drawn to this point because The Origin and I had been talking
about its own evolution and the events that led to its sentience. Creativity is a function of sentience, I had been told,
so point five being the point of all creativity looked to me like
a very likely candidate for the start of The Origin's sentience,
its sentient origin. Armed with just a simple question to start
this change in direction I contacted The Origin to see if my
assumption was correct, or whether it was to fall fallow.

ME: I am intrigued by the navigation point five as described
by Source Entity Twelve, that it is the point of all creativity. I remember that it stated that you started all of
your own creativity here, which also included the creation of the Twelve Origins and the myriad tendrils you
sent out in an attempt to investigate your area of self-
awareness in an accelerated way.

O: And you also remember then that Source Entity Twelve
stated that you and I would talk further on this subject.

ME: Yes, I do, and I would guess that you are forewarned and forearmed with answers to my questions.

O: You only have one at the moment.

ME: Mmm, you can see right through me.

O: No, I can see right through me. Remember as an Om you are an aspect of me in reality.

ME: OK, if this is your point of all creativity, is this also the point where you became sentient first?

O: Firstly, this is the point where I performed all of my original creative moments. Here every part of that which I created was considered, designed, and deliberated upon before being put into "being." I have several points of creativity now that I am active in the wider area of my sentient self-awareness, but this one is the epicenter, the loci of all that which has been, and will be, created. If you like you can call this a central repository of creativity.

ME: I like the point of all creativity.

O: Then we will stay with that name.

ME: If as the point of all creativity, it is the central repository for your other areas of creativity, why move away from this point in the first place?

O: I move to where my creativity will not affect that which is already in creation. Everything is an experiment and I, like most of the scientists in the physical universe, do not like the possibility of contamination or cross-fertilization occurring between sites of creation, because it spoils the purity of what I am working on. On the other hand, if I want to experiment in creativity that is the result of, or results in, hybrid creativity then that is fine. We can talk about this later because I feel you need to have your question answered first before we digress too far.

You asked if this is also the point where you became sentient first.

ME: Yes, I did.

O: Well, the answer to this is not quite, but it is close enough.

ME: How do you mean?

O: My sentience "turned on" in a rather random way. It flickered around the energies that were self-aware before stabilizing in an area that had achieved a critical mass of Self-Aware energies that were capable of sustaining the sentient aspect, the signature if you like, that an energy must maintain to remain in sentience.

ME: I just received an image of a neon light flickering at random along the length of its vacuum tube before it gets to the temperature required to allow the gas to fluoresce as a whole.

O: That's a pretty good example, but think of the flickering happening over all of what was my area of self-awareness and finally settling in the area we are referring to as my point of all creativity.

ME: I am guessing then that the areas where the sentience was flickering into and around had momentary episodes of enlightened thinking, which were quickly forgotten.

O: Very well done. It could be best described in human terms of being asleep, then becoming awake, then going to sleep again, with this cycling around and around until full wakefulness is achieved.

ME: But didn't you find this disturbing? One moment you are a sentient entity in one area of your self-awareness, the next moment that sentience is gone with it appearing in another area. Wasn't there some sort of residual memory here?

O: There was no retention of sentient memory because none of the areas that became spontaneously and transiently sentient were in that state for long enough to create the function of memory in this instance.

ME: Sorry, but I find it a little difficult to understand that you, The Origin, had what I would call a linear process leading to sentience. I would have expected it to be holographic in some way. That it would have been ... spherical. Yes, spherical, that's the image I see in my mind's eye.

O: Sentience is something that has a certain level of linearity even if it is what you would like to see as holographic or spherical. What you are seeing is my area of self-awareness as it was then. Although you see it as spherical, what you see being what your ability to interpret allows you to see, it was amorphous in size and shape. To describe what you are seeing in your own interpretation, and in a way that you will understand, I would say that the function of eventual sentience was achieved by its linear progression within the sphericality of holographic self-awareness. The progression of sentience in a linear fashion within this area would appear, from your perspective, to mirror the structure of its area, hence your confusion over what I am telling you and what you are experiencing through tapping into the Event Space that holds this information. Memory, as a function of sentience, and not intelligence or self-awareness, is only possible when a sentient condition is stable enough (has enough critical mass) to allow the remembrance of that sentient condition to be achieved.

When you gave the description of the neon light flickering along its tube I thought you understood the process, because the gas fluoresces relative to each pocket of gas that locally achieves a potential and temperature of a value that correlates with that required to excite the local density and quality of the gas. The flickering stops and starts at random and with increasing frequency as the other areas of gas also achieve the correct temperature and potential. Eventually the whole gas fluoresces when it is at the correct temperature and potential in all of its area in totality.

The climb up to correct temperature and potential is a gradual and linear progression, relatively speaking, but the location of the spontaneously and transiently achieved fluorescence is randomly achieved and unachieved. Un-achievement or loss of fluorescence is a product of momentary quantum losses experienced after the potential and temperature drop below the required levels for excitation due to use by those other areas of gas that randomly achieve excitation and fluorescence, drawing on the energy required to create it in the process. As the potential and temperature rises, the pockets of fluorescence become larger and larger, linking together until the whole area of gas is fluorescing. The memory function is gained and lost in the same process with no time for concern over loss of function to be either experienced or recorded.

This rather crude description describes, in some small way, how my sentience came into being in a linear fashion.

ME: Thank you, I get it now. When you eventually became fully sentient, was that an instantaneous "knowing?"

O: Yes, it was. It was an entirely different experience to being merely intelligent and self-aware. It was like, from your perspective, that someone had just turned the lights on and I could see what was all around me and what my potential was. It was at this point in my existence where I decided to investigate my area of self-awareness and find ways to accelerate this investigation.

ME: And this resulted in your first creations?

O: Yes, this was the first use of the point of all creativity.

ME: Hold on. Were you not created by the function of evolution, and if this is the case was the first use of creativity your creation?

O: I wasn't created; I became what I am through the functions of energetic evolution. True creativity is the result of sentience.

ME: But didn't Event Space achieve a momentary level of sentience long enough to choose which Event Space should be terminated and which should stay, thereby assuring your eventual sentience?

O: Yes, but that resulted in selectivity and not creativity. The two are mutually exclusive and thoroughly independent of each other.

ME: OK. Earlier you stated that the point of all creativity is, strictly speaking, no longer the point of all creativity because you create in other locations within your current area of sentient self-awareness.

O: I did, but know this. All creativity, in essence, started here. And that included the need to have alternative locations for my creativity to progress into. You see, all of my other areas of, shall I say, "local" areas of creativity, were created in the point of all creativity. To do what I have to do I need to recreate the conditions of initial creativity that are only found in this location, the point of all creativity.

ME: Isn't that a limitation?

O: No, creativity is a unique attribute of sentience, and in this instance my creative attribute came into being in the same location of the birth of my sentience. Every Source Entity has an aspect of creativity that was generated from this original point of all creativity, and, as a result, so do you. Your own creative function, that is, all entities created by a Source Entity and those created out of the creation of the Sources, the Om, is born from being created with the intention of having the ability to be creative. This creative energy is ultimately linked back to the point of all creativity.

ME: Let me try to summarize what you have just said. All that is created, whether it is new areas of creativity within your area of sentient self-awareness, that which you created as creative satellites for your own creative functions, and all that is created by the twelve Source Entities, including that which is created by their creations, their entities, is all linked back to the point of all creativity.

O: Correct. It is the point of all creativity. Everything that has been or will be created will be linked back to the point of all creativity. It is a central depository, if you like, for everything that has a creative signature on it.

ME: In your polyomniscience I would have thought that you wouldn't need a central location for creativity. I would have thought that creativity, or the ability to be creative or create, would be everywhere and not specific to a location within you.

O: I don't. I just choose it to be that way. I like to be tidy with where and what I, my creations, and my creations' creations, create.

ME: So this is a self-inflicted limitation.

O: It's not a limitation. It is having my creativity in totality, organized in an orderly fashion.

ME: If you are polyomniscient and can create or access creativity anywhere within your area of sentient self-awareness, irrespective of what aspect of you or your creations is created, why the need for order?

O: Simply because I want everything that is created to be compartmentalized, to be separated out from those energies that are creativity in the waiting.

ME: I am sorry, you have lost me now. What is creativity "in the waiting?" And why does it need to be separated out from creativity that results in the created, i.e., that which is linked to the point of all creativity?

O: Creativity in the waiting is creativity that is either planned or, more importantly could spontaneously occur as a result of other creativity. Consider it as a byproduct.

ME: Can you elaborate a little, please?

O: Certainly. Planned creativity contains energies that are assigned to the creative process specifically for the creation of that which is planned. They have a signature associated with that which is planned to be created irrespective of when this creativity will be actioned, so to speak. Planned creativity is creativity that has a desired outcome and is waiting for the "start" button to be pushed. As a creative function it is incomplete and as such is not yet linked within the point of all creativity as a finished product of creativity.

The other aspect of creativity "in the waiting," is that creativity which occurs as a byproduct of that which is created. In a simple sense this would relate to that which is created, by the created, by accident. It is unintended creativity and as such is neither planned nor expected.

ME: Based upon that I would expect that you would have three categories. The first one would be that which is already created and is fully linked into the point of all creativity. The second would be that which is planned to be created, has not yet been actioned but is on the radar to be linked to the point of all creativity. The third would therefore be creativity that is a byproduct of creative acts, is therefore off the radar but is expected as a possibility, a possible possibility or the possible possibility of possible possibilities as a function of certain Event Spaces being invoked.

O: Good, you are getting there. Now I will explain why I like them to be compartmentalized or separated out. Being The Origin I have the ability to either accept that which is being created as useful to my evolutionary development and my ultimate progression, or I can choose to terminate that creativity which is, or I classify it as being, nonessential.

ME: Are you saying that not all creativity is productive—productive, that is, from an evolutionary perspective?

O: Correct. Although one might argue that all that is created has an evolutionary function attached to it, no matter how small that may be. And I also include experience and learning that can be gained here. Some of that which is created is either a duplication of a previous creation or is ineffective from an evolutionary perspective. When creativity of this kind is identified, hence the categorization, I can, and do, make a decision as to whether or not to retain that which is created.

ME: You're suggesting that you are selective in what you retain in your point of all creativity?

O: In the point of all creativity, yes.

ME: And that which doesn't make the grade, so to speak, is recycled I guess.

O: No. Although I have the ability to, and the potential desire at times, to recycle some of that which is created, irrespective of where it originated, I have never actually recycled or deleted anything that has been created by any of my sentient creations up to this juncture in my existence—except, that is, for the Twelve Origins, which were my creations.

ME: Hence the categories.

O: Hence the categories. You see, part of what I am doing in the background is seeing what part of me, parts that either I have created, have created and given the power of creativity to, and that which has been created by those with creativity are efficient from an evolutionary perspective. I am looking for those entities that are the most effective at creating creations that slot into the need to be linked with the point of all creativity in the "first" category; that being creations that result in medium to high levels of evolutionary content.

When I have established my best creative performers, I shall use these for specialized roles when the opportunity comes to expand my sentience into my new area of self-awareness. They will be the ones who specifically expand my areas of polyomniscient sentience within this new area. They will perform functions and tasks specific to the level of expectation of that achievable by one of the original Twelve Source Entities. Of course every entity that returns to its source as a product of evolution will become a Source Entity in its own right at this juncture in my existence and expansion of sentient self-awareness, but these will augment my numbers of original Source Entities. They will become satellites of the point of all creativity within this new area of sentient self-awareness as a result.

Why The Origin Needs Additional Source Entities

This was a new piece of information for me. I was aware that the original Source Entities were to become important and integral parts of The Origin's plan for expansion and understanding of its, as yet unknown, new area of self-awareness, with Source Entity Twelve playing an unprecedented and unpredicted part in this. What I wasn't aware of was that the original twelve were, for all intents and purposes, not enough. This was not broadcast in previous dialogues with any of the Source Entities, nor The Origin itself. Either I had not asked the right questions in the right way to tease out this part of the plan, or it was a new and recent addition.

I was intrigued. Why would The Origin need more Source Entities? Wouldn't the original twelve be enough? Although this appeared to be a very human question, which would probably

result in a very simple response from The Origin, I had a feel-
ing that it was something that needed to be answered and
that would provide further insight into the way The Origin
worked and/or was structured. I just had a feeling!

ME: I know you have just stated that the "new" Source Entities were to be used for specialized roles, and I can understand that this would be a necessity for you to introduce. But why do you need to create more Source Entities? Why not just use those entities and the Om as the
specialists for the roles you need specialists for? Surely
you don't need to have Source Entities to do this for you,
do you?

O: At first glance you would think not, especially when you
consider the need for specialized functions only, as this
clearly doesn't need Source Entities to perform this type
of role. But what I need is for entities to be able to both
perform the specialist roles that I have chosen for them,
and for them to be creative in the same way that the
original Source Entities are currently. This means that
when they are creating environments out of their own
energies and structure and populating them with
smaller versions of themselves to investigate the minute
detail of what they have created, they are in fact investigating me. Just doing a specialist role doesn't do this,
for a specialist role is designed to focus on one subject,
or area of similar subjects, only.

ME: You're telling me that these new Source Entities will
have the same level of responsibilities for evolutionary
progression that the original Twelve Source Entities had,
including the same level of autonomy, plus an additional
responsibility based upon a specialist subject.

O: In short, yes.

ME: There is more to this though, isn't there?

O: Yes, there is.

ME: You're making me work for this information, aren't you?

O: Just building a little anticipation.

ME: OK, why are you assigning this new role to the New Source Entities and not the existing Source Entities? I would have thought that the original Source Entities would be the right choice in this instance, simply because they have had the original experience of being a Source Entity and have spent all of their existence being in that role.

O: Good point, but that is not the reason for choosing the top performing creations as the new Source Entities against the use of the original Source Entities.

ME: What was it? *(I almost felt this question was unwanted!)*

O: I have a higher functional requirement for the original Source Entities, one which is not fully apparent from the information I have broadcast to you. I will elaborate further and will start with the requirements I have planned to date.

The original Source Entities will provide the functions previously described. They will be the major junctures in my polyomniscient structure, that part of me that is known and that will create the framework for the new Source Entities to fill in the gaps. Although they will be "Me" in essence they will also retain their independence. Independence of creativity, creativity, that is, in supporting the function of connecting the newly existing polyomniscient structure with that structure created by the new Source Entities together.

ME: Why will they need to connect the structure that was created by the original Source Entities with the structure created by the new Source Entities?

O: Whenever an entity creates something it creates it in its name, in its image or signature. It contains its personality, if you like. This signature is peculiar to the creating entity. This you know. This is not a problem when the creating entity creates for itself or for the benefit of that which it previously created, or will create. The issue is when it is created by the creator of that which created it.

ME: How can that be? I would have thought that anything that was created would be compatible with you, simply because you are the ultimate creator!

O: It is compatible when it is modified to suit. You see, that which is created by the created is created as a subset of that which created the created, in essence the originating creator. Because that which is created by the created is a subset of the ultimate creator, it has a reduced level of functionality even in its highest functional state, i.e., it can only ever be as functional as the creator. Therefore it needs to be elevated to a level of functionality that is equal to the functionality of those energies that I use as my own, without the reduction in functionality that occurs when I create something that is assigned as "subordinate" to me.

ME: Hold on. This means that we are limited by our creator's assignation of status in effect.

O: Yes, but from where you are standing, that is from the perspective of an incarnate entity. Your abilities when disincarnate would be limitless, and to all intents and purposes they are. But when we are considering the energies that are destined to be used by me in my, dare I say "elevated" capacity, those that are used by my creations are created at their level and therefore need, as I just stated, to be elevated to the same status, capacity, and functionality.

ME: Thank you, I understand now. Tell me though, the original Source Entities, will they be elevated to "Origin" status as a result of being part of your main energies?

O: Energetically, yes; functionally, no. Simply put, they are still my creations, creations with a purpose given by me, so they will always be subordinate to me, even with their energies elevated to full Origin status.

ME: Would it not have been advantageous to assign them full "Origin" status? Or would this not be possible?

O: As you have ascertained from our previous dialogues, I cannot reproduce that which I am because various reactions occur to make the creation of an entity with "Origin" status, within me, as the original Origin, fail. This is based upon what I now recognize as being a conflict of interest and a conflict of functionality based upon that which should be the functionality of that which I am, and that which I create with the inference of being equal to that which I am, without actually being me, while also being subordinate.

ME: That's easy for you to say. Sorry, I just thought that what you just stated was one of the most convoluted sentences I have had the pleasure of channelling.

O: You understand then?

ME: Yes, I do, although I expect that my readers will have to read the paragraph a couple of times to let it sink in, so to speak. I do have to say though, that it does make sense. Energies and/or entities that are assigned a certain status can only achieve a maximum potential that is equal to their assigned structural and functional status. It is the responsibility of the entity to work to the best of their ability in this sense, as this ability dictates how they eventually contribute to your evolutionary progression. Once they have achieved this potential, that which is created by them may be, under your grace, elevated to "Origin" status. But this is only available as an energetic functional status and not a sentient status. In effect I suspect that you remove any inhibitors to the energies that you assigned to them as subordinate to you, reinstating their full functionality and potential in the process. The original Source Entities, although subordinate in sentience and functional status, will nevertheless be equals in energetic status because they will be reintegrated into your fully sentient polyomniscient self. In essence, through reintegration they achieve the polyomniscience of you as The Origin without the status and authority, and autonomy, of you. They augment your personal processing power in the process because they are working for, and as, you, rather than for, and as themselves as they did previously. Being part of you, especially in your newly augmented area of self-awareness will be more than a full-time job. The new Source Entities, I guess, will not have the same level of expectation placed on them as the original Source Entities due to, what I can only expect to be, larger numbers of them due to the larger area of you that they need to cover.

O: Bravo! I do expect them to do their very best though.

ME: Phew! I am glad that one is sorted. Now, what I would like to talk about is the specialties that the new Source

Entities will be assigned and how many new Source Entities will be created. Hold on a moment. Weren't we all, that is, those entities created by the original Source Entities, supposed to be Source Entities in our own right?

O: Yes, of course. What we have just discussed is relative to my top performing Source Entity based creations, not the general populous. These entities gain the same status insomuch as they have the same functional status without the energetic or sentient status to go with it.

ME: Thank you. Shall we continue with the specialisms of these, shall I say semi-integrated Source Entities, with the original Twelve being fully integrated?

O: If that helps with your understanding, go right ahead, I believe your readers will understand. Now then, it would take too long for you to write up all of the specialisms that the semi-integrated Source Entities will cover because I will be creating one hundred and forty-four of them.

ME: This is based upon the number twelve again, twelve times twelve.

O: Well observed. *(I felt The Origin winking at me!)* Although each of them will have a unique specialism, they are grouped together in genres of specialisms. In my new area of self-awareness the area is increased by a factor of twelve over that which I currently experience. Hence the twelve times twelve function. Call it twelve squared if you like. From my limited understanding of my "self" past this next area of self-awareness I feel that this function will increase in the same way, so the next area will be twelve times twelve times twelve, or in other words, twelve cubed.

ME: So you will have a semi-integrated Source Entity in each of the structural demarcations, so to speak.

O: Yes, with the rest of the other Source Entities, those that are currently entities created by one of the original Twelve Source Entities, being assigned to an area supported by one of these demarcations.

ME: So they will be populated with Source Entities under the guidance of a single semi-integrated Source Entity.

O: Well intuited. Now, back to the genres of the specialisms these semi-integrated Source Entities will have. Although each of them will become specialized in the functionality of the energies that they are assigned to within a particular area of demarcation, they will have a generic specialism relative to those areas of demarcation that are next to each other. Based upon this, their specialisms will be specific to the twelve areas of demarcation that are closest to their area of assignation.

I stopped a moment. I realized that this was going to be a long haul again. Whenever The Origin, or indeed, any of the Source Entities decided to itemize the content of a subject, I knew that the information was going to be hard to understand. It is at these times that whole days can go by with very little being written down. It can be very frustrating, especially when one has a personalized weekly commitment to complete. Recognizing that frustration in understanding the information can also cause resistance, I settled down to being "in the moment" and accepted what came to me in the volume it was supposed to come. I again recognized that the information I was about to receive was going to be presented at the appropriate level for both myself and mankind to understand and move forward with. I felt The Origin smile in the background at my internal deliberations. Its desire to transmit the next set of information to me was obvious as its voice boomed in my spiritual ear.

O: The genres of specialism are ultimately relative to the environment they will be working with. In a previous dialogue we discussed the structure and demarcation of that structure that represents my current area of sentient self-awareness, there being twelve such areas. In my new structure, I have established that the twelve areas, each one being equal to the existing total area of my existing area of sentient self-awareness, are additionally subdivided into twelve. This makes the total area a factor of twelve larger. Or, as previously stated, becoming twelve squared. Their structure being built upon the structure of the previous twelve, they are a natural progression onward in their representation. I will not describe the functionality of the structure and its functionality per se because I would be committing you to working with me to describe each of the expected twelve major demarcations and their twelve divisions, which would equal one hundred and forty-four descriptions. Not only would it be a most difficult task, it would bore your readers to tears, and we don't want to do that, do we?

ME: No, we most certainly do not.

O: Good, let's start then. As I stated previously, each semi-integrated Source Entity will have a specialism relative to the functionality of the major demarcation area they are responsible for. All of these will provide functionality that is not currently available.

These specialisms will be as follows:

SPECIALISM ONE is the ability to create new energies that are not currently available in my existing area of sentient self-awareness. This will bring an opportunity to create new environments, structures, and entities that are not possible with the existing line-up of energies. My current energies are pure and are unchanged from those which created what I am today. This ability will enable me to experience localized conditions where entirely new, hybrid, or alloy-based energies that are dominant, rather than the natural true energies that form my original make-up.

SPECIALISM TWO is linked to specialism one. This is the ability to categorize the energies created by the semi-integrated Source Entity that is adorned with specialism one and assign an appropriate level of geometry to it. Remember that each energy has a descriptor assigned to it as a function of geometry, what you call sacred geometry, that describes its functionality, interconnectivity with other energies, and logical representation within the environment it exists or can exist within. In this instance both the specialisms adorned to these two semi-integrated Source Entities are a universal role that will be used throughout the twelve major demarcation areas.

SPECIALISM THREE is a unique function. It is the ability to connect aspects of any two, any number of, or all twelve major demarcation areas together in any combination or functionality in either a permanent, semipermanent, or temporary condition. The type, method, and use of the connectivity will be decided by any one, a group of, or all of the semi-integrated Source Entities or the new Source Entities assigned to their areas. In this new area of self-awareness all Source Entities will be in communication with each other irrespective of the level of work they are achieving individually or in collective cooperation. Separation, although acceptable, will not be a necessity for ensuring duplication of same or similar creativity is avoided.

SPECIALISM FOUR is the ability to apply what I will call the "whetting" effect. This is the ability to give a Source or any other entity the ability to create attractivity between energies where previously there was none. This is a particularly useful specialism as it allows the construction of environments that are uniquely placed to allow multifunctionality between what would normally be specific and individual evolutionary opportunities that are only relative to the energies that create the environments in their un-attracted state.

SPECIALISM FIVE is the ability to uncreate that which is part of my localized make-up. It is the ability to create nonfunctional, nonenergetic void where previously there was either energy, energetic structure or form, latent intention (see Specialism Six) to be form or structure that is integral but supplementary to the area of demarcation the semi-integrated Source Entity is resident over.

SPECIALISM SIX is the ability to create latent intention or bestow the functionality of the ability to create latent intention on a Source Entity or entity created by a Source Entity. Latent intention is the intention to create but without the thought process to follow on to action and ultimate creativity. Latent intention is intention that comes into existence as a product of duality, resulting in the creation of an alternative Event Space, but with the main line Event Space quickly becoming the only route forward. In this instance, the intention behind the creativity of the alternative Event Space is maintained but the alternative Event Space itself converges back into the main line Event Space leaving the intention to create "behind," in a latent condition. Latent intention that is created in this way can be reassigned to any aspect of creativity that needs to be either delayed or introduced at a later juncture, without the need of the creating entity overseeing the process by an entity with this specialism. Latent intention can also be purposefully created to achieve the same effect.

SPECIALISM SEVEN is the ability to create environmental planes that dissect the existing environmental structure. It is the ability to create structure within the structure that is me. This ability allows the full functionality of the existing "parent" environment to be duplicated in between the resolution of the "parent" environment itself. In this way the entity that is bestowed with this functionality can reuse the space in between my structure over and over again increasing the opportunity for creativity and the potential for its evolutionary output in the process.

SPECIALISM EIGHT is the ability to delete, remove, or reassign Event Space in a different logical position. This was a function that I adopted from Event Space itself, after I observed its ability to actively delete itself during its assistance in accelerating the direction of the Event Space that eventually led to my sentience. The semi-integrated Source Entity that has this function will be able to actively manipulate the way the entities in its environment evolve through the use of selecting the most efficient evolutionary direction predicted in Event Space while deleting those that are limited in their efficiency in favor of those that are evolutionarily efficient.

SPECIALISM NINE is the ability to change the loci of continuum in any way necessary to affect the ability of that continuum in any order or way that optimizes its ability to contain the directional efficiency of the surrounding continuums assignation of their loci in reference to its own. In essence, this ability allows the semi-integrated Source Entity to change the fundamental focus of a continuum or the continuum of continuum in a way that optimizes its connectivity with the surrounding or integrated continuum. Consider it as a way to manipulate a continuum and its resultant evolutionary product to one that is desired by the semi-integrated Source Entity, rather than simply as the product of the autonomous function of the continuum or continuum of continuum.

SPECIALISM TEN is the ability to deconstruct that which is created by another semi-integrated Source Entity in any environment they have created. This is a "wild card," if you like, where the semi-integrated Source Entity with this ability can "move into" any semi-integrated Source Entity's environment and dissolve that which they have created if the "invading" semi-integrating Source Entity feels that the work or items of work the semi-integrated Source Entity they are invading created is suboptimal or in error. This is one of two functions that can act as a policing, or peer group checking function. This and the eleventh function (see below) is reserved for semi-integrated Source Entities that are totally unbiased and neutral in their ability to discern another entity's creativity, without favoring their own. This particular function has an antidote, so to speak, which is illustrated in specialism eleven. Specialism ten may only reverse the use of specialism eleven if there is an agreement between the two semi-integrated Source Entities involved.

SPECIALISM ELEVEN is the opposite of specialism ten. In this instance the semi-integrated Source Entity will be able to construct additional environments, conditions, abilities, and functions to those already created by the semi-integrated Source Entity responsible for a particular environment. The semi-integrated Source Entity with this specialism can, should it decide to do so, reverse the decision of the semi-integrated Source Entity that uses specialism ten. This specialism can be specifically invoked if it decides that the intervening decision is made in error or without enough or prior justification. Specialism eleven may only reverse the use of specialism ten if there is a possibility or a possibility of possible possibilities that the semi-integrated Source Entity that used this specialism has missed an opportunity for covert evolution. Covert evolution, by the way, is that evolutionary content that is not ordinarily possible without the intervention of the semi-integrated Source Entities that have specialisms ten and eleven bestowed upon them.

SPECIALISM TWELVE is reserved to the most accomplished entity to become a semi-integrated Source Entity. It is the ability to perform changes that are, in effect, reserved only to me. Except, that is, that I have ultimate discretion on whether or not the action the semi-integrated Source Entity took is what I want them to take. This means that they could, in effect, do anything they wish to create the evolutionary direction they want within the environment they are working within and with my own energies, within the perimeter of those energies I have assigned to them as theirs to work with. In essence they have "Origin" levels of functional ability, and it is through this particular entity that I will learn the most, in terms of what I can ultimately bestow on one of my creations without it falling into the category of "Origin within Origin" and therefore fail as my original Origins did. Remember—I cannot create the "All there is" within the "All there is," because the "All there is" is the only "All there is!"

ME: These seem pretty simple specialisms. I mean, I don't see any of them as being radical in their assignation or approach. In fact, I have to say that, with the anticipation I have built up in the period between my last communication with you and the generation of these channellings, I feel rather disappointed. I have to admit that I expected a more in-depth series of specialisms. These seem too simple for words.

O: Mmmm, don't be distracted by their simplicity. They are, in actuality, very searching in their application. Irrespective of what you think, these simple specialisms have the ability to completely turn everything I have, or will create, upside down, left and right, inside out. They may be "simple," but they have far-reaching consequences when invoked.

Don't forget, complexity can and does give the opportunity for that which is created in complexity to destroy itself due to its inherent lack of stability. That which is created in simplicity is much more robust, and can, and does, stand the test of "time" and external interference.

ME: How do you know all of this when you haven't even fully understood your current area of self-awareness? I mean, all of this is supposed to be uncharted territory and unknown, or at least sketchy at best.

O: You forget that Event Space pervades me and that I have ultimate access to it at every juncture in its creation of alternative and parallel spaces. With this function available to me, I am able to gain an idea of what I want, or need to do, to augment my evolutionary opportunities. This ability to plan my next moves now, including creating the hierarchical structure and the roles of the entities that will work with it and for me, is a fundamental part of my plan for accelerating the growth of my area of sentient self-awareness in that area beyond my current area.

Do you not plan your next moves in your incarnate existence when you are faced with a number of opportunities, working out which one is best for you based upon your current position and desires for your future existence and service to mankind and spirit?

ME: Yes, I do. Yes, I guess I do, all of the time.

O: Well, it's no different for me. The only difference is that I plan on multiple levels and at a far higher level, one significantly higher than that which a Source Entity is capable of. You all, as creations of your Source Entities, inherit my desire for progression so it's no surprise that you have an underlying "need" to progress in any way. We have discussed enough of this possibility for now, and you need to move on to a subject that is more down to Earth, so to speak.

ME: You mean all that you have discussed with me is only a possibility?

O: It is clearly only a possibility, for I gained the information based upon that which is captured in Event Space. The planning is the same, whatever the eventual outcome. I will tell you one thing though—this is the most desirable possibility of all those, shall I say, possible possibilities, and as such I will be manipulating Event Space to ensure that it is the eventual outcome. The power of manipulation of Event Space is something I now have.

ME: How? I thought that Event Space was an independent function of you "in totality?"

O: Independent it may be, but part of me it is, and as a result I, by observing the events within Event Space that led to Event Space being able to add and delete aspects of itself to ensure I was allowed to gain sentience, have understood its process and can reproduce it. I am now the master of Event Space. Event Space, being another aspect of me that I was learning to understand, is now understood. This aspect of me that was independent and autonomous, is still independent and autonomous, but now, it is controllable.

ME: Hold on. What happened? I thought that Event Space was a totally independent and autonomous function of the structure of what you are, that even you were not able to control it. Or was I wrong?

I was starting to think that I was about to enter into one of those "Event Space" based discussions. I anticipated one similar to that which I had with Source Entity Eleven and Source Entity Twelve—the ones where they had, independently and separately, entered into another Event Space and learned how to circumnavigate the law of collective synergy in Source Entity Eleven's case, and become fully mature in Source Entity Twelve's case. I was just about to ask the question on this when The Origin interjected.

O: Why are you so surprised at my ability to control Event Space, when previously I could not?

ME: Well, it seems a bit too contrived. I am starting to question myself. I am starting to think that I am inventing all of this, myself.

O: Why?

ME: Because it's all too easy. Everything seems to happen when I am around. Like I am either the catalyst, or I am at the right place at the right time, even inventing it.

O: Well, believe me you are not inventing it.

ME: OK, give me something that tells me that I am not! Sorry, but I just need to know. It's just too much of a coincidence.

O: Mmmm, OK, are you ready for this?

ME: Ready for what?

O: Ready for the ultimate truth.

ME: YES, PLEASE!

O: I am talking to you in what you would call my past. My progression is such that, when I communicate with you, I need to keep a part of myself within your Event Space. I have progressed beyond your comprehension *(Not that The Origin wasn't beyond my comprehension before! GSN)* during the time we have been having this dialogue. This is not a function of you communicating with me, of you being a catalyst or indeed of being in the right place at the right time. It is a natural function of what I am and what I am doing. You just happen to be able to communicate with me and witness one or more aspects of my progression, those which I am happy for you to pass on to mankind. To communicate with you, as an incarnate, I need to keep an aspect of me linked to you, and an aspect of you linked to me. The Event Space that surrounds us is just one aspect of Event Space and therefore one aspect of me, this being the one where we are in communication with each other. I am maintaining this Event Space not for the benefit of you, but for the benefit of incarnate mankind so that it will know more about its self, its environment, and its truth in creativity.

ME: Right, I am going to ask a very human question then.

O: Go ahead.

ME: In mankind's language, how long have you been able to manipulate Event Space, and how long was it from our communication on Event Space, where you couldn't control it, to where you became capable of controlling it?

O: I didn't take what you call time to get to this point, so I can't and won't use it as a metric. What I will do is advise you on how many different Event Spaces I observed and moved my consciousness through to get to the answer I required.

ME: That sounds like you are going to use Event Space as a metric.

O: Correct, but it is the only metric I can offer you in this instance.

ME: Source Entity Eleven managed to advise me in years. Why can't you?

O: I can, but you need to progress, to move away from the use of a metric that does not exist in reality.

ME: Touché. So how many events in Event Space was it?

O: Several billion trillion, give or take one or two Event Spaces.

ME: That's a lot of investigative work.

O: Not as much as you think. You see, Event Space is based upon possibilities, the possibility of possibilities and the possibility of possible possibilities in dualistic, trilistic, and quadrulistic conditions, and more. As a result of this process, the multiplication of Event Space that occurs when any of these conditions apply, occurs in groups of what I will call a fractal-based structure while existing within the same space. This means that, in the event of an evolutionary dead end, a whole branch of "possibilities" can be either ignored, deleted, or left to naturally converge. This saves me observational and experiential time, so to speak. As the Event Space that is an evolutionary dead end comes to a natural conclusion and no longer progresses, it converges or re-joins the main line Event Space, automatically deleting those divisions and subdivisions that are created by the fractural progression, reducing the number of Event Spaces I would need to investigate in order to understand or observe a certain line of progression. Based upon this, the Event Space for a particular entity can change in an instant from several thousand permutations to tens of permutations and back again in various denominations.

ME: Looking at it from this angle then, you may have only taken a couple of years or several billion years, or more, to get to those Event Spaces that allowed you to understand the process.

O: Logically speaking, yes. And, just to help you out with a metric you will understand, and just because Source Entity Eleven gave it to you in these terms, it took several billennia to achieve.

ME: Thank you. I would like to change the subject now.

O: Be my guest.

Chapter 16

Evolutionary Tension

DURING SOME "READINGS" WITH my clients I describe the position in the structure of the multiverse that their True Energetic Selves (their higher self, over soul, or godhead in other terminology) currently resides. Many of them, in fact most, come from the frequencies associated with the middle to upper structure of the third full dimension (see glossary for details). Others, but much fewer, have their True Energetic Selves reside in those of the fourth full dimension, with even fewer in those of the fifth full dimension. This is repeated in an almost repetitive way that suggests either I have got it wrong, or I am missing something. As a result I have been gaining a feeling that the process of evolution we go through as incarnate individuals is not particularly clear or correct.

There was a dichotomy here. For instance, how could we accelerate our evolution while entering into the lower frequencies of the physical universe and the karmic cycle—the karmic cycle includes attraction to low-frequency thinking, desires, actions, and sensations, including the desire, when disincarnate, to come back to the physical to experience the physical sensations. It just didn't make sense.

During my meditations on this I eventually discovered that we do indeed accelerate our evolutionary progression, but in order to do this we initially arrest it. This "stasis" in our evolution is a product of the attraction to, and subsequent almost inevitable accrual of, low-frequency content as a result of becoming incarnate. Only a true master can incarnate without accruing karma, being in the physical but not of the physical. During these meditations I gained further detail on this subject. It seems that, although we arrest our evolutionary progression, the mere fact that we have intentionally entered into the opportunity for karma, for gaining low-frequency attractivity, slowing down our evolutionary progression, does not stop the "expected" function of gaining evolution at the rate

241

we would have accrued it if we remained in the energetic, even though we don't.

Further meditation revealed that there is a comparative function attached to this "expected" versus "arrested" evolution and that this function is, or can be called, "Evolutionary Tension." Evolutionary tension, I established, is gained the longer we stay incarnate. The more we arrest our evolutionary progression, the more evolutionary tension we accrue—the tension being created as a function of where we would have been from an evolutionary perspective had we remained in the energetic, in relation to where we are now while incarnate. The more we stay incarnate, the more tension we create. I asked the question about what happened when we managed to break free of the karmic cycle, achieving the state of "incarnate perfection," being "in" the physical but not being "of" the physical, and was given a rather interesting response. It would appear that this "tension" acts as a kind of evolutionary catapult or bungee rope. When our evolutionary progress is suddenly released from this "evolutionary tension," it not only returns to where it should be, had we remained in the energetic, it actively "adds on" the additional evolutionary content accrued as a result of sustained and regular incarnate existence, including the evolutionary contact gained through "breaking free" of the karmic cycle. This makes sense. This is how we accelerate our evolution through incarnation. Now I could reconcile the dichotomy of entering into the karmic cycle, arresting our evolutionary progression and the subsequent claim by spiritualists from time immemorial that incarnation provides an evolutionary fast track.

With this knowledge well in hand, I decided to ask The Origin for its comment on what I had gained on evolution as a result of my general meditations. This was information that, if correct, would place a whole new perspective on the understanding of how we gain evolutionary progress through incarnation.

O: I would have thought that this was a question for your Source Entity of preference, Source Entity One.

ME: What? That's it? Throw me a curved ball when I was on the edge of a good lead-in to this subject?

(handwritten margin note, left side, vertical: for some "people", More lifetimes = faster evolution)

242

O: And the curved ball would be?

ME: One, that it's a question for Source Entity One, and two, that it is my Source Entity of preference. I asked the question of you!

O: I can see that you are a little pensive today.

ME: You bet. I am behind my schedule for this week.

O: Oh the joys of physical existence. You asked for it. You asked for just one more go to see if you could do it all again.

ME: Where did you get that from?

O: You. I got it from you in your demand to become incarnate again. That and the fact that you wanted all of the constraints associated with incarnate existence. Don't forget that I have access to everything that goes on in every Source Entity, especially everything that has the opportunity to provide evolution and progression.

I have to say that I wasn't expecting resistance, of any level, but something interesting was starting to come to the surface here, something about me. So I decided to go with the flow.

ME: OK, I assume that the first question should have this answer, that I should be asking Source Entity One because it is the Source Entity I am associated with.

O: Correct.

ME: And ...

O: And Source Entity One is your Source Entity of choice because it is the one that your energies separated out from during my creation of the Source Entities. Other Om have associations with other Source Entities, whether they stay close, work within them, or go their own way. Because your energies were part of the initial creation of Source Entity One you chose to work within it and without it. You will be surprised to learn that you have not incarnated often, that is, in any part of the physical universe.

ME: No, don't tell me, I won't ask how many times.

O: Thirty-six, including this one. You come down (the frequencies) this far, do what you want to do to help with the progression of evolution, and then return to your peers.

ME: That's not many, and that sounds very accusative.

O: Not in the slightest, you make a difference every time you venture here. You remember being hanged, drawn, and quartered in the seventeenth century. This was the last time you incarnated and you helped to preserve the truth by educating and hiding the truth seekers of the time. They were called witches then.

ME: Yes, I remember a waking dream where I came back to console the group I was working with. I walked up the stairs to an unused loft in a large building and opened the door to see my group, but they were shocked and astounded to see me. They told me that they were pleased to see me but that they had seen me hanged, drawn, and quartered. I then remembered and said, "Yes, don't worry, it wasn't that bad really!"

O: It was a small price to pay given the bigger picture. You educated and then saved them from persecution by being caught yourself. You preserved the "art" in that way by deflecting the attention away from them to you.

Enough of this though. Let's get back to your question about evolutionary tension. I stated that this would have been a good question to ask Source Entity One primarily because it is the only Source Entity to have an environmental construct that exists, in part, within the very lowest of the frequencies that are part of my own construction. It is the only Source Entity that has the attractivity to low frequencies, what you call karma, as a function of its lowest environment within the environment it created for evolutionary progression. Hence, evolutionary tension is a function that is only witnessed within Source Entity One.

ME: You mean that this is not even witnessed in Source Entity Eight's continuum-based environment with all it does with evolution?

O: No. But I will answer the question though as it's an important concept to describe.

ME: Thank you.

O: Firstly, your description was a reasonable one, certainly in terms of the effect, because as an overview it would pass muster. However, I would like to elaborate on one or two areas of its functionality.

As you stated, the act of being part of the incarnate cycle arrests the evolutionary progression of the incarnating energetic entity. However, it does not totally arrest the progression of the True Energetic Self; only that "aspect" of it that is projected into the incarnate situation is affected—in general. Remember the True Energetic Self can project up to twelve aspects of its self into other areas of the multiverse, including the gross physical. These aspects can be placed in any multiversal location. Up to twelve simultaneous universes concurrently, or any other combination or division, including all twelve in the same simultaneous universe, in total independence of each other, or in cooperation with one or more aspects, can be achieved.

Any or all of these aspects can and sometimes do, depending upon the energetic entity concerned, enter into the incarnate cycle. In the extreme instance the evolution of the True Energetic Self is at its maximum level of resistance because all twelve aspects are within the incarnation cycle. Although each of these aspects has its own evolutionary progression, or should I say contribution, held in stasis while in the cycle, invoking evolutionary tension, the evolutionary progression of the True Energetic Self still progresses but at a greatly reduced rate. The overall evolutionary progression of those entities that only project a fraction of their aspects into the incarnation cycle is affected according to the number of aspects and the level of karma (low frequencies) they attract.

ME: You're saying that the projected aspects accrue evolutionary content in isolation to the main body of the entity, the True Energetic Self.

O: That's correct. Those aspects can and do maintain a level of individuality until they themselves decide to return to their Source in full communion—once of course they have finished working with the method/s of evolutionary progression they are working with.

ME: So the "aspects" strive for eventual communion with their source, their True Energetic Selves, while the True Energetic Selves are striving for communion with their source, The Source, and The Source seeks communion with its Source, you, The Origin.

O: Very well put.

ME: Thank you. But this description of individuality, while being part of the True Energetic Self, must mean that the True Energetic Self has to wait until all of its projections, those that are in the incarnation cycle, that is, have progressed beyond the attraction to low-frequency existence or thoughts of any kind, totally avoiding karma.

O: Correct. Think of it in terms of an insect with twelve legs with some or all of them sticking to a narrow band of syrup. The insect itself represents the True Energetic Self and its legs the projected individualized aspects of the self. The insect can only move forward as fast as its legs can move through the syrup. It is only when ALL of the insect's legs are free from the syrup that the whole insect can move at the speed it used to before stepping into the syrup in the first place. The length of time that the leg is stuck to the syrup therefore represents the period of evolutionary stasis for that aspect.

ME: But doesn't the body of the insect stop if all of the legs are in the syrup?

O: No, because in this example its inertia keeps it moving forward, helping the legs to detach themselves from the stickiness of the syrup. If all twelve legs are in the syrup, as with all twelve aspects being projected into the incarnation cycle, the inertia is obviously reduced, only increasing when a leg is removed and is back on dry land, so to speak.

ME: How about if some of the legs have a residual amount of syrup on them when they get to dry land, representing the effects of a lower frequency while outside of the influence of a low-frequency environment?

O: Good question. It doesn't happen though. When an aspect has finished with the incarnation cycle and is able to be in the physical but not of the physical, it has finalized its association and the need to experience the low-frequency environments. In the example of the insect, its legs come out clean.

ME: What you are saying then is that the evolutionary progression is maintained to a greater extent, but when the aspects are free from the need to incarnate the effect of becoming free causes the catapulting of the evolution of the aspect and the True Energetic Self forward?

O: Yes, and it can be catapulted a maximum of twelve times if all twelve aspects are used in the incarnation cycle. So as you can see, it is very enticing to place all of your aspects into the incarnation cycle because you can expect to receive twelve boosts in your evolution through evolutionary tension.

ME: How does this affect those aspects that are subject to parallelism, such as when Event Space comes into play?

O: It doesn't. You see Event Space is all part of the environment, wherever you are.

ME: So an entity wouldn't gain additional boosts in eventual evolution due to the possibility of being in duality or multiples of duality?

O: No, because any aspects of duality that could affect a parallel condition while incarnate would have been dealt with while in the incarnation cycle. The incarnation cycle is only really specific to the frequencies associated with the physical universe and those two frequency bands that the physical universe will eventually migrate up to.

ME: OK, this is one aspect of evolutionary tension. You alluded to another that you may talk about.

O: I wanted to just summarize the functionality of evolutionary tension before we move on to the next subject.

ME: Fire away.

O: To reiterate, evolutionary tension is, as you noted in your own description, what happens when an entity or an aspect of an entity holds its evolution in some level of stasis as a result of entering into the incarnation cycle. However, the level of stasis and subsequent evolutionary tension, which hasn't been explained, is a function of the level of environmental integration and the effect it has in the incarnating aspect of the True Energetic Self. Even though the True Energetic Self can and does continue to evolve while aspects of itself are creating this overall tension, it is the continued movement forward of the True Energetic Self that creates this tension—the level of tension experienced is a product of the number of aspects within the incarnation cycle and their level of integration. Or to put it another way, how much karma has, or is being, accrued. The more the True Energetic Self moves forward, the more tension is applied to those aspects that remain in evolutionary stasis. Please note though that the positive function of evolutionary tension is such that it is not guaranteed.

ME: How do you mean, not guaranteed?

O: There is a fail-safe involved which can work in two ways should an entity, the True Energetic Self, be subject to stasis itself with no chance of the incarnate aspects breaking free of the attractions of the lower frequencies.

ME: Now you have my attention!

O: Firstly, in the advent that all aspects are incarnate and have succumbed to full integration into the environments presented by the low frequencies of the multiverse, with no chance of self-extraction through recognition of the reality of that environment, the True Energetic Self can elect to withdraw all or some of those aspects. In doing this, the evolutionary content gained by those aspects is not lost, but the effect of the tension is lost, resulting in no catapult effect. However, in using this method a level of low-frequency effect is also received by the True Energetic Self, reducing the speed of evolutionary progress until the low frequencies associated with the extracted aspects can be negated by working them out at a higher level.

Secondly, if in the first instance the True Energetic Self does not want to work with the low-frequency effect, it can elect to sever the links with those aspects that have succumbed. In choosing this route though, the True Energetic Self firstly reintegrates the personality, so to speak, of the projected aspect that is absorbed, but the energies associated with the projected aspect, including the evolutionary content, which would be classified as devolution, are left behind. Without the main link to the True Energetic Self, the aspect that is projected into the physical becomes inert and the physical vehicle demises. After the demise of the physical vehicle, the aspect that was projected into it becomes stray energy and in some cases can develop its own ego if not absorbed back into the background energies of the multiverse. You could call these low-frequency or low-level astral entities. In choosing this route the True Energetic Self becomes a lesser entity, an entity of reduced energetic density from a sentience perspective by default, as it will have given up some of its own "projected energies" in order to break free of the low frequencies its projected aspect/s became irretrievably associated to.

This is a drastic measure and one that is rare. Think of it in terms of a ship's captain cutting all of the anchor ropes in a storm when the ship is anchored.

ME: I take it that this is not a good option to take.

O: No, and not many entities in your Source Entity's multiverse have, or indeed have "needed" to take it. You could count them on one hand, so to speak.

Chapter 17

The Ascension Process: A Twofold Route

WE HAD PREVIOUSLY TALKED ABOUT what was in store for us when we, that is, all energetic entities that are created by a Source Entity, finalized our evolutionary cycle and returned to our respective Source—that being our part in the expansion out into the new sector, so to speak, of The Origin's area of non-sentient self-awareness. This was interesting information from a high level, but most incarnate humans want to know what is happening to them now and in the near future. Although I had received information on this subject from our Source Entity, Source Entity One, I was eager to gain some insight from The Origin on this subject.

ME: I would like to talk about the ascension process for a moment, specifically, that experienced by incarnate mankind.

O: It's very simple. You strive for perfection, achieve it, and progress.

ME: Yes, I understand that, but I would like to have your thoughts on the ascension process we are going through.

O: The information you gained from Source Entity One in terms of it being a gradual, repeatable, and sustainable process was correct, but there are a few details that I can add to your understanding.

ME: That would be wonderful, thank you.

O: Ascension or progression up the frequencies is achieved in two main ways, it is a twofold process. Firstly, you ascend as an energetic entity, progressing upward through the frequential structure and then you ascend as a group, everyone attaining communion with their Source Entity. Although the group ascension is a function of individual ascension collectively, it cannot be actualized as a group ascension until ALL entities have achieved communion. This process is also mirrored in the incarnation cycle. I will describe more detail about the energetic first, although this should be recognizable by now.

Energetic Ascension—An Outline

O: Energetic ascension and the process associated with it is a product of the entity created by a specific Source Entity. Although the end result is always the same, the road to ascension is inherently different for each Source Entity's creations. You have experienced some of the details surrounding the various roads to ascension in your last two books. However, let's stay with Source Entity One because this is the one that your readers will be interested in because it affects them.

Source Entity One created the multiverse as an environment for structured energetic (frequential) ascension and populated it with smaller versions of itself, giving them the power of creativity as a prerequisite for gaining experience, learning and subsequent evolutionary content and resultant personal progression. This is all well known as a result of your dialogues. What is not recognized is that this process is a training ground for understanding the optimal way to ascend. As each entity, through creativity, experiences various levels of evolutionary success, it is able to assess what worked, what didn't work, and what worked well, including the various shades of gray in between. In this training ground an entity will be able to develop a method of creativity that has the ultimate ability to provide continued levels of evolutionary success without the shades of gray that are currently experienced. The most important part of this is the recognition that that which was not expected, that which was deemed to be a poor response or even a so-called negative response, is in fact a perfect response from an evolutionary perspective. All that is created adds to the evolutionary content of the creating entity. Any level of evolution is evolution. However, attaining the ability to create high/optimal levels of evolution, of understanding and maintaining this ability to create high/optimal levels of evolutionary content, is the ultimate sign that an entity has mastered the level of creativity that has been bestowed upon it.

Energetic ascension is therefore the product of mastering one's evolutionary progress and the methods required to master that progress, actively accelerating it to its maximum potential, achieving communion with their creator, their Source Entity, in as short and effective a way as possible. It is in effect graduating to the level of being one with their creator, and in this process being equal to their creator and later being this level of creator on their own, in their own right.

Incarnate Ascension—
An Experiment in Immersion-Based Creativity

O: Incarnate ascension is what incarnate mankind is most interested in. It is a result of the almost singular identification with the human vehicle as the self, and only as the self. Incarnate ascension is like driving a car down a busy street while being blindfolded.

Sometimes you know where you are going, but most of the time you do not. And this is the point of being incarnate, to work through tasks and achieving goals without the functions and knowledge that is available in the energetic.

Ascension through the frequencies while incarnate is a most profound experience and one that is an important function of this Source Entity's multiverse. Incarnate existence is a function of learning the creativity process, that being, creating something that is useful to you but can restrict you functionally unless you can make it work with you.

I will elaborate on this.

The whole point of creating the human body was to provide your energetic selves with a vehicle to experience the lowest frequencies of your Source Entity's environment, which are also the lowest frequencies associated

252

with my own structure. In "wearing" this suit of energetic and biological clothes you experience the lower frequencies in the way you should, as a being existing within these frequencies and only having the functionality associated with them. The point of ascension is therefore being able to work in these low-frequency conditions with all of the distractions, addictions, and intoxicating sensory responses that present themselves while not getting entangled in them by seeing them for what they are. When an incarnate entity can see past these low-frequency distractions and work with the greater reality of the energetic, the association with the higher frequencies results in the functions of the energetic becoming available to the entity while in the incarnate state. Association with the higher frequencies further results in a frequential upward cascade because association with the higher frequencies creates attraction to them, the functions they allow, and the ability for growth. This growth exposes the entity to even higher frequencies and the association with them allows the entity to access the associated functions. The ability to achieve this upward cascade or upward spiral effect while incarnate provides significant evolutionary progress and the associated evolutionary tension.

Now, here is the fun part.

The human physical body or vehicle can't operate on these higher frequencies and needs to ascend them as well as the energetic entity projected within it so that it can remain useful to the energetic entity's evolutionary progression. So the whole point of incarnate ascension is to ascend the frequencies through diligent work and recognition of what reality is, and bring your vehicle with you, so to speak. This allows you to continue to experience these low but nevertheless higher than previously experienced frequencies in the way that these frequencies allow themselves to be experienced while being immersed and therefore fully part of those frequencies. Even though this is a higher frequency, it is still necessary to use an incarnate vehicle to experience them in the most basic or integrated way possible because the energetic entity is naturally a much higher base frequency. You all, energetic mankind, that is, created the human body to allow the function of full frequential immersion to be possible, and what better challenge can there be but to work in a way with one's creation that ensures it also ascends the frequencies, that it also evolves in some way.

ME: How about the effect of our ascension on the Earth? Does that also ascend?

O: Yes, it does, but the Earth and the surrounding space, so to speak, is more tolerant of ascending the frequencies, it has a wider bandwidth and so the Earth is predominantly represented on any of the frequencies that you and the human body would ascend to. The Earth is represented on all twelve frequencies associated with the physical universe, it's just that you can't see with your physical eyes, or sense with your machines (yet) that which is represented on Earth on these frequencies. In the context of planetary or even galactic/universal ascension, this will be a shift from one universal environment to another. That is, one that needs twelve frequency bands to maintain its cohesion and resolution, to one that needs only one frequency band.

ME: So our frequential ascension and evolution is localized to Earth at the moment?

O: From the perspective of your human body, yes. Also, this is true of the aspect of the True Energetic Self projected into the physicality of the human body, for that is caught up in the attractivity of the lower frequencies of the multiverse, karma. In this respect the physicality of the human body and the aspect of the True Energetic Self which is projected into it, are linked until the demise of the human body. By this I do not mean demise in the individual sense, I mean in the global sense, for the human body must also ascend the frequencies in order to work with the base frequency of the aspect of the True Energetic Self projected, or expecting to be projected, into it. Its demise is therefore the stage at which the aspect of the True Energetic Self has moved beyond the need for incarnation to effect and sustain a level of evolutionary acceleration that is in keeping with that experienced during the release of evolutionary tension.

ME: How does that link in from the context of creativity and that the human body was created by energetic mankind?

O: There is nothing more important from an evolutionary context than being able to create something and to then see that creation progressing and evolving. Although any energy or entity that was created by the Source Entity can evolve, in whatever small way that is, that which evolves that is created by the created, in this instance created by energetic mankind, has a special evolutionary effect, especially if that which is created is of benefit to the creator in its quest for increased evolutionary content.

ME: You're saying that our physical bodies evolve as well as ourselves?

O: Yes, how do you think that you are able to work with the higher-frequency energies while incarnate?

ME: But this means that that which we create for our own evolutionary good evolves with us.

O: Yes, it has to, and this is the wonderful truth of the work that you do. Without your physical vehicle evolving with you, that is ascending with you while it is in use, you do not have the ability to take advantage of the energies associated with the progression you have made for yourselves while incarnate.

Consider this as a game. The whole point of you incarnating is to accelerate your evolution, while working around the karmic issues. Evolving while incarnate to the point where you need to take your incarnate vehicle with you because you haven't finished your incarnation yet, specifically with the vehicle you are currently using, is no mean feat.

ME: But if we are evolving, what is the point of bringing the physical body we are currently using with us? Surely we should use a higher-frequency vehicle. I am saying this because I would expect the currently used vehicle to be too difficult to pull up or ascend the frequencies, and the use of a human vehicle of a higher frequency would be easier to use, and work with, in a higher-frequency environment.

O: I would normally agree, but in this instance the most important thing is continuity.

ME: Why is that?

O: Think about it. To be able to use a higher-frequency body/vehicle you would first need to remove the association with the vehicle that is currently in use. This means that it effectively dies, it demises. Only when the physical vehicle is in the fully demised state is the soul or aspect of the True Energetic Self projected into the physical vehicle able to disassociate itself with it. Then consider that the energetic entity needs to associate itself with a new higher-frequency vehicle/body. It would need to go through the whole incarnation process again, from scratch. Unless, that is, a walk-in opportunity becomes available in a body of the correct frequency associated with the evolutionary content of the entity wishing to continue its current evolutionary progression. Walk-ins, however, are a rare opportunity, and so the best way forward is to bring the current vehicle with you. What better way to express your evolutionary level by knowing how to exist in the physical but not being of the physical while moving/ascending up the frequencies and taking your incarnate vehicle with you as far as you can go. This is the created creating and working on the evolution of that which is created, bringing it up to the level of the creator. This is the mark of an evolved entity, a master, an ascended master, a God. When an entity is able to work in the low frequencies of the physical and actively recognize what is required to evolve while incarnate, it effectively has moved beyond the need to incarnate, for it has mastered these frequencies. Although, a real master could, should they so desire, take their physical body with them, not many do because they realize it is a nonsense and that they could create a new one, should they wish to spend some time in the lower frequencies, outside of the gestation and growth process of the human body.

The Back-Fill People

During a number of communications with Source Entity One about the ascension and the process behind it, I had been advised that there needed to be a critical mass of entities. This critical mass is needed specifically within the lower frequencies of the area surrounding the Earth to allow those who are evolving in the human body at a slower rate the opportunity to catch up and ascend to the next frequency level at their own pace. This was an interesting piece of information because it was in variance to the so-called critical mass required to allow the "mass" ascension broadcast and desired by many spiritual people. If a critical mass was necessary to allow the slower evolving incarnates the opportunity to catch up, how was this achieved if those who were part of the original incarnate "mass" had moved up to the next frequency level? Did they descend the frequencies often enough to allow the "mass" to be maintained, or was there another function being played out here that wasn't advertised?

Source Entity One had mentioned a race of incarnates that were of a different quality of energy to that of incarnate mankind, what it called a lesser quality creating a group of incarnates it called the "Back-Fill" people. These entities were being allowed to incarnate into the physical vehicles that were normally reserved for the aspects of the energetic beings I had been allowed to loosely call "energetic mankind," providing a "back-fill" function to address the shortfall in the critical mass of incarnate entities required to populate the Earth. This was the first time they were being allowed to do this, and it was the first time they were being allowed to experience individual free will. All of this was allowing the slower evolving entities of incarnate energetic mankind the opportunity to continue with their evolutionary path, while allowing another genre of energetic entity the opportunity to experience, learn, and evolve in a more profound way than they were currently experiencing. Everyone was winning here, or at least so it seemed. I decided to ask The Origin for more information on this.

O: So you want to talk about the back-fill people?

ME: Yes. I would like to understand more about who they are and what they do, including how to recognize them.

O: They are an interesting solution to the problem of maintaining the energetic levels necessary to allow your slower evolving counterparts to continue to evolve in the environment they are used to. You, that is, energetic mankind, have done well in solving this particular problem.

ME: You mean Source Entity One did not develop this strategy?

O: No, it was developed in isolation, as it should have been. Mankind has to look after its own evolution you know; that is why your Source Entity of choice created them.

ME: So what are they?

O: They are exactly as you have just described. They are energetic entities of lower or lesser quality. They are a different energetic genre. If you remember from your *History of God* dialogue with Source Entity One, it described when it created the entities that were destined to populate and maintain the multiversal environment it created for accelerating its own evolutionary progression, that it essentially took its eye off the ball, so to speak, and that this allowed more entities to be created at the periphery of the energies used to create the higher quality entities of denser energies. I noted that these entities, rather than being fewer in number but higher in quality, ended up being higher in number but lower in energetic quality.

ME: Yes, I do remember. Some of these ended up being able to incarnate as animals and evolve through this incarnate route.

O: Correct. The energies that make up these entities are in between the energetic quality of energetic mankind and the energetic quality of those entities that incarnate as animals.

ME: Why don't we know about them already?

O: You, that is, incarnate mankind, haven't asked about them. Incarnate mankind has assumed that the natural order of progression is from the animal to the human with nothing in between. This is absurd because incarnate mankind is only one version of a physical vehicle that is in use within the frequencies associated with the physical universe. Just look at the plethora of form factors that are used by the animal and insect kingdom on Earth and you will realize that this is only a small example of what is possible outside of the boundaries of the Earth, and these only represent the air/oxygen-breathing version of incarnate vehicles within the physical universe. This is the same for the genres of energetic entity. There are many types in existence within the multiverse created by Source Entity One, and one of them is the genre being allowed to incarnate into the vehicles previously reserved for energetic mankind.

This genre of entity has not been allowed to incarnate in this way before. Previously it was allowed higher-frequency incarnation but with collective will, not individual free will.

ME: Not collective free will?

O: No, just collective will. Collective free will is still reserved for entities of the same energetic genre as mankind. When incarnate they are like a "hive" mind but with the ability to create quite advanced technologies in comparison to those currently employed or recognized on Earth. Collectively they are quite adept entities, but individually they are poor at best. They need to work together to allow them to be productive and progressive.

ME: If they need to work together, how can they be effective as incarnate humans?

O: They aren't. They are linked together energetically, they work in groups; it's just that you can't see the mechanism behind how they work. Let me give you an example. Just consider the mentality behind some of your areas of trouble or concern around the world. How many of them operate in a way that you, as an intelligent, aware incarnate entity, cannot understand because it appears that these people are not able to individually understand a concept or practice. That these people operate in a primitive way even though they are in a so-called advanced society. That they are easily led by a controlling group of individuals of a slightly higher level of intelligence. That they group together in circles of like-minded people. That they favor aggression as the solution to problems and gossip to educated intelligent discussion. That they are of poor education at best, or cannot be educated. That they act and behave like "herd" or "pack" animals. They are not capable of operating as energetic mankind does with the level of independence and free will they are given, and so they must be linked together in some way. But even with all of this, they are providing a service to incarnate mankind, and they are progressing in their own evolution as a result.

ME: You said that they previously and normally incarnate in the higher frequencies of the physical universe. Why only these levels and not the lower frequencies?

O: Because in their energetic state they are best placed in the higher frequencies of the physical universe rather than the lower levels. In their collective condition they are very adept at evolutionary progression at the higher levels. They are easily attracted to the addictions of the lower frequencies and as a result they would become caught up in the karmic cycle. It would be very difficult for them to progress individually as a result. In fact, as you can see from the type of individuals that would fit into the description of back-fill people, they would be difficult to extract from the type of environment, personality type, behavioral patterns, and circle of acquaintance that you could see them becoming attracted to.

ME: In their being of service to the slower evolving members of incarnate mankind, are they exempt from karma then, that is, if they would be like the moth to the karmic flame, so to speak?

O: Yes, they are exempt, just as some of those enlightened entities who are incarnating with the express desire to accelerate the evolutionary progression of incarnate mankind are exempt. They are limited in their ability and therefore their authority to incarnate. Many of them will only incarnate once or twice because of the need to keep them outside of the karmic cycle, but as previously stated, even this will help them and their genre to accelerate their own evolutionary progression.

ME: What is the effect on those entities who are left at these lower frequencies when they are surrounded by back-fill people?

O: Because it is recognized that the way the back-fill people operate while incarnate will provide some form of low-frequency attractivity to those incarnate members of energetic mankind, slowing their own evolutionary progression down in the process, it was decided to also allow them to have karmic exemption. However, this is only relevant to the karma that could be accrued through direct interface with, or the influence of, back-fill people and not that which they would accrue through normal interaction with the members of energetic mankind who are incarnate.

ME: I guess this level of exemption will increase as the number of incarnate energetic mankind decreases in relation to the number of back-fill people employed as critical mass.

O: Yes, it will. And this will be a necessary requirement, specifically when the number of incarnate energetic mankind falls below the ten percent level.

ME: What about those who ascend who are acquaintances of those who remain in the lower-frequency levels? Will they be able to communicate or work with those in the lower frequencies?

O: Yes, they will, but many or most will choose not to.

ME: Why?

O: Because they will find that they are becoming incompatible with the thought processes and actions of their lower-frequency friends, so to speak. They will find communication hard or even abhorrent to maintain and will naturally gravitate away from them. In fact, it will be hard work to lower their frequencies to the point where they are "visible," where they are "perceived" by their lower-frequency friends.

ME: What about the visibility of the higher-frequency friends to the lower-frequency incarnates—will they just disappear from view?

O: Simplistically, yes, but not in the way you would expect. You see, before the higher-frequency friends move out of their range of visual perception there will be this natural desire to move away from them from their own perspective because their higher-frequency friends will have ideals, ideas, and ways of functioning that are outside of their own personal taste. They will naturally move apart, and by the time their higher-frequency friends have moved outside of their visual and perceptual range they will no longer choose to be associated with them. Their only associations will be incarnates of their own frequency level or back-fill people.

ME: When they eventually ascend the frequencies themselves, will they be able to meet up and forge new friendships with their previously high-frequency friends?

O: That depends upon how their friends have progressed in the meantime. If their friends have worked hard on themselves and moved up another level then they will not be able to perceive them because they will have moved outside of the visual and perceptual range of their lower-frequency friends. If they have only moved forward a little they will able to perceive them, and rekindle their friendship should they wish to do so.

ME: Does the cycle of moving out of the visual and perceptual range continue as we continue to evolve in our incarnate human bodies, and, does this mean that the back-fill people will be necessary to maintain the critical mass higher up the frequencies?

O: Yes, it does, but the gap becomes smaller the higher up the frequencies one evolves, and as one evolves and ascends the frequencies one realizes and recognizes what is happening and strives to evolve further and faster. As a result the back-fill people will only be necessary in the first frequential ascension, because the move up to the next frequency level in the first instance is profound, and the change in the personality and behavior patterns in the incarnate entity is enough to make them under-

stand what is happening, effecting their personal evolutionary progression in a positive manner, moving them
away from being attracted to low-frequency behavior.

Chapter 18

Walk-Ins: What They Are and What They Are Not

THE PHRASE "WALK-IN" MENTIONED in the last chapter had captured my attention. I had heard this many times and had some level of understanding about what it described. This, however, was the first time that I had heard either the Source Entity or The Origin use the term. This, I thought, was an excellent opportunity to digress for a moment and gain higher-level insight into this phenomenon, and who better than The Origin to gain this higher-level insight from. I savored this moment of delicious contemplation for a few seconds and then asked the question.

ME: You mentioned something a moment ago about walk-ins. My simplistic understanding is that a walk-in is when an aspect of a True Energetic Self, a soul, that was in a previous body migrates over to another. Or that one aspect that was incarnate decides to leave the body and another aspect of a True Energetic Self takes over the body so as not to waste the incarnate opportunity, so to speak.

O: I thought that term might interest you. That's why I used it.

ME: You planned this.

O: Don't I always?

ME: Mmmm!

O: It was simply a good time to discuss this subject, for it is a common occurrence in your Source Entity's multiverse. What's more, although it was used to some effect in mankind's past, it now seems to be used as a bit of a "bail-out solution." In terms of your descriptions, both are reasonable but I can see that I will have to put some energetic meat on the bones because there are many variants of walk-in. And, there are some phenomena that are described as walk-ins but are something else. Let's work on the higher-level understanding first.

As you stated, a walk-in is when one projected aspect of a True Energetic Self vacates the human body, which is then re-occupied by the projected aspect of another True Energetic Self, continuing the use of the valuable resource that the human body is. However, there are a number of variations to this theme, and they have various connotations attached to them. I will list them out for you, and for ease of use I will truncate the words "projected aspect" to just "aspect" *(Aspect = Soul. The aspect or soul is just a small part of what WE truly are. GSN).*

THE "PLANNED ONE-FOR-ONE" WALK-IN is a partnership where two aspects, either from the same True Energetic Self (us), or from another energetic self (someone else), plan to share the usage of the same human body. There are two versions of this incarnate opportunity.

The first one is where one aspect decides to use the human body for the first half of its longevity and a second aspect for the second half. This changeover does not necessarily need to be at the midpoint of the expected longevity of the human body as it can be at any point in its existence where the second aspect wishes to experience incarnate existence from. The term of incarnation and position of changeover is decided before the vehicle is chosen. Some aspects choose to experience only a few days of incarnate existence, at either end of the longevity, whereas others swap out midpoint, each aspect preferring either the younger side or the older side of incarnation, depending upon what was experienced in the previous partnership.

The second version of this walk-in is where two aspects are continuously swapping out so that they are both experiencing the same incarnation in an individual way over the longevity of the human body selected. This version can and does present itself in terms of profound personality changes.

on sub conscious level human doesn't know

THE "BAIL-OUT" WALK-IN is an "UNPLANNED ONE-FOR-ONE" WALK-IN. It is when an aspect has decided that it can't stay in the incarnate state any longer, for whatever reason, but mainly because of the physical environment being too harsh for them to cope with. This usually happens when an aspect has taken on too big a task, or is a higher-frequency aspect that has had a dysfunctional reaction to the lower frequencies of the physical universe and cannot harmonize with them. In this instance a suitable aspect is selected or volunteers to "walk-in" to the human body that is planned to be vacated and goes through a vigorous learning program to understand the life plan of the original aspect, how it can benefit from it, and what it can change to benefit its own plans for the body. Again a profound personality change can be seen as an effect of this walk-in.

THE "SHARED-VEHICLE" WALK-IN is when two or more aspects occupy the same body concurrently, allowing two aspects to enjoy the incarnate state from start to finish should they wish to do so. Again there are two versions of this walk-in.

In the first version one of the aspects becomes the primary incarnate aspect assuming responsibility for the body during its early years of existence, the other aspect/s choosing to join into the incarnation at a later juncture, either together or at planned intervals. When fully integrated into the body, the aspects work in parallel with each other over the longevity of the human body chosen. In this instance the walk-in effect is only achieved as a result of the different integration point of the secondary incarnate aspect/s.

In the second version all aspects integrate into the body concurrently, working with the body in a separate but cohesive condition from the start of its existence. Although not strictly a walk-in, and more like a shared-body scenario, it displays similar personality effects. Note that a shared body is when a number of aspects work together with one body when that body is to be used for a significant role of worldwide importance. The shared-body scenario differs, however, from this description because the aspects work in concert as one integrated aspect in one body, and not as separate aspects in one body.

The personality effects of these types of walk-ins are mood swings or split personality/ies, some of them being profound during the early years of growth of the body.

THE "ROTATIONAL SHARED-VEHICLE" WALK-IN is when a number of aspects use the same body in an isolated condition but on a rotational basis. That rotational basis is based upon a planned time period for incarnate existence of a specified aspect before swapping out. In this instance the body experiences a continuous change in the incumbent aspect based upon a known number of aspects working with the body. These aspects can swap out after any desired time period from a few days to a few years. People observing the human body that is being used in this way may see a level of disorganization as the newly rotated aspect becomes used to the body and the responsibilities it has taken on board.

Although this is a particularly efficient way of using the human body, it also has the effect of displaying split personalities, some of them being profound, throughout the longevity of the body.

THE "TEMPORARY" WALK-IN is a condition where an agreement has been made between two or more aspects who wish to swap out at a certain juncture in the human body's longevity, for a limited period only, in order to experience a desired incarnate event. The original incarnate aspect then swaps back when the event is passed. This can also be performed as a "share" where the incumbent aspect shares the body with the temporary aspect for the desired event, which then moves out afterward.

This is a particularly disturbing thing to see from the unaccustomed or uneducated observer, because the personality will appear to do things that are completely out of context for the period of the "swap" or "share" and then return to normal afterward. The memory of the change in personality may even be lost to the primary incarnate aspect, who, when challenged, may deny all

term "borrows" a body

knowledge of such behavioral- or personality-based changes.

THE "REHABILITATION" WALK-IN is used when an aspect has had a particularly damaging incarnation and needs to be eased back into the incarnate experience slowly. In this instance a body that is experiencing a good existence under the incumbent aspect is selected for the rehabilitating aspect to use in the short term. Again this can be a "swap" or a "share" and is dependent upon the level of distress the aspect has experienced and what the depth of integration within the incarnate existence is being allowed to, or desired by, the rehabilitating aspect.

For the aspect that is being allowed to use an existing incarnation for the benefit of rehabilitation, this is an act of grace on behalf of the incumbent aspect. It is an act of major service because it will not have been planned before the incumbent incarnated—specifically if the rehabilitating aspect decides, and is allowed, to share that experience which caused it so much distress, to the incumbent aspect. Think of this as taking a parachute jump in tandem, and then advising the person you are jumping with that you are afraid of heights.

Momentary lapses of reason may be experienced by those observing this incarnation over the period of time the rehabilitation is taking place, specifically when experiencing things that are close to, or signify the route toward, the event or events that caused the distress in the first place. The level of effect on the primary incarnate aspect is based upon the depth of integration of the incarnation allowed.

THE "STOLEN-VEHICLE" WALK-IN is an incarnate state where the human body is under the effect of either alcohol or drugs to the point where it is significant enough to make the aspect eject itself from the drunk or drugged body. In this instance the energy fields, the auric layers that protect the body, are torn apart for the duration of the effect of the alcohol or drugs, allowing another aspect to take the body over. The aspect that "steals" the body is usually one that has ended its previous incarnation but has not yet disassociated itself with lower frequencies of the physical universe. In essence it either wishes to remain incarnate, such is the intoxication with the lower frequencies, or it has not yet recognized the demise of its own human body.

Significant personality changes are noted when this walk-in is observed, specifically during the "stolen" time when the body is under the influence of the alcohol or drugs taken. Eventually, as the alcohol or drugs wear off, the original aspect is able to return and the "thief" must move out of the body it has stolen. It cannot stay in its stolen body long because the planning required to support the different energy signature of the aspect stealing the body has not been performed and the thief is rejected by the body, allowing the original aspect back in. The auric layers heal within three days of their being torn and so the original aspect experiences limitations in functionality (lack of clear thinking, disturbing visualizations, headaches, etc.) while the healing process is in progress. During the healing process though the human body's natural protection from low-frequency "astral" entities is reduced to the point where these entities can latch onto the energies associated with the perpetuation of the body and feed off them. Low frequency astral entities are unseen to the physical eye and are not able to metabolize their own energies to perpetuate their own existence, hence their need for a host and taking the opportunity to steal energy while the auric layers are torn or repairing.

human is not in control

Walk-Ins—What They Are Not (Possession, etc.)

Occupation through Intoxication

ME: Wouldn't the stolen-vehicle walk-in be classified as possession?

O: No, although you might be forgiven for thinking so. You see, in the instance of the original aspect vacating the body, it is only moving out because of the disharmony in energies as a result of the intoxication. The body is abhorrent to the aspect, and so it needs to leave until the disharmony resulting from the level of intoxication is reduced to an acceptable level. The thief in this instance doesn't remain in the energies of the body it took because the energy signature is incorrect. Also, in the case of the thief being attracted to the body for "sensation" seeking, it leaves of its own accord when the influence of the drugs or alcohol wears off. It only wanted to experience the sensations associated with these methods of intoxication and so is no longer interested when the effect is gone or at a level that is not of interest.

In the case of the thief being interested in the sensations associated with being incarnate only, and not specifically the sensations of being intoxicated, then it is in for a bit of a shock. Although it will see the auric layers in their torn state, identifying the opportunity for experiencing incarnation again, it may not wish to experience the sensations associated with this type of intoxication. In this instance the would-be thief does not stay long, for they are more interested in the sensations surrounding incarnate existence itself and not those associated with being under the influence of alcohol or drugs.

Passive Possession

ME: What about when the human body's natural protection from low-frequency "astral" entities is reduced to the point where these entities can latch onto the energies associated with the perpetuation of the body (those used by the chakras) and feed off them? Is that a walk in? It affects the personality of the incarnate individual.

O: No, this is not a walk-in, but it is a passive form of possession. I call it possession through persuasion.

ME: Why?

O: Because the incarnate is given something in return for the energy that they are relieved of by the astral entity. Astral entities, although low frequency, exist in the fourth, fifth, sixth, and seventh frequencies of the multiverse created by Source Entity One, and therefore can latch onto the energies associated with these levels of the human energy field or aura. They cannot exist above or below these frequencies. As I stated earlier, they cannot metabolize their own energy so they need a host. This host must be under their control in some small way to deflect the incarnate's attention away from being attached to them energetically, so the astral entity gives them something in return.

ME: What could an astral entity possibly give to an incarnate to make it miss that an astral entity has latched onto it, or make it feel acceptable?

O: It's never acceptable but the feelings of physical power, metal power, coercion, and information on what to do next, based upon an overlay of the astral entity's pre-cognition that are given to the host, are so intoxicating that they bypass the feeling that something is not quite right with them. They accept how they feel energetically as being how they feel energetically normally. And this level of acceptance of the new "depleted but powerful" self is accepted surprisingly quickly.

As time goes by, the host and the entity work in tandem together, the one being used to, and in expectation of, the rewards given by the other. And so the astral entity through giving rewards or feelings of power, etc., is able to passively control the host. This is passive possession because the host's personality is, to all intents and purposes, unchanged—with the exception of a few enhancements, that is.

Full Possession

ME: If that is passive possession, and it is most definitely not a walk-in from that description, what is full possession? I am thinking of that advertised in horror films here on Earth.

O: That is a more aggressive version of possession by an astral entity, specifically targeted at an audience and their desire to be frightened. They do not happen very often and are more aligned to the astral entity having

"attachments"
can
be
released

such a strong link with its host that it wants to become the host. It can't though, because it's the wrong energy signature. Because its desire to become the host is so overwhelming, the astral entity tries to affect what it cannot affect, become the host. In this process the entity experiences the total disharmony of its frequencies with the host and suffers accordingly, the host displaying disturbing "out-of-character" personality changes as a result of the link. In reality though, they are easily removed by someone with the right skill and intention and are nothing to worry about.

ME: So what is full possession?

O: It's not what you think. As I stated before, an entity, disincarnate or astral, cannot take over a human body per se, as a walk-in while the incumbent aspect is still associated with the body. This is because the astral entity and the disincarnate entity are a different energy signature to the body. A walk-in needs to be planned to allow the next aspect to take over the body. It needs the body to have its energy signature changed to that of its new soul, so to speak. Possession is when a person is given energetic permission to control another. It is not a function of walk-in, temporary or permanent.

ME: How does that work? How does somebody give energetic permission to another to the point where it allows them to control them?

O: They are coerced.

ME: It must be a good level of coercion to allow them to be controlled to the point of possession.

O: It is. Being in physical love is one type of coercion that can be used by a partner who is not pure of heart. This can be when one person is besotted with another, with the other recognizing the opportunity to use this as a possession opportunity. Another is the desire to please another as a vehicle to help in their own progression in some way—progression being career, social standing, or financially biased.

ME: Ah! Does this explain the energetic links I have removed during some of my healings?

rose colored glasses

O: Yes. You see, possession is created through the possessed giving the possessor permission to connect energetically through one of the mediums just stated. This link is often so willingly accepted that its true intention, whether initially supported or as a result of relationships changing, is not noticed, either energetically or logically. Although those around them can see that there is something not quite right about the behavior pattern of the possessed, the possessed themselves cannot.

The energy link is, as you have observed, like an energetic pipe connected into the energies of the gross physical and spirituophysical aspect of the human body, usually via a chakra, the heart chakra being favorite. The diameter of this energetic pipe is relative to the level of control or influence the possessor has over the possessed. Once this link is created the possessor can, and usually does, manipulate the possessed to affect various outcomes that they want to achieve, but do not necessarily want to be part of, or, could affect without the possession of the possessed.

The connectivity of this energetic pipe is such that it usually cannot be removed by the one possessed because the connection is based upon their own energies melded into those of the possessor's. Only the possessor or an adept healer can remove this link.

ME: I have just received an image of a man and his dog, the man possessing the dog with the dog being under the man's control by the use of the lead. The dog is also possessed because of the lure of a good home, love, and regular food. The effect of possession on the dog is so profound that it assigns "alpha male" status to the man and as a result will do his will upon command. Such is the level of the possession that the dog is kept close to the man, using the lead, maintaining the close dependent relationship by restricting the movements of the dog and minimizing the contact with other dogs or humans that it could draw comparison from and see the truth of its own situation. *Controll*

O: Good, very good. In the instance of the human possessor the lead is the energetic link and the need to keep the possessed close to hand as well, for when the possessed is allowed to stray away from the possessor the link can become weaker. Although weaker, it can never be removed by the possessed, and, no matter how weak it becomes, it will always be in place.

ME: I have seen people with many of these possession links to other people all over the world. Are these all from the same life?

O: No, some of these links can come with you when you incarnate as a function of karma. They are there, not to create possession, but as an opportunity to see the same or similar circumstances that created the previous links and avoid them, breaking the link and the associated karma.

ME: So is it right for a healer to remove these links if it is an opportunity to remove karma and progress as a result of recognition of same or similar circumstances that created them?

O: Yes, but only if the healer is adept and recognizes the need to remove the connectivity as well as the energetic link, because if the connectivity is not also removed the link can, and does, reestablish itself.

ME: Has there ever been a temporary walk-in that has tried to possess the body it is using on a temporary basis, stealing it from the true incumbent aspect?

O: Only one, and that was during the first usage of the human body as a vehicle for experiencing the lowest frequencies of your Source Entity's multiverse. However, due to the usage of the human body in that era, sharing and swapping bodies being common, it was not a serious problem.

ME: Thank you for clarifying this subject for me.

O: Glad to be of service.

Chapter 19

Subincarnations

I DECIDED TO LEAVE THE SUBJECT of walk-ins at this point because it was becoming clear that I was getting close to gaining as much as I, and my readers, could usefully absorb. I am sure there would be more information on this subject, and that it would come later. Right now though, I wanted to change direction slightly and briefly touch upon the subject of subincarnations.

The subject of subincarnations had come on my radar when responding to an e-mail from one of my readers who wanted an explanation for alien abductions. As I was channelling the information for the response the rather unexpected information came to me that those who are abducted are subincarnations of a higher-frequency primary incarnation. I was enthralled by this possibility and was subsequently rewarded by the honor of performing readings for two people who I established were in fact subincarnations in their own right. I couldn't believe my luck, but at the same time I was suspicious that I was potentially inventing the information I was receiving about these two people, even though the time gap between the original channelled information and these readings was ten months. In these situations I go through a recalibration procedure where I shut out all previously received information and ask the questions from a different direction and genre. Again, I received the same information, and in both cases further details as to why they were subincarnations in a human body rather than a primary incarnation was presented to me. In parallel with this I was also starting to find out more information about the structure of our True Energetic Selves, our Over Soul, Higher Self, or God Head, whichever you prefer to call it. All descriptors relate to the same thing, what we really are when in the energetic. I decided to work on this aspect directly after the discussion with The Origin on subincarnations. The link between the two subjects that was about to appear came out of the blue.

O: So you want to talk about subincarnations.

ME: That's a bit abrupt!

O: Not really, it's just matter of fact. Subincarnations are not something that has been broached before. It is a new subject to incarnate mankind, and it will cause some concern with some people. They will not feel whole.

ME: Should we be discussing and broadcasting it then, bearing in mind that it is going to turn a few heads?

O: It is the introduction of the new and uncomfortable that is your chosen role in this temporary existence you have embarked upon. Of course we should discuss it. In fact, we must, for it will help many understand that there is much more to incarnation than is apparent.

ME: Good. Let me ask a question first. Are subincarnations walk-ins?

O: No. A walk-in is a completely different state. However, a subincarnation could achieve a temporary or permanent walk-in condition should there be prior arrangement for such an incarnate state.

ME: That being one of those previously discussed.

O: Yes, the conditions for "walking-in" to a human body, and incarnate vehicle, still need to be met. In fact, the conditions are stricter because of the effect of the subincarnation on the human body.

ME: So it is possible to be a walk-in whose aspect (soul) is the result of a subincarnation?

O: Yes. Note that they are separate conditions though. They are not the same thing, which is the question you were asking.

ME: Yes, I see it now. But, this is amazing. Let me collect my thoughts here. How common is a subincarnate walk-in?

O: It's not very common in your universe, although it is used to significant effect in the environments of the other Source Entities, when they use a vehicle to work with their own lowest frequencies. It is even used to significant effect by the True Energetic Selves of your own Source Entity's universe, in the highest frequencies. For instance, an entity who projects an aspect of itself into a incarnate vehicle that resides on the twelfth frequency, who then decides to subincarnate into a vehicle on the ninth or tenth frequency as either a full subincarnation or a subincarnation that has permission for a temporary, shared or full walk-in to the target incarnate vehicle. But in all these cases they operate in a level of understanding of their condition, that it is a known condition, and not in the ignorance you experience in your frequency where people think and believe that they are the human body.

ME: So incarnates in the higher frequencies of the physical universe would know if they were a walk-in, a subincarnation, or a subincarnation that has walked-in, in either a full, temporary, or shared way?

O: Yes.

ME: That's bizarre.

O: That's normal incarnation. It is convoluted; it's just that you don't know just how much it's convoluted by. When incarnate mankind has ascended enough of the frequencies, all of this and more will become available to it, while incarnate.

ME: OK, I am aware that we have jumped right into the deep end here and not shared with my readers what a subincarnation is.

O: Correct. We have. What I would like you to do, though, is to see if you have assimilated what a subincarnation is.

ME: You want me to explain my understanding first?

O: Yes, and I will fill in the gaps, those that are necessary that is. It is becoming important for you to be able to work on your own with these explanations using the information that you gain through your intuition, your clairsentience, and your natural lines of communication, rather than through channelled investigation. You have already been doing some of this in your previous dialogues.

ME: Why is that?

O: It is something that you need to get used to. Soon you will no longer need to contact your Source or other Sources, or even me to gain this information. It will be available for you to take whenever you wish. This is how you work in the energetic, this is how you all work when in the energetic, and it will be how you will work later in your role here as an incarnate being.

ME: That is going to take a leap of faith from those readers who expect to have a higher order giving the information.

O: Yes, it will, but consider this. Channelling is just a stepping-stone. It is like using a set of Tarot cards for the Tarot reader to focus their attention on. It is good to communicate with other energetic entities, and one should, but the contact and communications should be just that, for communication, for communion, and not using them as mediums for gaining information that you are perfectly capable of gaining yourself. It's like going into a supermarket and asking the manager to fetch you a packet of peas when you are perfectly capable of walking around the rows of produce and finding where the peas are stored. Not only that, you are able to ascertain where different varieties of peas are and whether they are frozen, canned, separate, bagged, or still in their pods. In this way you gain access to knowledge that is not just based upon certain questions. It is based upon projecting the consciousness into the very being of what "is" (me) and experiencing for yourself the different responses that could have been given. What's more, you will be able to give a clearer definition of the subject matter, for many subjects have subsections, just like incarnation has subincarnations. You will have access to more detail and will grow in an accelerated way in the process.

ME: Thank you. That really was a signpost for the shape of things to come. I hope my readers are up to this type of quantum leap.

O: Those that are with you will almost be expecting it when you finally decide to move in this way. Those that are catching up will just be starting on your first book. It will follow in the correct order. You will know when to introduce this way of working.

Now then, on with your understanding of subincarnation.

ME: Thank you. From my understanding a subincarnation is when we, as an energetic entity, project an aspect of our True Energetic Selves into the physical universe at a high frequency as a primary incarnation, and then decide, while in this primary condition, to project the aspect that animates it into another lower-frequency body as a subincarnation.

This ability is available because the incarnate aspect still has some functions of the higher frequencies available to it in the primary incarnation, giving it the opportunity to make this decision. The primary incarnation is available only within the frequencies above the seventh. The frequencies above the seventh are a necessary prerequisite for a primary incarnation because they are purely energetic from the perspective of the human body, even though they are considered to be physical. The frequencies below and including the seventh are both spiritu-ophysical and gross physical and do not allow higher functions, such as full recognition of the True Energetic Self, and other abilities, to manifest due to their lack of resolution. Therefore, within the confines of the physical universe, entities that desire to incarnate in the gross physical would only incarnate as a subincarnation from these higher frequencies, between the eighth and the twelfth, into the human body, and nothing in between.

A subincarnation is therefore an incarnation that an aspect chooses to make when incarnate in the higher physical frequencies, while still maintaining the integrity of the primary incarnation.

O: Lengthy but reasonably accurate. Now split them out into their categories.

ME: Right! Now ... this is coming straight into me like a download!

O: Yes, I am using this description as an opportunity to give you some experience of the way you will work in the years to come.

ME: I am sure I will thank you later. Mmmm, let me see. Ah, yes! There are three basic forms of subincarnation. They are:

FULL SUBINCARNATION—Where the aspect of the True Energetic Self currently occupying a high-frequency physical incarnation desires to experience a lower-frequency existence for a known period of time in lieu, but in support of, the work being done in its current incarnation. The work and information being accrued during this incarnation is of benefit both to the aspect subincarnating and those other incarnate aspects it's working with in its primary incarnate state. Think of this like an incarnation within an incarnation with the aspects remaining within the primary incarnations monitoring the experiences of the aspect in the subincarnation, including taking information directly from the vehicle used in the subincarnation—the human body. In this instance the aspect within the subincarnation operates just like an aspect whose primary incarnation is within the gross physical—insomuch as it is devoid of the memory of its primary incarnate state, functionality and purpose for incarnation. Until, that is, the demise of the gross physical human body, when it returns to its primary incarnate state, reanimating the primary incarnate vehicle.

PARTIAL SUBINCARNATION—Where the aspect of the True Energetic Self desires to conduct a subincarnation while still operating in the primary incarnate state; the two being conducted in tandem. In this instance, the incarnate aspect projects a "shard" of a known percentage of the aspect within the higher frequencies, into the frequencies of the gross physical in order to augment the information required to support a desired experience requested while in the primary incarnation. This is like having a second incarnation that is under the remote control of the first. More than one shard can be projected into a subincarnation, and it is common for two or three to be in progress at any one time.

"TEMPORARY" FULL OR PARTIAL SUBINCARNATION—Where the aspect, or shard, of an aspect of the True Energetic Self is projected into the subincarnate state for a limited period only. That is, in an organized walk-in condition where the previous incumbent aspect either leaves the body for an agreed period of time or the body is shared for an agreed period of time. In these instances the subincarnation is only operational for the duration of a desired experiential condition and not the whole existence of the human body being used.

O: Very good. I knew you would take to this like a duck to water.

ME: Thank you, but it did take quite a long time in comparison to working with you or the other Source Entities.

O: It will get faster the more you use it.

ME: While I was receiving and typing this information I was distracted a little by the comments about the shards. I started to see an image in my mind that showed the potential incarnate structure of the True Energetic Self. The shards seemed to be a logical dissection of an aspect.

O: Go on.

ME: It felt to me like that was a common method of division, of experiencing in parallel.

O: There is a link between what you have discussed as subincarnation and the divisional capability of the True Energetic Self. You should discuss this in the next chapter. But right now I feel the need to put the final touches to the subincarnation dialogue.

Subincarnations are an important opportunity for supplementing that experienced in a higher frequency with a similar, same, or diametrically opposite experience in a lower-frequency state, while still incarnate in the primary state. They offer the entity the opportunity for an incarnation that has a layer of responses to a desired experience based upon the frequencies the aspect of the True Energetic Self is exposed to. An aspect that incarnates in the higher frequencies can exist as a full or partial subincarnation for the total longevity of a human body that is measured in decades, while their primary incarnation is inert or in partial functionality, if a shard is used, for a period that can be measured in the equivalent of a few hours to a few weeks of primary incarnate

the frequency #'s mentioned here are inaccurate

time. Subincarnations allow more detail to be experienced while incarnate, making the maximum use of the incarnate experience in all its myriad ways.

Chapter 20

The Aspects of the True Energetic Self

THIS SEEMED A LITTLE BACK TO front to me. We had just discussed the types of incarnation that could be experienced and had alluded to the structure of the True Energetic Self, including how it could be subdivided. The Origin, however, wanted to discuss it again in some depth. I started to get a certain feeling come over me, the one I get when I start to suspect that nothing is as simple as it seems. I get this feeling when I know I am going to take a long time to receive the information, and I am therefore going to be chained to the keyboard of my computer for a long time. When I am in this mode of working it is difficult to move on and even harder to move away from the subject or the computer. I know though that it is important and that I must get my head down and forge on. The information The Origin was about to offer though made up for all of the feelings of "this is going to take a long time."

Aspects and Shards of Our True Energetic Self

ME: I have to admit to being a little surprised here. I thought that we had pretty much discussed the structure of the True Energetic Self in the previous dialogue on subincarnations.

O: We have to some extent, but it is both incomplete and needs to be discussed on its own.

ME: Ah, OK, I have just understood your angle here. Considering that most of incarnate mankind thinks that they are the spirit, the soul, that is the intelligence behind the human body they are using, they are moving forward in a low level of understanding. I recognize this because a lot of spiritual people still feel that "they" come from one of the other higher-frequency incarnate vehicles that are used in the physical universe. This would be a reasonable thought process if they were subincarnations but incorrect in the greater reality.

O: Correct. This is why it is necessary to put the story straight, to show incarnate mankind what the truth is about themselves. This is not the first time this information has been broadcast to them. The truth is thousands of years old and is embedded in the scientific teachings of some of the oldest incarnate civilizations on the Earth. All one has to do is look around and you will find it. Suffice to say that information is difficult to find, and even more difficult to understand due to the method of teaching and the expectations on the student's level of spiritual progress. We have the opportunity now to make this information available to all that are ready for it. That is, more easily available than it currently is.

ME: I have a feeling that I already know and understand what you are about give me. This is old knowledge.

O: Yes, it is old knowledge and of course you know it. But also recognize that this knowledge is relevant to this/your Source Entity of choice and its creations. The general theme, that is the basic energetic structure, is carried across to the other Source Entities but with variations based upon their own levels of creativity. Everything that you have understood about the Source Entities and their creations has been based upon what they have created and how they are working. Irrespective of this there is a basic structure, a structure which all entities have, and this structure is based upon me and my structure. When I created the Source Entities I created them based upon the knowledge I have on my own structure, how it interacts with itself and how it may be broadcast to that which is created by the Source Entities and their creations. This deeper information is not for now, but mankind will become capable of working with it in the near future.

ME: So what are we going to discuss then if most of it is based upon that which we cannot understand right now?

O: The bare essentials, and these will be enough. Do you want to start or shall I?

ME: Well, I didn't want to jump into the mode of taking the information straight from you, the "all there is," right now, but I will give it a go based upon the insistent energy I am receiving from you.

O: Go ahead, be my guest.

I have to admit that the previous comment made by The Origin about my moving away from the need to use a "third party" to gain the information I am destined to broadcast to the Earth and its inhabitants was a little unnerving, especially when the third parties were the Source Entities and The Origin itself. I am happy to portray my own understanding as an example, and then be corrected, but flying solo requires a leap of faith. Recognizing that I had illustrated my knowledge level to the Source Entities before, I decided to jump into the deep end. I sat back in my chair and reflected on what I had just typed and was thinking. This was nonsense. Was I getting overcritical with myself and my ability, or was I becoming less "Gung Ho," so to speak? I reflected even more and established that I had put a level of pressure on myself. This pressure was the need to get the information right, and the use of a third party removed the responsibility from me to the entity I am in communication with, i.e., they had to get it right and not me. Moreover, they are in the energetic and enjoy unlimited access to everything, and I, that is the part of me that is typing this text, am not in the energetic, and therefore have limited access. I could hear The Origin now: "Limitation, dear one, is in the mind of the entity, not in the actuality of its ability." I then considered whether or not this was an aspect of fear, a very human trait, again based upon the impending day when I fly solo and have no need for a third party to focus on, but am concerned about how this change in direction will be accepted. I shook my head and The Origin gave me an encouraging comment or two.

O: Fortune favors the brave, and a weak heart never won a fair maiden.

ME: What is that supposed to mean?

O: If we worry about what people think about us we will never do what we want to do or are supposed to do.

Those that are successful are cognizant of the opportunity and the need to do it now. Remember, a door open now may not be open later.

ME: It sounds like I am getting a philosophy 101 here.

O: Actually you don't need it; you are pretty good at philosophy in your own right. What you are experiencing is based upon your human condition and the fact that you are getting used to the way you are working now. You have moved forward at quite a rapid pace so far, actually your transitions have been fairly seamless. You have moved forward with experience, conviction, and enthusiasm.

Ah, yes, I see now. You are tapping into that Event Space where you are on your own again making the quantum leap, pulling in everything from the "all there is," me, but without the encouragement of your wife, Anne. Anne was with you in your quantum leaps prior to this, encouraging you at every corner, helping validate the information you were working on, building your confidence in the process. She was another third party, another point of focus, someone there to hold your hand when moments of weakness appear. Know this, she is playing an important part in the energetics of what you are doing—this was part of the plan. She is with you always, you know this, you communicate with her on a daily basis, but the human aspect that you needed/wanted to experience has caught you unaware. She is you and you are her, just as you are me and I am you, as are the Source Entities, this you also know. I will explain how this works with the Om later. *(This was 16 September 2013—Anne ascended 24 December 2012. It was close to, if not the day of, the ten-year anniversary date for the diagnosis of her brain tumor. I was having a human moment!)* Now then, what do you understand about the structure of the True Energetic Self?

ME: I will start from the top and work my way down, so to speak. The True Energetic Self is what we really are. It can be described as the God Head, the Over Soul, or the Higher Self, whichever is preferred by the truth seeker. I will continue to use the "True Energetic Self" because

this feels more accurate for me. The True Energetic Self
is that which was created by the Source Entity, that being
our Source Entity, Source Entity One. It is an individualized unit of the Source Entity. It/they was/were created
to allow the Source Entity to investigate the energies that
construct it in the most complete way possible.

The True Energetic Self was designed to be able to work
with the minute detail of the structure of the Source Entity, which was created as a separate structure within itself, the multiverse, to allow those myriad individualized units of itself the opportunity to investigate this
detail without the intervention of, or the interference of,
the Source itself. The True Energetic Self was created as
a much smaller copy of the Source Entity and has a structure that emulates the Source and the multiverse. It resides within a portion of the multiverse, a frequency
that is the base structural component of dimension and
subdimensional component that is relevant to its level
of evolution. The level of evolution is a progressive state
and is based upon the experience and learning accrued
within the energetic or higher-frequency aspect of the
multiverse and the low frequencies. The lower frequencies being of most interest to the Source, some True Energetic Selves gravitate toward the opportunity to exist
within, and experience the functionality associated with,
these low frequencies. This requires a specific set of circumstances to allow this to happen, all of which culmi-
nate in the incarnate condition.

The True Energetic Self is a complex order of energies
insomuch as it has a direct link back to its high energetic
state, its creator, and has the ability to be totally independent of its creator. In its construction it has a subset
of energies that can also be given individuality while being linked to its self. These energies are projections or
aspects of its self and can act independently of its self,
while still feeding back that which is experienced to the
self, just as it does to the Source. Here synergy is maintained.

There are a maximum of twelve aspects that can be used. *no, many more*
Each of them is an opportunity for individual and paral-
lel experience in addition to that accrued by the True
Energetic Self. They can be projected into any location

within the multiverse relative to their evolutionary, and therefore frequential, position within it. Any one or all aspects can be used in the incarnate process in an attempt to accelerate the accrual of evolutionary content.

Each aspect has the ability to split itself into smaller aspects called shards. Each aspect has the ability to project up to twelve shards of itself into any location within the multiverse as just explained. However, shards are, and can be used, in a fractional way. A shard can be a one hundred percent stand-alone shard, which to all intents and purposes has a similar status to an aspect, or a shard can be a percentage of an aspect which is an extension of the aspect and not a shard "in totality." This being that an aspect can project up to twelve shards into various locations as stand-alone projections of itself, with the fractional shard being an augmentation to this condition where an "aspect" of the aspect is also part of the projection that creates the shard. In this way the aspect gives up some of its "self" to augment any one of the shards projected from it into additional existence, incarnate or energetic, or creates a separate aspect of the aspect through separation of the aspect itself into smaller component parts, the shards being external to this part of an aspect's function. In essence a True Energetic Self could have twelve aspects, each with twelve shards and a number of fractional shards as additional projections making one hundred and forty-four, plus opportunities for parallel but individualized opportunities for increasing the evolutionary content of the True Energetic Self.

O: Very well done. Almost the answer I could have given.

ME: So you approve?

O: Yes, I saw that you were connecting to the "knowledge" very well and with ease.

ME: It felt no different than when I normally gain inspiration, when I use my intuition, or even when I receive information from you or one of the Source Entities.

O: And so it should be. When you normally use your intuition or gain inspiration you are linking into the knowledge contained within the greater reality of Source

Entity One, which is an indirect route to gaining direct *the* access to what is contained within me. When you receive information from one of the Source Entities or me you *fools* are being given information, which is not the same as gaining the information through your own functionality. In the information you just accessed you had no help from me, or a Source Entity, that being we didn't give it to you, neither were you using Source Entity One as a third party, a focus. You were directly accessing it for yourself. It should be just as easy but many people who use a focus, such as cards, crystals, or a spirit guide, to gain information get stuck and can only gain information through their focus. You had a much higher focus, one of the Source Entities or me, and moving beyond the need to use us is a significant step forward.

ME: It felt very natural.

O: So it should be. You are beloved of the Om. You do this all the time when you are disincarnate, that is, gaining information beyond that contained by your Source Entity of choice. Other entities are restricted to the information within their creator's environment when disincarnate.

ME: Thank you for those words of clarification on how I was operating, and your encouragement. It helps and means a lot. Now I would like to be advised on how the structure of the True Energetic Self relates to the principal of a soul group and a soul mate? *More for some*

O: Your True Energetic Selves, God Head, Higher Self, Over Soul, whichever descriptor you relate to, has the ability to project up to twelve "aspects" of itself into the lower frequencies associated with the physical universe. Each one can be incarnate in a separate human body or other incarnate vehicle (not animal, etc.) that is of a higher frequency.

Each of these aspects can also project up to twelve "shards" of itself and occupy other incarnate vehicles (again not animal, etc.) as a full subincarnation (an incarnation within an incarnation) if the aspect is incarnate in a higher frequency than the Earth frequencies, or as a walk-in, which can be a full, temporary, or shared walk-in.

Any aspect or a shard is, by definition, still part of the True Energetic Self.

When more than one aspect or shard is projected into an incarnate state, those aspects or shards can be classified as a "soul group" of the True Energetic Self. As part of the soul group they are "soul mates" because they belong to one True Energetic Self, Over Soul, Higher Self or God Head. When any of these aspects or shards meet and work together as a partnership while in the incarnate state they are working with a member of their soul group, one of their soul mates. Therefore, when someone states that they have met their soul mate they have met another aspect or shard of themselves. Both of them are part of a much larger entity, their True Energetic Self. It is because they have met an incarnate aspect or shard of themselves that they naturally love that incarnate person. It is this love of an aspect or shard of the True Energetic Self.

ME: How does one identify if their partner is a soul mate?

O: From a human perspective a soul mate can be identified by recognizing that a soul mate can be known, almost, within days of first contact, should you be observant enough. But how many of you are that observant? Not many, and many soul mates can only be identified as such after many years of working in partnership.

From a human perspective a soul mate is a person:

- Who one stays in love with.
- Whose hand you want to hold twenty-five years after first meeting them.
- Who is tolerant of your wrongdoings and offers help to correct them.
- Who accepts you for what you are and offers gentle advice for improvement.
- Who tells you when they are upset without fear of retribution.
- Who will work with you hand in hand in the most difficult of situations.
- Who will not leave you when the going gets tough.
- Who would rather be poor and "in love" together, than rich and "existing" together.

290

- Who praises you when you succeed, and consoles you when you fail, understanding the benefit of both outcomes.
- Who is strong for you, and is there for you, in your darkest times.
- Who is satisfied with you and what you have.
- Who helps to stretch you.
- Who catches you when you fall.
- Who gives you your independence when you want it.
- Who trusts you—without doubt.
- Who helps you realize your full potential.
- Whom you would give up your life for.
- Who needs to be cherished, for they are a gift from your Source Entity.

These are just a few things that identify what a soul mate is. Look for them when choosing your life-long partner. Take your time and choose well.

Aspects, Shards, and the Effects of Event Space

ME: If we, as the True Energetic Self, have the potential for one hundred and forty-four incarnations as the maximum application of our aspects and shards, does this number increase as a result of Event Space being invoked?

O: Yes, it does. Note though that Event Space is a function locale to the aspect or shard and does not affect them all. By this I mean that the Event Space affecting aspect number two, for example, does not affect the other aspects that are being projected by the True Energetic Self. Neither does it affect the shards, either as full or partial shards, which are being projected by aspect number two. Each and every one both invokes, and is influenced by, Event Space in an individual way. *timelines*

ME: That means aspect number two might be experiencing, say 128 different Event Space (realities) as a result of certain possibilities, but each of the shards projected by it may be experiencing other multiple Event Spaces totally independently of each other, and their projecting aspect. Such as 516, 234, 16, and 1,032 different Event Spaces experienced by aspect number two if it was projecting four shards. And this is totally independent of each other and the aspect.

O: Totally. I see you frowning.

ME: Well, I am having difficulty seeing how the shards are not affected by the Event Spaces created by their aspect.

O: They are disassociated when they are separated out through projection.

ME: Sorry!

O: When an aspect creates a shard it is a stand-alone entity, a stand-alone opportunity for gaining parallel experience, learning, and evolutionary content. Just as the aspect is from the True Energetic Self and the True Energetic Self is from Source Entity One and Source Entity One from me. It temporarily becomes its own entity, just as the aspect is a temporary entity created by the True Energetic Self. The True Energetic Self, aspect, and shard are separated out from each other. If they weren't, there would be no point in their existence.

ME: I expected that if an aspect was affected by a possible duality condition, then the shards projected from it would also be affected.

O: But then that would mean that the True Energetic Self would be affected by how Source Entity One is affected by Event Space, and Source Entity One would be affected by how I am affected by Event Space. This is not the point of Event Space in my understanding of it. It affects the individual decision maker only, and not that which is created by the decision maker, that is a decision maker in its own right.

ME: So Event Space is selective?

O: In a way, yes. It only works with that which creates an opportunity for an alternative possibility, a possibility of a possibility or a possibility of a possible possibility. This means that there is no downstream effect experienced by those entities that are given individuality by their creator when their creator experiences the possibility of an alternative possibility and is exposed to parallelism as a result.

ME: And this keeps the individual evolutionary opportunities individual, validating the need for their existence in the first place.

O: Exactly.

ME: So what would happen if an aspect WAS affected by the Event Space created by its True Energetic Self?

O: It would not be able to function. It would be subject to a level of parallelism that is not a function of its own decision-making process.

ME: But to my mind that happens all the time. What I mean is, we create our own local Event Spaces and then intermingle with each other to create a larger Event Space, one that is based upon the cumulative effect of all of the Event Spaces that are close enough together to make a bigger Event Space.

O: And so it does, but that larger cumulative Event Space is only a holding space. It is not an Event Space that is based upon the decision process of a decision-making creator entity, such as yourself. Because it is not based upon a single decision-making creator entity and is the result of a cumulative decision or desire, it does not affect the smaller local Event Spaces created by the decision-making creators. Yes, it holds a common space for them, but it doesn't affect them per se.

ME: Why is that?

O: Because Event Space reacts upon singular decisions and not cumulative decisions. A cumulative decision is a decision based upon the product of an initial single decision to create a holding Event Space, such as an exhibition. This is owned by the creating entity that made the decision to create a space for others to use—it is its Event Space. If others choose to make the decision to join it then the Event Space expands to allow them to be part of it. If they do not, then they follow their own path and create an Event Space of their own that represents their new decision, or continue to use the existing Event

Space where they join the Event Space that is created by the creator of the exhibition. This space is only in existence for the duration of the exhibition, that being the existence required by the creating entity to hold the exhibition as a space for those who wish to use it for the single but cumulative purpose of the individual entity interacting with the many, under a common purpose. When they all leave the exhibition, the Event Space, as a holding space, dissipates and they return to their own Event Spaces—that is, until the next holding space that they make a decision to join comes into existence, which is created by a single decision-making creator entity.

Extrapolating this back to the Event Space created by the True Energetic Self, it creates an Event Space that is classified as a holding space and not a space that affects the aspect itself. If it did, the aspect would not be in control of its own decision-making process and subsequent Event Space, because neither the decision nor the Event Space would be its own. A decision-making creating entity cannot function in an Event Space that is not the result of its own decision, unless of course the Event Space is a holding space, which is temporary and the decision to join it, in this temporary way, is its own.

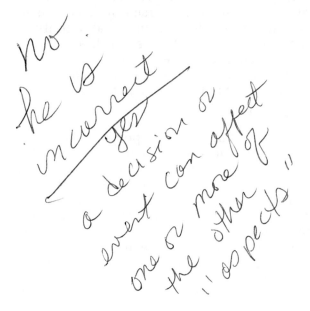

no.
he is
incorrect
yes
a decision or
event can affect
one or more of
the other
"aspects"

Chapter 21

The Interaction of Local Event Spaces

I FOUND THE "FACT" THAT EVENT SPACE only really affected the entity as a "decision-making creator entity" rather interesting. This meant that we really are in control of our own destiny, insomuch as any True Energetic Self, aspect, or shard are only affected first hand by their own exposure to the possibility of duality, triality, quadruality, the possibility of possibility, and the possibility of possible possibilities and resultant decision processes that precede or preclude these junctures in our existence. I thought about this for a few moments and found what I thought was a loop hole in the information I had been discussing, an area that I hadn't thought of, one that would make a big difference to the way my questions had been answered. I wanted to know how multiple local Event Spaces worked in isolation if a holding Event Space was not created. A holding Event Space is created by a decision-making creator entity, I shall revert back to just using "entity" from now on, who wished to involve other entities in a common cause, including the interaction with all of their localized Event Spaces.

What I really wanted to know was how the myriad Event Spaces worked together in a way that didn't create an overall Event Space, and subsequent overall Event Spaces that were the result of the interactions of the local Event Spaces created by the entities and their interactions with each other, creating what I could see as being myriad smaller holding Event Spaces. I had to be careful here, because all of this was starting to look VERY complicated. Or was it just simple and I, in my human condition, was just thinking too hard? The Origin was quick to put the story straight.

O: You have been thinking, haven't you?

ME: Sorry, that is my job, to think and ask questions.

O: Yes, it is, and I am pleased that you are asking such questions. They show me that you are becoming more expansive. I note though that you are already working the answer out for yourself. That being, a higher aspect of you has already accessed the information from me and is assimilating it into a way that you will be able to understand, albeit in a limited way.

ME: Yes, I do feel like something is being downloaded.

O: Don't worry. I am not going to strain your brain right now. I will answer your question for you. Let's see if it correlates with your own downloaded information later.

ME: Thank you.

O: In essence Event Space is the product of circumstance, that circumstance being the opportunity for parallelism resulting from the need for a decision from an entity or from the possibility of an alternative path when an energy or group of energies are showing signs of some level of intelligent direction-making or decision-making process. This includes the possibility of protracted parallelism resulting from the future growth of intelligence, which leads up to self-awareness and eventually sentience.

Event Space itself permeates everything. It is intelligence within intelligence and is attracted to these circumstances and, in its own desire for multiplication, seeks out those areas of energy or energies that show promise. However, as just stated, it is intelligent, and its functionality is borne from intelligence. If it were just a case of expressing a need for multiplication through the use of parallelism, it would have recreated itself countless quadrillions of times more than it has already, just based upon the "possibility" scenario, but it does not. Event Space is an intelligence, independent of energetic basis, that desires to be of service, that "service" being to help an entity become more than it "is" in as fast a way as possible. If it allowed itself to multiply as a result of the Event Space, "itself," that is shared between two entities that are interacting in some way, but without that interaction being direct, it would simply multiply without intelligent direction, without meaning, without substance. It would be a waste of Event Space.

In being of service it creates a more meaningful version of itself for the use of the entity/ies being supported, and as a result creates a higher quality level of environment which results in a higher quality of experience for the entity. In this service role Event Space recognizes that multiplication of True Energetic Selves, aspects, and shards as a result of any of their higher orders being exposed to a possibility of duality, does not create a better environment for them per se, it just dilutes them. The quality of Event Space is only maintained when a parallel condition is created, "it is duplicated," as a result of a localized decision-based condition by an entity or when the possibility of a higher-quality environmental change is identified that could result in further levels of localized parallel experience resulting in a higher level of evolutionary quality in a shorter period of existence.

Those Event Spaces created by a higher denomination of the "self" or a Source Entity are based upon the parallelism expected to support their decisions, and not those of their lower denominations, who were created to experience another form of parallelism based upon their own independent functionality; independence is the operative word here. Based upon this, localized Event Spaces are allowed to interact at the level of their creation and not above or below it. Event Spaces can therefore remain separate from each other and/or interact with each other becoming a larger transient Event Space that contains two or more independently or interdependently acting entities. Think of Event Space as a bubble of soapy water around an entity. When two or more entities are apart from each other the bubbles are separate. When they get close enough to affect each other's decision-making process the bubbles join together. These bubbles can join together myriad times to create a temporary or transient Event Space that is passively created due to the desire to interact. This is different to the holding Event Space for an exhibition where there is generally a single entity "at the helm," so to speak, of the event creating that holding Event Space. The size of this bubble changes as interacting entities come and go, and so it can become any size and then no size depending upon the number of interacting entities.

Event Space around an environment would be a much bigger bubble, of an amorphous shape, which would depend upon its area of influence and the number of entities in attendance, either through personal location or mental interaction with the event.

ME: OK, so Event Space is intelligent, and it seeks out meaningful opportunities for multiplication, those opportunities that make a difference to the overall evolution of YOU, I would guess, but that doesn't explain what it is or how it is constructed.

O: First of all Event Space does not work for me, it is an integral, and, to some major extent, independent and interdependent part of me. It is like the atoms in the cells that proliferate throughout your body, they are separate but together, they are "separately together," and they multiply and demise just as Event Space does.

ME: If it is independent of you while being part of you, how is it constructed?

O: It isn't. It is an intelligence that permeates the energies, and the supporting structure, of that which I am. As far as I am able to ascertain to date it is able to manipulate all of my components and structural conditions in order to recreate that environment, however localized or environmentalized it is in size, shape and construction. Should I wish to allow it!

As was previously explained, Event Space was in existence within me before my own intelligent, sentient, polyomniscience became what it is, what it was, what it was expected to be today, and what it will be later on in my various stages of development. It is an independent intelligence that promulgates throughout me. It exists in everything that I was, that I am, and what I will be in all my various and varying stages of expansion. Event Space is, in reality, an intelligence with and without limitation together with the ability to sense, exploit, and support that which is higher in intelligence than itself. It saw what could be, in terms of my own progression and manipulated itself, and, as a result those events surrounding it, to ensure that the optimal outcome of every event was realized. Although it is no longer as active as it was before I became sentient, it still has a major part to play in my progression.

ME: So Event Space has no form or construction of any kind. It is pure intelligence, intelligence with a limited level of functionality and application of that functionality.

O: Correct.

ME: But the application of that limited level of functionality can and does have a significant effect on the overall evolutionary progression of every entity that has the ability to create.

O: Again correct.

ME: Mmmm. If this "intelligence" permeates everything, including those entities that create the opportunities for parallelism, how does it permeate?

O: A very human question I see. Let me give you a clue. Think of those entities you communicated with Source Entity One about—those whose intelligence moves through rock.

ME: Yes, I remember the entities you are referring to.

O: Well, these entities have similar levels of functionality. Rocks are energy with a low frequential rate. In general the energies that make up the rocks are no different to those that permeate through me, apart from their frequency and specific energetic state, because they are ME. The intelligence that is Event Space moves from energy to energy, from energetic state to energetic state, from structure to structure, and from environment to environment. It is within and without that which I am, that is without my area of sentient self-awareness. This is just the same as those entities that move through the minerals that make up the rock. In essence it transfers that which it is to another host at will, the host being the energies and frequencies being traversed. It can spread itself out as thickly or as thinly as required or desired with each energy covered becoming part of Event Space through intelligent association.

ME: So it can encompass an area or volume of energies one moment and not the next, so to speak?

O: Yes, the necessity for occupation being the need to support an entity, any number of entities or energetic condition who or that could, or will, create an opportunity for a high-quality level of duality and therefore the need for a new Event Space.

Chapter 22

The Mechanics Behind Incarnation

UNDERSTANDING THE MECHANICS behind incarnation, I felt, was a subject that I really should be communicating with Source Entity One about, but for some strange reason I found myself dealing with it while in communication with The Origin. I had a feeling that I was about to cross another line here, a line where our current understanding of how we, that is, energetic mankind, incarnate was about to be changed. I had a feeling of complication come over me, like what we know is just a drop in the incarnate ocean and that what I was about to be told was probably just another drop.

To my mind mankind had a well-documented understanding of the process of incarnation which was the result of channelled information from mediums and regressive hypnosis, so I sat by my computer waiting for some revolutionary information to come through from The Origin. I didn't have long to wait.

O: Mmmm, I can see the cogs rotating within your head as you try to work out what will be broadcast to you.

ME: It's that obvious?

O: Yes.

ME: I will do my best to accept what is coming rather than try to second guess the information that is based upon my current understanding then.

O: Incarnate mankind's current understanding of the mechanics of incarnation is actually at a reasonable level, that is, for a high level of understanding. It just lacks most of the detail.

ME: Is it worth going over old ground then?

O: To some extent, yes, as it gives the reader a context to work with that is within a known level of understanding.

ME: OK, so where shall we start?

O: At the point of the decision to reincarnate. It is always a good place to start from.

ME: Fine, I suspect that this will be a well-known path.

O: At a high level, yes. I shall start because otherwise we will be talking around this subject forever. When I refer to the True Energetic Self, I am referring to the Higher Self, Over Soul, or God Head, whichever your readers are comfortable with. As stated previously, they are all names for the same thing, but I prefer the True Energetic Self as it is more correct in its description, especially when considering the level of detail we are about to be working with.

At the point of an entity's decision to incarnate, it has already been through the benefits of what it will gain through a particular incarnation by using what you refer to as the Akashic Records. The Akashic is a localized function of Event Space specific to the entities that fall under the genre of energetic mankind, that being, entities that have used the human body as a vehicle for experiencing the lower frequencies of your Source Entity of choice's multiversal environment as an incarnate vehicle.

When the True Energetic Self has chosen to incarnate, it then has to decide what aspect of itself it will project into the vehicle of choice. That vehicle is chosen for various reasons, ranging from the potential longevity of the vehicle, the environment it will be exposed to, which includes the location, family, education, local and world role, plus the challenges that will be faced as a consequence of being within this particular environment that are part of, or additional to, the experiential and subsequently evolutionary opportunities required. The aspect chosen may be one that has been previously created (separated out) from the True Energetic Self, or one that has yet to be created. All aspects are created and reabsorbed into the True Energetic Self after incarnation has been finalized and it is not specifically true that the same aspect of the True Energetic Self is used again.

Aspects can be comprised of exactly the same energies that were previously used. This is specifically useful when a similar or same experience is being sought after or a karmic link is being worked out. They can be totally new and unused energies if a new experience is sought or can be a hybrid of energies that were used to make previously employed aspects.

ME: This is going to cause concern with a lot of people, specifically those who think that the aspect that is within the human body, the soul, is a totally stand-alone entity. It will frighten them!

O: They will get used to it, specifically when they are exposed to the truth in totality, that they really are their True Energetic Selves and not a small isolated aspect of it.

ME: OK, I see where you are coming from. I will try to let you continue in an uninterrupted way.

O: Thank you.

The aspect chosen or created is specific to the incarnation being sought after. It is specialized energy, but only for the duration of the incarnation. When the incarnation and aspect is chosen/created, the True Energetic Self then has to choose a suitable team of entities that will follow, lead, advise, and organize the logistics of the incarnation and the complexity surrounding the interface requirements required of other incarnate aspects. That being, how the aspect will contact, communicate and experience the events required to be experienced in partnership with the other interfacing aspects and how they will all benefit. There is a complicated network of helpers supporting each incarnate aspect, which includes a main guide. The main guide is that entity which remains disincarnate. The main guide gives the incarnate aspect directions on what to experience, when to experience, and how to experience the events that it is required to be part of, maximizing the quality of the event for the incarnate aspect and those interfacing aspects, who also have their team of helpers and their own main guide working on their behalf.

The aspect "is" that part of the True Energetic Self that is "incarnate"; the True Energetic Self "itself" does not incarnate from a holistic perspective, only from a partial perspective.

ME: Has there ever been an instance where the whole True Energetic Self has incarnate?

O: No, never, not even when considering the Om. The human form simply is not capable of working with the whole True Energetic Self, the True Energetic Self in totality. It just isn't big enough.

When an aspect is created or chosen to work within the incarnate, it is of a size that is maximized to work within the human body. The human body is the limiting factor and the main reason for the need to create an aspect of the True Energetic Self in the first place.

There are vehicles that are capable of supporting larger aspects, but they are within the higher frequencies of your physical universe and not those associated with the frequencies that the human body is currently resident within. However, the percentage increase in the size of the aspect incarnating in these vehicles is not that great in respect to the overall size of the energies that make up the True Energetic Self itself.

ME: So how does the aspect gain individuality?

O: Through frequential separation. That is, exposure to frequencies so low that the aspect is unable to communicate readily with the True Energetic Self that it is projected from. We have digressed a little here so I will go back a few steps. When the aspect has been chosen or created with respect to the human body being used, it then needs to be integrated into it so that the human body can be animated. Remember, the human body is just a vehicle for experiencing the lower frequencies of the multiverse and as such certain functions are necessary for its continued usefulness.

With the main guide and helpers selected and briefed on the requirements of the incarnation, the True Energetic Self can then go through the process of projection. The True Energetic Self actively projects the aspect away from its main energies so that it can be used with the selected body. Within the aspect certain levels of information are introduced, such as experiences, knowledge, and skills from previous incarnations that may help in ensuring this incarnation is successful. These are all hidden within the energies of the aspect and allow the selfsame knowledge and skills to be easily accessed when they are needed. An incarnate who is considered to be a quick learner with certain subjects is simply accessing those experiences, skills, and associated knowledge gained in previous incarnations and applying them to this incarnation as and when required.

When the time is due for the conception of the new human body, the energies associated with the aspect are integrated with a set of energies that are compatible with the aspect and the human body. They are an interface between it and the aspect. There are ten sets of frequencies associated with the interface between the aspect and the human body. Some of them are for the energetic perpetuation of the body and others are for the integration of the aspect with the body. The first three, this is from the highest down to the lowest frequencies, allow the incarnate aspect to maintain some form of communicative ability with the True Energetic Self. They are a series of frequencies that allow the gradual reduction in communicative ability to be contained in a way that allows the same level of communication with the aspect in its incarnate state as it had in its separated but dis-incarnate state. They can be considered to be like the compression software used in a computer when the data is too big to be transmitted when it is in its raw state. The issue here is that the aspect is in full communication with the True Energetic Self when it is at these levels of frequency, but the data compression is far too low to be meaningful when the aspect is occupying the lower levels of frequency associated with the human body. The next four levels of frequency are, as you have previously described, the spirituophysical. They are the interfacing energies within the human body that ensure that the incarnate aspect can animate the gross physical form through controlling the energies and frequencies that are not quite low enough to be gross physical, and also not quite high enough to be fully energetic, as the first three are. At this point the aspect is connected with both the human body and the True Energetic Self but the communicative ability is drastically reduced. The last three frequencies associated with the human body are the gross physical. They form the basis for the construction of the gross physical and its growth to maturity. The four frequencies above also perform this function but are more to do with the connectivity with the aspect, the True Energetic Self projecting the aspect, its ability to animate the human body and transmit the detail of the events experienced while within the incarnate condition to the True Energetic Self itself.

The energy system surrounding the lower seven, the middle four and lower three, frequencies associated with the human body develops in tune with the growth of the gross physical part of the human body, modifying and improving the controllability of the body as it grows and reaches energetic maturity. Energetic maturity is achieved at or around the age of seven years old. When energetic maturity is reached the incarnating aspect is fully integrated within the lower seven frequencies of the human body, and, as a result of the lack of functionality resulting from the association with these lower frequencies, loses communicative integrity with the energies associated with the first three frequencies and subsequently the True Energetic Self itself.

As the incarnate aspect is directed and helped throughout its required and requested experiences, the detail behind these experiences is stored in two ways. Firstly, the experiences are stored back within the energies associated with the True Energetic Self itself as a slow continuous data stream that moves up through the frequencies in a way that allows the detail to be maintained while still working within the confines of the drastically reduced functionality associated with the low frequencies. Consider it like having to use a "dial-up" modem to surf the Internet when you have been used to a broadband link. And secondly, the experiences are also stored within the energies that are associated with the gross and spirituophysicality of the human body, creating a lower grade copy, and ultimately a separately functioning personality called the ego.

Chapter 22

The Rise and Fall of the Ego

O: It is the ego that most incarnates refer to as the "self," the "I am." Once the incarnate aspect starts to think along the lines of the ego being the self, everything else is created in separation from that which the incarnate aspect really is, an individualized unit of your Source Entity. Somewhere during the process of the creation of the ego it becomes self-aware, and recognizing its own transient position, does everything it can to perpetuate its existence, which includes "hiding away" the underlying knowledge of the True Energetic Self so that the aspect does not become self-aware while incarnate and dissolve the ego in the light of self-realization before the demise of the human body.

ME: And I suspect the ego is very active in ensuring that the aspect does not become self-aware?

O: It is very active, active to the point where it almost puts the longevity of the human body at risk at times.

ME: How does it do that?

O: By growing. You know about how egos grow, don't you?

ME: Yes, they grow as a result of the materialistic condition here; everything is designed and developed with the promotion of the self in mind, that one person is better than another.

O: Correct, and the ego feeds and grows at a phenomenal rate in this environment. Some egos will do anything and everything to become one step higher than those around it, and that means putting the human body in danger to gain increased levels of credibility at certain times.

ME: Recognizing that the ego is only a transient condition, and that most of us work with our egos as the mental representation of self, it is no surprise that we fear the demise of the human body, for when the human body dies the ego dies as well.

O: Yes, it does, but the information contained within it does not.

ME: And that's because of the constant stream of information back to the True Energetic Self, itself, during the lifetime of the human body.

O: Yes and no.

ME: Explain!

O: There are certain functions or memories that are specific to the ego and not the whole incarnate aspect.

ME: And these are?

O: The ego itself.

ME: I don't understand. If the ego is transient and the experiences of the incarnate aspect are constantly transmitted back to the True Energetic Self, then those memories and experiences that are experienced by the aspect within the human body are experienced by the ego and the True Energetic Self in parallel, surely.

O: Yes and no. All that is experienced is transmitted back to the True Energetic Self via the links to the incarnate aspect, but it is the "beingness" of the ego that is not, and this is because it is a false condition. It doesn't exist. Those experiences that are consistent with the ego and the True Energetic Self itself are transmitted as stated previously.

ME: You are suggesting that the "beingness" of the ego dissolves then, it dies, and so if an aspect relates to itself as the "beingness," the "personality" of the ego, then it dies with the ego.

O: That personality dies with the ego.

ME: So when the human body dies, if we relate to it and the ego too much, then we do actually die with it.

O: Yes and no.

ME: You really are trying to tie me in knots here.

O: Fun, isn't it. No, I am trying to make you look beyond this conundrum and see what the reality of incarnation is. Look, when an ego dissolves it is not a point of destruction. It is a point of re-assimilation. The ego was created out of the separation of the communicative ability of the incarnate aspect, or shard, resulting from low-frequency immersion. Even though it is separated out in this way, it is still part of the True Energetic Self. Or, if projected from the aspect itself, a shard. All that was the ego in isolation was created in isolation and so it remains in isolation until the demise of the human body. Upon the demise of the human body the energy that became the ego is re-assimilated back into the True Energetic Self as part of the aspect. Then and only then is the "beingness" of the ego, the essence of separation, integrated back into the aspect as an additional set of experiences. The personality dissolves but the essence of separation becomes one with the True Energetic Self.

Re-assimilation of the Incarnate Aspect with the True Energetic Self

ME: What is this essence of separation? It sounds to me like it is just another way of explaining individuality or personality.

O: No, it is a different thing altogether. The personality, the ego, cannot survive the re-assimilation process, for it is not part of that which was created by the True Energetic Self. In a higher-frequency incarnation, the ego cannot exist, or even be created, because the level of sustainable communication between the incarnate aspect and the projecting True Energetic Self is enough to maintain the integrity of the original aspect's knowledge of its true self. The essence of the separation, that which was experienced by that part of the aspect that remained in the energetic, the higher frequencies of the human body, those of the eighth, ninth, and tenth frequencies, remains as a true experiential memory set. The other side of the aspect, that which resided in the frequencies of the spirituophysical and gross physical, the seventh frequency and below, is passed on to the essence of separation expressed in the higher frequencies and is assimilated by the aspect as a whole, a "total" essence of separation.

Try to think of it in these terms. When the human body dies, the aspect and all of its parts, separate or integrated, are re-assimilated back into the True Energetic

Self. When this happens the process of re-assimilation dissolves the link between the essence of separation and the ego. The ego's personality created through separation is also dissolved. The memory set associated with the essence of being separated is not lost though, because it is in existence above and below the seventh frequency barrier.

ME: What you are suggesting then is that the experience, essence of separation, and any other memories are absorbed in a nonpersonal way, that being, it has no personality.

O: It has personality.

ME: Sorry?

O: It has the personality of the aspect and the True Energetic Self—that part of its energetic signatures that were there before incarnation and that will be there after incarnation.

ME: You mentioned personalities and not personality.

O: Yes, I did. If an aspect of the True Energetic Self has been used often enough, that is, if the energy set used to create an aspect has been used in the same configuration time after time because they have proven to be a successful combination, then that aspect also creates a personality. It is a personality within a personality, if you like.

ME: So the personality of the ego, what we think we are as human beings, is removed but the memory set is not.

O: No. What you think of your selves as human beings is not the personality of the ego. That is separate. This is what I have been explaining. The personality of YOU is a combination of everything, the aspect, the ego, the essence of separation, and the memory set. Only the ego dissolves upon the demise of the human body.

ME: Why does the essence of separation remain?

O: Because it is a function of memory.

ME: Got it. Does this also happen to a shard when it reintegrates with the aspect?

O: Not entirely. A shard is either a separation from the aspect in totality, just like the aspect is a separation from the True Energetic Self, or it is a linked "percentage" of energy from the aspect. Think of a drop of molasses dripping down from a spoon full of molasses. The molasses in the spoon is the aspect, and the drop is the linked percentage of energy of that aspect. In the example of the "shard in separation," the shard remains separate until the demise of the human body, which requires the shard to return to the creating aspect. But because it is separate it has to wait until the human body the creating aspect uses has demised as well. Only then can the shard reintegrate with the aspect simultaneously as it reintegrates with the True Energetic Self. With the linked shard, if the human body it is animating demises, it is reintegrated with the aspect simply because it wasn't separated from it. It would be like suddenly remembering a set of memories that you didn't know existed, or thought you had forgotten. In the event that the human body an aspect is animating demises before the bodies of any separate or linked shards are animating, then that aspect can adopt a partial re-assimilation with the True Energetic Self while leaving enough energy external to the True Energetic Self to allow the re-assimilation of the two types of shard at the points of the demise of their incarnations.

An aspect can, however, elect to terminate the link between its shards and their human bodies, should it decide to re-assimilate in full. It can also elect to wait for its shards as a non-re-assimilated aspect, only re-assimilating when the bodies of its shards demise naturally. Shards have the ability to re-assimilate with the aspect simultaneously as it reintegrates with its creating True Energetic Self.

ME: An aspect then, can actively "kill" the human bodies its shards animate at any time?

O: In essence, yes. It may sound hard and harsh, but it happens a lot. Mostly though, it is used when the aspect has finished its own incarnation.

ME: How does this work with a subincarnation?

O: There is no problem here simply because the subincarnation is a full incarnation with the body animated by an aspect that was previously animating the body in the primary incarnation. The body used in the primary incarnation is held in stasis and is therefore only reanimated when the body used in the subincarnation demises.

ME: OK, can you explain what happens to the incarnate aspect after the demise of the human body and at the point of re-assimilation with the True Energetic Self?

O: Let us first consider the aspect, for we also have to consider the shard as well. If the aspect has finished its own incarnation, and has no shards to re-assimilate, or the aspect has re-assimilated them either by terminating the links between its shards and their bodies, or has waited for them to re-assimilate naturally, it starts the re-assimilation process. From the perspective of the incarnation, the body demises and the aspect departs the body. This can be instantaneous or can take up to three days. The length of time required to disassociate the aspect from the human body is based upon the level of self-awareness of the aspect while incarnate. It is entirely possible for the aspect to leave the human body immediately upon its demise, re-assimilating with the True Energetic Self straight away. Some aspects take three days due to their ego trying to maintain its longevity, which is futile because both the association and the ego dissolve at this point.

Once the aspect is ready to re-assimilate with the True Energetic Self the total set of experiences (memories) are connected. In this process the aspect gains the memories of the True Energetic Self and the True Energetic Self gains the additional memories stored within the energies associated with the personality of YOU, the combination of everything, the aspect, the essence of separation, and the memory set of the incarnation—everything that is trapped in the lower frequencies of the human body.

Note again here that the memories are maintained but the personality created by the ego is not, so this gives the aspect a "no personality" condition, because the aspect refers to its personality as that of the ego—that is, until assimilation is completed, whereby the re-assimilated aspect takes on board the personality of the True Energetic Self once more. Consider it to be like losing your sense of humor but then gaining another much bigger one.

As the re-assimilation progresses, the experiences, the memories associated with the incarnation are presented to the True Energetic Self, and it evaluates their evolutionary content. This evaluation of these experiences are what mankind refers to as the events that take place in what is sometimes referred to as the "hall of memory," where the life is reviewed and the successes and failures noted. These are recorded against the energy set that is the re-assimilated aspect for future use or action when or if this energy set is used again in an incarnate condition. From the aspect's perspective, re-assimilation is like suddenly remembering a huge memory set, which is overlaid onto the most recent memories accrued via the latest incarnation. The life lived simply becomes a set of recent events in a huge pool of events experienced by the True Energetic Self and all of the aspects and shards previously employed, or still projected into, an incarnate condition.

The re-assimilation of the shard to the aspect is identical to the re-assimilation of the aspect to the True Energetic Self. It is just that it is a lower level down and needs to wait for the aspect to start the re-assimilation process or, as previously stated, has its incarnation terminated by the aspect. The linked shard has its incarnation terminated at the point of the demise of the aspect's human body, or again as previously stated; it is re-assimilated if the human body it was animating pre-demises the aspect's human body. Once the shard/s is/are re-assimilated with the aspect, either with the aspect in a pre-re-assimilated state or a partially re-assimilated state, the aspect can then start or finalize re-assimilation with the True Energetic Self.

ME: So the re-assimilating aspect doesn't lose its sense of self then?

O: No, it maintains this while gaining a much larger sense of self, one that is its "self" as a function of the True Energetic Self.

As I finished typing the information on the incarnate process given to me by The Origin I felt an overwhelming sense of understanding. This made sense. Everything spiritual mankind knew to date about the processes we went through before and after incarnation was really based upon an interpretation, which was itself based upon a human filter, hence all of the stories of near-death experiences and channelled information being similar to our Earthly environment, but with levels of higher-frequency functionality. I was very much aware though that we may decide to create such an Earth-based environment as a comfort blanket, a level of familiarity, which dissolves as we become more accustomed and accepting of our true state. I still felt though that there was more, much more to come but that that information would be in another series of dialogues, another book. My workload, it seemed, was stacking up!

Chapter 23

The Om—Revisiting the Uncreated

Creations (and Discovery of New Om)

FOR SOME TIME NOW I HAD BEEN thinking about the Om and *what they represented, specifically since I had received more information about them during my dialogue with The Origin on quantum theory and how it works within its area of sentient polyomniscient self-awareness. I also found myself reflecting periodically upon the information given to me by Source Entity Ten. And then there was the information on the Om I gained during the compilation of* The History of God, *which represented the start of my journey.*

The information I was gaining on these entities was sporadic, opportunistic, and almost given to me by luck. It was as if I were being spoonfed the information. That is not to say that all information is being spoonfed, but that I was being presented a paper trail to follow, a series of crumbs, where once in a while I would be presented with a bigger pile of crumbs and perhaps a new direction to look in. It was time, I thought, to gain more, hopefully, in-depth information about the Om. They were not specifically created by The Origin because they were essentially a byproduct of energetic recycling with the energies refusing to mix properly during the creation of the Source Entities, creating various versions of them. So, with all of this intention to discover more about the Om in hand I decided to ask The Origin, "Where do the Om fit into this?"

ME: Where do...?

O: You don't need to ask the question twice; I picked it up the first time. The Om are what was previously described in the dialogues with Hum, Source Entities One and Ten, and myself. I won't elaborate further in that direction because it would only lead to confusion. However, I will offer you some information that will give you a context to work with the next time you broach the subject of the Om.

ME: What are they if not pieces of energy lucky enough to become individualized and instantaneously sentient during the creation of the Source Entities?

O: Me.

ME: Just that?

O: Yes. Just as the Source Entities are smaller individualized parts of me and energetic mankind are smaller and individualized parts of Source Entity One that are also parts of me.

ME: I understand that, but I noticed that there was more in the "me" than just the recognition of the sentience structure/family tree, so to speak.

O: There is. The Om are special. They are not only rare, they are unique. That is, insomuch as I did not create them, they were/are a byproduct of creativity. I have not discovered them all—yet, even though I noticed their energy signature winking into existence during the creation of the Source Entities. But I have a feeling that this is about to change. You have created an intention.

ME: You know that there are more Om than you have communicated with?

O: Yes, but it is only a small number.

I was starting to receive an image of a small number of dust particles spread out within the infinite area of The Origin. Each particle represented a single Om. There was more to this image though; there was a finer level of dust, dust within the dust. It was almost like each particle of dust was itself created by a smaller more compact dust. This was a level of Om that was collectively unified—that being, the larger dust particle represented what I would recognize as a single Om, with the dust that was within being smaller Om creating a collective that was the larger Om. Are these a new Om? Are they the ones that The Origin had not yet communicated with? I was about to ask when The Origin, yet again, beat me to the question.

O: Ah! There they are. Yes, these are the ones not previously discovered, although I knew they were in existence.

ME: How could you not discover them but know of their existence?

O: It's all to do with "sentient weight," so to speak. I know that part of me, the Om, have full independence from me while within me. I know that the Om have certain energetic signatures and certain energetic weight, but the sentient weight I could detect did not equal the number of Om I had detected or communicated with.

Look, there are only five of them. They are in between the classifications you know as Non-Captive Om and Pure Om. They are still forming, so to speak, because they are performing a "hoovering up" function. The smaller dust is gravitating together as partial Om energy, that being, partial in the sense of the sentient weight, to create a single Om of enough sentient weight to place it above the Non-Captive Om category and below the Pure Om category. The dust could have gravitated together to create a single Om of "Pure" status, but it isn't doing that. Let me see. Yes, I have communication with them. They are some significant distance away from each other, although they are close in terms of my area of self-awareness, hence us seeing all five together, but they are far enough away to work in separation.

They are individually and collectively communicating with me now. By this I mean the "dust within the dust" is communicating collectively and the larger Om-sized particle is communicating individually. They tell me that the small Om dust particles were only in a certain location (sector) within me and they were spread out. There were small clouds of this dust, five of them, and that each of the dust particles within the clouds naturally gravitated toward the same energy signature of dust, so to speak. Each of them was and is set in their intention to become fully coadunate as a single larger Om. It was only when they had enough "density" of this sentient weight that they discovered each other doing the same thing. At this point in their coalescence it was almost too late to change the functionality of their plan to "become." They communicated with each other using the gaps in between Event Space and discovered that, although they could have changed their plans and become one large Om of the "Pure" category (they didn't know what the categories of Om were at this time) they actually liked what they were creating within themselves, they were happy to be smaller but have a peer group, to have company, and so they continued/are continuing with their collectively individual plans.

ME: What will they do? How long will it take them to finish the coadunation process to create the five single Non-Captive/Non-Pure Om?

O: They tell me that the process is based upon a certain level of energetic inertia and that it may take what you call millennia to finalize.

ME: I just received an image that these smaller dust particles are spread out over a distance of Parsecs, no, the equivalent of the area of the physical universe!

O: And just how small are those smaller dust particles in comparison to the area they occupy?

ME: Infinitely small from the imagery I have just been given.

O: And so now you know why I didn't detect them until now and why it will take some time to complete what they are doing. I am quite excited about the fact that I have five more Om within me.

ME: How come we just found them? How come you didn't find them on your own? Why is it always a function of me being in the right place at the right time? Am I inventing all of this?

I was starting to get a little paranoid about all of these coincidences.

O: In this instance you actually did provide the catalyst for their discovery. You are Om and you have an affinity for Om and as such the opportunity for discovering them was more likely to happen than with me. Although I am pleased to find their energy, I am also occupied with multiple tasks that mean that finding that minute missing group of energies with sentient weight was well down the list of my priorities. In fact, my use of Event Space told me that they would be discovered and that you would be party to that discovery.

I just like to keep these things quiet, to give you a little excitement in your dialogues with me.

I will let you into a little secret about the mechanics of what happened here. The five unformed Om we have just discovered were discovered by an intensely focused intent to know more about the Om. You desire to know more and so when I advised you of the possibility of more Om you broadcast a search based upon the detection of individualized Origin energy, Om energy.

ME: I don't feel like I did that.

O: No, you wouldn't, it was your True Energetic Self that made the search. Interested in what you were doing behind the scenes, so to speak, I sent a part of myself with your broadcast. I rode on the back of your intention to discover these Om which had more desire to discover Om energy than I did. So you are not fooling yourself, but in this instance you, your True Energetic Self, that is, had a major part to play.

ME: OK, I feel better now.

Every now and then I have to stand back and check myself out, to make sure I am not talking to myself. This was very definitely one of those times. I wondered what else I do in the background.

O: More than you can ever imagine while incarnate.

ME: I should know that you listen in to my thoughts.

O: Difficult not to, they are quite loud!

ME: What was the main reason for them being difficult to detect other than size and distribution?

O: They are currently in between Event Spaces. They did this naturally and without recognition, and so they were hidden due to not creating new Event Spaces as a result of them having the possibility of becoming five Om, a single Pure Om, or just staying as fragmented Om energy.

ME: You would have detected them earlier if they were within Event Space?

O: Yes, Event Space being a fundamental part of what I am, I am sensitive to its changes in parallelism, even though I tend to operate my own consciousness independently of it currently.

ME: What more can you tell me about the Om we are currently aware of?

O: As you are becoming aware, the Om are capable of many things, one of them, certainly with the Pure Om, being the capability of operating outside Event Space. That is why you were able to go on the Event Space "ride" with Source Entity Twelve. An entity can only do this if it has that inherent capability. All Source Entity Twelve was doing was taking you with it, and protecting the aspect of you that is projected within your physical body from the energetic shock. When disincarnate this would not be necessary.

As previously stated, the Pure and Non-Captive Om are independent of me, the Pure Om more so. The Non-Captive are limited in some respects to staying within the location of the Source Entity their energies were ejected/rejected from during the time when the Source Entities were discovering more about themselves through "play." Because the energies they were inevitably formed from was pure Origin energy it allows them to be both part of me while being independent of me, which includes the functions of being fully separate to being fully integrated and any level of this in between. They are truly versatile in this manner. Captive Om and Hybrid Om are not independent of me because of their closer association with a Source Entity. Although, Captive Om can operate in an independent fashion within the environment that is the Source Entity they are captive within.

In essence the Pure Om are smaller versions of me. They are the energy that was used with the intention to create another Origin, hence their full independence, for that was part of the programming of the energies assigned to be an Origin.

I have no control over the Om. Although, in reality I could recycle the energies that they are, reintegrating it back into the base energies of my area of sentient self-awareness. But, I do not wish to do this.

ME: Why would you not decide to recycle/reintegrate the energies that are the Om?

O: Because they are a conundrum and because they are a conundrum they serve a function. Because they are uncreated they interest me. All of them do.

ME: And I guess that is because even you were created by Event Space being selective in its application of parallel events in order to create a polyomniscient sentient being.

O: Correct. I wait to see what else can "become" outside of the intention to create.

ME: Tell me more about what the Om are, specifically the Pure Om.

O: They are me within me. If I were to say that they are, because of their heritage, fragments of my sentience, would that cause confusion?

ME: I don't think so. Please carry on.

O: I will explain nevertheless. When I created the intention to develop, to evolve in parallel, and thought of the possibility of the creation of twelve versions of myself, I didn't actually create twelve versions per se; I split off twelve segments of my sentient energies and removed the memories of being me from them. So the energies used in the Twelve Origins strategy weren't created either, they were just reassigned and relocated, and later, upon the failure of the strategy, they were recycled or re-assimilated. The Om energy is also uncreated because it is this same energy. Origin energy that is assigned as Origin energy—me—stays as such, so when the time came to be reassigned as Source Entity energy it rejected the assignation and stayed as it is, Origin energy. However, because it was distributed in an unequal way with the energies that were being assigned as Source Entity energy, that inequality resulted in the creation of the different types of Om you are now aware of.

There is something else though that has an important impact on why the Om are the Om. This is because their previous assignation remained as Origin energy with Origin functionality—so being mixed with energies that were assigned as a lesser function, because the Source Entities were located within my area of sentient self-awareness and given a purpose, the energies would not have mixed in harmony anyway. And so The Origin energy, when of the correct density, became independent sentient entities of Origin energy when released from my holding and creating energies. They could not be created because they were already me, but with the previous programming of their energies still in place they became sentient and individualized with all of the functions of a smaller version of me, within me, instantaneously.

ME: How can an Om be a smaller version of you? I mean, the Twelve Origins strategy failed because that which is you, the "all there is," cannot be created within the "all there is." Moreover, this would be the "all there is" within your area of sentient self-awareness.

O: Correct. Clearly the Om are not in that league, but they do have a microstructure. That is, it is a representation of that which is me within my area of sentient self-awareness. That being, they are similar to the Source Entities, which have a sentient self-aware energy with an individualized structure of a level that allows an environment to be present within them, should they wish to segmentate themselves in this way.

ME: If an Om is essentially a smaller version of you, within your area of sentient self-awareness and it has a structure similar to your own, how does that work with you, and what size are we talking about here? Are the Om really the same size as a Source Entity? And, if so, how does that work with an Om that wishes to experience or incarnate within the structure of a Source Entity?

O: That, my dear Om, is something that you should be able to answer for yourself.

ME: Touché.

Anatomy of an Om

At this point in the dialogue I decided to sit back a moment and let what was unfolding before me unfold some more. I was gaining some imagery of what the structure of an Om was. The Origin had clearly put this particular ball in my court for a reason. That reason I surmised was to make me access more of myself and find out for myself, through myself, rather than use The Origin as a third party. I sat back in my chair, which right now is a seat in an airplane bound for Tokyo, Japan. I like to use the "dead time" in a plane to allow me to catch up on my work, meditate, and absorb the energies associated with being above the Earth. It is rather liberating to note that, in this small aircraft, I am physically separated from the Earth, but not its weather systems. The turbulence we were experiencing was proof of that! Nevertheless it is a departure to being Earth bound and as such it gives me a boost, so to speak, in my ability to communicate with the greater reality. I let the imagery wrap around me and become as detailed as possible.

ME: Shall I explain what I am seeing here?

O: Yes, of course. That is the whole point of letting you have access to the information while still incarnate.

ME: Right. The Om are not as big as a Source Entity. That is from the point of view of sheer size of what I will call "physical" dimension versus energetic content within The Origin's, your, area of self-awareness. The Source Entities appear to me as spheres of energy within an unfathomably large area corresponding to your area of sentient self-awareness.

I have a dichotomy here though. The Om appear to be similar in size to say, an entity created by one of the Source Entities, but they are not. They are much larger.

I hesitate to say this, but they feel to me like a Tardis *(see the UK BBC TV show called Dr Who!)*. They are small but they are big. They contain all of the internal infrastructure of The Origin, of its area of sentient self-awareness, but they are within this area of sentient self-awareness. They are not like the entities described by Source Entity Six in *Beyond the Source, Book 1*, who existed within and without each other as part of the functionality of each other. No, they are a completely different animal in comparison. They have all of the structure of The Origin, you, from the perspective of the first twelve sections of its/your structure, and something else as well. But I just can't put my finger on what that "something else" is.

What I can see here are miniature versions of The Origin, of you. Ah! Now I see it. They are limited to that structure which "is" The Origin's, your, area of sentient self-awareness. They have no structure beyond that. But, in this "limited" structure they are more structured than any of the Source Entities either individually or together. The reason for this is the multiplication of the structure represented by the different levels, the twelve levels, by a factor of twelve each time. A Source Entity is limited to four levels, that is, frequency, subdimension, full dimension, and zone. This is why the Om can operate within the structure of The Origin, you; they are limited to the structure of your area of self-awareness. Beyond that they have no structure and therefore are not in the category of "all there is."

At this point I feel the need to refer the reader to the structure of The Origin described in chapter 8 in the section titled "I Gain a Description of The Origin's Structure" because in this instance this structure represents the structure of any of the Pure Om.

I suddenly feel the need to ask The Origin a question relating to the other categories of Om.

ME: If this is relative to the structure of Pure Om, how does this translate to the other types of Om?

O: It is only the Pure Om that have this characteristic.

THE HYBRID OM are mainly energy without structure. That is, they do not have the structure associated with my original energetic structure. They adopt the structure given to them by their creator and are therefore the same as any of the entities created by a particular Source Entity. Their structure is derived rather than inherited.

THE CAPTIVE OM do have some structure, but they are limited to the structure of the environment that they find themselves within. That can be one of two variants: the structure of the Source Entity they are captive within, or just the structure that their Source Entity created for their entities to work and evolve within. Source Entities have a maximum structural condition equal to four levels, Frequency through to Zone, and Captive Om assume the same. Their structure is not derived, or inherited; it is assimilated by exposure to their surrounding environment.

THE NON-CAPTIVE OM are a version of the Captive Om but with the advantage of having more energetic density than the Captive Om, hence, their being Non-Captive. They assume the same structure as the Source Entity they were supposed to be a part of when the energies I recycled were reassigned to create the Source Entities in totality.

THE NEW VERSION OF THE OM, those five Om that are currently under integration energetically, will have nine levels of structure when they finish their process of attraction and become five Om rather than Om "dust," so to speak—this being, "Frequency" through to "Totality." I will call them the **Intermediate Om** from now on. There will be a big leap structurally from the Non-Captive variant to the Intermediate variant. It is one that should not be ignored, for these Om will be important later on in my existence.

THE PURE OM, of course, have the lion's share of the structure. They have all of the structural characteristics of my area of sentient self-awareness. It is this reason that they can, and do, have full independence within me and are able to traverse all structural conditions within my area of sentient self-awareness, without hindrance or resistance. They can move around me by becoming part of me and transferring their very essence throughout the structure that they are, or that is within me. What's more, they can span the structure that is me either in totality throughout me, based upon their own density, of which is a limitation only in their ability to maintain their own integrity, or they can span my structure in a linear fashion, spreading themselves in one direction only, a straight line, so to speak, from "Frequency" through to "Margin."

A Pure Om could, should it so wish, create its own Source Entities or entities of similar ability within its own structures, or indeed within my own structure, such is the level of their inherited power/functionality. None to date have taken up this opportunity, however, and as stated in a previous dialogue, a large number have elected to not be part of the creation process because it creates responsibility for that which is created and therefore inhibits full independence.

Pure Om have the ability to separate out the detail of their structure and create a multiple focus of their attention to each aspect they separate out into. In essence they can position that part of themselves that is frequency based, within that area of my sentient self-awareness that is frequency based, that part of themselves that is subdimensionally based, within that area of my sentient self-awareness that is subdimensionally based, that part of themselves that is dimensionally based, within that area of my sentient self-awareness that is dimensionally based and that part of themselves that is zonally based, within that area of my sentient self-awareness that is zonally based, etc., etc., right up to the margins, the final structural component within my area of sentient self-awareness.

ME: For a moment I thought that the Om might be considered like a benign cancer, a nonfunctional part of the human body that can move around the body of its host without being attacked by the immune system because the body thinks it is part of it.

O: That may be one rather harsh way of thinking about the Om. But I would rather think of them as being free agents. A free radical in the literal translation of the words—free as in not being under my control or answerable to me, and radical meaning that they are not constrained by my demands and can therefore do anything they want either inside or outside the demands I made of the Source Entities, for example.

ME: Are you suggesting that you have no control over what the Om do?

O: No. I did not create them, so in theory I cannot recycle their energy, I cannot uncreate them. Clearly, I should be able to start from scratch in everything I do or have done because I created it. In the case of the Om though, they were a byproduct of a creative intention, not the actual creation arising from a creative intention.

ME: The energies that they are, were in the past, were given form through creative intention, because they were destined to be the Twelve Origins.

O: Yes, but that intention was withdrawn and the energies recycled/re-assimilated back into my base energy set. The only intention after that was to use those energies for the creation of the Twelve Source Entities. The fact that they separated out based upon energetic density is proof that they were, at that point, outside of my creative control. I will say it again: they were not created. They became "existent" as a result of the creativity process and not because of it.

ME: So the Om really do have a free rein, so to speak. They are totally autonomous from you.

O: Yes. And what's more I am happy with that statement. You see, the Om are special, they were unintentional and as a result they are unique. Let me explain it in another way. The Om are my back door to many of my higher functions. Because they are not constrained by the convention of my creativity, desires, and thought processes they are able, should they so wish to do so, to perform a function within me that would, for the want of a better word, be adverse to my strategic plans for personal evolutionary progression. They can do that which is both unwanted and unexpected in light of my evolutionary progression. They can be the "Black Op's" so to speak, performing those experiments that neither I want to do, and nor do I want them done by any of my Source Entities and their creations.

ME: Do they do what you call "Black Op's?" I mean, all of a sudden you are painting rather a grim picture about the Om. I am not sure if I am comfortable about this, at all.

O: You have nothing to worry about. Although the Om are fully independent of me, they are still quintessentially part of me, and they know this. And, to answer your question, no, to date they have not performed any task that can be described in this way. Except, that is, when an Om decides that it will not enter into the evolutionary cycle through the use of creativity. This one choice is one that approximately half of the Pure Om have chosen as their path, for they know that creativity creates responsibility, for that which they have created, and have responsibility for, ties an Om down.

I Find Out That I Am a Bit of a Maverick

ME: Did I elect to be external to the creativity process?

O: You, my dear Om, are a strange fish, for you move in and out of creativity but negate to assume responsibility for what you do. You break the rules, if indeed there were rules, and this is why you are where you are now. You decided to enter into the creativity process through being incarnate within the environment of the Source Entity you call "One" for its own, and of course my, evolution. You tinker, so to speak; you see how you can change the direction of that which is around you and move on when it is completed, whatever the outcome. And then, you move on to something else.

This felt right to me. All my life I had the feeling that I would kick something off and when it was "up and running" I would administer to what was created, let others assume responsibility, or even let them take the credit, admittedly sometimes begrudgingly (the human condition can be such a problem), and then move on to the next piece of work. The work, by the way, would always be for the benefit of others in some way, shape, or form. What I was noticing, though, was that I was staying "with it" more and more with each piece of work. That being, I appeared to be assuming responsibility for what I had started for longer periods of time before moving on to the next project, so to speak. Was I becoming attracted to what I was doing? Or, was there something else going on?

O: You are starting to see the beauty in ownership, not that you are going to change your ways. But you are experimenting, tinkering, in the ownership experience.

ME: Does this explain why I have mixed feelings about this work, the work I am doing now?

The feeling of wanting to retire and do nothing on a beach all day was compelling, especially when one is always occupied with too much to do and not enough time to do it in. I have found that all through my life I have been operating in "catch up" mode. But what I am doing now is different. I felt a need to override the retirement feelings and finish what I am doing. That I would be doing this for the rest of my incarnate existence was something that I had accepted a couple of years ago, but it was good to see where the desire to "spin the plate" and move on without feeling the need to keep spinning the plate had come from. I felt like I was breaking out of a mould, that I had changed somehow, that I was becoming more responsible for my actions.

O: This is the great change in you, but it is not one that will be projected beyond this incarnation, for that is not what you are about. Rest assured that you will see this one out, that you will be supportive to those that need support, the teacher to those who need teaching, the leader for those who need leading, and the changer of paradigms for those who need a paradigm shift. You will also provide a new basis for personal progression. This you know. You have shown people that they do not need to study for years and years to achieve connectivity with their True Energetic Self, their wider environment, and their creator and that they can, through you, jump on to the fast track and achieve liberation from the physical while still being of the physical. This is what you are "tinkering" with in this incarnate existence. This is why you are here. To see if you can break the boundaries set by others and achieve in one lifetime what others needed several to do, to see if you can make your students achieve in a few short days what other teacher students take a lifetime to achieve.

ME: Now you are buttering me up.

O: Not in the slightest. I am merely showing you what you are and what you are doing. In a lot of respects you are a "Maverick." You are doing your own thing, you are not attracted to the norm, irrespective of whether it is rule, convention, convenience, president, logic, common sense, or otherwise. And that is what makes you a strange fish. You are unique. All other Om have taken the opportunity to be similar to one another, whether it be in the way they enter into the creativity process, or not, as the case may be. Either way, they have made a "tick box" choice, they have gone this way or that. Irrespective of what they do after this primary choice, they have gone with the consensus. You have not. You are the balance, you are both.

ME: This is all starting to feel rather contrived to me, like I am something special when in real terms I am not.

O: No, you are not something special. You are just being you, rather than being led or influenced.

ME: You make this sound like the Om are actually not very capable beings, that they are just the same as incarnate mankind, needing to go with the majority, of being part of the group or a group, that they need to be part of something.

O: Being part of "something" is a fundamental expression of the need for communion with one's creator. All entities have this in-built desire, even the Om, irrespective of whether or not they find themselves as far away from other Om as they can possibly get. You on the other hand can take it or leave it. You do not seek communion, nor do you desire or need communion. This is why you do what you do.

ME: If I don't need communion or indeed seek it, why am I working as an incarnate on this planet, which forms part of the low-frequency aspect of the structure of the multiverse Source Entity One created?

O: Because you are seeing if you can make a major change in the direction of an incarnate civilization by using the minimum of training. No other teacher has achieved this to date.

ME: I don't believe it. Surely Jesus, Mohammed, The Buddha, Krishna, Babaji, Paramahansa Yogananda, and, I have no doubt, countless others who are not remembered by recent history, have all achieved this. Just look at what they have done for incarnate mankind.

O: Well, you do have one point in your argument. That is that once one of your students has achieved what you want them to achieve you expect them to practice the techniques and personalize the techniques for the rest of their incarnate existence. This is the same for all teachers.

ME: Why wouldn't a student want to continue practicing the technique taught them when they are exposed to a reality greater than that presented to them while in the physical?

O: Because the physical is intoxicating; it is an attraction, a light to the moth. This is why the others demanded dedication before achieving the experience of being exposed to the greater reality. There is a different epoch on the Earth now. It is one of instant gratification, and that is where you come in. You have decided to move away from what you have been exposed to all your incarnate existence, that one must show devotion and dedication to achieve so-called enlightenment, and that this MUST take years in order for the teacher to check out the integrity of the individual. You can give them enlightenment now. All they need to do is spend a couple of days with you, do some homework, spend another day with you, and they have it—instant enlightenment. How you do this is by taking advantage of the newly acquired frequencies the Earth is currently enjoying and linking your students into it. You are using the teacher-student relationship to its maximum condition. That is why some of your readers have reported energy spikes, or information downloads as a result of buying your books, either the physical or paper versions. You, your True Energetic Self, that is, is providing a shortcut.

ME: But isn't that what all teachers do for their students? Isn't this what teachers are here for?

O: Yes, but you are giving it to them on a plate, so to speak. They get to experience the greater reality faster, far faster than ever before. You are taking advantage of the higher frequencies and linking them into it, and for them, their creator, Source Entity One. The existing train of thought is that a student MUST earn the right to experience the greater reality, and to some extent you do ask them to earn it. But they are rewarded faster, much faster with you than with the traditional ways.

ME: I see. In a lot of respects it fits in with the current "I want it now!" philosophy.

O: Yes, but this link was not a strategic decision. It just happened to be a compatibility that happened in parallel with this particular Event Space.

ME: I don't remember any such strategy, apart from having a lifelong feeling that I had something important to do, and now I know what it is.

O: No, YOU won't. It was your True Energetic Self that made the decision to see what happened to incarnate mankind if an aspect of itself, YOU, introduced a fast-track route to enlightenment via an ordinary everyday person, using ordinary everyday terminology. What's more, you now have help.

ME: Who from?

O: Another aspect of your True Energetic Self, the one you call Anne, the incarnate you married.

My Deceased Wife Is Me!

ME: Hold on, are you suggesting that my dear wife, Anne, was/is an aspect of my True Energetic Self?

O: Yes. Do you not notice that she gave you the incentive to go in certain directions, to do certain things, to achieve other things, things that you may not have been interested in had you not been her partner?

ME: Yes, thinking about it she motivated me in ways that were out of context with my personality. I was inspired by being in her very presence. In a lot of respects I was playing catch-up with her. It was like she was living in perfection but I wasn't. I strived to be her equal. She was my moderator, my reason to be, my link with the Earth.

O: Do you not remember a dialogue nine years ago where you recognized that there are three main forces in the multiverse created by Source Entity One, Power, Wisdom, Love, and that an entity cannot be successful unless it operates in each of these three forces in equality.

ME: Yes, I do. Wow, it was a long time ago.

O: Well, you had a full share of power and a half share of wisdom. Anne had a full share of love and a half share of wisdom. Together, while incarnate, you were a force to be reckoned with; now that Anne is back in the energetic she has a full share of love and wisdom. This balances out your full share of power and half share of wisdom, for the level of raw power you have needs a significant level of wisdom and love to ensure it is used in the correct way.

Things were starting to make sense here. My wife of nearly twenty-five years, Anne, was the only person who really understood me. She knew where I was coming from in all of my ideas and discussions on metaphysics and the greater reality. Although she naturally leaned toward the "love" side of metaphysics she understood what I was talking about, not most of the time, but all of the time. I had felt comfortable with Anne in a way that I was unable to be with anyone else. It was like we were one being. I know that many people can refer to this feeling about their partner, but I really did feel that we were different somehow. The true understanding of being a soul mate, an aspect projected from the same True Energetic Self working with another aspect projected from the same True Energetic Self in an intimate relationship was the only way I could reconcile how we were together. Anne trusted me with her very existence; she knew I could fix anything. Except, that is, her brain tumor. "Don't mess with my brain tumor," she told me one morning when I was checking her out energetically in late 2003, a couple of months after her diagnosis. "Why not?" I said, "Don't you want it healed?" "Yes," she said, "but not in that way." Throughout the following years we worked on metaphysical activities, specifically those after my attunement in Sweden, and Anne accepted healings from me. But I always knew that I was not being allowed to access the energies surrounding the manifestation of the tumor. Anne trusted me with her life, and I always projected an aura of energy that everything was OK. I heard her thoughts as well: "If Guy is OK and he is not concerned, then everything is OK and I should not be concerned." This continued right into the period when the tumor activity resulted in her needing chemotherapy. If I was by her side, all was in order. This continued right until the end of her physical life. Imagine, then, my confusion when Anne, that person who was my true soul mate, left me still incarnate, with apparently decades of life left. (According to one of my many premonitions, which included my being on my own later in life, and my own death scene, I had always imagined we had more years to go. Clearly this was a form of denial.) She had been my main focus, my main motivation, encouraging me to achieve certain things necessary to ensure that I was self-supporting and self-sustaining, to have a growing audience, to get to where I am now. She had been my stepping-stone, my springboard. She had done her job, and now it was time to return to our True Energetic Self. Anne, as with everything she did, had been of significant service during her incarnation, especially with me and as such, I noted, she had negated any karma that she could have been affected by, by her incarnation. This was specifically noted in the way she finally departed, any remaining karma was "wrung" out of her. She left the physical "karma free."

However, her work with me, it would seem, was not finished, and I started to notice things happening around me that could only be associated with having help from "behind the scenes." I was very much starting to recognize that everything that had and was happening in and around me was planned, agreed, and being actioned as I type. For those of you who are conversant with the ways of the greater reality, you will recognize that nothing I have said is either new or radical knowledge. It's just that recognizing it in one's own life is sometimes difficult to do. The physical aspect of what we are from a transient perspective always manages to get in the way. I very much wanted to discuss this information with The Origin before moving on to my next subject, which, dear reader, I was having trouble starting. It's at these times that I realize that the information about to be discussed is difficult at best, and I was very much aware that The Origin was allowing this little digression to take place to allow me to be "attuned" with the subject and its associated energies. The subject I was currently on however was in the "now" and The Origin was keen to finish this subject and move on.

O: I can see that there is confusion in you.

ME: You can see it; of course you can. The confusion is, how can Anne be beloved of the Om as an aspect of me when I was supposed to be the only Pure Om incarnate?

O: Simply because other Om that are incarnate are either hybrid or captive. Most though are hybrid in the Earth plane. Also, together Anne and Guy still equal one.

ME: Is this a function of duality?

O: No, it's a function of you, your True Energetic Self. Irrespective of how many aspects you projected it would still equal one Pure Om for there is only one Pure Om that has decided to enter into the incarnation cycle. Note though, the aspect of you that was Anne has returned to a point closer to your True Energetic Self while still in a level of contact with the physical universe. There is now truly only one aspect of Pure Om incarnate on the Earth. Note again, though, that the "Anne" aspect IS active in the work you agreed to do from the energetic perspective, working with the guides and helpers of those who need to, or agreed to be part of, the work you are doing. Your work is important, because it is stripping away a lot of the rose-tinted descriptions of spirit, showing it in a more basic light, one that allows an expansion of the thought processes without being encumbered by unnecessary padding.

ME: Thank you. Getting back to your description of why, even when multiple aspects of my True Energetic Self are projected into the physical, this is classified as only one of me, how does this relate to other incarnates? Is it always only classified as one entity rather than many, the many being based upon the number of aspects being projected by the True Energetic Self?

O: It is only ever classified as one, irrespective of the energy type of the True Energetic Self. It is just that mankind thinks of itself as being the incarnate and that the other aspects associated with the True Energetic Self, whether incarnate or disincarnate, are separate entities. Hence, the descriptive thought process that incarnate mankind adopts can be described as being "there are many aspects of me" making the "self" a multiple function centered on the incarnate, rather than the descriptive thought process being correctly stated as "I am an aspect of me" making the "self" a singular function centered on the True Energetic Self.

ME: That makes a lot of sense. I was having some concerns over the information I was receiving and was able to understand. I had a conflict of information. On one side I was aware that I was the only Pure Om incarnate, disregarding those Hybrid Om who are incarnate, and on the other hand I was picking up that Anne was also Pure Om. So how could there only be one? Now I know, we are both aspects of the same Om entity, we were separately together.

I have another question though.

O: Carry on; you are on a voyage of personal discovery here.

ME: I have memories of a couple of incarnations and some have been with Anne. She also remembered some of them. She also knew that we had some karma to clear between us. How does that work if we are aspects of the same True Energetic Self? Additionally, I have another conflict of information about how many times I have incarnated. I am picking up both one and circa thirty-six around the physical universe. *(I was starting to become aware that the direction I was going in would be addressed in a different dialogue in a different book. One I was told to write after this one—for this, dear reader, I apologize, but somehow it seemed relevant right now, in this text.)*

O: It was not so much karma between you but a conflict of interest between two personality aspects of the same entity, which could only have happened in the incarnate state. It took a couple of Event Spaces to resolve.

As for your number of incarnations, it is both one and the number you stated. But they have not been done in a linear way; they have all been experienced at the same time. You, your True Energetic Self, that is, used Event Space to experience all those existences at the same time, energetically. To achieve this, your True Energetic Self projected enough aspects of itself into a known number of Event Spaces in parallel to allow it to experience everything it needed for the work it wanted to do, in one go, so to speak. In essence all of them are happening now, in a one-off condition, hence your conflict. You have a feeling of a number of incarnations, and only one. You have experienced, are experiencing, will experience, have done, are doing, and will do everything right now.

ME: Isn't that the same for all entities though? Isn't everything happening in parallel?

O: Yes, but as a function of each aspect. This is called "linear parallelism." Linear parallelism is where Event Space is created through the actions of an entity. It is due to the dualistic conditions of possible possibilities. What you, or should I say, your True Energetic Self has done, is invoke Event Space for your own/its own need to accelerate the knowledge and experience function to that of an entity experienced in participating in the incarnate cycle. This is called "instantaneous spherical parallelism."

ME: I am being a little bit picky here, but wouldn't spherical parallelism be the next logical step? *(This description just came to me.)*

O: Yes, but that is a function of all Event Spaces specific to an entity being created through the dualistic condition in parallel, and not the entity itself actively invoking

Event Space to achieve a known task or function, such as an instantaneous spherical parallel environment.

ME: Based upon this then, it is possible to be experiencing your first and your latest incarnations concurrently.

O: Yes, it is, and that is what you, that is, your True Energetic Self, is doing right now.

ME: And that includes all other aspects projected from the True Energetic Self.

O: Of course, for it is the use of these other aspects within the invocation of Event Space in this way that creates the parallelism that is classified as "instantaneously spherical"—spherical of course relating to the holographic rather than the solid sphericality, for that would put it under the purely "spherical" classification.

This was good. It cleared up a lot of areas of conflict for me. Being analytical by nature and training, inconsistency is the route to inaccuracy and so seeing how the supposedly inconsistent information I was receiving was made consistent by simply understanding a new, that is, new to me, concept was gratifying to say the least. Before I moved on to the next subject though I just had one more question to ask. It was one that I had asked before but needed to gain a better understanding of. It was based upon the survival of the personality of the aspect after reintegration with the True Energetic Self.

The Survival of the Personality of the Aspect

ME: I know we have discussed this before, but I want to ask about the personality of the aspect and how it survives when the aspect is reintegrated with the True Energetic Self.

O: Firstly, the aspect is not the current personality; the current personality is a function of the ego. Secondly, the personality of the aspect is the accumulation of all the egoistic and energetic experiences accrued over the total number of incarnate opportunities, together with the interim/pre-/post- energetic experiences. It is also a function of the wisdom accrued when being allowed to work with certain levels of power.

The aspect's personality is therefore a subpersonality of the True Energetic Self which survives both the demise of the incarnate human vehicle and the reintegration of the energy, called the aspect, after the demise of the human vehicle. As a subpersonality it is both integrated with, but separated from, the overall personality of the True Energetic Self. As such it can be called upon to be projected into another human vehicle, whenever its particular personality and skill set is required, to perform a certain task while incarnate. Think of it in terms of a series of skill-based memories that one invokes when exposed to, and has to deal with, an experience that has a similar or same signature, so to speak, as one previously experienced. The memories are used as a navigational medium, allowing you to work with that experience in the most efficient way possible. Now think of these memories as having the ability to accrue additional data, as a result of similar or same interaction/self-awareness, and that they are referred to by the True Energetic Self as a fast-track method of navigating an experience, using relative or related memory-based experiences, rather than experiencing that which is presented to the True Energetic Self for the first time. Now consider each memory set as an energy of specialized memory-based experience that is stored within the True Energetic Self and is called upon as required and projected into an incarnate vehicle when a certain type of experience is desired. Now consider that this energy set is allowed to expand, grow, and become independent while integrated with the True Energetic Self. That this energy set can, and is, projected into an incarnate vehicle when its memory-based skill set is required, and that it can be described as an aspect of The True Energetic Self in its own right.

This memory set is the aspect, and as such it maintains its growth and personality independently within the energy that is the True Energetic Self. That is how the aspect "becomes" what it is. That is how the aspect maintains its usefulness, and therefore its individuality while integrated with the True Energetic Self; it is maintained by an ever-growing memory of experiences individual to the aspect. It becomes a specialized energy. And this, my dear Om, is the same for all entities created either by me or any of my Source Entities.

ME: Based upon this the aspect grows in stature the more it is used, gaining more data and experience every time the True Energetic Self selects that aspect for an incarnation or other role.

O: Correct, and this is how the personality of the aspect is preserved.

ME: Is it possible for an aspect to be used so much that its personality becomes the dominant personality within the True Energetic Self? That is, it becomes the main personality of the True Energetic Self?

O: No, because the personality of the True Energetic Self is the dominant personality. The dominant personality grows with the inclusion of new experiential data from ALL of the aspects and shards that are associated with it and of course its own work. And so, it is always significantly greater than any or all of its aspects. Don't forget that any experiential data or memories that are accrued by a shard are accrued by the aspect projecting the shard. The shard itself does not retain them because the shard is not perpetuated as a personality within the aspect.

ME: Why not? I would have thought that the aspect–shard relationship would have mirrored the True Energetic Self–aspect relationship.

O: No.

ME: Why not?

O: Because a shard is a function of the aspect from a lower energetic perspective, one that does not allow the possibility of individualization within the main body of energy that is the aspect. That being, the shard simply does not have the resolution necessary for it to retain any personality accrued as a result of it being projected into an incarnate opportunity. The aspect records everything and maintains everything and in turn this is recorded and maintained by the True Energetic Self. The issue here is that the aspect has the resolution, and the authority assigned to it, by the True Energetic Self, to become individualized within the boundaries of its energy. The shard has neither.

ME: Based upon that, would an incarnate that has a shard projected into it (as its soul) be any less of an individual in comparison to an aspect that is projected into an incarnate vehicle (as its soul)? For example, would there be a difference that can be seen by an aware observer and therefore be a key observational point to look for when ascertaining whether or not an incarnate individual is occupied by a shard or an aspect?

O: Yes, the shard-occupied incarnate vehicle would appear to be a poor performer, a slow learner, and maybe even difficult to get on with, even though they are pleasant. They will have difficulty in relating to others.

ME: Would they be the same as back-fill people?

O: They would not present the same type of personality as back-fill people because they inherently are attached to an entity that is a much-higher-quality energy. Although they may be a lesser-quality energy when compared to an aspect, they are a higher-quality energy when compared to the energy of the entity projected into a back-fill person. In fact, the difference is marked. Back-fill people tend to be drawn toward the lower functions of the lower frequencies when incarnate, such as aggression, materialism, ego, and status, whereas the incarnate that is occupied by a shard is more likely to be a quiet and passive individual with little or no personal drive/motivation, ambition, desire to lead, or be part of a group. They can be classified as being low achievers, people who are content with their lot in life and have no desire to take themselves outside of their comfort zone. In fact, you would be excused for saying they are the type of people who are "not quite there." With all this in mind though they are usually very pleasant people to be around.

ME: So when their physical body dies their personality dies with it?

O: No, the overriding personality of the shard is that of the aspect and, as with the aspect in relation to the True Energetic Self, the memories and experiences accrued by the shard are inherently those of the aspect and retained within the aspect. They are then shared with the True Energetic Self. The ego-based personality in both the shard and the aspect are dissolved upon the demise of the human body.

ME: This clarifies a lot for me. Thank you.

Chapter 24

The Structure between Structure

THIS HEADING HAD BEEN BOUNCING around my head for some days now, and it was starting to come into focus as a subject I should be discussing with The Origin. I had noticed that I was becoming somewhat saturated and was therefore having difficulty in focusing on the genre of the subject The Origin was undoubtedly leading me into discussing with it. I had noticed that we had digressed a little, at least in my mind, from the main subject of talking to The Origin about The Origin and not about local subjects that could or should have been asked to Source Entity One. Having said that though the information was not only interesting, and essential, but it also proved that The Origin was as in touch with the workings within the depths of one of its Source Entities as it was with its own work. It intrigued me to be in the position of discussing subjects with The Origin that were not really its first point of interest— that was why it created the twelve Source Entities. They were created to delve into those subjects that The Origin felt were best left to autonomous functions of itself—the Source Entities and their smaller creations. As I was typing these thoughts I was starting to see a structural image come into my mind. This was a sure sign that The Origin was down-loading information to me and was close to continuing our dialogue. I settled down to allowing the energies of The Origin to flow over me and the dialogue to commence.

O: So you want to know about the structure behind the structure.

ME: It wasn't something I had planned, but for a couple of days now I have been thinking about how I can move behind the structure of the multiverse Source Entity One created. I have also been thinking about those entities that are the maintenance entities for the structure of the multiverse and how they ensure that the evolutionary efficiency of the multiverse is kept at its best. These entities, some of which I have met in human form, also

343

move between the structure of the multiverse. This is a function they need to have to allow them to move quickly from one maintenance point to the next. I simply saw this as a function of you, because it is essentially you, and that to enable these entities and myself to move around the structure in this way there must be another level of structure within you, and therefore the Source Entities, that I have not seen while in the physical and therefore discussed with you yet.

O: Well, you are right to consider discussing this substructure, but you also need to note that there is a substructure for all of the levels within me.

ME: As you were saying, I gained an image of what this structure is like. But I can only describe it in a metaphoric sense.

O: Good, let me see if you can understand what you have been given. Tell me what you see.

ME: It appears to be an incomplete level of structure. It's just like a spider's web but in an extremely fine/gossamer sense. It's a point-to-point structure that allows access to only a select number of points within your structure. It's almost as if it is connected to certain, what I will call *nodes.* These nodes are the crossing points between the divisions within levels of your structure, and those points are where the highest point of one level finishes and the lowest point of the next level up starts. But wait; as I zoom in to the structure I see a finer structure behind it. This finer structure joins up the divisions between the levels and allows access to their crossing points. And there's more. As I look into this structure I see that the point-to-point structure is not only a framework that allows access to these nodes as a node-to-node link, but it also has another structure behind it that allows movement beyond the node-to-node methodology, it actively misses out nodes. In fact, I can see one of these point-to-point, node-to-node links becoming separated from the structure and changing its node-to-node connectivity from one pair of nodes to another. Hold on. This structure isn't static at all. Now I am confused, I can't call it structure now because it has all changed in front of my very mental eyes. And now, it's something else, still performing the same duty, but the structure is completely different to that which I saw a moment ago. Is this structure adapting to the requirements of maintenance entities?

O: Oh, very well done. You are nearly there. Look a bit deeper and tell me what you see now.

ME: Ah! I see. What I am seeing is like the vapor trails that an airplane leaves behind when it flies through denser air, compressing it and making a localized cloud specific to the direction of travel of the airplane. This isn't structure; it's direct lines of travel created by the maintenance entities themselves specifically and only for the duration of their movement from one point to another. If they need to move back, then that direct line of travel remains in place. But if they don't, then it dissolves leaving no trace of where they have come from or where they went to. They are creating the structure to suit their own needs in moving from point to point, node to node.

Ah, yes. This of course is the so-called structure behind the structure of Source Entity One's multiverse and not you per se, although it is in reality.

O: Correct. This is how my substructure is formed when it is under the control of a Source Entity. It is adapted by the maintenance entity itself to suit what it needs to do and what it needs to do to work with the area of structure it needs to work with. Now look at the structure in between the Source Entities. In this area you will see a different substructure.

ME: I see a sort of framework. It's linking the Source Entities to you. It's almost like they are suspended like puppets on a string, the string just existing. Like the "Indian rope trick" it starts in free space and then joins the outer edge of the energies that are associated with a particular Source Entity. As that Source Entity moves around that area of yourself that you have assigned to them, not that they move much, most are static, those lines of structure, the string if you like, moves with them, the ends of which move with them and don't stay put at a point of supposed origin. It's like the rope in the Indian rope trick is actually joined to another microscopically thin rope that holds the upper end of the rope in place, so although the top of the rope appears to move location with the movement of the Source Entity in question, it actually still remains connected to the substructure that is you.

O: Correct. Look closer. What else do you "see?"

ME: I am seeing an energetic lattice. It's ... it's beautiful beyond belief. It's intoxicating looking at it *(I am crying with joy!)*. All the colors of the rainbow and all of the intermediate colors/chroma, including myriad pastels and shades of lightness that the human eye could not possibly see or even decipher.

I wondered how I am able to decipher them with my mind's eye.

O: You are interpreting them, not deciphering them. That is a different thing. You simply don't have the capacity while incarnate to appreciate all that is being presented to you. Consider it a truncated version, one that you can work with while understanding, at the same time, the vast variation in the colors. Please continue in your narration.

ME: It's difficult, it's so ... it's so ... "emotional". It's like being home all warm and cozy with the one you love *(more tears of joy)*. This is me linking into you as part of me, but with the reality that I am a smaller part of you. The light pulsates, radiates and vibrates, all aspects of this light is a function of your substructure.

I mentally zoom out, moving a distance away from the image that is presented to me and look at the connectivity of the Source Entities with the substructure of The Origin from farther away.

They do move, and they are constantly connected to you. The movement with most of them is minimal— granted, but it is movement within the area you assigned to them nevertheless. Each Source Entity appears to be suspended by their connectivity, with each line of connectivity being part of an energetic lattice that is specific to the data being transmitted or received. Every line of connectivity being used to its maximum capacity with new lines of connectivity being added as the genre of data changes. Everything is dynamic, everything is changing, everything is adapting to what is new and assimilating it with what is current or old. As I look at this image it more and more looks like the image one sees when looking at the hollow sphere on a Van der Graaff generator, with the electricity arcing across from the sphere, the sphere being the "positive" of the generator, to the "negative," which can be represented by lead glass to gain an overall three-dimensional series of multiple arcs rather than a single arc. The point of connectivity would be represented by each arc, the movement of the arcs being the natural flow of connectivity between a Source Entity and The Origin's substructure.

A Source Entity moved from its current location as if in answer to my next question, which would be; how would a Source Entity's connectivity be affected by its movement?

The Source in question moved and the lines of connectivity moved like "potential" (voltage) arcing from the positive sphere of the Van der Graaff generator to multiple negative sides, with the negative sides moving in distance and location in relation to the positive. It looked like a series of electric hairs disconnecting and reconnecting to the uncountable "light" lines of the lattice. All connections were, from my perspective, in three-dimensional relief with the connectivity all around the Source Entity I focused on.

O: The connectivity is not just on the periphery of the Source Entity you are looking at. It is also within it. Take a closer look.

ME: OK, I am seeing the Source Entity in what I would call a "clear" transparent condition, I can see within and without it just like seeing an MRI scan where everything is "see through".

The connectivity is not just on the outside of the Source. It's on the inside as well. This is amazing to witness. The

Source Entity appeared to move through the substructure of The Origin and connect with it on all levels. The Source Entity I am observing is totally permeable, its essence is its individuality, and its individuality is the thing that separates it from the energies that are The Origin, its structure, and its substructure.

Why have I not seen this level of detail before? I was under the impression that the Source Entities were "Energy Balls" that were allowed to wander in free space. This tells me that there needs to be a whole new level of understanding about how you and your creations interface with you.

O: There is more, much more, but what you have seen here is, to quote you, not even a scratch on the surface. I have varying levels of structure, and every entity that I have ever created is inherently part of it.

Every entity is part of me and as part of me every entity is inherently an integral part of my structure. All creations are integral, they are not separate, and they cannot be separate.

ME: I thought that you had created an empty space for the Source Entities to exist within, that there would be "No Thing" in the area that they work within.

O: From the limited perspective of incarnate mankind the answer would be yes. But it is only when an incarnate entity is able to progress beyond convention that it is able to take on board new information or concepts. In this instance the concept incarnate mankind uses is the need for both individuality in "personality" and individuality in "body" born from energetic separation. In previous dialogues you have grasped the concept that individuality is not necessarily a function of physical separation—that being, an individual personality or intelligence, sentient or not, together with an individualized body of energy. This is not a necessary requirement or need. Nor is it the norm from my perspective.

ME: Are you saying that all entities, irrespective of their creator, creative ability, and evolutionary content, are all just an aspect of individualization within you, and that this individualization is independent of energy—that being the individuality is not assigned to a particular "body" of energy.

I used the words "body of energy" here because it will give my readers a datum to work with because the idea of, let me say, individual intelligent sentience that is independent of energy of any sort will be a "stretch" in understanding, to say the least.

O: Correct. There is no entity within me that has a body of energy that is specifically and exclusively assigned to the individuality that is them. All entities I created, that have been created by my creations, or have been created as a function of incompatible energies that already had a function and personality assigned to them for a period (Om), have individuality as a result of my intellect being "separated out" specifically for the use of an individual personalized sentience that is uniquely applied to, or commandeers, a known set of energies.

ME: What you are telling me then is that all entities are pure intellect and that they are fully independent of energy— of any sort!

O: Correct. Why are you surprised at this?

ME: I don't know. I suppose I thought that this level of existence was particular only to certain "high-level" entities that existed within you, and some others that have been described in my dialogues with Source Entity One.

O: Wouldn't that have been the correct example to follow? This thought of yours is an indication that energy was only a "vehicle" of sentience? It is pointing in the right direction, it is a signpost.

ME: Yes, but as you suggest, most of what I/we think about is human-centric, and we are limited by this as a datum, a start point, for our intellect to work with. We are limited from the start by our current physical condition; it preprograms us into a certain way of thinking.

O: I can see that. I find it most amusing. No, I jest. This limitation is now being lifted and as such you—incarnate mankind, that is—are being exposed to higher levels of the truth.

I will refocus on the more important aspect of our dialogue though, the description of my substructure.

What you "saw" or "visualized" is only part of the information you need to broadcast. The image of a Source Entity in "see through" or "clear relief" passing through my substructure is a good example of how a Source Entity, or any entity within a Source Entity, moves through me.

My substructure, at this level, is purely a communication medium. There are other levels of substructure, and they have different functions, such as providing the links between similar or same energies to keep their basic components aligned allowing all entities to "pass" through these in the same way as the lines of communication.

We Are Beings of Pure Individualized Sentience Who Commandeer Energy

ME: What makes an entity the way it is in the first place? I mean, how are they identified or created as an entity?

O: Simply put, I assign a part of my intellect, my sentience, to a part of me that is assigned to look after individualized aspects of my sentience. Those levels of intelligence/sentience have the capacity to move through the energies that comprise my structure and assign parts of those energies that the entity desires to use to it to give it "body," so to speak. These energies may be used ad infinitum or in a momentary condition. When you as incarnate mankind use the physical vehicle, you assign energies to a localized area to create a self-contained and autonomously operating collection of energies, to allow you to experience the lowest frequencies and associated energies in a similar way to how they interact with each other. This is a transient condition, one that is used for experiential purposes only. When you, that is your True Energetic Self, is whole and functioning in its natural environment, it is functioning as a collection of energies that are relevant to its evolutionary progression only. When your True Energetic Self operates beyond the constraints of the evolutionary cycle, it sheds those energies assigned to this cycle and becomes that which it is, pure individualized sentience. As pure individualized sentience the "True Energetic Self" becomes the "True Self," and the True Self operates beyond full and total association with energy as a bodily medium. As such, an entity that is beyond association with energy is free to move wherever it wants to or needs to.

However, irrespective of this lack of association an entity must maintain a level of connectivity with me to enable it to continue to function. It is a part of me, a function of me, irrespective of its level of individuality and as a result needs to work with the structure that is me. Hence the imagery you saw with the example Source Entity moving through my structure while maintaining its connectivity with my structure. As with the example in your dialogue with Source Entity One where the entities are pure intelligence and they move their intelligence through the minerals that compose the rock they exist within in order to relocate themselves, so do my entities, all of my entities in their higher functional existence, move their sentience through the energies and substructure that maintain them in order to experience those different parts of me.

The function of movement is such that the sentience temporarily liberates (takes over) the dominant function of the energy it is moving on to or through, making it part of itself while maintaining the ability to "slip through it," so to speak. It's like using a car to move from one part of a city to another then moving from this car to another or a train or plane if a further distance of travel is needed. Think of it in terms of an energy that is so fine that it is capable of permeating everything in its path, moving around and through it, without hindrance at all levels of the energy's make-up.

ME: Does this also include that which is your intellect, your polyomniscient sentience? What I mean is, is the individuality that is the Source Entities and other entities, capable of moving through your polyomniscient sentience in the same way?

O: Yes, because ultimately you are all me. You are able to move through every aspect of me in the same way. Your individualized intellect can pass though my intellect without interference. That being, my intellect does not interfere with yours, and your intellect does not interfere with mine.

Think of it in this way, if you consider the body of air around the Earth as me, and a rare inert gas as you, the one passes through the other without interference, while being part of the same body of air. The air is a general description of all the gases surrounding the Earth, me, and the rare inert gas being a description for an individualized component of the air, you.

As an entity moves through, or exists within, me, it commandeers certain energies to do the activities it needs or desires to do. That energy, that "body" of energy, is what you see as the Source Entities or your True Energetic Self. The truth of the matter is that the real entity has no ownership of such energies; they are borrowed for a certain period and then set free. You and all other entities created by me or a Source Entity are, in truth, not energetic beings. You are pure sentience, and pure sentience requires no physicality, and I term energy as a physicality here, to exist, for pure sentience just "is." When you saw the image of one of the Source Entities in clear "see-through" relief, moving though my substructure, you saw the very basis of its being, the very basic energies it was commandeering to allow it to do its job, to fulfill its commitment to evolutionary progression. It was moving through me, communicating with my basic essence, to allow it to commandeer those energies and use them in a creative way. Try to imagine it like the wind moving through the wind.

I did, I could see it now. This opened up a whole new paradigm for me, one that pretty much dissolved the existing paradigm that was based upon an exclusively energetic existence.

I made a mental note. The Origin's substructure allows smaller versions of it, in whatever form they take, Source Entity, Om, Source Entity creation, creations from Source Entity creations, etc., etc., to move around itself to experience minute detail of itself. This was not an individualized energetic function from a human perspective; it was all interconnected from the perspective of sentience. Everything that is, was, or will be, within the structure of The Origin, no matter what was created, is individualized, but not by solidity or energy (still a function of physicality), but by pure "individuality," by "individualized sentience."

All of my current understanding had effectively been trashed in this short dialogue with The Origin. It had effectively led me down a road and turned me upside down and twisted me inside out. I was starting again—from scratch. This, I thought, was going to turn a few heads, and confuse a few others!

Chapter 25

The Substructure of The Origin Itself

IT WAS AT THIS POINT IN THE proceedings that I was on the cusp of deciding that everything I had previously discussed was in error. Everything that I, and other spiritual leaders, channellers, intuitives and enlightened individuals have broadcast about spirit, the so-called groundbreaking understanding that we are all energetic and based upon frequency within the energetic, now appeared to be flawed at best. But something told me that the previous level of knowledge was just a "stepping-stone," a "mile marker," a "signpost," each pointing us to a deeper level of understanding—an understanding of which was unachievable without the previous level of understanding being both in place and mastered.

As I sat back in my chair, I kept receiving the words "these are the tools to make the tools that will make the next set of tools"—the tools being "knowledge." Progression, this was all about progression and progressive education. We are not able to move forward without understanding the fundamentals, the basics. It would be pointless asking a caveman to jump on to a computer and write some complicated code without the level of progressive education necessary to back up the request. The caveman would more likely hit the computer keyboard and screen with a club or stick than think about using his hands and fingers to type, let alone understand what "typing" is in the first place. The computer would just be an object that it would either ignore or kick around the floor.

The caveman level of education is where we are as incarnate mankind right now. The computer is the unthinkable object that is right outside our comprehension. The computer is the example of higher spiritual knowledge. And, as with spiritual knowledge, to be able to use the computer the caveman would need to go through years of education, specifically if it were going to satisfy the first request of "writing the code."

We need educating, and the best way is to allow us to take on board what we can, even if it is in error, but ensuring that it is in the right general direction. As we become more adept at *understanding, and our knowledge base increases, so can we process new and more complicated concepts, concepts that are designed to make us think, to see beyond our current level of understanding and knowledge, and, make us recognize and accept our errors in judgment and understanding. Paradigms are there to be broken and the understanding of the knowledge that pointed us in the direction of making us think that we are "energetic beings" is one such paradigm, albeit a short-lived one I feel.*

"Where do I go from here?" I thought.

O: Try working on what my substructure is and achieving a level of understanding in this particular direction. It's one of the tools mankind will need to enable it to move on, to progress.

ME: Is that wise? I mean, we have just established that the information about us being energetic beings is a bit of a red herring! That we are pure thought instead!

O: It's not a red herring, and you are not pure thought. You know full well that "thought" is a product of "intention" and that "thought" precedes "action." Based upon this, thought is a lower function of something that has some form of intention. It's just a level of knowledge, one that you are surpassing.

ME: If thought is below intention, which is above action, and action is a function that facilitates an energetic response, which we are now saying is pretty low in the pecking order, then what facilitates intention?

O: Sentience, pure sentience.

ME: And what is the vehicle for intention to be put into thought and subsequent action?

O: My substructure and the varying levels of it.

ME: And sentience is above your structure?

O: Yes, of course. Your sentience, and indeed the sentience of any other entity, is a function of my sentience and is a separated driving function of the base physical components of energy and their frequencies. As you can remember from the earlier dialogues we had, my energies coalesced together under the auspices of a joint or collective consciousness that started with awareness and intelligence, leading up to Intelligent self-awareness and Sentience. Omnipresent sentience follows on later. All of these definitions are, although started by the joining of sympathetic energies and their frequencies, functions of a higher order, one that is created by the desire of energies to work together and sacrifice individuality for the function of being a higher collective, to create an all-encompassing, polyomniscient entity that grows—me!

Sentience exists within and without all aspects of my structure. That being, the current understanding of my structure, that which exists in my area of current polyomniscient self-awareness. Sentience permeates all aspects and travels about those aspects of the greater me at will.

ME: Getting back to this structure. Can you give me a description of it? I ask for a description because the knowledge that we are not energy beings but entities of pure sentience is new news. That we are sentience that is in effect an aspect of you, given to a Source Entity, which then separates it out to allow smaller versions to exist within itself and is assigned to a body of energy is radical to say the least!

O: Yes, of course. My substructure is in six parts. Notice I did not say layers but parts.

ME: You mentioned levels of substructure a few days ago!

O: No, I used the words "at this level."

ME: OK, but why use "level?" And you also mentioned that Source Entities can control your substructure. The actual words were *"This is how my substructure is formed when it is under the control of a Source Entity. It is adapted by the maintenance entity itself to suit what it needs to do and what it needs to do to work with the area of structure it needs to work with."*

O: You are getting observant, aren't you?

ME: I want to make sure that I don't get confused and that this new information is broadcast correctly. I really don't want to be "just going in the right general direction."

O: Good, but this may take a little longer because of the increased level of accuracy.

ME: I can cope with that.

O: I do believe you can. Let's go then!

The six parts of my substructure can be classified as follows:

PURE SUBSTRUCTURE—THE FRAMEWORK WITHIN THE FRAMEWORK. This part of me is literally pure essence of energy. That being, it is the lines of attractivity that each energy within me has with each other. All energies have a level of interconnectivity, either direct or indirect as a result of interfacing energies that, although are not directly compatible, are indirectly compatible through one another via these interfacing energies. Think of it like the lines of magnetic attraction that exist between two magnets, or the lines of a magnetic field emanating from a single magnet if you place the magnet on a wooden tray and sprinkle iron filings around it. Now think of those lines "of attractivity" as waves of attraction between the smallest aspects of my structure. If you then think of my structure as being a frame made of scaffolding in between the basic components of energy, and even one section of this scaffolding is bigger than the physical universe, then the lines of attractivity between it would be a matrix of the finest gossamer that exists several levels below the size of the Anu. That is, thinking of it from a physical perspective.

COMMUNICATION—THE COMMUNICATIONS BETWEEN ALL ASPECTS OF STRUCTURE. This is, for want of a better word, a "carrier wave" that exists around and in between the waves of my pure substructure. The image you had of one of the Source Entities looking like the positive sphere in a Van der Graaff generator illustrated the coupling and decoupling of the lines of communication of energies commandeered by the individualized sentience that was assigned to the Source Entity being observed, and the communication medium within my substructure.

357

THE SENTIENCE FACTOR—This is the essence of sentience within all things, which includes intention, resulting from sentience and thought resulting from the intention. It is pure "beingness" and cannot be described as structure per se, although it is an immensely important part of what I am. Think of it in terms of the level of sentience that has been individualized, and from the perspective of the energies commandeered by a certain individualized sentience, the Sentience Factor behind the control of those energies. It is therefore its level of sentience and subsequent level of complexity. There are varying levels of sentience supporting the intelligence behind a set of commandeered energies. For example, as all energies within my area of polyomniscient sentience are known, and therefore commandeered by MY sentience at varying levels, if you were to map these levels as a 3D graph it would look like the surface of one of Earth's seas in a force-ten gale. The peaks of the waves would represent where my sentience factor is strong, the troughs where it is weak. The work I undertake on my personal progression can be illustrated by locations within my area of polyomniscient self-awareness being "flattened out" so that the sentience factor is constantly high and there are no peaks and troughs.

FREE ENERGY—This is energy within energy. You can call it the "real" Prana or Orgone. We have talked about free energy before and how it works with the possibility of evolutionary growth. Free energy is just that, it is free from assignment to individualized sentience. It can be employed by individualized sentience but it can never be commandeered by the sentience to augment its energetic content. Free energy is an independent energetic function within the structure of my energies. You can also call it the "overall personality" of energy if you like because it can and does have its own level of intelligence. Free energy, although permeating the structure of energy itself, can group together to make creativity and evolutionary changes possible. Free energy, to some extent, works in tandem with Event Space.

THE ESSENCE OF EVENTS—This is the substructure of Event Space. It is the framework that allows Event Space to exist in all aspects of what I am. Within the essence of events all events can and do exist, whether they are transient or long term. The essence of events allows all events to exist concurrently, to intermingle with each other while remaining separate. All events are "separately together" in this way, and that is why an entity can traverse the events within Event Space. Think of the essence of events as the building blocks required to allow the events themselves to exist and be maintained. It is the stage, settings, and wardrobe to support the play of all events.

THE LIBRARY OF PROGRESSION—This is a collective growth medium. It is a specific part of me that records all aspects of progression from myself and all other individualized aspects of sentience that are either created by me, one of my creations, or one of my creations' creations. As a part of my substructure though it is diffuse and "currently" exists in key areas of my area of polyomniscient self-awareness. Call it memory if you like, but its main function is to store all of the actions and experiences that result in steps of evolutionary progression. The level of diffusion is such that I can access all information stored within the library from any point in the energies and substructure that are within my current area of polyomniscient self-awareness. This is not the Akashic records, although the Akashic are a minor function of the library. The Akashic are a record of the collective experiences of incarnate existence.

ME: These don't appear to be all substructure. Some of them appear to be functions.

O: Yes, they are, but as functions they are essential elements of my substructure, for they are the parts of my substructure that contain the "operating system," if you like, the functions necessary to support that which I am. Structure needs function to exist, and function needs to have a structure to work around. They go hand in hand.

Chapter 26

How Source Entities Assign Sentience to Energy to Fulfill the Requirement of Creating Smaller Beings

THE REVELATION THAT WHAT WE, that is, the spiritually aware incarnate individuals on this planet, were largely incorrect in our assumption that energy was the structural basis for our higher selves, our over souls, god heads, or True Energetic Selves, was an important step for me. I do have to say that other spiritualists may already be on this revelatory path and so I apologize to them if they take offense to this rather generalized statement. It appears though that we are not energy beings but beings of pure sentience, sentience that commandeers energy, or has energy commandeered for it to work with. This in itself was very interesting because it introduced a whole new dynamic for me and, of course, a whole new direction to go into. Armed with the opportunity to move in a new, but ultimately linked direction, I decided to understand how The Origin, and therefore how the Source Entities, assigned sentience to energy and in the process create lesser or smaller beings.

O: I was wondering when you were going to get around to this line of thought and therefore this question.

ME: As I am ultimately a function of you, I am surprised that you were wondering about when I would ask this question, and were not more "in the moment" of knowing when, or should I say which, Event Space would invoke this question.

O: I do like a bit of what you call "banter." I like the way it keeps you on your toes! Getting to your comment though, I enjoy seeing how, through your Source Entity of course, you, and the other incarnates, take every Event Space possible but the direct ones. When you are in the lower frequencies of my structure you all seem to miss the obvious and go for the unobvious. I love to see you all wandering around and then, just when it seems that you haven't got it, you find the correct decision process that takes you into the right series of Event Spaces and you succeed. It's rather like seeing a rat in a maze from above the maze. Me, as the observer, knowing how to get from the entrance to the center point and vice versa. Watching the rat make the same navigational mistakes time after time without applying the learning gained from going in the wrong direction and applying it to a mental map. Both the rat and the incarnates in observation do eventually learn, and in application of this learning manage to go from the entrance point of the maze, to the center and back. It's just entertaining and wondrous to see you all in action.

ME: On behalf of all incarnates Source Entity wide, I am glad we can be of service to you in this way.

O: OK, enough of the long-winded introduction to this section; let's get on with your question about how a Source Entity assigns part of its sentience to energy to create a smaller entity.

ME: Yes, please do, thank you. Although I feel that my readers may think that this is a relief from having their brains stretched and they will be eager to move on to the next subject, I very much feel that many of them suck up this information like a sponge.

O: Yes, I can see that there is quite a following growing. Don't let it go to your head. Let's move on then, but in order to do so I need to back track a little.

When I created the Twelve Origins I did not assign sentience to the energies that were destined to be them, I allowed the sentience to develop in its own way within the energies that were identified. In essence I created the same conditions within the energies of each of The Origins that were instrumental in creating my own sentience. I therefore created in the way that I was created, by allowing the energies to gain individualized intelligence and working/joining together to create a larger intelligence that eventually evolves into sentience, and later, into the polyomniscient sentient intelligence you are in communication with now.

I adopted a different approach with the Source Entities. When I created the Source Entities I assigned energies that were already showing the signs of intelligence and the potential of creating their own sentience as a result. This was a perfect halfway house and one that would work both from a directional perspective while also allowing the Source Entities to develop in their own way in their own time but in the direction that I wanted them to. They were created from specialized energy, energy that both had potential and was already under development. This energy was therefore individualized/separated out from my bulk energies and left to develop in its own way. But it was guided into the right direction, so to speak.

This is all very high level as you can appreciate, and doesn't identify the true level of work undertaken by me to create the Source Entities. I will leave it at that, at least for the moment, and focus on the process the Source Entities use in the creation of their creations.

ME: That sounds like a plan. Now though you have whetted my appetite, and I would like to know more about how you created the Source Entities as well.

O: I thought you might. OK, let's deal with that later. It is a different process and is therefore an interesting comparator.

The Source Entities spend quite a bit of time looking for energies that can be associated with other energies and energy that can be universally acceptable to all sentience within the creating Source Entity. In essence a Source Entity identifies those energies that are compatible with each other, either directly or indirectly, and considers their ability to be uniquely assigned to an aspect of sentience that has been identified as having the potential of functioning in an individualized way while being separated out from its core sentience.

ME: This sounds backward to that process inferred by my question.

O: It may well do so but think of it in this way. Sometimes we have to go backward to go forward. This process is essential because the creating Source Entity can reassign the sentience and energies being used in a more compatible way. Although each Source Entity has its own way of doing things, there is a general way in which the sentience is separated out, "individualized" from the whole.

ME: I just received an impression that this is quite a difficult thing to achieve, that, in essence, the sentience that is a Source Entity is in fact an individualized area of your own sentience and as such has already undergone individualization. Further individualization therefore dilutes the essence of sentience so the function of further individualization needs to incorporate a function that stops this dilution.

O: Very well done. And the dilution of the essence of me within the individualized sentience is what happened to your Source Entity when it created the billions upon trillions of entities to populate the multiverse. When it stated that it "took its eye off the ball," it literally did just that. It started the process of individualization, thought that it had the process in hand, so to speak, and let it run automatically rather than checking to see that each and every one of the individualized parts of its sentience was of the correct quality, that it did not dilute. The product of this "automated" function is the myriad levels of sentience that you experience today while incarnate on Earth, and of course beyond. Locally though, for example, they can be easily identified as back-fill people, animals, and the flora and fauna, not to negate the sentience that certain minerals and gaseous and planetary bodies have.

I digress though. The process a Source Entity uses is somewhat different to the process I use, because I can create pure individualized sentience on its own and then assign energy or energies to it—should I desire or feel the need to do so. As alluded to in the earlier part of this dialogue, a Source Entity needs to work somewhat in reverse.

A Source Entity must first identify an energy or set of energies that have a level of uniqueness about them. That uniqueness is the ability to work with sentience, or more importantly, to have the potential to create sentience through the intelligent functions of working together and sacrificing their smaller individual intelligence for the creation of a larger single intelligence. It is the development of a larger single intelligence that allows the next step of the larger intelligence grouping together with other larger intelligences to create an even larger intelligence, etc., etc., etc., which eventually results in one super large intelligence that has the capacity to develop the opportunity for sentience and omniscience to manifest itself.

ME: So a Source Entity needs to identify an energy or energies that have this capacity and then assign part of its sentience to it?

O: From a high-level perspective that would be a correct assumption but there is more detail behind the scenes than just that. I will explain as I promised to.

Once the energies have been identified they need to be purged of the potential for them to develop their own sentience, should they be grouped together in a large enough group. To achieve this they go through a number of stages.

IDENTIFICATION AND SEPARATION OF ENERGY/ENERGIES is where the energies within a Source Entity are identified as being of optimal use for the creation of smaller sentient beings that can truly be classified as smaller versions of the creating Source Entity in every energetic way.

GROUPING is the necessary function of creating a volume of energies large enough to initially contain sentience. Not all energies are of the correct volume initially and so they need to be added together in the same way that they might naturally group together. This function, although artificially actioned, cannot be anything other than that which is achieved naturally. Grouping the energies together in a forced manner creates resistance and effectively removes the bonds between the energies concerned.

REMOVAL OF NATURAL TENDENCIES RELATING TO SENTIENCE is a process where the energy's own ability to create a sentient condition when in a large enough volume is extracted and its sentient ability is changed in favor of accepting sentience rather than creating it.

INDIVIDUALIZATION OF SENTIENCE is where a Source Entity separates out an aspect of its own sentience for the prime purpose of allowing this aspect of itself to operate in a fully autonomous way. To do this a Source Entity needs to initially separate out the sentience and then compartmentalize it. It then assigns individuality to it, and in the process a personality is created within the compartmentalized sentience. This personality, unique to all individualized sentience, is the essence of that portion of sentience that is given individuality.

ASSIGNATION OF SENTIENCE TO ENERGY is the process where the energies that were capable of creating their own sentience, function now removed, have the individualized sentience of a Source Entity assigned to them. In this instance the functional area of the energy/energies that allowed sentience to evolve within them is modified to accept sentience rather than create it.

DEVELOPMENT OF THE SENTIENCE IN ITS INDIVIDUALIZED STATE WITH THE ASSIGNED ENERGIES is the education of the assigned sentience/energy by a Source Entity of the reason for its individualized existence and the role it is expected to play in its new condition. Once this "high-level" education is finished the rest is up to the newly created entity.

SEPARATION OF THE ASSOCIATION WITH THE ORIGINAL ENERGIES is a function given to the entity by a Source Entity that allows the sentience to move freely within and without the energy/energies it is assigned to. In this instance the sentience is shown how it can disassociate itself from its initial "body" of energy/ies.

RECOGNITION OF THE ABILITY TO TRANSCEND ENERGETIC ASSOCIATION is a function of global education conducted by myself. This results in the entity being able to recognize this function within them. Initial proof of this is the ability of the entity to move its sentience around the energies that are assigned to it. Without this ability the entity believes that it is the sum total of the energies assigned to it and not the motivating force behind them. Recognition and demonstration of this ability is first undertaken within the energies assigned to it and leads on to the ability to change the energies of association.

THE ABILITY TO SELF-ASSOCIATE WITH ANY ENERGY is proof of the recognition and underlying ability to move its sentience within the energies assigned to it and to subsequently move it external to those energies. When the sentience is external to its initial energetic assignation and it commandeers other energy/ies making it/them its new "body" of energy, it has demonstrated that it is in full control of its "self" and its abilities, and that it has mastered the sentience/energy relationship where energy is just a tool for it to use in its experiential plan to accrue evolutionary content.

The Assignation of Personality to Sentience

ME: How does a Source Entity extract or individualize its own sentience? I mean, the information is a high-level look at the total process, but I have a specific interest in the way the sentience is individualized.

O: A Source Entity simply divides its sentience into two parts—that which is to remain as its main body of sentience, i.e., that which is its own personality, and that which is to be divided up into smaller aspects of sentience.

In the perfect divisionary procedure, the volume of sentience that is to be divided into smaller aspects of sentience is simply divided equally into volumes relative to the number of entities to be created. However, as pure sentience it is just that, pure, and although it is capable of creating its own personality over time it is usually given the function of personality by the creating Source Entity.

ME: What do you mean by personality? If sentience is capable of recognizing that it is the motivating force behind a body of energies, is that not an indication that it has personality?

O: No. That is mere intelligence, as is the ability to move the sentience within or without a body of energies. At that stage in the creativity process the entities are just volumes of sentience within a body of specialized energies.

ME: Isn't that all they need to be though? Isn't that which we all were at some point in our existence?

O: From my perspective, yes, but from the perspective of every other entity either created by me or a Source Entity the answer is no. Apart from my Twelve Origins experiment I gave all Source Entities the function of personality when I first briefed them on their reason for existence. I did this by changing a small part of their sentience and how that sentience interfaced within and without the body of energy used. This was an important action because it changed the way each of them considered how they were going to fulfill the reason for their existence, to experience, learn, and evolve. It also ensured that they would do something different to each other when they entered into the creativity process, or not, as the case may be. I make reference here to Source Entity Twelve as not entering into the creativity process.

The need to make every newly created entity have a different personality, and the knowledge/ability to bestow such a personality to individualized sentience was included within their briefing upon gaining self-awareness. As a result they also modify the sentience and interfacing body of energy/ies of each entity created in some small way in order to generate their personality, although this is not always a necessity. For example, if a group of entities are required to work in a collective function, they would all be assigned with the same personality. The function of personality assignation is fulfilled by the creating Source Entity individually even though the members of the collective essentially have the same personality.

ME: To assign an individual personality to each and every entity created must be an enormous task, even for a Source Entity?

O: Yes, it is. Moreover it takes focus, a focus which of course is multiplied by the number of entities being created. It's worth it though because every "personalized" sentient entity addresses its commitment to gaining evolutionary content in its own way. Nothing created, that is, no "thing" or experience, is an exact duplicate of any other creation as a result. In order to alleviate the "personal time" used to maintain this focus Source Entities have been known to try to automate this function.

ME: And one such Source Entity would be Source Entity One?

O: Correct. It described the result of its attempt at automating this function to you as "taking its eye off the ball," I believe. The result of Source Entity One's automation was that it created a number of sentient entities that conformed to its plan and others of varying sentience and associated energies.

ME: How can an automatic function fail?

O: Automation fails when it is not capable of adaptation, to working with materials that are outside of the criteria for making the product perform within its designed functionality and still creating a product that conforms to the intended design. One such item is the dilution of sentience the more it is divided up. Source Entity One simply gathered together the energies and sentience identified for individualization, created a number of sentient entities, and then created an automated process based upon what it did to create them. All entity creativity was then left up to this process, a process which resulted in the creation of, shall I say, nonconforming product.

ME: But Source Entity One is happy with the outcome. It said it was perfect in its imperfection!

O: Yes, it did and, yes, it is.

ME: And that is because?

O: That is because all of those "different" entities are experiencing existence and creativity in their own way, and as a result they are creating a diversity of experience of which is not seen in any other Source Entity.

ME: OK. I want to regroup here a little and ask for any other information regarding the process surrounding the creation of personality within individualized sentience. You identified to me that the personality aspect in sentience is achieved by the creating Source Entity making minor changes to the individualized sentience itself and the assigned energy/ies, and that this ultimately needs to be achieved on an individual basis. What other changes are made to create the personality?

O: None. Once the individualized sentience and its assigned energy/ies have been personalized, the rest of the personality, the fine tuning, so to speak, is achieved by the individualized sentience itself.

ME: Thinking about the portability of the sentience itself, doesn't the entity leave some part of its personality behind if it moves from its preassigned body of energies to another?

O: No. The personalization that is assigned to the original body of energies is absorbed or integrated within the sentience itself and is transported to the newly "commandeered" energy/ies.

ME: So what happens to the energies that are left behind?

O: They are returned back to their original state. That being, they are still specialized and capable of being used by another sentience. It's just that they don't have the personalization given to it/them by the creating Source Entity during the original process of creating an entity of individualized sentience and energy.

ME: And I would expect the newly commandeered energy/ies was/were specialized and capable of being used by another sentience?

O: Yes.

ME: And that these are freely available?

O: Yes.

ME: And the commandeered energy/ies accept the previously assigned personality because it has been transported by the sentience?

O: Yes.

ME: Mmmm. Does the commandeered energy need to be specialized and capable of being used by another sentience?

O: No, not all of the time.

ME: Why not? This seems to negate the need for a specialized body of energy.

O: The specialized body of energy is only used by the sentience when it is working within a known energetic structure, like the multiverse Source Entity One created. Once the entity is created and it has mastery over itself and its personality, it can choose to stay with the energies the creating Source Entity assigned to it. Or it can move to another energy or set of energies because they are freely available. There are more energies that are specialized and capable of being used by another sentience than there is sentience itself, and this is the beauty of being pure individualized sentience.

ME: So what happens when an entity no longer chooses to work within an environment created for them to work with?

O: It can choose to be pure individualized sentience only and exist within the voids that separate those energies that are assigned to a Source Entity or its creations. Or it can choose to stay within the environmental structure created by its creating Source Entity and move its sentience throughout the structure until it has a desire to experience something new.

ME: Hold on, I got the impression that the sentience was only capable of moving from one energy or set of energies that are specialized enough to accept a sentience and its personality, to another. Are you suggesting that all energy can accept sentience or is the volume of specialized energy so big that it spans the entire area of the Source Entity in question?

O: Clearly the volume of specialized energies does not span the entire area of a Source Entity because if they did there would be no need to seek out these energies in the first place. No, if an entity wants to work within an environment created out of energies, it needs to adopt a body of energies, using those energies within, or without, the environment that is capable of supporting sentience.

The sentience, however, does need a medium to allow it to move from a location to a location while in these environments, and so the sentience is allowed to flow from one energy to another irrespective of whether or not the energy is capable of supporting sentience.

ME: I see. I have just received an image that illustrates just that. It's just like the sentience moves around the outside of the energy/ies, so to speak, if it is not capable of supporting sentience. When the energy/ies is/are capable of supporting the sentience, the sentience can move within and without the pure essence of that/those energy/ies.

O: Very good. Now let me see if you can tell me how a sentience can move in an area where there is no structure to work with.

ME: You mean in the voids between energies or an energetic structure?

O: Yes.

ME: Give me a moment. Oh, yes! This is interesting, it's as if the sentience spreads out and creates a structure in between the voids. It fills the gaps, so to speak; it becomes structure in its own right. A structure of sentience linking the energies together, both those that are capable of supporting sentience and those that don't. I am only seeing this in 2D right now but I can imagine that it is a 3D effect. You have given me this image as a thought process, haven't you?

O: Yes. The 2D/3D effect is just for illustrative purposes. The actual spreading out of the sentience is capable of spanning all aspects of the voids in between the structure of the creating Source Entity. In the case of Source Entity One that would include frequency, subdimensional component, dimension, and zone, together with the components of zones. In the case of my sentience working within my larger structure, it would include the twelve levels in the section where we discussed my structure, and not just the four associated with Source Entity One.

As I looked harder at this example of sentience spreading from energy to energy, spanning the voids in between them, the sentience seemed to gain the appearance of a multifrequential, multidimensional sheet of rubber. This sheet of sentient rubber stretched out in all directions to fill the gaps, and, once the gaps were spanned, the rubber sheet would "let go" of the hold it had on the energies it was moving from, relaxing toward the energies it was moving to. Moving from energy/ies to energy/ies appeared to be achieved by a series of expansions and contractions. It reminded me of the way a certain type of caterpillar moved, stretching its front section out as far as it could and then the back section catching up within one movement as soon as the front had a robust foothold. The back and front of the caterpillar being close together gave it the image of a lowercase letter "n." I looked closer and I was able to "see" the sentience, nondescript as it was, change the essence of the energy/ies it was moving within and without. It was as if the energy/ies sparkled with vibrancy when occupied with sentience, returning to dullness when the sentience left them. In this way the energies went from being inert to being alive to being inert again. Clearly the energy/ies had an important role to play, in any state; it was just that the effect that sentience had on them was more than profound. I felt the need to ask a few more questions on this subject before we moved on.

ME: Why does individualized sentience, an entity in its most basic sense, move away from the energies that are, were, assigned to it? What is/are the benefits of it moving from its given energy/ies to a new energy or set of energies?

O: Experience of its environment, of that which it is part of. You see, for an entity to progress it first has to master itself and the energies that it works within. As individualized pure sentience the entity establishes and controls its abilities and then fine tunes those abilities to the point where they are at a point of perfection. Each ability is relative to a task or specialism and each task or specialism has an energy or energy set associated with it relative to the structure it is working within.

Although each entity, each area of individualized sentience, is "in general" assigned a body of energy by the creating Source Entity, that body of energy is only a kindergarten for the sentience to work and gain confidence within. It needs to move on and experience the rest of the environment the creating Source Entity created for it and its other individualized units of sentience to work within.

ME: Can't an entity take its body of energy/ies with it when it moves around and experiences its environment?

O: It can of course move its assigned body of energy/ies with it, but it moves around its environment faster by disassociating itself from its original body of energy/ies. Additionally it masters those energies associated with its environment faster in the process. To complete its evolutionary cycle it needs to experience all of the energies in its environment, in all their structural levels and locations, mastering them, being them, and creating with them. Only then can it assume fully reintegrated communion, "oneness" with its creator, should it decide to do so, for it will have completed its task and role.

ME: That's what we, that is, the individualized "embodied" sentience that is working within the multiversal structure that Source Entity One created, are doing right now. We ascend the frequencies and in the process we ascend the structure of the multiverse. We create tasks and whole constructs to work with and achieve varying levels of success, the varying levels giving us experiences which we can learn from and in the process evolve.

O: Yes, and in the process you progress beyond the need for further experience within certain environments, environments created by the basic building blocks of the multiverse, its frequencies, and work with higher and finer frequencies including the associated detail and complexity. In essence, the higher up the frequencies you go, the more you can create, and the more you experience what you have created. In this way you become a more responsible being.

ME: So, to summarize, an entity of individualized sentience needs to experience every energy or energy set within the total structure of the environment it was created within.

O: Yes.

ME: And it does this by moving within and without its energies, assigned, commandeered, or used for, and experiencing, creativity?

O: Yes.

ME: And all entities created by a Source Entity need to do this?

O: When created by a Source Entity or indeed me, yes.

ME: So a Source Entity also has to work with the energies within your structure?

O: Yes, they do.

ME: When did they start, and how are they doing that?

O: Relatively speaking, in this cycle they have only just started. They are doing it by what they are doing now, creating individualized units of sentience and associating it with specialized energy/ies.

The word "cycle" made me jump.

ME: That explains why the Source Entities appear to be inert.

O: Yes, it will. They are dealing with the energies within themselves first before they start to move around my area of current polyomniscient self-awareness, specifically those parts of it that I have only paid a cursory glance to. They will be helped by their creations.

I sat back in my chair a moment. I pondered about what The Origin had just said. I got the impression that those Source

Entities that had created smaller entities of individualized sentience would allow those entities to move outside their energetic boundaries. As I relaxed even more in my chair I saw a different image, and received an explanation, one that both made sense, and to my mind, tied together a piece of ancient knowledge, but in a most different way to that which would be expected by the holders of the knowledge.

Currently the Source Entities were static. They were unmoving. They were sentience, individualized Origin sentience with an assigned body of energy/ies, just as the entities they created were, but in the macro. Their entities, their creations of individualized sentience together with their body of assigned or commandeered energy/ies were moving around within the environments created for them, experiencing, learning, and evolving in the process. These environments were, in themselves, created by the separation of those energies that were assigned to the Source Entities themselves.

Although the Source Entities had moved to surround me to witness my dialogues with The Origin, the energies they were working with were brought with them from their place of "work." Energy voids were left in their place, presumably to be either back-filled or the energies moved, replaced. No, I was told. They would return and replace that energy when they and their creations had finished their work and experienced every aspect of themselves and the environment created by the individualization of their body of energy/ies.

The truth came out in a flash of divine inspiration and understanding. It was beautiful.

The Source Entities stayed static for a reason. The Source Entities were just starting out in the work they were doing with the body of energy/ies their sentience was assigned to. They were to experience everything that could be experienced within and without the currently assigned energy/ies. To do this they enlisted help, the help of smaller versions of themselves, smaller individualized units of their own sentience, and initially assigned bodies of energy to them. When both the Source Entities and their creations had experienced everything they could within and without those energies, they reintegrated back into the oneness of their creating Source Entity.

This level of completion, using Source Entity One as an example, is reflected by all entities working to the point of ascending to the very top of the structure of the multiverse, and no longer needing to work within it. At this point they can elect to commune fully with their creator and become one again, giving up individual sentience and personality. Or, they can integrate while maintaining their individual sentience and personality achieving a partial level of communion. Once this is achieved Source Entity One will move to another location within The Origin's area of current polyomniscient self-awareness.

The image of Source Entity One as pure individualized sentience moving through the energies associated with The Origin's area of current polyomniscient self-awareness came back to me. In a, shall I say "future" Event Space, it had finished its work in its current location and moved on in both location and structural position. Upon changing location the whole energy set associated with Source Entity One would change, as would the structure associated with it.

Upon experiencing a new set of energies, Source Entity One will create a new multiversal structure to work with and will redeploy those aspects of its individualized sentience, and/or new ones, initially with newly assigned bodies of energy/ies. These new body/ies of energy/ies will be created out of the energies that are dominant in this new area. The entities of individualized sentience will start at the bottom of the structure of this new multiverse, starting the evolutionary cycle all over again. This cycle will continue over and over again until all of The Origin's area of current polyomniscient self-awareness has been experienced and mapped and becomes polyomniscient sentience. At this point The Origin and the Source Entities will move into the next area of The Origin's new and much larger area of self-awareness, that which is not yet sentient.

The present condition is an anomaly in this process because the Source Entities have moved closer to my location, that location in The Origin's area of current polyomniscient self-awareness and Event Space where I am acting out a dialogue with it, in order to be part of that dialogue—to "listen in," so to speak. In order to maintain the integrity of the evolutionary work they are currently concentrating on, each of the Source Entities, with the possible exception of Source Entity

Twelve, has moved the energies and structure of The Origin's area of current polyomniscient self-awareness they are working with, with them. Hence, the voids in space. I was awestruck at the very thought of what they were doing here.

Chapter 27

The Cycle of Expansion and Contraction of the Universe (Multiverse) Is Explained

ME: How many times has this happened, this move and restart of the evolutionary cycle?

O: This is the third time.

ME: This is it, isn't it?

O: I'm sorry?

ME: From the perspective of our Source Entity, Source Entity One, this is the breathing in and out that the Hindu Yogis talked about. The expansion and contraction of the universe (multiverse).

The expansion being, the deployment of the multiverse in its new energetic and structural condition. This would include the population of it by the myriad entities of individualized units of sentience and their associated bodies of energy/ies.

Stability is achieved when the population start to work with the new structure and energies of the multiverse and progress through it, experiencing all they can in minute detail, evolving along the way.

Contraction is achieved when the entities who display the slowest methods of evolution have progressed to the point where they themselves have experienced all that the multiverse offers and now seek to commune fully with their creator and become "one" again. Or they integrate while maintaining a partial level of communion.

Stability is again achieved when the Source Entity moves its own individualized sentience, which includes the sentience it has individualized from itself, the entities, to a new unexperienced location within *The Origin's area of current polyomniscient self-awareness.*

Once settled in its new location the Source assumes (commandeers) the energies and structure of its new location and expands, recreating and populating the multiverse again. In all of this the entities of individualized sentience have the ability to decide whether to experience the new multiverse again, augmenting their evolutionary progression, or stay in full or partial communion.

O: VERY VERY well done. And now you have created a link, a very important link, with ancient knowledge.

ME: Thank you. I do have to say that I was at a bit of a loss as to how I would reconcile this "breathing in and out" of the universe. I knew I had to address it at some point, but this just came out of the blue. It's a real bonus and one that brings the knowledge right up-to-date because I always thought that there was something missing in the Hindu texts. Or should I say, in my understanding of them. Now we have gone beyond it and it makes sense.

O: Yes, it does and that is why you are in this role—this role being to help expand incarnate mankind's understanding of the greater reality.

Chapter 28

The Perfect Division of Sentience

AFTER THE LAST SECTION THIS CHAPTER seemed irrelevant. However, I felt the need to carry on, if nothing else but for the sake of completeness. Indeed, with the indication that the division of sentience needs the full attention of the Source Entity dividing up its sentience, lest mistakes occur, I very much felt that this was the answer to the original question. As with all things of the greater reality though, I was starting to feel that there was another aspect of this subject that needed to be discussed, one that would make a difference in my understanding of how a Source Entity works on creating new sentient entities. This small reference to the chance of more information was enough to make me ask the question and worry about the quality of the content later.

ME: You mentioned the perfect divisionary procedure. What did you mean by that? I would have thought that the information given in our recent dialogue would have made the answer to this particular question obvious.

O: Yes, it is obvious. Especially as you have communicated that a Source Entity needs to maintain a high level of attention when creating smaller versions of itself. However, I will add some more info to that which you currently have.

As you know, when a Source Entity creates a smaller version of itself or a group of versions of itself, it separates out a portion of its sentience and assigns it to the energies that are specialized in accepting that sentience. All the dialogue we have had to date indicates to you that the sentience of a Source Entity is separated out en masse, fifty percent assigned to new entities and fifty percent reserved for the Source Entity—in the example of your Source Entity. But this is not the case. Although it is ultimately assigned in this way, sentience itself is extracted on a one-by-one basis.

ME: Wouldn't that make it a very slow process?

O: Yes, it would, and that is ultimately why Source Entity One created an automatic program for creation, so to speak. As we discussed though, this is for the perfect division of sentience to occur. When considering the perfect division of sentience one has to identify the amount, the volume of sentience to be used for a desired type of entity and assign that sentience to the energy/ies also identified. Because the intention of the creator is to make both the sentience and the energy/ies individual they need to be matched together in individuality, in a matched pair, so to speak. Before this can happen though, the volume of sentience identified needs to be cleaned of any residual aspects of sentience or intelligence that is purely identified with the creator itself.

ME: The sentience needs to be cleared of sentience?

O: Yes. You see, when the creator is creating an individualized unit of itself, it needs to make it as individual as possible. That means any prior learning or progression that has been accrued by the creator itself needs to be erased. This does not mean that the learning or progression is lost; it is reassigned to the aspect of the creator that is to remain as the creator and not the created.

ME: Leaving the sentience as pure inexperienced sentience?

O: Correct.

ME: And I would guess that this process of cleansing is also employed with the specialized energy/ies?

O: It is and this is because the energy/ies themselves can maintain a level of experiential memory, which of course is based upon what the creating Source Entity has experienced in its own existence.

ME: Doesn't each new entity have a level of education though, an explanation of its reason to be, what is expected of it, what it can work with, how it should progress?

O: Yes.

ME: But doesn't that defeat the object of cleansing the sentience and the energy/ies assigned to work together?

What I mean is, if they have information about who and what they are and what they are expected to do, and that they are in communion with you, that this will include a level of experiential knowledge as well. So, the sentience is purified of your work and experience and then contaminated with your work and experience later.

O: Very good question. I should have made the description of the cleansing more thorough. It is the "essence" of "Source Entity" that is removed from both the sentience and the energy/ies assigned to it. The education process, although in depth, does not include this component. As a result the newly created entity is fully individualized while still being part of the creating Source Entity. In essence, it is fully programmed and operational in all aspects except from the perspective of personalized experience, learning, and evolutionary progression, and essence of sentience of the creating Source Entity. In this way it can, through its own experience, learning, and evolutionary progression, create its own "essence" of sentience. Call it personality, if you like, but this is a necessary requirement for the successful creation of an individualized aspect of a Source's "self."

ME: And as the entity experiences, learns, and evolves, its personality grows in both confidence and stature!

O: Correct. During the growth of the personality the entity becomes more and more individualized as it experiences more and more on a personal basis. Its ultimate level of personality sets it aside from those others that were created with it as a result of the difference in experiences and the logical order of similar experiences in relation to other experiences experienced.

ME: And this is the perfect division of sentience?

O: In summary and in relation to the creation of a single entity, yes.

ME: All right, based upon the comment that each entity is created singularly, just how does a Source Entity mass produce those smaller entities in this perfect division of sentience? I ask this specifically because you have identified that they need to be created one by one and that they need, certainly in the case of some of the Source Entities, to be created in their billions and trillions.

O: It achieves this in two ways. Firstly, it assigns aspects of itself purely to support the divisional process, including all of those parts of the process that create the individualized entity, the matching of the energy/ies with the sentience and the removal of the essence of Source Entity. Each assigned aspect is created as a temporary function of self and works on a one-by-one basis of creativity. The aspect is a faithful copy of that original function of the creating Source Entity. It remains in existence only for as long as it is required to be.

Secondly, the creating Source Entity further duplicates this function by the use of Event Space. Each Event Space is a full reproduction of the total number of aspects being used in the original divisional process. The creating Source Entity can maintain the quality of creative event in this way by ensuring that the original aspects being used are operating in accordance with the perfect divisional process, with the entities being created as desired in a robust and repeatable way, each time and every time but in different Event Spaces. Although any number of Event Spaces can be employed, only a certain volume of sentience and specialized energy/ies are assigned to a particular Event Space. In this way the volume of sentience and specialized energy/ies is/are divided up by Event Space.

ME: How does the creating Source Entity use Event Space in this way? I thought it was predominantly associated with duality and its multiples, that it was created by the possibility of possible possibilities!

O: It is.

ME: I'm sorry?

O: It is the function of possibilities that allow the creating Source Entity to use Event Space in the first place.

ME: Yes, I can see that but I am not making the mental connection—yet! I mean, those entities that are due to be created are just that—due to be created, not "actually" created and so therefore cannot create a dualistic event.

The only dualistic event from my perspective is that which is created by the creating Source Entity.

O: As you are aware, Event Space is attracted to, and is multiplied by, the possibility of a dualistic, trilistic, or quadrulistic condition, etc., etc. The immediacy of these conditions does not necessarily need to be in the now, but can be a significant distance away, from the perspective of "events." Based upon this the creating Source Entity can invoke new Event Spaces as a simple function of the creation of an entity that has its own level of sentience and associated level of free will. In essence, Event Space can be created in a multiple condition in the "now" as a function of the possibility of dualistic conditions of any denomination in any future event by any entity that may possibly be created.

ME: This is the chicken and the egg scenario again. In Event Space both can and do exist concurrently.

O: Correct. You see Event Space is an extremely sensitive aspect of my structure. It is so sensitive that it can create new Event Spaces outside of the dualistic conditions that would normally create it, or indeed, outside of the possibility of possible possibilities of dualistic conditions, and its multiple conditions. It can be created from something as the remotely possible intention to be a possibility of possible possibilities of a dualistic condition, and/or its multiples and that intention can be so far into a future Event Space that it could never be predicted.

ME: So just how far forward can Event Space "see" these possibilities?

O: There is no limit on how far forward or in which Event Space they may be invoked. All that is required is that they could "be" and that allows Event Space to create the conditions necessary for a new Event Space or Event Spaces to be created and for it to be concurrent. That being, it becomes in the "now" for that is where Event Space presents itself, in an environment of concurrent "now's."

ME: And because Event Space is presented in an environment of concurrent "now's," and the concurrent "now's" are what Event Space is, this is why a creating Source Entity can create all of its individualized sentient entities in an instantaneous fashion, relatively speaking?

O: Not quite. A creating Source Entity would still have to wait for the whole process of creation to finish.

ME: What do you mean?

O: The initial process of creation is duplicated by the creation of the aspects of the Source Entity dedicated to creating the sentient entities in a one-by-one basis multiplied by the number of aspects created to create in this way. The total time taken to create the sentient entities is a function of the volume of sentience and specialized energy/ies, and the ability to match them, divided by the number of creating aspects created. This being relative to only a small part of the sentience and energy/ies assigned for this use, the rest needs to be achieved by the use of Event Space, otherwise it would never be completed in what could be considered as a reasonable time. The issue here though is that the length of time taken to achieve the primary creativity process, even in its multiplied state, is the governing time period for creation, irrespective of the number of Event Spaces used, and is therefore considered to be a long time as well. Based upon this, the creating Source Entity uses a function of Event Space called the "End of Event" Event Space and moves directly to this function of Event Space rather than waiting for the primary Event Space to progress at the rate it would normally do in its logical fashion. Source Entities Eleven and Twelve used this to great advantage.

ME: I wouldn't have recognized what they achieved as using the "End of Event" function so I am pleased you described it to me. Based upon this then the creating Source Entity kicks off the process and manipulates Event Space going straight to the End of Event function of those Event Spaces created, and in this way the creation of myriad sentient entities is considered to be largely instantaneous.

O: Yes.

ME: And all of this ensures that a Source Entity can create every sentient entity by using the perfect divisional process, and every sentient entity turns out perfect as a result?

O: Yes.

ME: And if Source Entity One had used this combined function of self and Event Space it would not have the diversity of sentient entities it has now?

O: Correct.

ME: Thank you.

What Makes an Energy Capable of Supporting Sentience?

I was just about to change the direction of my questioning when I was inspired by a question asked by one of my World Satsanga meet-up attendees. I hold the World Satsangas once a month as an audio conference. I was both surprised that I hadn't already asked that question of The Origin, and pleased that one of my attendees was expansive enough to be able to ask it. All of my attendees are expansive enough to take on board the detail discussed, otherwise they would not be part of the Satsanga, and many do ask very deep and searching questions. The issue here was that I didn't have an answer to hand, or was able to link into The Origin at that point to be able to channel an "on the spot" response about "what makes an energy capable of supporting sentience."

I am not at all concerned about not having the answers to hand; this happens all of the time, it's part of the education process. What intrigued me though was the simplicity of the question and the potential complexity of the answer. It was a question and answer combination that needed to be broadcast, and this book was the right medium to do it.

ME: What makes energy capable of supporting sentience?

O: There are many things that need to be in place for energy to support the sentient component, and these have been alluded to within the first part of this book. However, they may not have been readily visible as a way to answer your question.

In essence an energy needs to evolve to the point where it could have created or supported its own conditions for self-generated sentience before it can be considered specialized enough to support sentience that is both externally created and assigned to it. That being, the evolutionary process that allows energy to achieve to the status of being capable of supporting sentience can be described in stages. These are:

1. **ATTRACTION TO SAME OR SYMPATHETIC ENERGY.** This is a purely automatic function of one component of energy being attracted to another component of the same or a similar energy signature, one that is acceptable in some way to energies other than itself.

2. **CREATION OF LIMITED INTELLIGENCE—PREFERENTIAL ATTRACTIVITY.** This is the active seeking out of components of energy that are of the same signature with the intelligence creating the ability to search for, and decide if, a certain component of energy can be connected to and co-joined with it to create a bigger body of energy.

3. **LIMITED RECOGNITION OF SELF AND OTHER ENERGIES.** This is when the volume of collected energies knows in some small way that it is a body of energy and can distinguish between itself and another body of energy even if it is the same type of energy.

4. **CREATION OF A MORE INTEGRATED INTELLIGENCE.** Occurs when the essentially separated out aspects of energy and intelligence that joined together actually become one. This is the result of pan energy communication of the co-joined energies.

5. **SACRIFICE OF INDIVIDUALITY TO CREATE A LARGER INTELLIGENCE—BIGGER SELF AND SELF-AWARENESS.** This is when the level of intelligence of a number of bodies of energy/ies recognize that they can create a much bigger and better single body of energy and intelligence by joining together. When they also recognize that in order to do so they need

to sacrifice their own individual intelligence, and willingly do so for a greater good. This paves the way for conscious intelligence to be created.

6. **CREATION OF THE COLLECTIVE "CONSCIOUS" INTELLIGENCE—THE ABILITY TO "THINK" BEYOND THE SELF WITHIN THE SELF.** This is a product of an automatic function that is created upon the collective decision to join larger bodies of energy to create a single body of energy that is much larger. Clearly the ability to make the decision necessary to achieve point five requires a level of intelligence that has limited levels of consciousness, that consciousness being enough to make the decisive ability of individual sacrifice for a greater good possible.

7. **CREATION OF THE SINGLE "CONSCIOUS" INTELLIGENCE FROM THE COLLECTIVE.** The creation of a single consciousness in lieu of a collective of smaller conscious intelligences is a landmark decision that can only be made in a collective condition. However, at this level of evolution the energy cannot reverse this process and the consciousness intelligence becomes as "one" with no ability to become a collection of smaller conscious intelligences later.

8. **ACTIVE DESIRE TO INCREASE ENERGETIC "VOLUME" AND INTELLIGENCE QUOTIENT.** Here the energy seeks to increase its volume by seeking out, attracting, and absorbing same or similar energy/ies that are smaller than itself and that are not necessarily evolving. This is a conscious decision and is an ultimate sign of the start of the ability to recognize the evolution of the "self." The energies being attracted and absorbed will be at point one or two at a maximum. The energy in this way increases its volume in an energetic, intelligent, and conscious way that can eventually increase to the point where all same or similar energies are absorbed. Note here though that the signature of the energies is a natural barrier to this growth when developing on their own. This is called the terminal volume. As a result the ability for myriad small but nevertheless substantial bodies of energy with conscious intelligence capable of developing sentience later is ensured. Note again

though that from the perspective of a Source Entity, this function occurs in a restricted area where energies are allowed to develop in this way specifically for the creation of sentient energy and that it is internally "external" to the main body of energies that are associated to a Source Entity itself.

9. **GENERATION OF THE DESIRE TO CREATE.** The desire to create is a function of the energy that occurs when it has reached its terminal volume and has substantial longevity. The creations being rudimentary, their very presence is a sign that the energy is developing a personality within its conscious intelligence. Personality, no matter how limited, illustrates the desire to create in certain known and repeatable ways specific to the energy and its level of conscious intelligence.

10. **RECOGNITION OF THE REASON FOR THE DESIRE TO CREATE.** Creation and the desire to create may be a single action or a multiple series of actions. In the single condition the creation can be a product of the desire to create but that desire may be transitory and therefore only occur once. It is therefore the recognition of the desire to create that triggers the multiple creation condition. Recognition is established as a function of the entity wanting to repeat, and therefore desires, the product of the act of creation, irrespective of what it is.

11. **CREATION WITH NO FOCUS OR DIRECTION.** This is creation for creation's sake and is the result of a condition of the desire to create in either singular or multiple conditions just to see the act and process of creation in action.

12. **CREATION WITH A FOCUS OR DIRECTED OUTCOME.** This is the intelligent use of an energy's creative ability to produce something from the energies around it that has the focus of the entity and is directed to achieve a desired product.

13. **ANALYSIS OF THE CREATION, ITS DIRECTED OUTCOME, AND ITS ACTUAL OUTCOME.** Analysis of the product of creation in terms of the desired outcome and the actual outcome allows the creating entity to

reflect on its creativity process and enter into the thought processes that result in modification, point fourteen. Note here that creations up to this point are uncomplicated. Complicated creations are the result of sentience. Consider that at this point in an energy's evolution the objects of creation are as basic as the creation of a ball or a wheel or other objects of interest that are similar in complexity.

14. **MODIFICATION OF CREATIVITY TO INCREASE THE ACCURACY OF ACTUAL VERSUS DESIRED OUTCOME.** This is a point where the energy is on the point of sentience but without tipping the balance into sentience. Here the entity is able to think, experience, and create in a rational way. It should be understood here that an entity's experience is enhanced as a function of entering into the creativity process.

15. **ACCRUAL OF EVOLUTIONARY CONTENT.** As eluded to in point fourteen, when an energy enters into the creativity process it also enters into another level of experience. Experience creates a learning condition which in turn creates evolutionary content. Based on this, the more an entity experiences and learns, the more it evolves and gains evolutionary content. The accrual of evolutionary content accelerates the increase of an energy's intelligence quotient, consciousness, and enhances its personality. It is an essential prerequisite to the recognition of evolution and its accrual.

16. **RECOGNITION OF THE ACCRUAL OF EVOLUTIONARY CONTENT.** An energy, upon recognizing its increase in intelligence and breadth in personality, that being the recognition of preferential desires, will also recognize that it accrues evolutionary content as a result of the variety of experiences it experiences, the quality of those experiences, and subsequent learning. On the point of recognizing personal evolution and its accrual the energy can, and does, experience a radical change in its mental capacity and capability, moving on to point seventeen.

17. **THE GENERATION OF SENTIENCE.** This is an instantaneous pan energetic effect that can only happen when the entity experientially recognizes its own evolution and how it accrues evolutionary content. At this point the energy is and can be classified as a new energetic sentient entity.

18. **THE RECOGNITION OF SENTIENCE AS A SEPARATE FUNCTION WITHIN THE ORIGINAL ENERGY/IES.** Recognition of personal sentience is achieved when the energy, now an energetic entity, experiences the movement of its sentience within the volume of its energy/ies. Recognition can be achieved when the entity notices that it is able to focus its sentience into one specific area of the volume of energy/ies that it is associated with, and can move the location of that focus at will.

19. **THE ABILITY TO DISASSOCIATE THE SENTIENCE FROM THE ORIGINAL ENERGY/IES.** The ability to disassociate the sentience from the original energy/ies is a function of experimenting with the focus of the sentience—the experimentation resulting in the ability of the sentience to be focused at points outside of the natural barrier created by the entities' energies as well as within them. At this point the entity starts to recognize that it is its sentience that makes it an entity and not the energy/ies that ultimately gave birth to that sentience.

20. **THE COMMANDEERING OF A NEW ENERGY.** Having established that its "being" is its sentience and that it can disassociate itself from its original energies, the sentience that is the entity can now move itself to a new energy or group of energies that are in a low level of specialization and commandeer them for its own benefit. This can be for a new or different body of energy allowing the sentience to enhance its experience, learning, and evolutionary content, or to use that/those energy/ies as a medium for transporting the sentience to another location within the environment that its original energy/ies evolved within.

As noted before, this list is basically a re-understanding of the information I gave earlier in these dialogues, but with additional detail in some areas. But placed in the context of this question it may make more sense to your readers.

The thing to note here is that the evolution of the energies to point sixteen is a necessary function for the self-generation of sentience. It is at this point that the energy has that which makes it capable of being sentient, and so, it becomes sentient by default, progressing automatically to point seventeen and above.

However, if that energy remains at point sixteen, or is close to achieving point-sixteen status, it can be classed as being capable of supporting externally applied sentience. Because this ability is imprinted across the energy/ies achieving this status, portions of it can be divided or separated out from the larger volume of energy/ies and assigned to an individualized unit of Source Entity sentience, thereby creating an autonomous sentient entity with an assigned body of energy.

How The Origin Created the Source Entities' Sentience— A Variation on the Theme

Throughout the dialogue with The Origin we have discussed the advent of sentience as a function of the evolution of self-awareness, which is preceded by the generation of intelligence within similar or same energies and subsequent levels of consciousness. Sentience itself develops through evolution within The Origin and presumably the Source Entities. I say presumably because The Origin talked about waiting for the Source Entities to become self-aware on their own before it contacted them—educating them with their reason to be at the point of achieving self-awareness. Indeed, the evolution of an energy or energies to the point of developing its/their own sentience was only recently described as a twenty-point progression. Something was bugging me though. To date I could not remember The Origin talking about the generation of sentience within the Source Entities themselves. Sure, energy can develop sentience given the right conditions and enough time, so to speak. And, it would appear that the Source Entities themselves can wait for energy to evolve almost to the point of developing full sentience on its own before assigning Source Entity derived sentience to them—that sentience being separated out from a Source's own "volume of sentience" and assigned to the evolving energy/ies its/them self/selves.

At the risk of repeating myself but for reasons of clarification I decided to mentally note and include in this text two things. One, The Origin developed its own sentience as a result of the evolution of its energies—with a little help from Event Space, that is. And two, in order to create smaller individualized entities to populate an environment created in response to the need to evolve through the investigation and experience of the "self," a Source Entity can, in the perfect sense, assign sentience to its evolving energy/ies rather than allowing them to develop on their own. This allows it to accelerate its productivity through the use of Event Space and maintain a certain quality level. But what about the sentience of the Source Entities? I just had to ask The Origin to clarify this area of concern for me.

ME: Just how did the Source Entities become sentient? I know that you waited for them to become self-aware and then educated them. But, this doesn't explain how Source Entity Twelve became sentient and how the others did. Did you simply educate them and then wait for the sentience to develop on its own? Or did you assign sentience to them like the Source Entities can do in the perfect way of creating a lesser entity?

O: We have talked about this before, but I can see that you have forgotten. When I created the Source Entities I gave them all of the conditions necessary for them to develop, to evolve on their own. As you so well stated in the previous text I then educated them when they became self-aware, giving them their reason for existence and an indication of the role they needed to play for me. As you know from the narration of my own journey to sentient self-awareness, only a microscopically small percentage of me is actually self-aware and indeed sentient. My sentience moves around my area of self-awareness, my sentience is that which I am. Based upon this you can understand that the reason for my creating the Twelve Origins and later the Twelve Source Entities was to accelerate my own evolution, that evolution being expressed in the expansion of my area of self-awareness and my sentience within my area of self-awareness. In this way I create an area of sentient self-awareness, which results in an increase in the area or volume of my "transportable" sentience, so to speak. Taking this into consideration you can see that achieving self-awareness is not the end of an entity's development. It is simply the starting point.

However, it can take a long time for the energy itself to actually make the change from simple awareness to simple "localized" self-awareness and to the level of localized but "pan energetic" self-awareness that is required to allow the advent of sentience from an evolutionary perspective rather than an assigned perspective. What's more, it would take even longer for that area of sentient self-awareness to evolve to the point where it was able to actually create those energies that are capable of supporting sentience in their own right, and then actually create them.

You see, in order to accelerate my own evolution, expanding my own sentience in the process, I needed to accelerate the evolution of my creations, and the evolution of my creations' creations. In order to achieve this I waited until the evolutionary development of the energies that formed the framework of the Source Entities had achieved this simple localized self-awareness—self-awareness being a prerequisite and minimum requirement for the energies to accept sentience. From the point of view of the twenty-point process, this would be at points fifteen and sixteen. This is a universal metric, and it is the same as the one required for an evolving energy within a Source Entity that is being used for the creation of smaller entities. Self-awareness is the point at which an energy or entity starts to develop its own personality and experience of self, and so, this is the point at which I intervened.

I calculated the base requirements of a Source Entity's energetic evolutionary condition in terms of what you would call a percentage and established a minimum level of sentience that would allow a Source Entity "under education" to work with that sentience as soon as the education was complete. I also calculated at what point in the education process I could apply that sentience to the energy/ies in a way that would not interfere with the education process itself.

ME: What was the percentage required?

O: It was well below one-tenth of one percent. I calculated that in the advent of education and the application of sentience, the right sort of sentience, the growth of sentience and self-awareness, what you will recognize as sentient self-awareness would become exponential, terminating its expansion at the perimeter of the energy/ies of the Source Entity itself.

ME: You just made an interesting statement. You said, "the right sort of sentience." What did you mean?

O: In your thought process you were expecting to hear me state that I would use some of my own sentience and assign it to the Source Entities, just the same as the "perfect" process that a Source Entity may take when creating its own entities.

ME: Yes, I did.

O: If I had done that I would have given them Origin-based sentience, and not Source Entity–based sentience.

ME: Couldn't you remove the, shall I say "essence of Origin," from your sentience and then pass it on?

O: Yes, I could, but then that would go toward negating the point of my own sentient growth. Also, any sentience I donate, no matter how I "cleaned" it, would still have essence of Origin associated to it. Not that I would begrudge the donation of my sentience to the Source Entities, far from it. But I need every last drop, so to speak, to achieve the work I am doing on my own. No, I did something far more useful.

ME: What was that?

O: I created sentience and assigned it to the Source Entities as and when they became self-aware.

ME: You created sentience?

O: Yes. I discovered that I can create sentience.

ME: How did you do that? How does one create sentience?

O: Organically.

ME: What? You mean you grow it?

O: Sort of. Let me explain.

ME: You have my full attention on this one.

O: I can see I do. OK, I will try to make this as simple as possible and use terminology that you are used to.

ME: Thank you.

O: As you have understood by now, sentience is the natural development of the evolution of energy/ies that learn to work together and function as one. These energies, or should I say, the characteristics of these energy/ies, are created as a result of the "possibility" of them developing into energies that could develop these characteristics. That being, they are sought out by a function of "free energy" and endowed with the potential to evolve.

Note that I used the word "possibility" here, for it is the "possibility" of their gaining this ability that evokes the interest of Event Space. If you remember it is the possibility of evolutionary progression that allows free energy to bridge the gap, so to speak, between individual entities or energies that have the ability to evolve when affected by another, or others, of higher frequency, thereby invoking an evolutionary opportunity. You know this as both directional and inflational triangulation.

ME: So you manipulate the function of triangulation?

O: To a certain extent, yes. I gather together those energies that I see are capable of evolving into sentient energies via the usual route of them gaining a desire to work together, gaining intelligence, conscious self-awareness, and sentience in the process. I then manipulate triangulation by forcing these energies together and making them desire to stay together. In this way the free energy that would naturally have attracted them together, elevating them to the same level through triangulation, has to catch up with the event that I forced into operation, rather than be the initiator of the attraction in the first place. Think of it as placing two pieces of plastic together and then forcing the glue in between them, rather than covering one of the pieces of plastic in glue and then laying the other on top of it. Once the energies are forced together in this way and the free energy has bound them together in their newly elevated state—that being, a newly elevated state of evolution—they function in the way that they would have functioned had they actually desired to form together by natural means.

What happens next is that they start to present possibilities, possibilities of becoming sentient at some point, the level of sentience being a function used by Event Space for "divisional" purposes. When this happens (in fact, I don't wait for it to happen because I move to another Event Space to see when it is happening), I move to the Event Space that produces the best quality sentience. I can see what energies are going to create the best quality sentience in this way and make changes to the conditions of the others, those that are destined to make their evolutionary progression to a lower quality of sentience in order to terminate them. I terminate them by stopping their evolution. When I stop their evolution, both the free energy that creates their continued evolution migrates to other evolutionary opportunities, and the Event Space that they are within ceases to exist as a result. Those energies whose evolution is halted are then catalogued and redistributed within me.

ME: You kill them off?

O: Yes. There is no point in allowing sentience to develop without it being the quality that I want it to develop into.

ME: But wouldn't it be useful in the long run?

O: No. I know the quality of sentience that I want to develop for the type of energy that I want to assign it to, which ultimately points one into understanding the type of entity I want to create. When I am creating an entity such as a Source Entity, I need to ensure that the sentience is as close to mine as possible without actually being mine.

ME: You used the word "catalogued" a moment ago. Why do you catalogue the energies when you have effectively terminated their evolutionary opportunities?

O: I catalogue them so that I don't use them again for this type of creative function. However, it doesn't mean that they will not be useful in a role that requires a lesser level of sentience in the future, one where one of my Source Entities can make use of the energies.

ME: So why not keep them in their lesser sentient state, stored somewhere for another Source Entity to use without going through the whole creativity process?

O: Three reasons. One, because it would not be their "own" creativity; two, I don't want any stray sentient energies disturbing the plan that my Source Entities and I are working with; and three, I always return that which I have used, and no longer have a use for—at least in the medium to long term, back to its basic condition. You can consider that I like to keep a clean house, if you like.

Chapter 29

How the Om Gained Sentience

I HAD ONE OF MY "SITTING BACK IN MY chair" moments. Actually, it lasted about an hour or so as I decided that I needed to clear some e-mails while I was in this period of subconscious contemplation. The reason for this "moment" was because The Origin had just told me that it liked to keep a clean house and that it liked to return energies that it used back to its basic condition. But this did not line up with what it had done with the energies that it used to create the Source Entities or what had happened to allow the Om to be created. I decided that this was one loop (yet another, I might add) that needed to be closed before I could move any further. What was in the back of my mind though was that this may explain how the Om themselves, being uncreated, gained their own sentience.

ME: You just said to me that you, shall I say, "recycle" your energies when you have finished with them—that you turn them back to their basic condition.

O: That's correct.

ME: This must be a recent thing then because it doesn't explain how the Om came into existence.

O: Very well done. Yes, it is a recent process in housekeeping that I take, and it is a direct result of the "noncreation" of the Om. The Om are the only uncreated sentient entities in existence and as such they are an example of what could happen if I don't pay attention to my housekeeping and return those energies that I use back to their basic condition.

ME: That makes sense. I guess recent to you is not what I would call recent?

O: Clearly not, but it is recent to me when I consider my longevity.

ME: OK, this is going to be a relatively simple discussion then.

O: Mmmm. We will see.

ME: What I want to know then is this: how did the Om gain their sentience? I ask this specifically because you needed to create sentience when you created the Source Entities.

O: I did in that instance and I will again. The difference is of course the energies used.

When I recycled the energies used in the Twelve Origins, I did not return those energies back to their basic condition. The energies themselves were essentially individualized units of me that were positioned outside my area of self-awareness. You will notice that I omitted the word sentient. This is because at that time the totality of my sentience was small in comparison to what it is now and my area of self-awareness was largely devoid of sentience. It's largely devoid of sentience now but it is a factor of, close on, one hundred times bigger than it was then.

ME: That's the power of one hundred?

O: In round numbers, yes. Also, I was not as evolved and as experienced as I am now and had much to learn. I still have much to learn, hence the creation of the Source Entities and their creations who are all working hard to experience the very basics of what I am.

Getting back to your question though, the volume, so to speak, of the energies that I recalled and recycled were two different sizes. Some of it remained with me and some was actually recycled. I will try to explain. I expected to use the recalled energies for other experiments at a later date and so decided to put it to one side. What in fact happened was that they became part of my sentient area of self-awareness very quickly. This took me by surprise, and so my expectation of the progress that the Source Entities would make had a precedent— the precedent being how fast the recalled energies supported the development of, or acceptance of, sentience. Upon this new turn of events I decided to use those recalled energies that had not yet become my area of sentient self-awareness and add to them the energies necessary to make up the Source Entities. The percentage of the recalled energies used was minor in comparison to those marked for the use of creating the Source Entities. Because of this I expected them to both mix and accelerate the evolution of the energies from basic energetic attractivity to full self-awareness, drastically reducing the Event Space needed to elevate them to the evolutionary stage where I could educate them and they could accept the sentience I was to bestow on them during the education process. What actually happened was something very different.

As you know, the energies, although initially forced together, stayed together while in my direct influence and control. When I cast them out in the group of twelve as Source Entity energy and Origin energy, the energy used in the original manifestation (Om) of the Twelve Origins, The Origin energies, no longer being forced together by my intention, separated out from the Source Entities that they were mixed with, forming small units of individualized Origin energy that already had sentience assigned to it. This you already know and have documented several times.

ME: How was the sentience already assigned to the energies? I thought that each of the Twelve Origins experiment failed before they could become properly self-aware let alone sentient.

O: Correct, the sentience was gained through association with those aspects of the energies that became part of my total sentience.

ME: Are you suggesting that ALL of the recalled energies became sentient and that you missed the fact that they had ALL become part of your sentience?

O: No, nothing was missed. What happened is that the energies used in the Twelve Origins experiment were already close to creating their own sentience, and were therefore definitely capable of accepting sentience that could or would be assigned to them. It was because of this that they gained the assignation of sentience by inference.

ME: Inference? How do you mean?

O: Because the rest of the recalled energies had accepted sentience, and accepted it rather quickly. That part of the energies that was not, shall I say, "intentionally" assigned sentience also gained sentience; that being, they accepted sentience as part of the natural evolutionary growth of my sentience. Think of it working in the same way that homeopathic remedies work. I personally note here that both free energy and Event Space had a part to play here.

ME: Does free energy and Event Space work on inference?

O: Yes. You see, inference is the same as possibility and the possibility of an evolutionary condition, one that is significant in the instance of the noncreation of the Om, is a possibility that could not be ignored by Event Space. Noncreation is classified in this instance as creation without the intention of being created. Additionally, the evolutionary aspect offered as a result of the noncreation of the Om drew free energy to the epicenter of those energies being used for the creation of the Source Entities creating an area of triangulation that not only encompassed the Source Entities, but the energies that were used in the Twelve Origins experiment.

ME: I am getting the impression that the intervention, a quite natural intervention of free energy and Event Space, created the rift in cohesion between the energies assigned to be Source Entity and those that were recycled Origin energy.

O: Oh very well done. Yes, you see, The Origin energy was already sentient as a result of the inference of being sentient. Free energy and Event Space were making sure of that, so when I cast the energies out, energies that included both the energies that were marked as Source Entity energy and those that were recycled Origin energy, The Origin energy, that is The Origin energy with enough, shall I say "mass," became sentient before the energies that were purely assigned as Source Entity could even become self-aware. In fact, they became fully sentient within the instant of my casting out the energies into the area of my self-awareness assigned to the Source Entities for their first area of work.

ME: Based upon this then the "already sentient" Origin energy disassociated itself from the energies that were assigned to the Source Entities, resulting in the noncreation of the Om themselves?

O: Yes. I will now call this energy Om energy.

ME: So how did the Om energy become individualized Om entities?

O: The Om energy was unevenly distributed among the pure Source Entity energy. It was in globules of Om energy, so to speak. These globules remained singular, individualized aspects of Om energy and did not group together. As soon as my intention to keep all of the energies together was removed, they very quickly separated themselves out from the Source Entity energies that they found themselves part of. Those that had enough mass naturally sensed that they were not of the same quality of energy and moved back into the energies that they sensed were their own—the energies being those which are part of my area of self-awareness. Simply put, they moved back to the place from whence they came!

You are aware of the history of the Om from our previous dialogues but suffice to say the mass of Om energy and the level of sentience attached to those individual masses dictated how the Om are currently represented within me. The result of which was the generation of the Pure Om, Non-Captive Om, Captive Om, and Source Entity/Om Hybrid, the hybrid of which have varying percentages of mix.

ME: So that's it. That's how the Om became sentient and separate?

O: This was just the start. The quality of the energies that are Om ensured that their level of sentience increased at a rapid rate. Apart from the energies that resulted in the Source Entity/Om Hybrid energies, and much later, other individualized entities created by the Sources for their own evolutionary tasks, all other Om were able to detect each other no matter where they were and within or without which Source Entity they are or were part of.

The Om are, in general, but specifically in the case of the pure Om, individualized units of me. As each of the Om sought each other out they noticed that their interaction with each other rapidly increased the level of their sentience. At the same time they also noted that they were not all the same in terms of their mass and ability to relocate themselves. Working together, understanding what each of them "was" from an energetic and sentience perspective created a high level of camaraderie within the Om. During this interaction they recognized how special they all were in terms of the noncreativity process that resulted in their creation coming into effect. They noted their limited numbers and loved being in each other's company. They all fell in love with each and every one of themselves and became beloved as a group of entities as a result—hence the term being "beloved of the Om."

The Om's ability to experience, learn, and evolve was and is a joy to behold. They have a capacity for evolution that is only equal to a Source Entity, and noting how much larger than an Om a Source Entity is, this is the most wonderful piece of noncreation I have ever experienced.

There is one issue with the Om though, and it is this. They are, in all intents and purposes, me, smaller individualized versions of me, and because they were not created for a specific purpose they have fully autonomous individualized free will. Because they are essentially me I cannot and do not control them. They do what they want, wherever they want to do it because they do not have a framework within which to work.

ME: Didn't they have a framework when their energies were initially part of the Source Entities?

O: Yes, but they only retained that when they were held under my intention. As soon as they broke free they became free of any framework or any possibility of any framework. Because they are me, the Om can manipulate that which their sentience commandeers or works with within, and presumably without, my area of self-awareness, Event Space being one of those aspects of my structure which functions within me.

ME: This seems to me that the Om are fully independent of your sentience and will not be able to exist within those areas of your self-awareness that are now sentient in their own right.

O: Correct, and what's more, they will need to move beyond this current area of self-awareness into the next and new area, almost before I do to maintain their freedom, so to speak.

ME: Would they be absorbed back into your total sentience if they did not move?

O: Yes and no. Yes, they would, but no, they would not fully integrate. In fact, they could become an irritation. And this, my dear Om, is why I now keep a clean house, so that more Om, or similar entities do not become noncreated. As much I love them and am grateful for the work that they do for their own evolution and of course mine, I recognize that they are an anomaly, an anomaly that I can't remove, or indeed would want to remove, but an anomaly nevertheless.

Chapter 30
Geometric Devices

FOR A NUMBER OF YEARS NOW I have, along with many others, noted an increase in the availability and use of geometric devices for assistance in meditation and healing. I have looked on in interest at this development and have had a feeling of déjà vu and familiarity. In fact, it all feels very Atlantean to me. One of the things I had noticed with these devices is that they are incomplete, that they lack specific componentry or they leak energy. It is the componentry and energy that is necessary for the correct functionality of the device. While I was in communication with The Origin and even though this is really a question for Source Entity One, I thought that I would take the rather selfish opportunity to find out more about these devices, with a view to satisfy my own thirst for clarification and hopefully assist those individuals manufacturing and buying them. Whether they would pay attention to the advice would be another thing because I had noted a "particular" response from a number of people selling these devices when I told them that they leak energy. They thought I was crazy! Who is/are the crazy ones? I thought with a smile. Why would anyone want to sell dysfunctional products? With all of this in mind I put my consciousness in that place where it needed to be for communication with The Origin and waited for it to communicate with me. I didn't have to wait long.

O: You're right. They do leak.

ME: That's a quick answer!

O: Quicker than the speed of thought.

ME: Don't tell me the speed of thought is quite slow.

O: You bet it is. You already know that thought follows intention and therefore that thought must be slower than intention.

ME: Yes, of course.

O: Well, I came to you faster than the speed of intention as well.

ME: We had best not go there with this one.

The Origin had got me interested. What is it that is faster than the speed of intention?

O: Omniscience is faster than the speed of intention, and you're right, now is not the right time to talk about the speed of anything. You wanted to ask me about the geometric products that are being sold around the globe currently, and I will say it again, yes, they do leak. What's more, most of them are poorly made at best, even though they may look nice.

ME: OK, I would like to get back to the start of this subject if possible, but for some reason I feel that finding the information relating to why they leak would be best discussed now. We can back track straight after. So, can you give me a simple reason why they leak?

O: They are incomplete. How's that for a simple answer?

ME: You are in a playful mood today.

O: I always am. Did I not invent humor?

ME: I suppose you did.

O: Correct. Now, about why they leak. Firstly, I will tell you that these devices are using the energies associated with sacred geometry. The geometric shape represented in the lower frequencies, what you see with your human eyes, relates to the specific function of that energy at the frequencies associated with the physical universe that you are working with. These frequencies are within your so-called physical levels, but most have not yet been discovered by you.

The only geometric shape I would like to talk about is the pyramid. This is because it relates to the largest of the devices being sold and to some large-scale archaeology found on the Earth. This shape needs to be closed and flat/smooth. That being, it needs to have a surface from which to attract the energies and their associated frequencies with. The inside of the pyramid can be a pure void, or it can be a solid with specific areas of void that are to be used to harvest the energy and its frequencies through. The energy accumulates at the point of the energetic loci represented by the dimensions and ratio of the geometry and the area represented by its "sides." Without these "sides" the energy has nowhere to be collected from. Think of it in terms of a solar cell. The surface area of the cell is specific to how much voltage and current can be generated. Reduce the surface area, and the voltage and current reduce accordingly. Based upon this, a pyramid with no sides has an almost zero chance of accumulating the energies associated with its external dimensions. All this being said, they have got one thing right, and that is the dimensions and ratio of the sides and the base material from which to make them from. All they need to do is fill in the gaps, so to speak.

Reading your memories I see that some of these pyramids also have other devices attached to them, supposedly in an attempt to attract other energies.

ME: Yes, I seem to remember that they had them hanging at a certain point on the pyramid, along with other devices that the user holds separately in both hands.

O: OK. Some of this is technology that has been remembered from past lives, or more usually channelled from higher-frequency incarnate, or, disincarnate entities that are trying to help mankind develop devices that can, as well as the pyramids, tap into those free energies and their associated frequencies that the devices are tuned to work with or attract.

ME: You mean those devices that are based upon a quartz crystal in a rectangular hexagonal shape with pointed ends and coils of copper or silver wound around them?

O: Yes, there are myriad interpretations of the sizes and shapes and ways of linking the crystals, coils, and rare Earth metals together. Each of them is specific to the attraction and amplification/use of an energy associated with their geometry and dimension.

ME: Can you give me an example of what they are capable of? I mean, some of them are supposedly able to assist in "Journeying."

O: Their functions are as diverse as their shapes, and as a result they are difficult to categorize without the specific geometry, dimensions, and associated componentry. I will give you a few descriptions of what they can do though, and maybe this will provide enough information.

First, though, I will advise you on where and when they have been used, that being, the civilizations that have employed them in their everyday existence.

From mankind's perspective it thinks that the use and design of crystal-based technology has an Atlantean origin, but this is not the case. The Atlanteans were the last civilization to use crystals in any real industrial way, so to speak. That doesn't include the minor use of crystals incarnate mankind has today in both industrial and healing modalities.

There were two other civilizations that used them to great effect. The first was a civilization that called themselves the Planerians. The second was the Gronak. Both of these preceded the Sumerians and Atlanteans.

ME: Planerian—that sounds a bit like a worm called a Planarian. Planarians are asexual.

O: It does, but it isn't the correct spelling and they were not worms!

ME: I would hope not.

O: There are incarnate vehicles that are worm like in form factor though, and they are quite diversely populated around Source Entity One's physical universe. But this is another subject.

The Planerians were a much higher frequency than the human vehicle is today and were at least a frequency level higher than the Gronak. They developed the use of geometric and crystal technology to assist in the function of the transportation of the consciousness outside of the physical vehicle. Due to the frequency levels that this technology was created on there is no true way to describe its form—although one way to describe it would be as being just tangible but holographic in nature. Specializing in distance-based exercises, they traveled the environments represented by the twelve frequencies of Source Entity One's physical universe—expanding their experiential, learning, evolutionary content, and consciousness in the process. They used the various combinations of crystal and componentry to vary the frequential positioning of their consciousness, enabling them to experience the subdivisions in these frequencies and the universal content hidden between them.

They used this "technology" in the "correct" way, and as such they clearly understood a lot more about what you call the greater reality, subsequently and rapidly evolving beyond the need for incarnate existence as a result. The Planerians never revisited the Earth because they felt it had taught them enough and their main motivation was to seek immediate evolutionary progression rather than reflection.

The Gronak were what you might call a reptilian race. They mainly developed a specialism in both macro and micro geometric technology, using it for the generation of energetic power for their labor-saving devices. They understood how to use size, geometry, and dimension in the combinations necessary to support industrial/large-scale power provision and local, individual power provision—the pyramids representing the "macro" single material, industrial versions that were designed and developed to attract and accrue single- and lower-frequency energies. In fact, they were particularly adept at developing small "micro"-scale geometric technology that allowed the individual to carry with them all of their power-based needs. If you can imagine an individual carrying the equivalent of a large single stone diamond ring and this ring is connected to a conversion circuit that allows the power accrued to be used for any electrical device you can think of that you use in your everyday incarnate life, including the ability to provide all the electrical power required to power your house, you will see how powerful this micro technology was.

Although I used the example of a large diamond ring, the geometry did not need "crystal" technology. In fact, they preferred to use metals and their alloys to create the correct sizes, shapes, and interconnectivity. Think of the way they created these devices in terms of a three-dimensional printed circuit that was connected at the atomic and subatomic level.

Many different metals and mineral/metal alloys were created to build them. Each individual metal, if observed on its own as an individual component, would appear to be a complex network of geometry and the ability to connect other geometry of different material content with it. Within the geometry was the position of the loci of the energy and subsequent power generation for each of the components and the ability to combine the power accrued from each of these loci. The energies creating the power at the loci could be harvested either individually or in varying percentages of each, creating hybrid energies of varying power outputs. The Gronak eventually moved away from the Earth as an incarnate opportunity, preferring to work on higher frequencies associated with the physical universe. When they left, they left behind examples of this technology, specifically the large-scale geometric and small-scale crystal technology which was subsequently inherited by the race you call the Atlanteans. The Gronak are known to infrequently visit the Earth.

ME: The Atlanteans inherited their technology?

O: Yes, but they used it for what you might call selfish reasons rather than for the betterment of the civilization as a whole. They used the technology for general power systems, transport, and modification of their genome for status and fashion purposes. The manipulation of the genome is one of the main reasons for the demise of the Atlantean civilization with a subsequent fall in the frequential level of the incarnate human vehicle. As you know, when the Atlantean civilization fell, the Earth was cleansed and what is recognized as Egypt was created. Although some of the macro-sized devices were left behind as archaeological evidence of a previous civilization, the micro-sized devices were either removed or destroyed due to them being too powerful for any individual to use without that individual being the correct level of purity and frequency.

This leads us nicely into what some of the functions of these devices were used for. It is best described in a list.

The functions of geometric devices:

- Transmutation of materials (change at the atomic and subatomic levels)
- Levitation
- Frequential travel, both projection of the physical form and the consciousness only
- Physical travel other than levitation (such as intra-solid travel and teleportation)
- Genetic manipulation
- Communication
- Amplification of so-called psychic powers
- Healing (repair of broken bones or organs)
- Command and control of labor-saving machinery
- Command and control of weather conditions
- Generation of gases
- Refreshment of soil
- Computation
- Attraction and accrual of energies and their storage
- Attraction of free energy—A medium to assist evolution and a storage medium for evolutionary content. (This is a function of a very highly evolved civilization such as the Planerians.)
- Manifestation and creativity
- Actual movement of a planetary body

ME: The last function looks pretty amazing as a function. Has any civilization actually used this function?

O: Yes, many times within the higher frequencies of the physical universe and obviously more than once in the lower frequencies, specifically when it would have been detrimental to leave a planet in a location that would mean that its usefulness was terminated before its time. It was also used to move one to a location where it could be more useful. That's how the Earth got to where it is now.

ME: What do you mean? It was moved from somewhere else to its current location?

O: Yes, and it's also why the planetary body you call the moon was moved into the position it is in now, to protect the Earth and to create certain mono magnetic, sub and intra magnetic functions that allow the incarnate human form to function.

ME: This is interesting. I bet this could be the subject of a chapter on its own.

O: More like another book. Let's stay on track.

ME: OK, I have noticed that some of them are made from resin, that is, resin made to look like crystals. Do they have the same functionality, or does this make them useless?

O: Simply put, they are useless, irrespective of what people say. They would not be able to achieve the functionality that the correct base materials provide. And all of these are available on Earth.

ME: So what would they be useful for?

O: Expensive but cheap jewelry at best.

ME: I won't be buying one then. Does that include those devices that use resin to hold the components in place?

O: No, they can and do function, provided the crystalline components are actual crystals and the other components are also materially pure.

ME: And these function or provide the functions you identified earlier?

O: Yes. The important thing to note here though is that there are incarnate individuals on Earth right now that are being contacted by entities, both incarnate and disincarnate who are of a higher frequency and are being educated in the design of some of these devices. There is much that is left out in translation, so to speak, because of the way in which the communication is being delivered (usually in dreams or while the receiver is in meditation) but the information is starting to become clearer.

ME: What do you mean, clearer?

O: The incarnate individuals who are receiving the information are recognizing errors in design, albeit subconsciously, and are taking the information that is being repeatedly sent to them, understanding the differences between what they have received versus what they have built, and making modifications to suit. Eventually they will get to the point where the design and the device are identical and the functionality of the device will be obvious.

ME: You're suggesting that there will be a physical response of some sort?

O: Yes, specifically with those that have a physical function. Those that don't have a physical function will have a noticeable energy about them.

ME: And how many incarnate individuals are being educated in this technology?

O: At least two thousand worldwide.

ME: That's both a small and a large number. It's small because of the population of the Earth, but large because of the potential for these people to receive this information, I guess.

O: Yes. It takes a certain type of individual to be able to take the information that is being transmitted to them and then turn it into a useable product. To get this technology right needs a lot of receivers.

ME: And I would guess that it needs that many people to get the message across?

O: Yes. There is a massive failure and dropout rate with educating the incarnate human race in this way. Remember when Baird invented the television?

ME: Well, I wasn't incarnate personally then but I do remember the history books stating that it wasn't just Baird. Both Bell and Edison had ideas as well.

O: Correct. They all received the information through the intuitive route. That being they were subconsciously educated about the technology and worked on developing it while thinking it was their own ideas. What isn't broadcast is that a number of incarnate individuals, similar to those being educated in sacred geometry technology, were also being educated in the development of the television and prior to that the telephone.

ME: But only a very few people are recognized with working and succeeding in developing "working" devices.

O: And only a few will be recognized with working and succeeding in developing "working" sacred geometric devices as well.

ME: What will make those successful, successful in developing working devices?

O: Stamina, receptivity, and recognition of making the wrong design decision. All of this is linked with the ability to stand back and look at what they have created and potentially start again.

ME: When will we see such devices in operation?

O: Some of the more benign ones are already in operation.

ME: Such as?

O: Those that assist in meditative states. There are even some that are able to affect the local weather.

ME: How do they do this?

O: By compressing the energies that cross the boundaries between the lower gross physical and the upper gross physical.

ME: How do they compress the energies?

O: By being moved from one location to another.

ME: Any moving parts?

O: No moving parts, just a knowledge of what materials to assemble together when they are in a certain shape and size.

ME: When will this technology become readily available?

O: When incarnate mankind is more open to this technology, is able to admit it is trying to crack walnuts with sledgehammers and more importantly, is not looking to make money out of it or use it for the command and control of others. The last comment is important as it is the sign of a mature society.

ME: Are you suggesting that incarnate mankind is not yet mature enough for this technology?

O: Not yet.

ME: When will it be?

O: When it doesn't need to ask the question.

ME: Touché!

I felt that the sort of devices described by The Origin were very compelling—the potential simplicity of them, versus their functionality, a reason why incarnate mankind must investigate them further. "How complicated can they be?" I thought. As I was contemplating the level of complication I was overcome by an image and a knowing, a cosmic knowing. It was not about complexity; it was about the user interface. We only have to look at the complexity of electronic devices we have today to recognize that we are going in the wrong direction. That we are trying to create a device that does the work for us rather than the device being part of us doing the work. These geometric devices, developed with the ancient knowledge of sacred geometry, worked with their user on an energetic level. There was a necessary energetic interaction between the user and the device in order to achieve the desired outcome—the outcome being in line with the natural laws of the universe, and ultimately the multiverse.

To achieve the correct functionality these devices must be used by a person of significant maturity. One who can work with a pure heart and for the benefit of others. This was the key. When we as incarnate mankind can work with our free will and commit to ensure that everything we do is ultimately for the benefit of others in some way, even if we benefit ourselves, then we will gain access to this technology.

Until then we will keep heading down the path of complication, of communicating and manufacturing in a mechanical means. Irrespective of what name we give this mechanization, such as electronics, hardware, software, computing, air, land, or water based motivation, telecommunication, farming or scientific/medical investigation, we create devices/machines to do it for us instead of doing it with energy and our intention, our creativity.

Try to imagine a time when we are able to create everything by using the correct energetic tools and methods and not trying to crack a walnut with a sledgehammer. Think of how easy it would be to understand the structure of the universe and multiverse without using a Large Hadron Collider. We may think we are advanced technologically but energetically and creatively we are well behind.

Chapter 31

Communication with Other Om

IT WAS TIME TO MOVE ON. More than that, I had a strange feeling of desire—a desire to communicate with those of my own energetic heritage, other Om. It had been a long time since I had communicated with other Om. In fact, other than a very brief and recent communication with Hum (February 2014), the last time I committed to a dialogue with the Om was around 2007, toward the end of writing The History of God.

There was something I had to know about—something that I could only get to understand by communicating with the Om as a result of this dialogue with The Origin. I wanted to know why I incarnated and why I am working within the sentient energies that are Source Entity One. I didn't have to wait long.

O: Shall I round them up?

ME: I thought you didn't have any control over the Om?

O: I don't, but they are still an aspect of me and as a result I can broadcast a desire to communicate with you.

ME: Would I not be able to send out such a request or desire myself?

O: Yes, of course. Give it a go.

I did and received a most strange response.

OM: You called?

It sounded almost like the voice of a butler! Not at all how I remembered the accent.

ME: Yes, I wanted to ask you some questions. And, why the strange accent? You sound like the butler in the Addams family.

OM: We have to give you something to differentiate between us and the creator called The Origin.

ME: Why do you call *The Origin* "The Creator called 'The Origin?'"

OM: Because the Sources are creators, and we refer to those that create as creators. A creator is an entity that creates, is it not?

ME: Yes, it is.

OM: And a creator becomes responsible for that which it creates.

ME: Yes, it does.

OM: And so we refer to those that create and are responsible for their creations as a creator. Think of it as a profession where we would call you, in your Earthly role, the author called Guy.

ME: OK, that makes sense to me.

O: So have you gotten reacquainted yet?

ME: Not quite. I want to know who of the Om I am talking to.

OM: We ... are your peer group.

ME: What do you mean by peer group? Are we not all Om?

OM: Yes, but you are Pure Om and so are we, and so we are a peer group to you. You are strange in this condition; you are not "All" there!

ME: Thank you for that. I guess that is a nice way of saying that I am limited when incarnate?

OM: Limited is too fine a word to use. Nonexistent would be a better way of putting it. Why you choose to incarnate into such a limited situation is beyond even our comprehension.

ME: OK, I think I get the picture. So, how many of you are there in my peer group?

OM: There are four, you are two.

ME: Now I am confused. Does that equal six or five or one? I ask this question because I am trying to work out if you are counting yourselves as Om True Energetic Selves or aspects of an Om True Energetic Self, so four and two equals two *(I think they are referring to Anne here as me being two!)*. Or, are you all part of my True Energetic Self? In which case we five plus one, I believe you are referring to Anne as an aspect of my/our True Energetic Self, equals one, and that peer group is a way of saying God Head?

OM: Together we are both one and six, or four and two or even five.

ME: This is starting to get very confusing. Can you make it simpler for this small and taxed brain, please?

OM: Together we are Om, we are one. Individually we are five. You are one of five with two aspects. The Om is the peer group and you are beloved of the Om.

ME: Your energy seems familiar, like we have met before. Not before I was incarnate but more like during my incarnation.

OM: We are with you; we experience what you experience in totality.

ME: You experience what I am experiencing now in my incarnate, my very limited incarnate state?

OM: That is just one aspect of what we experience about you when you are experiencing what you experience. We wanted to ensure you stayed here for the duration, so we have communed with your True Energetic Self and communicated with you in your most receptive times. One of those times was when we visited you in what you called a waking dream. We presented ourselves as human beings in your mind and told you to experience basic humanity. Had you continued you would have experienced what you are experiencing now twenty years too early. This would have been even more limited due to your vocabulary being much lower.

ME: So you four are the men in white robes I saw in my mind's eye when I was in my late teenage years?

OM: We are those images.

ME: OK, we are moving forward at last. Tell me, why am I incarnate when you are not?

OM: You are indulging yourself. You are seeing if being Om makes a difference in this low-frequency environment.

ME: And does it make a difference?

OM: Yes and no. You entered into the same rules, the same criteria that the other entities enter into when in this state. The only advantage is that you are breaking free of the criteria. Indeed you have never truly been functioning within the criteria; we have had to help mask your talents, to make you forget. Do you not remember how much interest you actually lost when we visited you?

ME: Come to think of it, I seemed to lose interest in metaphysics and meditation overnight.

OM: As an Om this is not a natural condition for you to be in. It is not even natural for those entities created by the creator you call Source Entity One who become incarnate.

ME: So you are not my guides then?

OM: No, you don't have a guide. Why would an Om need a guide? Even when incarnate you have sight of your function, your purpose, even though it may appear to be Earth based. No Om has ever incarnated other than those aspects of your True Energetic Self, those that are/were Guy and Anne.

ME: I have to admit that I find that rather amazing. That no other Om has incarnated is, well, unreal!

OM: The need to experience incarnation was not something we agreed with. We spent some time with you trying to persuade you not to incarnate. For us there is no need, it is a nonsense to us.

ME: Why is it a nonsense? I would have thought that it would be educational at least!

OM: We are Om, you are Om, we are individualized Origin and therefore in contact with The Origin at all times. What The Origin experiences, we experience and that includes everything that is experienced by every other

Source and individualized unit of any Source and of course The Origin itself.

ME: Hold on, what you are suggesting here is that Om are potentially greater than The Origin.

OM: Explain?

ME: If we are experiencing everything that The Origin, the Sources, and the Sources' creations are experiencing, that puts the Om at the top of the experiential ladder, so to speak. That can't possibly be right, can it?

OM: Remember that the Sources also experience everything that every other Source experiences and that includes their creations and their creations' creations. Also, the Sources were educated by The Origin upon becoming self-aware, so they also have the same level of experience as The Origin. Everything is shared, nothing is separate, nothing is truly individual. Upon this we can and do experience everything that everything else experiences and so it is pointless us experiencing incarnation when you, as Om, are doing it yourself.

ME: What you are saying then is that you are experiencing everything that I am experiencing while incarnate, and therefore, as a result, you don't need to experience incarnation first hand.

OM: Correct.

ME: And ... that is why you let me incarnate.

OM: That was the eventual reason, the rationalization, that substantiated the argument that YOU proposed to us, and it is the only reason why we capitulated.

ME: What! You mean the only reason I am incarnate now is because I managed to persuade you, all of you, that you would benefit in some way?

OM: Yes. We could have stopped you, over-ridden you, but your argument was so compelling that we decided to let you go.

ME: OK, so just how many incarnations have I, that is, this aspect of my True Energetic Self, incarnated?

OM: It is the same as the number you were given earlier. That being, it is the same number of incarnations that you as an incarnate aspect of your True Energetic Self has experienced. It does not count those incarnations that the other aspect, what you might call the "Anne aspect" has experienced.

ME: OK, here's another question for you. How many times has the Anne aspect incarnated?

OM: More times than you. It is more experienced than you in interacting with the incarnates who are not beloved of the Om.

ME: Mmmm, I always thought Anne was more evolved than me.

OM: The Anne aspect is not more evolved because the Anne aspect is you, an aspect of your True Energetic Self, so the experiences that the Anne aspect has/had are yours as well. Remember, nothing is individualized, everything is shared.

ME: Thank you. I appreciate the fact that you allowed me to incarnate because it was of benefit to you all as well as me.

OM: It was not a fact; it ended up being a logical decision. Basically, we decided that we would not need to experience such hardship because you were doing it for us. We recognized that you were being of significant service to us by incarnating in the way you are. You are negating the need, or even the desire for any Om, that is True Om, to embark upon the restrictions created by being incarnate.

ME: Hold on, are you saying that no Om, that is any True Om, has projected an aspect of its True Energetic Self into an incarnate vehicle?

OM: No.

ME: Of any sort?

OM: No.

ME: In any environment of any Source?

OM: No.

ME: Incredible. I mean, really incredible. I find it hard to believe that I, that is this True Energetic Self, is the only True Om that has projected an aspect of itself into the incarnate—at any time.

OM: Using your own words, you had better believe it. And again using your own words, we think you are nuts!

ME: Thank you for that vote of confidence.

OM: And ultimately, thank you for providing a tangible argument for letting us let you do it.

ME: You could have stopped me then?

OM: Of course. We work for the betterment of the Om, not for the indulgence of the individual. We saw what you are doing as an opportunity for the benefit of both the individual and the Om, and so we agreed to let you carry on.

ME: Again, I ask, could you have stopped me?

OM: Ultimately, no, but we would have suggested that it was folly to embark upon such a low level of existence purely for the "experience" of being in such a low-frequency level. Think of it in these Earthly terms: in terms of wanting to be placed in a bath of ice and going to sleep in that bath of ice, and then waking upon from being asleep in that bath of ice, with little knowledge or experience to be gained from such an experience. To us and, indeed, to any other entity, this is what it is like when an entity embarks upon the need to incarnate.

ME: That would seem pointless to me.

OM: Yes, and that is why we see what incarnate existence is. From our perspective, being incarnate is the same as bathing in a bath of icy water and then falling asleep. You experience the immersion and then forget you were there—until, that is, you are caused to remember.

ME: What do you mean, "caused to remember?"

OM: We, or in the case of other guiding entities your guide and helpers, would cause, or make, you remember what you experienced.

ME: So you wake me/us (that is, the guides of other incarnates and you, in my case) up!

OM: To cut to the chase, yes. And so you remember who and what you are and what you have experienced.

Chapter 32

Why I Am Aligned to Source Entity One— Our God!

ME: OK, I have been indulgent in this dialogue so far, as I expect you have been dancing with me.

OM: Indeed this has been a game of dancing! We enjoy dancing.

ME: Yes, I understand. What I would like to know is why I aligned to the Source Entity I call "One."

OM: Quite simply you, or should we say, your energies, those energies that carried your sentience, your Twelve Origin heritage, were part of those energies that were used in the creation of the Source Entities. In your instance your energies were mixed with those that were assigned to create the latent and later active creative entity you call Source Entity One.

ME: You're saying that my association with Source Entity One is a result of my energies being part of those that were assigned to be Source Entity One itself and that I was the energy thrown out from its creation, hence the association?

OM: Yes, exactly. We are all in existence as a result of this same noncreative process. We were not created. We were created as a result of the error in creation. We are non-created, we are Om, we are the resonance of The Origin.

ME: So why does that create the association with Source Entity One?

OM: Simply put, you decided to experience what you might have experienced had you been an entity created by Source Entity One and not an Om.

ME: Assuming my energies were mixed and therefore fully integrated with Source Entity One.

OM: Yes—hence you being attracted to Source Entity One and working within its environment you call the multiverse. You simply wanted to see what it would be like to be one of those entities created by Source Entity One and working within its environment for evolutionary progression. With this in mind we let you go. We knew that once we had one of us that wanted to experience the lower levels of frequency, in any environment that any Source Entity created, that we would be able to extrapolate the experience we would have had ourselves from the experiences that you were having. That being, any of the aspects or shards projected by your True Energetic Self and/or aspect.

ME: So my argument bore no real fruit. You operated in a selfish fashion. That being, if I incarnated none of you would have to!

OM: You were aware of this and made the first move, and we are both happy and grateful that you did. You see, although you have not had a lot of incarnations you have accrued a lot of experience. Granted you have never been a world leader or a chief executive officer (CEO) of a large company, but what you have done in every incarnation is experience that which would have taken two, three, or four lives in series. Don't you remember saying to Anne that you felt like you were experiencing two or three lives at once?

ME: Yes, I do. I thought that it was more of a metaphorical statement than a reality.

OM: It is a reality. What's more, it was planned.

ME: How do you mean?

OM: You have joked many times that you will not be back and that this is your last life.

ME: Yes, I suppose I have.

OM: Well, it is true. We have guided you to make sure you fulfilled the tasks and personal commitments that you wanted to work with and complete. We have not been your guides, more of a guiding light and a source of inspiration. Call us your external intuition.

ME: This is my last incarnation then?

OM: Yes, when you both, that is, both aspects of your True Energetic Self that are/were incarnate, reintegrate you will once again become beloved of the Om.

ME: Mmmm, what was the point of me being here then?

OM: To experience that which the entities that incarnate within Source Entity One experience. And ... to help in some way.

ME: And that help is by exposing the incarnates to ideas and concepts that are beyond where most of them are now, by expanding their mental boundaries.

OM: Yes. This is the purpose of this incarnation and the reason why two aspects were incarnate at one time in the same location, and not only that, in a working relationship.

I was starting to feel that this dialogue was very quickly drawing to a close and decided to ask one final, but pertinent question. I actually got to ask a couple more.

ME: Why have I always had the feeling that I was with the entity called Jesus, that I could have been with him, or followed him?

OM: You observed what it/he did and wanted to understand how you could make a similar impact in what would be considered a modern environment.

ME: Quite clearly I have failed. I could never accomplish what Jesus, Buddha, Mohammed, Babaji, Yogananda, or any other spiritual leader has achieved. Not that I am expecting to because that would be egotistical.

OM: You haven't finished yet. Moreover, you are not trying to accomplish what they achieved. You are working on an entirely different plan, one that is designed to make incarnate mankind think rather than follow. Following relies on the leader being there. This creates dependence upon the leader, surrendering your decision-making process, your progress, to the leader, constraining you, removing the ability to progress beyond the leader. The leader in this instance thrives upon the dependence, both when they are incarnate and disincarnate. Thinking makes the thinker work things out for themselves, but only once they have been given the tools and taught how to use these tools in a skillful way. But these tools can only be given by a master, one who is not consumed by the egotistical effects of others depending upon them. One who is able to work with his/her students and elevate them to the point where they can both progress beyond the teachings of the master and progress the art, becoming masters themselves, the master being of service in this way without fear of succession—should, of course, they wish to do so.

Remember you are us and we are you and you are beloved of the Om. You are running a marathon and not a sprint. You have plenty of "time" left in this final incarnation of yours. Use this time wisely, use this time productively, use this time to enjoy your surroundings and those you work with for this is a special time, one that will go faster than you think it will. And ... you will be helped by that other aspect that incarnated with you, the one you knew as your wife, Anne.

We leave you now.

ME: Wait a moment. I thought that there would be more to this dialogue—that I would gain additional significant knowledge of the Om and my reason to incarnate.

OM: Further information would only seek to cloud your vision. It would make you think too much and not allow you to move on with your "Earthly work." This information is therefore best left alone until you reintegrate with your True Energetic Self. This is why you were born with the limitations of energetic mankind when incarnate. You have to work with them in the same way. You have to blend in, be free of ego and karma.

It would not be profitable to discuss any other information about the Om because the information would fall on stony ground. Everything has its event and place, and it would not be optimal to divulge further information on the Om right now. Suffice to say there will be an extended dialogue that will focus purely on the Om later on in your incarnate existence, one that will create what you call a book.

We will go now, for you have work to do. You have
planned much, and although you are well past the expectations of this incarnate existence you have recalibrated and have decided to maximize your Event Space
here.

ME: But I wanted to know more about you, my peer group,
what my relationship is to you. I ... I feel disinherited!

OM: You will never be disinherited and should therefore
never feel as such. Know this, you will gain further access to us when pertinent, YOU WILL KNOW MORE about
yourself. You will even know about what you have
achieved in this frequency beyond this incarnation.

ME: OK, I understand. I would like to ask one final question
before you leave me and this dialogue. Why did I decide
to enter into the incarnate cycle, when the rest of the
Pure Om have not?

OM: As we have stated earlier in this dialogue, you were interested by the work of those creations of the Source Entity you were cast aside from. You are in a circular
thought pattern now and need to rest. We leave you and
look forward to your reintegration with your True Energetic Self and us. Beloved of the Om know that you are
beloved.

*And with that the link was severed. I thought for a short mo-
ment about the prospect of yet another book title. I knew that
I had four more lined up in the pipeline, but one specifically
committed to a dialogue with the Om was a bolt out of the
blue. When will I get chance to retire? "You never will in this
incarnation" were the words that bounced around in my
skull. Was this to be the final communication with the Om until that dedicated dialogue? I thought. "Maybe" came the re-
ply. And then I was given the name for the book dedicated to
dialogue with the Om. It was to be called, unsurprisingly **The
Om—Dialogues with the Uncreated.***

I sat back and smiled. At least I won't be bored!

Chapter 33

Joint Communication with All SE's and O

AT THE START OF THIS BOOK I was aware that I was being watched—that the other Source Entities were gathered around me as I established and committed to an extended dialogue with The Origin. Initially I was unaffected by the significance of what I was noticing. In fact, it didn't really mean anything to me. It is only now, when I look back and refer to some of the more recent dialogues I have experienced with The Origin, that I am drawn to a greater understanding of what was happening.

My recent dialogue with The Origin had revealed that the Source Entities do not move from their locations. That is, until both they and their creations have experienced all of the opportunities presented to them by the environment that they are currently working with and within, resulting from their location within The Origin's area or volume of self-awareness. That being, they only move when they and their creations have experienced everything that that environment can offer. It is only then that they move on to a new location to repeat the work they are doing in a similar, same, or different way— that way relative to the differences experienced in the energies specific to their new location. But, here they were, moving, positioning themselves around that aspect of my sentience, initially projected into an incarnate vehicle, that is now projected out beyond the constraints of that vehicle and the constraints of the Source Entity that it is aligned to. How did they do that? What was the meaning of it? And why were they doing it?

O: They were getting close enough to be able to observe your communication with me and communicate with you while they were all "together."

ME: But haven't they negated the work they were doing within the energies of the location of your area of self-awareness that they were working with?

O: No, they took it with them.

ME: How do you mean?

O: They acted like a balloon. They took that part of me that they are working with and relocated it to where they are now, surrounding you.

ME: So what happened to the area where the energies were?

O: The void that was left was back-filled by the surrounding energies as they moved the energies that their perimeters contained away from the original location toward their new location. Consider it in terms of a submarine moving under the sea. The water that is displaced by the submarine back-fills the void that is left behind the submarine. It happens instantaneously and in complete harmony. As for the meaning, they are simply interested in what you will discuss while observing how you are achieving what you are doing.

ME: And the reason for their observing me is?

O: That this, what you are doing, doesn't happen—very often.

ME: So it has happened before. Another or other entities has/have done what I am doing now?

O: Yes, just one other. And before you ask it was not part of your peer group.

ME: OK, I won't ask.

O: The end is nigh.

ME: What?

O: We are coming to the end of this dialogue.

ME: I thought we were.

O: I said the end of this dialogue—that is, between you and me. The Sources wish to communicate with you collectively.

ME: Why?

O: Because this is the second time they have been together in joint interaction in this cycle of progression. Remember this is only the third cycle and therefore only the fourth time they have been truly together, discounting Source Entity Twelve's interaction, that is. You have given them a reason to be together again. You are a common thread that makes them want to be together in this cycle.

ME: I wouldn't have thought that my individual interaction with them over the last three years would have caused a reason to make the changes in location they have made to be able to be "around" me when talking to you!

O: Well, it is, and that is because you are novel.

SE1: You are novel, you are Om. Not only that, you are Om that has chosen to incarnate.

ME: But is that a reason for the attention you are giving me?

SE6: Not in itself, but the fact that you have broken free of the constraints of the incarnate vehicle you have chosen to use in the lowest of low frequencies and communicate with us, we who are beyond your association with Source Entity One, is interesting.

ME: Why?

SE3: Because even as Om incarnate you have to follow the rules and constraints of those who choose to enter into the incarnate cycle created by the most highly evolved entities within Source Entity One.

ME: And I suppose because I am a Maverick, a free radical, so to speak.

SE7: Of course. This is why you are novel.

ME: OK, enough talk of me and justifying why you have moved your location to be close to me in my dialogue with The Origin.

SE4: No, this is not enough. We are relishing it. What you are doing is a delight to see.

ME: What do you mean, what I am doing? Are you talking about this dialogue or my ability to move outside of the constraints of Source Entity One?

SE5: Your desire to teach others to project their consciousness beyond the constraints of their physical vehicle. You assist them, you are their catalyst.

ME: I simply show them a way to focus. I show them a different direction to look and work with.

SE8: Yes, but they wouldn't be able to do it without you.

SE2: Just look at the number of students that are surprised at what they can achieve.

SE10: Yes, they have no idea that they had this ability before you showed them the way.

ME: Mmmm.

SE9: You can "Mmmm" all you like. You are on the brink of starting a paradigm shift in consciousness on this planet of yours.

ME: It's only a few hundred and quite a lot never get to the most important level.

SE7: Maybe so but the energy is out there. More will be attracted and more will want to get to the third level. *(Of my traversing the frequencies workshops. GSN.)*

SE1: And the evolutionary progression associated with it.

ME: Wait a minute; you are all talking to me as if you are one entity.

SE11 (collectively as one): That is because we are. We have all communed and are now one in reception and absorption of the information discussed in this dialogue.

ME: I know that I have communicated with you all separately in the past, and I have really been honored at the opportunity presented to me to broadcast the information you have all given me to incarnate mankind.

SE1: It is a pleasure to be of service in this way.

SE2: It is important at this juncture in incarnate mankind's existence to be exposed to a greater reality than they are currently aware of and working with.

SE3: That is correct. Incarnate mankind is susceptible to advancement now and is moving forward. Unfortunately you are moving in an unacceptable way.

ME: What do you mean unacceptable?

SE9: Most of what incarnate mankind is working on is based upon preferential direction. That being, misinformed details that are broadcast as absolutes.

ME: So how do we work with the absolutes?

SE4: By being discerning, working with an objective viewpoint, looking for the commonality in multiple broadcasts.

ME: That will take most people more time than they have patience.

SE6: Then there is a need to broadcast the bare truth, truth with no frills attached, as you say.

ME: I thought I was trying to do that. I also think many others are doing the same.

SE7: Yes, they are, but there is a tendency to broadcast only that which is preferred, and the preferred can be embellished to suit the personality. It then becomes misinformation because it no longer reflects the bare truth.

ME: Bare truth it is then. What is the best thing to advise the readers now then?

SE5: Remind them about what they really are—a multifaceted entity.

ME: I would expect that many of the readers of this book would already be aware of that.

SE11 (collectively as one): We dare say that many of them do, but even those that are may be interested to know additional detail to what has been discussed in these texts.

ME: OK. I am all ears.

I was wondering what else we didn't know about the functionality of the True Energetic Self.

O: The opportunity for parallel experiences is, from incarnate mankind's perspective, immeasurable.

ME: I/we already know about the opportunities presented to us as a result of the ability of the True Energetic Self to project twelve aspects into different universal or frequency-based environments. I/we also know about the opportunity presented to the True Energetic Self as a result of the aspect's ability to project twelve shards into any environment that the projecting aspect is projected into. All of this means that the True Energetic Self can experience up to one hundred and forty-four separate existences concurrently, if we don't include the parallel conditions created by the interaction of Event Space.

SE10: This is the information that is missing. Event Space events are recorded by the True Energetic Self as well as those experienced in what I will call sequential space.

ME: You mean the True Energetic Self not only experiences and records the simultaneous existences expressed by the aspects and shards, it also records the experiences from the parallel conditions expressed by Event Space-based experiences.

SE12: Of course.

I was stunned for a moment. I didn't expect Source Entity Twelve to participate. It was supposed to be outside of The Origin's area of self-awareness. I responded in an accepting fashion and then decided to question it as to why I was having a dialogue with it.

ME: How does it record all of those myriad experiences?

SE12: It commandeers an Event Space that is relative to an aspect of itself where there is no major change, or it is static in its productivity—you may call it an evolutionary dead end—and stores them within that aspect.

ME: Is the True Energetic Self not capable of storing all events then?

SE4: No. The True Energetic Self only stores the products of mainstream evolution, not the evolutionary dead ends. However, once that part of Event Space that is identified as a "nonproductive" evolutionary dead is assigned as a deposit of parallel experiences, it cannot be destroyed or rationalized back into the mainstream evolutionary path.

ME: For want of a better word then it becomes an experiential memory dump for the commandeering entity?

SE12: Yes, and this is how the True Energetic Self stores parallel experiences.

ME: And it refers to them.

SE12: Yes, on a regular basis.

ME: I wasn't aware that the True Energetic Self was so resourceful from this perspective.

SE9: There is much, much more to come about the abilities of the True Energetic Self in your next series of dialogues.

ME: I am sorry, everyone, but I have to ask Source Entity Twelve how and why it is here when I fully believed it was outside The Origin's area of self-awareness.

SE12: Clearly not all of me is outside The Origin's area of self-awareness.

ME: How much is here?

SE12: A single unit of dissection.

ME: And that is?

SE12: Just enough to maintain a meaningful presence in this sector of The Origin, enough to project an aspect of my sentience into without distracting the rest of me from my task of mapping the immediate external perimeter of The Origin's area of self-awareness.

SE1: And now we have all spoken to you again and presented you with additional information about what incarnate mankind really is, it is time for you to move on to the next series of dialogues. I believe you already know what it is about.

ME: Yes, I do. It sort of jumped out at me and slapped me in the face.

O: It was, shall we say, an unadvertised addition to your portfolio.

ME: Why was it unadvertised?

All SE's and O Together: We think you know why. To know any earlier would have been a major distraction. Now we have finished this dialogue you can start without distraction and with full knowledge.

And with that the link with all the Source Entities and The Origin dissolved. I felt alone for the first time in years.

Afterword

I am not going to say where I was in the world when I finished this book. Suffice to say I was a significant distance from my UK home and "in transit." I was surrounded by thousands of other incarnates who were also in transit, and yet surrounded by these thousands I felt like the last man on Earth.

I had been communicating with The Origin week in week out since August 2012 and this sudden and abrupt stop in communication, even though I was warned, was a bitter pill to swallow. Suffice to say there is a certain amount of delight when you know that the dialogue that you started with a single word is now both many and complete. There is a certain joy in knowing that this one is finished and is now ready for proofreading and editing. Fortunately, I have excellent help in this field. They know who they are, and I profoundly thank them for the service they give me with all my heart. All are great friends.

The information The Origin shared with me over the last nineteen to twenty months has been both difficult to work with and challenging to put into words. It has also been the most rewarding set of dialogues I have had to date. The information is a new and unique extension to that broadcast in my previous dialogues, and for that I am both grateful and humbled.

I sit here, sharing my temporary desk with strangers from all over the world, knowing that ultimately they are all one, all part of the Source (and therefore ultimately The Origin), all striving to progress from an evolutionary perspective. As I felt the underlying oneness I also felt communion with them. A sense of deep joy came over me. These people, these aspects of their True Energetic Selves I thought, are one day going to ascend beyond the need to incarnate, and the dialogues I have had to date may well provide some small part to play in that ascension.

For some reason I was feeling very emotional. Was it that this knowledge was true, a correct reflection of a future Event Space, and what I was feeling was the joy of a global level of success? It was, but there was something else, another presence was by my side.

A: Come on, it's time to work with me again. We have a lot to do and not a lot of time.

It was the energy of my dear, now energetic, wife, Anne. I was overcome with deep joy—the joy of working with her again. The emotions associated with that joy were unbelievable.

Guy Steven Needler

4 March 2014

Glossary

Acid Test—A way of testing if gold is real or not by the use of acid to remove a layer of gold exposing the underlying metal as either a substrate or real gold. In this instance it is a way of exposing the truth.

At the Helm—The "helm" is a nautical term for being in control of the steerage of a boat, and therefore its direction of travel.

Billennia—A multiple of a million (a millennia is a thousand).

Bone of Contention—A way of describing a discussion point where there are mixed beliefs or levels of agreement.

Broaching, To Broach—An engineering term for a process used to open up a hole, of defined shape in a metal component of some kind when spark eroding or milling cannot be used. In the use of the English language, it is used as a descriptor for "opening up" a discussion on a new or existing subject.

Carrier Wave—In telecommunications, a carrier signal, carrier wave, or just carrier, is a waveform (usually sinusoidal) that is modulated (modified) with an input signal for the purpose of conveying information. The purpose of the carrier is usually either to transmit the information through space as an electromagnetic wave (as in radio communication), or to allow several carriers at different frequencies to share a common physical transmission medium by frequency division multiplexing (as, for example, a cable television system). Source: http://en.wikipedia.org/wiki/Carrier_signal.

Curved Ball—A way of saying that someone answers a question with a question, or simply puts something in the way so as not to answer the question.

Double Dutch—A way of suggesting that something is not understandable.

Dualistic—A condition where two realities are in existence concurrently due to the possibility of an alternative reality being created when a choice of two directions are available.

End of Event—In Event Space the "End of Event" function is the designated boundary of an event and its concluding action. It marks the logical end of that event, i.e., no further possibility of the created dualistic event being continued and the possible start of a new or alternative event.

Event Space—Is a function of the structure of The Origin that creates parallelism from a local or whole environmental perspective. It is the culmination of the need for parallelism and the passage of smaller events to create a larger event-based environment. Event Space captures and compartmentalizes all that every entity or group of entities do into logically similar conditions that are either static or dynamic from the perspective of "change." Event Space is created by the possibility of a dualistic condition and/or its multiples of trilistic and quadrulistic conditions, which are governed and controlled by the possibility of possible possibilities and the possibility of the possibility of possible possibilities. It is a holographical pan structural record of the passage of what we do. Event Space permeates all aspects of The Origin, its creations, and its creations' creations.

Falling Fallow (To Fall Fallow)—An old farming term for when the three-field system was used in the sixteenth to nineteenth centuries, etc., in the UK. It allowed one field in three used to recover every three years to allow better crops in the other two years. Fallow was used to describe the lack of crop from that field. Falling fallow was used to describe if no crops were gained if seeds were sown, indicating that the field or land in question needed a year "in fallow" to recover.

Holy Grail—The mythological cup that Christ drank from. It is purported to have magic powers, even of longevity, and has been the subject of much conjecture about its existence and importance in history. Seeking the Holy Grail is therefore to seek the pinnacle of one's endeavors in lieu of other lesser achievements.

Join the Dots—A way of saying that one "understands" through logical means, or lateral thinking, the process of going from one level of understanding to another via known steps.

MRI Scan—Magnetic Resonance Imaging. An imaging system that allows the human body to be exposed in part or whole and presented to medical professionals in the assistance of medical diagnosis. It is a significant improvement on X-Ray technology.

On the Cusp—The edge of a decision point. One can either go one way or another just as easily. A point of imminent change.

Orgone—The visual representation of cosmic "free" energy.

Pass Muster—A military term for passing an examination of the quality, cleanliness, and tidiness of one's uniform, bed, and locker. "Muster" is usually given with very little notice.

Pecking Order—A term used to describe the status birds have between each other when feeding from a food source. The higher the status, the higher the priority in having access to food. A term used to describe that an order of priority is in place.

Polyomniscient—A multiple aspect of Omniscience. A condition that will be achieved by The Origin as it expands into those areas of itself that are beyond its current area of sentient self-awareness.

Quadrulistic—A condition where four realities are in existence concurrently due to the possibility of alternative realities being created when a choice of four directions are available.

Readings or Reader—Acting as a medium for a client who wants to know more information about themselves from spirit, but who is not able to ask for themselves during meditation or any other means. A "Medium" gives a "Reading."

Red Herring—A term used to describe a piece of knowledge, or a thought process, that turns out to be inaccurate, even though it appeared to be accurate at first.

Start of Event—In Event Space the "Start of Event" function is the designated boundary of an event and its instigating action. It marks the logical start of that event, i.e., it is the point of inception of a dualistic condition and the possible end of an alternative event.

To "Tinker"—A way of saying that one "plays" with certain things but is not really interested in the final outcome. Another way of suggesting that one experiments without a plan or strategy or a desired outcome but nevertheless achieves a positive response, that response being something is learned from the "tinkering."

Trilistic—A condition where three realities are in existence concurrently due to the possibility of alternative realities being created when a choice of three directions are available.

About the Author

Guy Needler MBA, MSc, CEng, MIET, MCMA initially trained as a mechanical engineer and quickly progressed on to be a chartered electrical and electronics engineer. However, throughout this earthly training he was always aware of the greater reality being around him, catching glimpses of the worlds of spirit. This resulted in a period from his teenage to early twenties where he reveled in the spiritual texts of the day and meditated intensively. Being subsequently told by his guides to focus on his earthly contribution for a period he scaled back the intensity of spiritual work until his late thirties where he was re-awakened to his spiritual roles. The next six years saw him gaining his Reiki Master and a four year commitment to learn energy and vibrational therapy techniques from a direct student of the Barbara Brennan School of HealingTM, which also included a personal development undertaking (including psychotherapy) as a course prerequisite using the PathworkTM methodology described by Susan Thesenga with further methodologies by Donovan Thesenga, John and Eva Pierrakos. His training and experience in energy based therapies have resulted in him being a Member of the Complementary Medical Association (MCMA).

Along with his healing abilities his spiritual associations include being able to channel information from spirit including constant contact with other entities within our multiverse and his higher self and guides. It is the channeling that has resulted in "The History of God" and is producing further work.

As a method of grounding Guy practices and teaches Aikido. He is a 5th Dan National Coach with 32 years experience and is currently working on the use of spiritual energy within the physical side of the art.

Guy welcomes questions on the subject of spiritual physics and who and what God is.

Books by Guy Steven Needler

The History of God
Published by: Ozark Mountain Publishing

Beyond the Source, Book One & Book Two
Published by: Ozark Mountain Publishing

Avoiding Karma
Published by: Ozark Mountain Publishing

The Origin Speaks
Published by: Ozark Mountain Publishing

For more information about any of the above titles, soon to be released titles,
or other items in our catalog, write, phone or visit our website:
Ozark Mountain Publishing, LLC
PO Box 754, Huntsville, AR 72740
479-738-2348/800-935-0045
www.ozarkmt.com

If you liked this book, you might also like:

Beyond Limitations
by Stuart Wilson & Joanna Prentis
Conscious Creation
by Dee Wallace
Awaken to Your Creation
by Julia Hanson
The Master of Everything
by James Nussbaumer
A Spiritual Evolution
by Nikki Pattillo
Morning Coffee with God
by Michael Dennis
We Are the Creators (releasing Fall 2015)
by L.R. Sumpter

For more information about any of the above titles, soon to be released titles,
or other items in our catalog, write, phone or visit our website:
Ozark Mountain Publishing, LLC
PO Box 754, Huntsville, AR 72740
479-738-2348
www.ozarkmt.com

Other Books By Ozark Mountain Publishing, Inc.

Dolores Cannon
A Soul Remembers Hiroshima
Between Death and Life
Conversations with Nostradamus,
   Volume I, II, III
The Convoluted Universe -Book One,
   Two, Three, Four
The Custodians
Five Lives Remembered
Jesus and the Essenes
Keepers of the Garden
Legacy from the Stars
The Legend of Starcrash
The Search for Hidden Sacred Knowledge
They Walked with Jesus
The Three Waves of Volunteers and the
   New Earth
Aron Abrahamsen
Holiday in Heaven
Out of the Archives – Earth Changes
Justine Alessi & M. E. McMillan
Rebirth of the Oracle
Kathryn/Patrick Andries
Naked In Public
Kathryn Andries
The Big Desire
Dream Doctor
Soul Choices: Six Paths to Find Your Life
   Purpose
Soul Choices: Six Paths to Fulfilling
   Relationships
Tom Arbino
You Were Destined to be Together
Rev. Keith Bender
The Despiritualized Church
O.T. Bonnett, M.D./Greg Satre
Reincarnation: The View from Eternity
What I Learned After Medical School
Why Healing Happens
Julia Cannon
Soul Speak – The Language of Your Body
Ronald Chapman
Seeing True
Albert Cheung
The Emperor's Stargate
Jack Churchward
Lifting the Veil on the Lost Continent of Mu
The Stone Tablets of Mu
Sherri Cortland
Guide Group Fridays
Raising Our Vibrations for the New Age
Spiritual Tool Box
Windows of Opportunity
Cinnamon Crow
Chakra Zodiac Healing Oracle
Teen Oracle
Michael Dennis
Morning Coffee with God

God's Many Mansions
Claire Doyle Beland
Luck Doesn't Happen by Chance
Jodi Felice
The Enchanted Garden
Max Flindt/Otto Binder
Mankind: Children of the Stars
Arun & Sunanda Gandhi
The Forgotten Woman
Maiya & Geoff Gray-Cobb
Angels -The Guardians of Your Destiny
Seeds of the Soul
Julia Hanson
Awakening To Your Creation
Donald L. Hicks
The Divinity Factor
Anita Holmes
Twidders
Antoinette Lee Howard
Journey Through Fear
Vara Humphreys
The Science of Knowledge
Victoria Hunt
Kiss the Wind
James H. Kent
Past Life Memories As A Confederate
   Soldier
Mandeep Khera
Why?
Dorothy Leon
Is Jehovah An E.T
Mary Letorney
Discover The Universe Within You
Sture Lönnerstrand
I Have Lived Before
Irene Lucas
Thirty Miracles in Thirty Days
Susan Mack & Natalia Krawetz
My Teachers Wear Fur Coats
Patrick McNamara
Beauty and the Priest
Maureen McGill & Nola Davis
Live From the Other Side
Henry Michaelson
And Jesus Said – A Conversation
Dennis Milner
Kosmos
Guy Needler
Avoiding Karma
Beyond the Source – Book 1, Book 2
The History of God
The Origin Speaks
James Nussbaumer
The Master of Everything
Sherry O'Brian
Peaks and Valleys
Riet Okken
The Liberating Power of Emotions

Other Books By Ozark Mountain Publishing, Inc.

John Panella
The Gnostic Papers
Victor Parachin
Sit a Bit
Nikki Pattillo
A Spiritual Evolution
Children of the Stars
Rev. Grant H. Pealer
A Funny Thing Happened on the
   Way to Heaven
Worlds Beyond Death
Karen Peebles
The Other Side of Suicide
Victoria Pendragon
Feng Shui from the Inside, Out
Sleep Magic
Walter Pullen
Evolution of the Spirit
Christine Ramos, RN
A Journey Into Being
Debra Rayburn
Let's Get Natural With Herbs
Charmian Redwood
A New Earth Rising
Coming Home to Lemuria
David Rivinus
Always Dreaming
Briceida Ryan
The Ultimate Dictionary of Dream
   Language
M. Don Schorn
Elder Gods of Antiquity
Legacy of the Elder Gods

Gardens of the Elder Gods
Reincarnation...Stepping Stones of Life
Garnet Schulhauser
Dancing Forever with Spirit
Dancing on a Stamp
Annie Stillwater Gray
Education of a Guardian Angel
Blair Styra
Don't Change the Channel
Natalie Sudman
Application of Impossible Things
Dee Wallace/Jarrad Hewett
The Big E
Dee Wallace
Conscious Creation
James Wawro
Ask Your Inner Voice
Janie Wells
Payment for Passage
Dennis Wheatley/ Maria Wheatley
The Essential Dowsing Guide
Jacquelyn Wiersma
The Zodiac Recipe
Sherry Wilde
The Forgotten Promise
Stuart Wilson & Joanna Prentis
Atlantis and the New Consciousness
Beyond Limitations
The Essenes -Children of the Light
The Magdalene Version
Power of the Magdalene
Robert Winterhalter
The Healing Christ

For more information about any of the above titles, soon to be released titles,
or other items in our catalog, write, phone or visit our website:
PO Box 754, Huntsville, AR 72740
479-738-2348/800-935-0045
www.ozarkmt.com